AF600580

EXHIBITING THE GERMAN PAST

Museums, Film, and Musealization

Exhibiting the German Past

Museums, Film, and Musealization

EDITED BY PETER M. McISAAC
AND GABRIELE MUELLER

UNIVERSITY OF TORONTO PRESS
Toronto Buffalo London

Toronto Buffalo London
www.utppublishing.com

ISBN 978-1-4426-4965-1

Library and Archives Canada Cataloguing in Publication

Exhibiting the German past : museums, film, and musealization / edited by Peter M. McIsaac and Gabriele Mueller.

Includes bibliographical references and index.
ISBN 978-1-4426-4965-1 (bound)

1. Museums – Social aspects – Germany. 2. Museum exhibits – Social aspects – Germany. 3. Motion pictures – Social aspects – Germany. 4. Germany – In motion pictures. 5. Germany – In popular culture. 6. Collective memory – Germany. I. Mueller, Gabriele, editor II. McIsaac, Peter M., 1968 –, editor III. Series: German and European studies

AM7.E95 2015 069.0943 C2015-902241-X

This book has been published with the support of grants from the Social Sciences and Humanities Research Council of Canada, the University of Michigan Office of Research, and the University of Michigan College of Literature, Science and the Arts.

University of Toronto Press acknowledges the financial assistance to its publishing program of the Canada Council for the Arts and the Ontario Arts Council, an agency of the Government of Ontario.

Canada Council for the Arts Conseil des Arts du Canada

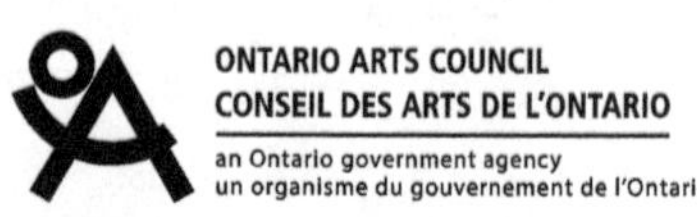

Funded by the Government of Canada Financé par le gouvernement du Canada Canada

Contents

Illustrations

Acknowledgments

We would like to thank those agencies and people who have enabled and supported this project in its various stages. The germinal idea for *Exhibiting the German Past* came out of a surprise discovery of common research interests that became the basis for a research network based at the Canadian Centre for German and European Studies at York University. Thanks to generous funding from the German Academic Exchange Service (DAAD), this network came into existence for the span of a year and a half and engaged scholars working on museums, film, and musealization within 500 km of Toronto. After two workshops, this network was expanded for an international conference, which was supported by both the DAAD and SSHRC funding. The publication resulted from a selection of high-quality papers that, together, are able to illuminate the problems of musealization in films and museums in ways no single paper would manage to do. To CCGES and York, the DAAD and SSHRC, we are most grateful.

At CCGES, we were blessed to have the unflagging brilliance and critical acumen of John Paul Kleiner behind the organization of this project in all its iterations. We were also fortunate to have Joshua Synenko's involvement in the conference and at most stages of the manuscript's compilation and development. At UTP, we would like to thank Richard Ratzlaff for his enthusiasm, support, and guidance from the very early stages of the project through to the volume's production.

Finally, we would also like to thank SSHRC, the University of Michigan Office of Research, and the University of Michigan College of Literature, Science and the Arts for their generous publication subventions.

EXHIBITING THE GERMAN PAST

Museums, Film, and Musealization

Introduction

PETER M. MCISAAC AND GABRIELE MUELLER

Both museums and films have for some time been individually recognized in German Studies as key sites for the production of historical knowledge and the construction of cultural memory, but what they share in how they present the world has only recently begun to figure as an important scholarly question. Driven in part by directions that museums and films have themselves taken in the past decade, scholars have perhaps been quickest to note that transfers between the two have become increasingly commonplace and intellectually productive in recent years.

During the last two decades, academic awareness has increased of the interrelation among academic, institutional, and popular forms of historical representation on the one hand and the all-pervasiveness of images on the other. This growing interest in media engaged in discourses on history has resulted in a proliferation of scholarly research that investigates the role of the visual in the production of historical consciousness in a number of disciplines, including museum studies, film studies, and media studies. Together with a wide range of other forms of narrating the past, both the museum and cinema are understood as part of what Vivian Sobchack calls the "historical field" (1997, 8) of different layers of historicized images and overlapping and contradictory narratives that are present simultaneously and contribute to the social production of historical knowledge. The essays in this volume engage with such processes of historical representation in German culture; they highlight the increasing intersections between and interdependence of museal and cinematic strategies and discuss both media's roles in their construction of the past and of historical consciousness.

Museum, Film, Television, and History

Even though sustained academic attention to the perceived "history/ memory boom" and to representations of history in museums and on screens is a relatively recent development in academic discourses, the museum and film have always shared important characteristics in the way in which they narrated history and addressed the spectator. Both the museum and film are visual media that work through processes of (guided) looking and seeing. They mediate the world of objects in a perceptual field that often privileges unified and coherent narratives in the service of knowledge production. In both the museum and in film, meaning is produced through the assembly of objects in a frame, mise-en-scène or context. Through the careful editing, arranging, sequencing, and labelling of the artefacts or images they put on display, both media affect the production of knowledge in that they work through ways of showing and shaping the process of seeing, which has to be understood as "a product of the tensions between external images or objects, and internal thought processes" (Hooper-Greenhill 2000, 14).

As the work of Alison Griffiths, Michelle Henning, Charlotte Klonk, and Haidee Wasson has made clear in different ways, the convergences and reciprocal borrowings that mark museums and film since the late twentieth century have significant historical precedents. Long before the third millennium, new visual media and museums have mutually served as sources of inspiration and points of reference, whether in the form of early-twentieth-century debates about the introduction of new visual media (Griffiths 375–89), avant-garde installation techniques from the 1920s and 1930s that incorporated a whole range of visual media (Henning 2007, 25–46; Klonk 218–23), or MOMA's attempt to invest cinema with high art status via its Film Library (Wasson). As this work has also shown, many of the goals surrounding these exchanges – for instance, the desire to improve spectators' experiences through novel modes of interactivity and the activation of affective registers – resonate powerfully with many prevailing positions in contemporary debates, with many of the stakes and concerns also anticipating those of the recent past.

In recent years, film and media scholars have also become ever more attentive to cinema increasingly exploring the valences of objects, commodities, and cultural products that have passed from regular use, in the process appropriating techniques and concerns traditionally in the domain of museums. Yet, the idea of cinema fulfilling an archiving and preserving function similar to that of the museum is not new either, but rather inherent in the medium of film which – through its very nature – captures "fragments of time" to record, preserve, display, and store for future use. And like museal display, the filmmaking process of selecting images for preservation, archiving, and public exhibition bestows significance on them as objects in the service of transforming social memory into long-term collective memory and historical consciousness. Films and museums work as part of the institutional network that forms the foundations of the cultural memory of a society: they both engage in processes of representation, interpretation, and canonization that, according to Aleida Assmann, are necessary to render ephemeral forms of social memory into more durable symbols and practices, thus shaping collective remembering and contributing to the construction of institutionalized top-down memory and historical master narratives.

The museum as well as film and television are media whose institutional role has traditionally been tied to an educational mandate to transmit historical information and knowledge and to the construction and dissemination of legitimizing narratives of national history. To be sure, the perception of the museum's roles, practices, and purposes have changed significantly during the last few decades, with an orientation on objects increasingly giving way to one that prioritizes emotional and sensorial "visitor experience" (e.g., Weil; Gurian; Hein, *Museum in Transition*; Simon). Yet even in this changing paradigm, education, learning, and the transfer and shaping of historical knowledge remain central to museums' mandates (Hooper-Greenhill *Museums and Education*). Similarly, film has always played an important part in modern configurations of knowledge production, and the proliferation of history programming on television (see, e.g., Bell), and the increasing use and exploitation of history films for school curricula are an indication of continuing and even increasing investments in the educational potential of the moving image.

Yet despite the many similarities that now seem apparent, the museum and film have been viewed differently in the past, mainly in the way in which they relate to historical authority and authenticity. The traditional museum derived its claims on authority and authenticity predominantly from its collection of objects whose uniqueness and documented provenance provided the aura and scientific confirmation needed to construct convincing narratives of the past. Since the sixties, museum practitioners have increasingly relinquished established claims to scientific objectivity and elitist approaches to the interpretation of history, mainly in acknowledgment of the discursive nature of historical truth narratives and of the discursively produced dichotomy between original and copy. However, this perceived trustworthiness in the museum's ability to capture the "truth" still seems to linger with museum visitors, and often their expectation of reliable historical narratives is continuing to be a dominant motivating factor for museum visits (see, e.g., Crane; Pirker and Rüdiger).

Films, and even more so television, by contrast, have traditionally been associated with visual, often trivial entertainment and emotional engagement that seemed incompatible with the seriousness of detached historical enquiry. While the museum's exhibition space required from the visitor a physical presence and with it a certain amount of attention to the objects on display, film and television have been perceived to allow for much more distracted and, therefore, less intellectually engaging viewing (e.g., Corner; J. Bennett). In particular, television's forays into historical representation have often attracted criticism for their tendency to reduce, distort, condense, and simplify history into bite-sized stories accessible to and palatable for a broad range of spectators. Nevertheless, the filmic medium also makes claims on the notion of authenticity despite its inherent reproductive nature, but it defines the authentic as a function of subjective experience rather than a category tied to objects. Through their main focus on the pleasure of experiencing history, of what history felt like rather than on what history was, film and television address the spectator emotionally and thus offer a form of authenticity derived from empathetic involvement and the privileging of memory over history (Engell). While this tendency to favour affective over distancing modes of spectator address is often bemoaned by historians, who doubt the medium's ability to produce accurate and scholarly reputable versions of history, scholars nevertheless agree that historical knowledge seems more and more generated by cinematic and television images of the past and popular and affectively engaging forms of historical representation rather than academic written histories (see, e.g., Rosenstone).

Indeed, it is not really new for museums and cinema professionals to reflect on and debate ways that seriousness and scholarly rigour might be combined with accessibility and spectator pleasure, with perceptions of exclusivity and high cultural status predicated not just on an institution's internal practices, but also on their relationship to the perceived status of other media. As Tony Bennett emphatically notes, museums' investments in what he calls "civic seeing" – projects of defining civic or community affiliation in relation to the ability to access and decode information through particular modes of visual presentation – have at times worked to regulate or outright oppose modes of spectatorship associated with popular visual technologies such as film (263–4, 271–3).[1] Or one could think of the insights of French writer, art historian, and cultural administrator André Malraux, whose mid-twentieth-century notion of the "imaginary museum" takes shape in response to the transformative effects that photographic reproductions of art objects were having on museums, art objects, knowledge, and memory (16–20). Sometimes rendered in English as the "museum without walls," Malraux's notion is particularly suggestive for its regard of photography as infinitely expanding the museum paradigm (an argument with renewed resonance in an age of digital reproduction and the lure of unbounded "virtual museums"), even as photography indelibly changes visitors' relationship to museums and the objects they preserve and display (17). While it thus seems manifest that filmic and photographic media and the institution of the museum have in fact existed in dialectical and historical exchange with one another since the advent of modernity (see also Klonk 214–15), far too little is known about the contours of these exchanges and what they reveal about the ways German-speaking culture has engaged with the challenges of modernity. But as much more historical and comparative work continues to be needed, categories capable of illuminating these complex exchanges, how visuality figures in them, and the way they link past and present with analytical and historical precision have also needed development. The chapters of this volume demonstrate that the concepts of remediation and musealization represent such categories.

Convergence and Remediation

Focusing on these media exchanges as part of discourses on history, the essays in this volume provide discussions of a broad range of cultural products. In their analyses, the authors examine ways in which both museums and cinema are implicated in musealization practices within and outside of their traditional spheres and how they contribute to the social production of historical consciousness. They investigate the ways in which the museum and film have responded to democratization processes in the construction of historical narratives as well as to changing notions and expectations of authenticity, authorship, and spectator involvement. In their engagement with both media's attempts to satisfy the modern consumer's contradictory desires for different forms of authenticity simultaneously, the essays illuminate the blurring of boundaries between the media and the increasing convergence between them. In reading the exchanges between the media as processes of remediation, Jay David Bolter offers a very productive concept for understanding representational processes that put the past on display. He contends that the practice of borrowing formal elements and representational strategies between the media are part of their cultural and economic competition. Bolter argues that "this competition takes the form of a dispute over the 'real' or the 'authentic' – not in any metaphysical sense, but rather in terms of how segments of our culture define the authenticity of the different media forms" (80). In their struggle to consolidate their claims to the most accurate and authentic version of history, the media appropriate and repurpose strategies and forms of authenticity associated with other media.

Film and television, for example, increasingly challenge the museum's claim to provide scientific objectivity and an auratic experience. Using extra-textual elements such as websites and actual exhibitions, filmmakers frequently emphasize the object authenticity and materiality of their texts, for example by location shooting at historical places or the use of historical objects whose provenance and historical relevance is documented and widely discussed in promotional material. Often, fictional television dramas explicitly cite reputable scholars and witnesses to the historical period in question as curators or consultants, not only in the credits, but, for instance, in interviews spliced into the film itself, added to the DVD versions or in widely publicized additional television programs, thus blending different forms of authenticity.

Museums, by contrast, have in recent decades appropriated more affective and experiential strategies that borrow from literature or theatre, or share characteristics with classic narrative conventions of the cinema (Bal 2010). Mieke Bal's examination of Ydessa Hendele's 2003 exhibition *Partners* at Munich's Haus der Kunst serves as just one example of the way in which museal and cinematic strategies of representation intersect. Heralding the rise of what she calls a "cinematic vision of art presentation," Bal's analysis helps to show that whole exhibition concepts, and not just piecemeal adjustments to museum layouts, have been emerging from the entry of film and digital media into the museum (2007, 71–2). Also, in their attempts to provide a sense of "felt history" similar to the approaches of cinema and television, museums offer visitors the opportunity to immerse themselves in a historical period, for example by spending a day in a reconstructed village populated by actors in historical costumes. Thus, they provide an almost theatrical spectacle and sensory experience, and they appeal to the visitors' emotions. In addition, more and more museums have begun to dematerialize and use film screens, digital media, and mobile devices for installations that allow for a higher degree of interactivity, emotional involvement, and visitor independence (Henning, *Museums, Media and Cultural Theory*; Simon; Parry).

These examples sharpen the expectation that a thorough investigation of remediation practices throughout German cultural history will yield important insights into the changing (national) discourses on the validity of master narratives and more pluralistic notions of historiography.

Musealization

In their engagement with intermedial exchanges and remediation, the essays in this volume illuminate processes of knowledge production and highlight the mechanisms and the central role museums and films play in contributing to what some scholars have referred to as a global "history boom" and to the increasing commodification of history. Far from being a phenomenon occurring in isolation from the convergence of film and museums, these effects can be illuminated analytically with the category of musealization.

A relatively new critical term, musealization was first deployed by Hermann Lübbe and Odo Marquard in the early 1980s as a means of understanding culture in an emerging postmodern, globalizing world (Lübbe 13–29; Marquard 13–18). Partly developed as a response to an unprecedented museum boom that began to emerge as the Cold War wound down, musealization referred to a pervasive, altered sense of temporality, manifested in part through an ever-faster atrophying of traditional practices and objects. As they fell out of use, traditional practices and objects became subject to preservation in historically novel ways, markedly expanding the boundaries of what museums could collect and show. In these years, seemingly "uncollectable" phenomena rapidly became germane topics for exhibition and made it appear that, in postmodern culture, nothing seemed to escape the museum. As Andreas Huyssen writes, musealization likewise figured more generally with regard to "the shifting temporal sensibility of our time. Lübbe showed how musealization was no longer bound to the institution of the museum, narrowly understood, but had infiltrated all areas of everyday life" (*Present Pasts* 14). In this analysis, disparate cultural phenomena such as the historicizing restoration of old urban centres, museum villages, and landscapes, and the growing propensity for recording and archiving snippets of everyday life and knowledge in myriad ways (from video cameras to computer databases) all share a sensibility with roots in museum processes (*Twilight Memories* 14). This sensibility likewise pervades other media such as film, for instance when film focuses on its own patterns of change or when it addresses monuments in its own history, when it takes up historical moments with a significant visual record (for instance, Anton Kaes's argument in *From Hitler to Heimat* [ix] that cultural memory of the Second World War resides primarily in images), when artefacts and images of a lost era are revisited in memory through filmic means, or when filmmakers employ exhibition techniques to challenge traditional modes of film spectatorship (see the chapter by Christine Sprengler in this volume). With the Internet, from virtual museums to social media and sites such as YouTube, the give and take between museums and visual media has become more intense and more complex. While fault lines between old and new media will no doubt go on shifting as a result of these changes, the rise of the Internet confirms the sense that musealization represents a phenomenon whose expansion seems certain to continue.

The concept of musealization offers critical purchase in that it helps to illuminate how museum practices and processes of film production and distribution develop within broader cultural discourses involved with the production of historical knowledge and memory. Because it engages the core processes of modernity and especially accelerating cycles of commercial culture, musealization is fundamentally concerned with the issue of cultural and material transformation and obsolescence. This conception speaks in particular to the arguments of French scholar Pierre Nora, for whom the transition to modern society has irrevocably shifted the balance between history and collective memory. Conceived as a form of preserving and transmitting knowledge of the past in traditional societies, in Nora's thinking collective memory (*milieux de mémoire*) represents a sensibility that collapses under the disruptive pressure of modernization and awareness of temporal change (7). Once lost, the sense of organic connection to the past is provided by a number of historical operations, techniques, and sites (*lieux de mémoire*), with museums and monuments figuring as the chief exemplars of the latter. Though often critiqued for its nostalgic lamentation that moderns' relationship to the past can only ever be mediated and thus somehow inauthentic, Nora's conceptions have nonetheless stimulated interest in the question of how, by saving, preserving, and interpreting the past, modern institutions of history and memory work to shape collective identities. For while collective memory remained foremost a narrow question of national identity for Nora, in the work of other scholars, the notions of collective identity and memory have been expanded so as to consider local, national, and transnational dimensions.

With respect to German-speaking memory culture, these correctives have of course been crucial as a means of detecting and critiquing the myriad evasions and enduring attachments to problematic forms of national belonging that took shape in the post-fascist era. Yet on the global scale, public memory culture now also needs to be seen as a phenomenon in complex dialogue with practices and dilemmas that have played out in Germany following the post-Holocaust injunction to "never forget" (for an exemplary discussion of this, see P. Williams 3–7). Though these efforts at first relied foremost on ruins and historical sites, built memorials, and (counter)monuments in an attempt to educate general publics, their dependence on processes of preservation, documentation, and display has inflected memory in ways that resonate with the practices and challenges faced – and also posed – by museums and allied media.

Such an approach to the relationship of musealization to museums and visual media in the context of global memory culture serves not only to focus attention on the impact cultural media have had on shaping memory. It also seizes on the effects of the changing roles that museums and media exert on the notion of musealization. If, as Andreas Huyssen has argued, musealization itself is not immune to the temporal and spatial effects of technological modernization, then the stabilizing effects musealization provides cannot be regarded as secure or constant over time (*Present Pasts* 24). With even conventional preservation techniques subject to occasional failures, as events like the burning of Weimar's Anna Amalia library in 2004 or the collapse of the Historical Archive of the city of Cologne in 2009 remind us, it cannot be assumed that the material past will always remain available. While this kind of loss might of course be mitigated to some extent by copies, the challenges encountered in adequately preserving and archiving decaying celluloid film stock – not to mention the unreliability of electronic records or the speed with which data formats and computer operating systems become obsolete – suggest that new media might well be more fragile than the old.

Yet with regard to stabilizing effects of musealization, it is not just that the remnants of the past cannot be assumed to be secure, but that the temporality of musealized experience may vary in significant ways. As environments at some remove from the flows of information and goods in modern consumer society, exhibition spaces might be considered to offer opportunities to move and think at paces other than those of the present. But if this temporal difference holds out the possibility, for instance, of gaining new vantages for considering how past and present relate, nothing is to say that this temporal difference has been or will remain fixed over time. Michelle Henning's argument that the inclusion of artist films in art galleries has forced changes to the way visitors linger and use the museum represents a single instance in which the museum temporality depends on its interpenetration with the media (*Museums, Media and Cultural History* 25–6; for a similar discussion in different terms, see Klonk). On one level, this temporal variability raises the possibility that musealization itself might get "sucked into the vortex of an ever-accelerating circulation of images, spectacles, [and] events," in the words of Andreas Huyssen (*Present Pasts* 14). Yet on another level, it raises more general questions about the temporalities at stake in the ways museums and visual media put the past on display. For more than relate past and present, musealization also involves passing the past on to the future in a process Sharon MacDonald has called "past presencing," with the term foregrounding "the implications of past presencing for imaging futures" front and centre (*Memorylands* 17). With its linkage of imagining and remembrance yet to take place, MacDonald's formulation signals an open-ended, pending quality to musealization that depends not only on the survival of objects in particular states and contexts, but also on the anticipation of how objects and contexts might be viewed and experienced by future spectators.

The Structure of This Volume: Salient Threads and Shared Emphases in the Exploration of Musealization in German Museums and Film

In organizing the essays in this volume, we have attempted to create an arc that does justice to the complexity and richness of each individual approach to musealization, museums, and film while simultaneously drawing out resonances in concepts and cases that emerge from the juxtaposition of particular essays. Leading off the volume, the opening essays by Simon Ward and Mark Rectanus shed new light on how films, museums, and urban spaces have worked to construct specific ways of seeing in the cultural centres of Berlin and Munich, respectively. Critically engaging the work of Tony Bennett, Andreas Huyssen, and Michel de Certeau, Ward's "The 'Museal Gaze' and 'Civic Seeing': City, Film and Museum in Wim Wenders's *Der Himmel über Berlin*" argues that the phenomenon of musealization relies upon what he calls an "urban museal gaze." With this concept, which he elucidates in terms of the dialectic of preservation and activation of artefact and image enacted in Wenders's 1987 film, Ward is able to discern a mode of active spectatorship that becomes pervasive in the urban upheaval that remade Berlin from 1989 on.

Also engaging the archival moment of *Der Himmel über Berlin* in addition to the theorizations of Bennett, Huyssen, and others, Rectanus's "Refracted Memory: Museums, Film, and Visual Culture in Urban Space" explores the very different built environment of twenty-first-century Munich in terms of what he calls "mobile mise-en-scène." A mode of audience engagement prevalent across once disparate cultural zones, mobile mise-en-scène speaks to visitors capable of moving through physical and virtual spaces of display as well as media such as television and cinema. With this framework, Rectanus masterfully maps the complex exchanges taking place over some fifty years of visual cultural practices, enabling him to illuminate the contexts and exhibition strategies of relatively new additions to Munich's cultural scene, the BMW Welt and the Jewish Museum Munich. Taken together, Ward's and Rectanus's theoretically rich analyses present a multifaceted account of musealized medial convergence in two of Germany's leading cultural centres as they have emerged over the span of many decades.

With Alice Kuzniar's and Catriona Firth's paired essays, the volume shifts its focus to sustained consideration of the way musealizing techniques inform important examples of contemporary documentary and mainstream filmmaking. In her essay "Nikolaus Geyrhalter's *Unser täglich Brot:* Preservation, the Food Industry, and the Interrogation of Visual Evidence," Kuzniar shows the 2005 Austrian production to engage with dilemmas that, while specifically cinematic in the way they are expressed in Geyrhalter's film, generally accompany exhibitory media today. After framing Geyrhalter's project as being aware of the high pedagogical and ethical stakes involved in the musealizing process of recovering and presenting gruesome images otherwise hidden from view, Kuzniar argues that *Unser täglich Brot* employs strategies of spectator engagement that ultimately seek to render its portrayal of suffering and slaughter fundamentally incomprehensible. With this in mind, Kuzniar avers that while driven to avoid the ethical and aesthetic impasses involved in visualizing death after Auschwitz, the film's aesthetic and technological choices paradoxically leave the viewer unable to re-establish a meaningful relationship to the animal and natural life that has been lost. In this way, Kuzniar regards Geyrhalter's film as operating in a photographic mode whose qualities exemplify a contemporary visual culture "under the sign of Saturn," to recall Susan Sontag's diagnosis of culture governed by the melancholy of the collector.

If Kuzniar's essay reveals *Unser täglich Brot* to be a self-conscious, if ultimately flawed attempt to engage the problems contemporary documentary film faces when employing musealizing techniques, Catriona Firth's analysis shows musealization made to serve nearly diametrically opposed purposes in the 2010 film *Der Baader-Meinhof Komplex*. Employing a notion of the curator that she carefully deploys as shorthand for the processes that go into the selection, arrangement, and presentation of images based on historical events and artefacts, Firth's essay seeks to think about filmmaking techniques made to evoke experiential reactions in line with those more commonly experienced in museum contexts. With this framework, "The Concealed Curator: Constructed Authenticity in Uli Edel's *Der Baader-Meinhof Komplex*" questions the premises upon which filmmakers convert highly charged historical events into easily consumable forms of cinematic heritage. Firth develops a meticulous account of the specific strategies filmmakers use to efface their curatorial agency through a comparative analysis of the curatorial strategies used in the main source for the film, Stefan Aust's identically titled 2008 book on German left-wing terrorism. By referring to a range of theoretical perspectives including that of museum theorist Mieke Bal, Firth is able to demonstrate in precise terms how filmmakers substantiate historical veracity through speech acts whose truth is constituted by gestures of exposure, a rhetorical strategy whose deep resonance with museal "truth claims" results in a program in which experiential affect stands in for reflexive knowledge and heritage stands in for history. Yet insofar as *Der Baader-Meinhof Komplex* succeeds in engaging viewers, particularly young ones, in a recent past that might otherwise be ignored, Edel's pursuit of the past would be less problematic for Firth were the film willing to put its curatorial apparatus on full display.

Following Firth's essay on the recent RAF (Red Army Faction) past, Anne Winkler's and Jonathan Bach's respective contributions to the volume constitute two different, yet resonant approaches to the musealization of the GDR past. Focusing exclusively on the preservation and display of non-official and non-commercial collections of GDR material culture, Winkler's "Remembering and Historicizing Socialism: The Private and Amateur Musealization of East Germany's Everyday Life" analyses the forces driving a phenomenon that began practically with the fall of the Berlin wall, collections of culturally obsolete quotidian objects. Calling attention to the mind-boggling pace of the demise of GDR socialism, Winkler frames musealization of the GDR every day in terms of temporal crisis and the concomitant threat of extreme cultural amnesia. But whereas musealization of the GDR thus shares many features with general millennial trends in material and memory culture, the museums in Winkler's essay also need to be seen for their counter-hegemonic dimension. As Winkler shows, amateur GDR museums operate at a grass-roots level, marshalling particular forms of installation that challenge significant lacunae in state-sanctioned collections and hegemonic narratives of everyday life in the GDR. Driven by the intersecting needs of Easterners who create and those who visit these spaces, amateur GDR museums are shown to enable certain productive forms of individual memory precisely because they eschew techniques such as interpretive labels characteristic of professionally curated museum spaces and attempts to collect artefacts from early eras of the GDR. Though they cannot address the need for a complex narrative of forty years of social, economic, and political change in the GDR, for Winkler these museums nonetheless offer a crucial corrective to the official version of life in the GDR presented in state-sanctioned venues.

Considering official and private museums excluded from Winkler's study as well as those she studies, Jonathan Bach's "Object Lessons: Visuality and Tactility in Museums of the Socialist Everyday" points to strategies of interactivity and tactility that he argues increasingly mark the whole spectrum of GDR museums. Drawing on the perspectives of Marshall McLuhan and Walter Benjamin, Bach shows how GDR museums of all stripes are increasingly devoted to providing intimate, multi-sensorial visitor experiences whose features address German topics using techniques prevailing in global museum culture. With his approach, Bach's work both resonates with Winkler's analysis of the fault lines running through post-*Wende* Germany at the same time as it illuminates key manifestations of a global museum culture that increasingly takes visitor experience as a cornerstone of effective museum work. In this way, Bach's essay draws out important complexities of GDR musealization, particularly for the way some displays engage the moral quandaries of surveilled life in the GDR. At the same time, Bach's chapter enriches the volume with an account that offers new ways of thinking about the impact of sound, touch, and multimedia on authenticity in museum display.

The next grouping of essays in the volume, by Stephan Jaeger, Annika Orich and Florentine Strzelczyk, and Kathryn M. Floyd, take up the problems of remediating the history and memory of the Second World War and the Nazi era using musealizing and cinematic techniques. Picking up the issues of visitor experience and authenticity that also figured in Jonathan Bach's contribution, Jaeger's essay, "Historical Museum meets Docu-Drama: The Recipient's Experiential Involvement in the Second World War," engages the growing production of Second World War history for lay German audiences. Examining two docudramas, two uses of film in the Deutsches Historisches Museum (DHM) of Berlin, and a 2010 exhibition in the Oskar Schindler factory in Krakow, Jaeger argues that television productions and museum installations increasingly share techniques designed to promote a sense of authenticity and immersive, emotional response in viewers/visitors. In the TV documentaries, which focus on the sensitive topic of the Allied air war on Germany, Jaeger demonstrates how fragmented witness testimony, archival footage, and shots of "authentic" spaces and ruins are edited into a kind of *Gesamtkunstwerk* with a marked tendency to simulate progression through multidimensional museum space. Noting that film increasingly informs the exhibited content and layout of museum exhibits, Jaeger traces several uses of film in German museums that point to a kind of unease. While the DHM has gone so far as to use film clips to explore how cinematic media have shaped collective memories of the Second World War in its 2004–5 exhibit *Myths of the Nations: 1945 – Arena of Memories,* in its permanent exhibition the DHM limits itself to using "authentic" film stock in order to provide an atmospheric ambience. Contrasting the DHM and several other German examples with a discussion of the exhibit 2010 *Krakow under Nazi Occupation,* in which the exhibition layout takes the form of a series of experiential moments that place visitors in several moments leading up to the Holocaust, Jaeger observes that German curators in the DHM and elsewhere seem highly reluctant to allow Second World War films to become deeply immersive. While immersive experience has become prevalent in films that appropriate museum techniques to broach topics as thorny as the Allied air war, images from Second World War cinema remain taboo material for historical museums, perhaps because experiencing the position of the perpetrator remains too fraught to contemplate in a museum setting.

Approaching another difficult National Socialist legacy, Annika Orich and Florentine Strzelczyk explore the contours of the recent archival fascination with Veit Harlan's notorious propaganda film *Jud Süß* (1940) in their analysis of Felix Moeller's *Harlan – Im Schatten von Jud Süß* (2008) and Oskar Roehler's *Jud Süß – Film ohne Gewissen* (2009/10). Noting that Harlan's motion picture has figured in multiple exhibitions, screenings, and two major cinematic projects since 2001, Orich and Strzelczyk pay particular attention to the divergent ways the latter – Moeller's *and* Roehler's films – use museal techniques to assemble, exhibit, contextualize, and didacticize the images in Harlan's film. As they explain, Orich and Strzelczyk regard the musealizing techniques employed by the two filmmakers as attempts to satisfy the desire to use authentic materials to educate subsequent generations about the conditions that made the Second World War and the Holocaust possible without running the risk of falling prey to the allegedly seductive power of Nazi propaganda. Though engaged by comparable strategies designed to isolate, contextualize, and thereby explain the images and conditions surrounding Harlan's production, the dangers of Harlan's images are explicated in different terms in the two contemporary films. Whereas Moeller's range of contextualizing techniques work from the premise that Harlan's images remain forever inseparable from virulent anti-Semitism and the spread of genocidal ideology, Roehler's film recreates the making of Harlan's film with the goal of generating affective excess in viewers. This strategy is thought plausible because for Roehler, the power of fascism lies not in the seductiveness of images, but in Nazism's ideological content and cultural context. In accord with their differing conceptions, then, the films develop curatorial strategies that respectively inhibit (Moeller) and invite (Roehler) affective visitor engagements that are both available using musealizing techniques. How cinema operates as archive and gallery, Orich and Strzelczyk suggest, depends as much on a filmmaker's premises and genre as it does on the past it displays.

The third of the volume's three essays that engage with legacies of the Third Reich, Kathryn M. Floyd's "Moving Statues: Arthur Grimm, The *Entartete Kunst* Exhibition, and Installation Photography as *Standfotografie*," uses surviving installation photographs as a point of entry into the complex dynamics leading up to the Nazis' most notorious exhibition. Driven to reverse the neglect that has befallen installation photography, Floyd's essay offers fresh perspectives on this infamous exhibition by showing how integral installation photography was to art, media, and museum practices in the first four decades of the twentieth century. As Floyd demonstrates, photographers such as Arthur Grimm worked alongside artists, filmmakers such as Leni Riefenstahl, and curatorial commissions such as those headed by Adolf Ziegler that mounted the *Degenerate Art* exhibition. By adroitly unravelling and illuminating multiple strands that come together in Grimm's photographs of the gallery floor, Floyd is able to relate the nuanced ways in which photography was able to musealize what is typically grasped primarily as a high-profile moment of de-musealization. While highly sensitive to the deadly politics involved in Nazi museum culture, Floyd nonetheless presents novel ways of understanding both the way photography has been deemed capable of preserving and even enlivening gallery space and the challenges and rewards of using musealization as a privileged vantage point for the study of art in medial and institutional contexts.

Based on a sustained engagement with Harun Farocki's 2006 reinvention of his 1996 film *Arbeiter verlassen die Fabrik* for multi-monitor gallery installation, Christine Sprengler offers a sophisticated account of Farocki's unlocking of the archival possibilities and limits of filmic and gallery-based media. Building on the critical commonplace that Farocki's 1996 film represents an archival project and/or "essay film," Sprengler's essay on his work greatly expands our understanding of the ways in which its terms – particularly the ways varying cinematic technologies represent and preserve notions of contested space – fundamentally involve concerns of musealization, remediation of history, and memory. These concerns Sprengler traces in the transformation of Farocki's project into a looped presentation on twelve monitors for the 2008 Hirshhorn exhibition, *The Cinema Effect*. Coining the term "expanded essay film" in order to elucidate the highly nuanced ways in which Farocki's installation operates in exhibitory context, Sprengler unpacks two sets of insights. The first, which she shows with respect to the installation itself, reveals how cinema, television, and museum offer distinct conduits to the past, even as they simultaneously and necessarily frame other media engaged in similar projects, whose basis is an underlying museal impulse. The second, which she generates by attending to the particularities of Farocki's installation in the Hirshhorn's gallery space, works to understand what Sprengler calls the spectator's co-performance of Farocki's analysis. Against this backdrop, Farocki's project is valorized a "thinking" work of art, an embedded and institutionally aware but also argumentative project capable of transforming the very way we conceive of the institutions of cinema and museum and their practices in the first place.

The final pairing of essays in the volume move from the photographic and filmic engagement with gallery space analysed by Floyd and Sprengler to the views of curators who have mounted exhibitions whose core concerns involved the themes of this volume. In their essay "Sex on Display: Sexual Science and the Exhibition *PopSex!*," historians and curators Michael Thomas Taylor and Annette F. Timm use their staging of the *PopSex!* exhibition at the Alberta College of Art + Design in 2011 to think through the role that exhibiting sex and sexuality has played in the development of sexual science. Looking to expose the work of early sexual scientist Magnus Hirschfeld to audiences largely unfamiliar with it, Taylor and Timm's exhibition contained museal gestures that amplified the place of collecting and exhibition at the centre of Hirschfeld's endeavours. The founder of what could be called the world's first well-known sex museum, Hirschfeld displayed objects and images throughout his Institute for Sexual Research in emulation of contemporary anthropological, biological, and medical collections that legitimized and furthered serious forms of knowledge production at the turn of the nineteenth to the twentieth centuries. Yet an institution whose boundaries with freak shows, panoptica, *Völkerschauen*, and other spectacles of the displayed body were more permeable than Hirschfeld might have wanted, Hirschfeld's sex museum offered Taylor and Timm a rich vehicle for engaging the sex museum in complex ways. Key in this regard was the object-driven driven film *N.O.Body*. Originally made as part of the 2008 *Sex Burns* exhibition in Berlin, this film deployed archival strategies designed to illuminate Hirschfeld's museum as an institution that, in carving out its own niche in the museum world of its day, anticipated the contemporary museum's turn to visitor experience. Yet in drawing out and itself working with visitor experience as a central category, precisely this aspect of the film required deep reflection on the problems of musealization and spectator engagement, since Western Canadians could not be assumed to share Berliners' assumptions about sex, Berliners' knowledge of history, and Berliners' expectations with regard to museum display. As Taylor and Timm detail in their concluding pages, their approach to *N.O.Body* carried over to the exhibition as a whole, with the curators employing open gestures of archival intervention and recovery in ways that envisioned musealization as an unfolding, future-oriented process in which visitors are left to produce knowledge and meaning on their own terms.

As the final contribution to this volume on film, museums, and musealization, curator Peter Mänz analyses the impetus and the strategies employed in the permanent exhibition of the Deutsche Kinemathek (German Cinemathek) in Berlin. As Mänz makes very clear, his museum's mission of using material artefacts to relate film history derives directly from the state of today's media. The ubiquity of moving images, made omnipresent via television, computers, and mobile devices, makes it ever harder to step back and reflect on their origin and function. At the same time, an approach to film history based solely on screenings cannot provide an overview that can be taken in in the span of a museum visit. But however strong the rationale for an object-based narrative of film history is, therefore, the challenge of representing cinema in exhibitory terms led designers to spatial and material metaphors that work in several registers. Drawing on the conventions of feature films, for instance, the visitor walk-through was conceived in terms of a single film, with the welcome gallery built to operate as a kind of "opening credits." On more abstract levels, the aura and authenticity of cinematic experience associated with screening needed to be translated into forms that can be carried by evocative objects, artefacts, and apparatus whose contours shaped what films could do in relation to the political, cultural, and commercial exigencies that drove their making. As Mänz shows in his analytical walk-through, screenings do not disappear in this environment. Rather, they become evidentiary elements that functionally recall historical documentary even as they reside in a context driven by the serendipity and open-endedness of a museum visit, in which the visitor is invited to become his or her own museal director, editor, and/or cinematographer.

NOTE

1 Bennett refers in part to the work of Griffiths.

1 The "Museal Gaze" and "Civic Seeing": City, Film, and Museum in Wim Wenders's *Der Himmel über Berlin*

SIMON WARD

Wim Wenders's 1987 film *Der Himmel über Berlin* (*Wings of Desire*) was made at a point where history seemed to have stagnated, and the division of Berlin seemed permanently enshrined in the Wall that carved through the city. Since 1989, Berlin has been radically transformed, an urban transformation that has brought with it a renewed focus on urban memory, and the display of many parts of the city as "open air museums." In order to begin to understand how urban memory and the city as museum is structured, it is instructive to return to Wenders's film, as a close analysis of its engagement with the city and its past reveals modes of encounter that can be identified in contemporary Berlin.

The Expanded Museum and the Museal Gaze

In *Twilight Memories*, his 1995 study of memory in an age of amnesia, Andreas Huyssen observed that the boundaries of the contemporary museum were becoming ever less distinct. Huyssen embraced this development, arguing that it undid the traditional mission of the museum as the purveyor of an exclusionary, conservative narrative of nationhood (35). In this, Huyssen is in line with Tony Bennett, who in his essay "Civic Seeing: Museums and the Organization of Vision," charts the shifting "regimes of vision" in museums, whereby "the directed forms of vision that have dominated Western museum practices since the Enlightenment" have "given way to more dialogic practices of seeing which, in enabling a greater degree of visual give-and-take between different perspectives, might prove more conducive to the requirements of 'civic seeing' in culturally diverse societies" ("Civic Seeing" 264).

Beyond this embracing of diversity, there was another positive element that Huyssen identified in this expansion of the museum, a "newfound strength of the museum and the monument in the public sphere" (*Twilight Memories* 255). This strength has, on the surface, little to do with Huyssen's celebration of the post-national museum. Rather, Huyssen surmised that it might have "something to do with the fact that they both offer something that television denies: the material quality of the object" (255). Huyssen theorized this, rather cursorily, in terms of "the museal gaze" (34).

Huyssen privileged this particular aspect of the museum experience in reaction to postmodern theorizations of the museum in the 1980s, responding in particular to Baudrillard's assertion that musealization is "the pathological attempt of contemporary culture to preserve, to control [and] to dominate the real" (*Twilight Memories* 30). Musealization, in this critique, "simulates the real" (30). For Huyssen, by contrast, the "museal gaze" redeems the idea of the "museal" as that which enables a connection to the real. In the case of both the museum and the monument in public space, there is a "live gaze" (31) that interacts with the object. For Huyssen, crucially, this live gaze produces the auratic power of the object: "Objects of the past have always been pulled into present via the gaze that hit them, and the irritation, the seduction, the secret they may hold is never only on the side of the object in some state of purity, as it were; it is always and intensely located on the side of the viewer and the present as well" (31).

It is the live gaze that endows the object with its aura, much as Pierre Nora argues of "lieux de memoire," that "even an apparently purely material site becomes a lieu de memoire only if the imagination invests it with a symbolic aura" (19). For Huyssen, however, the museal gaze is dependent on the live presence both of the observer and of an object, whose key qualities are its materiality and its opacity, and the fact that, as he writes:

> The more mummified an object is, the more intense its ability to yield experience, a sense of the authentic. No matter how fragile or dim the relation between museum object and the reality it documents may be, either in the way it is exhibited or in the mind of the spectator, as object it carries the register of reality which even the live television broadcast cannot match. (33)

In the process of distancing himself from Baudrillard and the postmodern critique of the museum, Huyssen is clearly still invested in the ideal of the rational, attentive, well-ordered museum-going public, an ideal which is founded on the rejection of "the clouding, diverting, hypnotic, dazzling, numbing, or shock effects of more popular visual technologies" (Bennett, "Civic Seeing" 273). Huyssen's museal gaze is a counterpoint to the "television gaze," and its encounter with this "register of reality" defines the anamnestic dimension of the material object. This anamnestic dimension, which Huyssen terms "memory value" (*Twilight Memories* 33), residing as it does in the object's opacity, needs to be distinguished from the transmission of critical historical knowledge and understanding. Rather, the museal gaze "may be said to … reclaim a sense of non-synchronicity and of the past" (*Twilight Memories* 34): that "sense," which becomes "presence" and "experience" in the following quotation, incorporates precisely a form of attentiveness.

> The older an object, the more presence it can command, the more distinct it is from current-and-soon-to-be obsolete as well as recent-and-already obsolete objects. That also may be enough to lend them an aura, to reenchant them beyond any instrumental functions they may have had at an earlier time. It may be precisely the isolation of the object from its genealogical context that permits the experience via the museal glance of reenchantment. (*Twilight Memories* 33)

The object at this point in Huyssen's description closely resembles Alois Riegl's early-twentieth-century conception of the "unintended monument," an object or building that had lost its original function. For Riegl, the unintended monument had a democratic significance, and in that it was located outside the (Germanic) national monumental canon, took the "curation" of objects out of the realm of the expert; the object was in a "natural" state of decline (Riegl 144).

In identifying the "memory value" of the material object, Huyssen is also close to Alois Riegl's definition of "age value" in his discussion of the unintended monument, where the "age value" of the object had nothing to do with its previous function (and thus to an understanding of the object's place in history), and much more to do with its contrast, for the spectator, with the surrounding modern buildings (Riegl 145). The age value of the material object testifies to the passing of time, rendering historical time visible where it would otherwise be invisible.

Huyssen's museal gaze produces, in the interaction between live spectator and opaque material object, an awareness of past time that is at odds with a synchronous present. Riegl's monuments were situated in public space, and, crucially, Huyssen sees his museal gaze as operating both in the museum and in the museum in an expanded, amorphous sense, in relation to monuments' "reclaimed public space, in pedestrian zones, in restored urban centres, or in pre-existing memorial spaces" (*Twilight Memories* 255).

By the time he published *Present Pasts: Urban Palimpsests and the Politics of Memory* (2003), Huyssen had dropped the perhaps too positive concept of the "museal gaze" from his analysis of how memory operates in urban spaces. If we wish to take up the question of the museal gaze within urban space, Michel de Certeau's essay "Walking in the City" is especially helpful. De Certeau contrasts the ostensible visual mastery of the solar eye, which designs the "concept-city" (hereafter paraphrased as the "synchronic gaze"), with the "tactile" heterogeneous practices of "walking the city" at ground level, which "resist" the rationalist logic of the planners. De Certeau allows us to formulate a particular "regime of seeing" which emerges from the synchronic gaze, or, in Bennett's terms, "the civic lessons embodied in those arrangements," which "are to be seen, understood, and performed" by the citizens ("Civic Seeing" 263). Gaze might imply a static vantage-point, but it is more useful to think this stasis in temporal, rather than spatial, terms. To modify and expand Bennett's terms, the synchronic gaze produces a form of "civic seeing" which produces the "good citizen" as one who is best adapted to the most efficient circulation of goods and consumers, to which a more differentiated perception of time (one including past and future, rather than synchronic present) would then be an "obstacle." In "Walking in the City," this is precisely how de Certeau formulates the presence of the past in the city.

In a later essay, "Ghosts in the City," de Certeau identifies a historical development that echoes Huyssen's view of the expanded museum. Whereas before, "the technicians [had been] supposed to make a tabula rasa of the opacities that disrupted the plans for a city of glass," now they were working at "extending the museum out of its walls, at museifying the city" ("Ghosts" 133). The expansion of the museum is not read positively by de Certeau, for he rejects this process of musealization, the "taming of the strangeness of the past with meaning" in favour of the evocative power of what, with Riegl, we can read as unintended monuments. He singles out the "seemingly sleepy, old-fashioned things," "these inanimate objects," which, "by eluding the law of the present, ... acquire a certain autonomy" ("Ghosts" 133). "These ... defaced houses, closed-down factories, the debris of shipwrecked histories still today raise up the ruins of an unknown, strange city. They burst forth within the modernist, massive, homogeneous city like slips of the tongue from an unknown, perhaps unconscious, language" (ibid.).

Here de Certeau celebrates the unconscious immediacy by which the objects of the past "burst forth": they are not invoked, but they evoke. De Certeau does not seek to explain how these ghosts become recognizable in a visual regime dominated by the synchronic urban gaze. On the one hand, they are "slips of the tongue," on the other, like Riegl's unintended monuments, they are anomalous, obsolescent material presences, simply "there, closed in on themselves, silent forces." Their virtue, in an era when other objects are "ennobled and ... see themselves recognized with a place and a sort of insurance on life," is to "actually ... function as history" ("Ghosts" 137). This is not "history" in the negative sense employed by Pierre Nora in contrast to "true memory," for it consists in "opening a certain depth within the present, but they no longer have the contents that tame the strangeness of the past with meaning. Their histories cease to be pedagogical; they are no longer 'pacified,' nor colonized by semantics – as if returned to their existence, wild, delinquent" (135).

This "opening of depth" suggests how "past time" is inserted into the present "nowhen" ("Walking" 94), but, importantly, it is the object that "does" this itself. It is the lack of intentional signification, the absence of pacifying, pedagogical semantics that enables their delinquency, much as for Nora, the investment of symbolic aura should achieve maximum meaning through the fewest of signs (19).

In discussing the expansion of the museum into urban space, de Certeau's key distinction is one that is not made by Huyssen: between the access to the past that is limited by the "ennobling" musealization process in the city, which constructs monuments in the service of a technocratic synchronicity, and the access to a strange past that is made possible by the ruin. De Certeau crucially excludes both the curator and the spectator from his description of this latter encounter: this past is not put on display, but is simply present.

We need to differentiate this form of encounter with the opaque, material object (aka the unintended monument) in urban space from the encounter with material objects in the museum or in reclaimed public space, but also with material objects in an urban space that has/have not (yet) been reclaimed. This will enable us to expand the implications of Huyssen's museal gaze, where the "live"-ness of Huyssen's "live gaze" is crucial in the recuperation of the museal gaze from the negative connotations of the object's "musealized" presence. Huyssen is also more honest, unlike de Certeau, in fundamentally implying that a "seeing eye" has a key role to play (even if he does not investigate the implication that this seeing eye's vision might be organized, or even, really, how, as Hilde Hein writes in her brief consideration of Huyssen's concept, "the aura-conferring gaze rests upon an object's musealized presence" (*Public Art* 118). De Certeau, by contrast, suggests that the unintended (i.e., non-pacified) object possesses a potential sense of the past and non-synchronicity. At the heart of the distinction is a question about the agency of the spectator and of the object, and, beyond that, how we think that relation between spectator and object, and what shapes that relation.

Film and the Museal Gaze

The following discussion proposes that the "urban museal gaze" is one way of formulating a particular form of encounter with the past in the city, a way of thinking the non-musealized object not as a discrete object, but as the product of a moment of encounter which is at the same time a moment of discovery and a moment of preservation. This "urban museal gaze" is investigated through the medium of film by Wim Wenders in *Der Himmel über Berlin* (*Wings of Desire*, 1987). After reading the work done by this gaze, I develop the insights offered by Wenders's film in the final section that examines a paradigm shift in regimes of vision whose contours are still changing in the years after the fall of the Wall. This sea change manifests in various practices (urban planning, preservation, installation art) in the city, and produces a different form of seeing as attention in the city, which one might describe as a form of urban memory. The fact that this city is Berlin is not insignificant. If, following the implications of de Certeau's argument, non-museified ruins themselves shape an implicit form of seeing, then the urban museal gaze that emerges in Berlin in the 1970s and 1980s is perhaps also shaped by the city itself. Wenders said in an interview around the time of the release of *Der Himmel über Berlin*: "Berlin has a lot of empty spaces ... I like the city for its wounds. They show its history better than any history book or document ... [The] empty spaces allow the visitor and the people of Berlin to see through the cityscape ..., through these gaps in a sense they can see through *time*" (Wenders, *Act of Seeing* 98–9).

Wenders's claim for Berlin has many resonances with de Certeau's version of the museal object: the wounds of the city give immediate access to the past and counteract the synchronic cityscape. In consort with

Huyssen's formulation of the museal gaze, however, there is a symbiotic relationship between spectator and material object in the production of a gaze that can perceive a sense of the past and of non-synchronicity. As with Riegl, the immediate experience of temporality is privileged over the transmission of historical knowledge and understanding. Wenders's quotation implies an immediate experience of the cityscape by the visitor/citizen. This elision is significant; the visitor does not have the immediate relationship that binds the citizen to place, as Maurice Halbwachs argues in his essay "Space and the Collective Memory," but is *in* the city, and therefore subject to the practices of "civic seeing." Wenders here proposes a decontextualized observer of the opaque, material object that can be extended to the cinematic spectatorial situation (one that is heavily implied by *Der Himmel über Berlin*'s interest in Berlin's cityscape). Emma Wilson has brought Huyssen's "museal gaze" into contact with cinema in her discussion of Alain Resnais's use of tracking shots in *Night and Fog* (1955). For Wilson, these shots produce "a more mobile, three-dimensional, even haptic encounter with history and its material relics than the conventional museum provides," which "might be aligned with Andreas Huyssen's reflections on the new possibilities of the museal gaze" ("Material Remains" 108). Wilson does not subject her problematic association of Huyssen's contemporary observations with a film from 1955 to further elaboration. Nevertheless, such extended tracking shots, as well as powerfully haptic close-ups, are also a striking feature of Resnais's next film, *Hiroshima Mon Amour* (1959). This film can be read as a prime example of cinematic scepticism towards the "conventional" museum (for which the Hiroshima museum stands in, despite, or perhaps precisely because of the way in which Resnais's camera encounters it, namely, in fluid sweeps that undermine "the singular and fixed spectatorial position that museums sought to arrange as the ideal vantage point from which to see and understand the logic underlying the exhibition arrangements" ("Civic Seeing" 276). Indeed, the opening dialogue between the two principal characters (Elle and Lui) expresses the conventional critique of musealization, summarized by Andreas Huyssen as a process that is "freezing, sterilizing, dehistoricizing and decontextualizing" (30), the reduction of the past to a framed image, "drained of life" (30).

In Laura Marks's terms, the haptic encounter in cinema undoes "visual mastery" (152), but also the mastery of the past; it runs counter to clarified historical seeing as comprehension, which is constructed in *Hiroshima Mon Amour* as the museum's mission and ultimate failing. Through their refusal to frame the object, the tracking shots point not only to the limits of historical understanding, but also to the *necessity* of the encounter for any *beginning* of understanding. The extended tracking shot draws our attention to the duration of the encounter with the object, the material extent of the object, and frames, or rather constantly reframes, our gaze upon the object. This stands in contrast to the conventional museum's static framing, which compels the visitor's body to halt in order to gaze upon the framed object.

The camera in *Hiroshima Mon Amour* travels not only through the museum in the city, but also constructs an encounter with the past, a speaking and a listening at the *site of trauma*. Emma Wilson, writing on *Hiroshima Mon Amour*, argues that "the film seems here to be fitted to the city, to bear the impression of the city's spaces and topography, its past and present" (*Alain Resnais* 62). The key to these sequences is that "the camera imitates the woman's blind, mnemonic pacing through these ..., urban spaces [of Nevers and Hiroshima]" (63). The camera mimics a mobile gaze, imitating the very particular psychological state the film investigates, the gradual recovery of a repressed memory, in which the ostensibly secure borders of the subject are rendered permeable to both space and time, expressed most clearly in the fractured flashbacks from the death of Elle's German lover, which can be described, with de Certeau, "like slips of the tongue from an ... unconscious language." Who sees these flashbacks? Perhaps Elle, but she is hardly in a state of visual mastery – these images happen *to* her – but certainly the cinema spectator, who, in Wenders's terms, sees *through* time, without comprehending what they have seen.

Film, or Resnais's film-making at least, is able to give us a way of thinking about the position of the spectator in the "museal encounter" with the opaque, material object, a spectator who has surrendered the synchronic visual mastery that de Certeau identifies in "Walking in the City."

Cinema and the Museum versus Television

Before discussing *Der Himmel über Berlin* in detail, one further point of correlation between Wenders and Huyssen needs to be elucidated. The oppositions of Huyssen's argument, in particular the museum versus television, seem somewhat obsolete given the recent advances in new media (though they do not necessarily diminish the relevance of his insistence on the compensatory power of the material object). Similarly, to think, in this digital era, about the relation between cinema and the "museal gaze" could be seen as a merely historical exercise. Yet it is crucial to an understanding of the historical moment out of which the museal gaze emerges, and from where it has evolved. Like Huyssen, Wenders is sceptical about television, which brings "the new idea of being able to view distant events 'live,' as they happened ... It [is] colder, less emotional than the movies, and it [takes] us further away from the idea that an image has a direct link with 'reality'" (*Act of Seeing* 94). Televisual hyperreality could "only be opposed by our European images, our common art and language, our European cinema" (146–7). Cinema thus emerges as a medium for Wenders that can counteract Huyssen's "television gaze," with its more direct link with reality. This argument has its roots in Bazin's essay on the "ontology of the photographic image," which founds the value of the photographic image (and by extension the cinematic image) on its automatic, indexical link with reality.

Wenders's faith in the photographic image as an indexical record of reality is borne out by his observations on the buildings in Berlin that were being sacrificed to urban planning. When asked in an interview whether he saw film-making as an archival activity, Wenders replied that the fact that a building is about to disappear is always a good reason to include it in a scene. This implies another way in which the city and its form shapes the film, but *Der Himmel über Berlin* does not just include ruins and threatened buildings in its scenes in acts of celluloid preservation. Those acts of preservation are simultaneously framed as active encounters between spectator/camera and the material, opaque remnants that litter the Berlin cityscape.

Museal Encounters in *Der Himmel über Berlin*

Wenders proposes the city(scape) as a repository of the past that is activated into a space of museal encounter through the live gaze of the camera/viewer. This "live gaze" is foregrounded in an early sequence in the film. The angel Damiel, atop the ruin of the war-damaged Kaiser Wilhelm Memorial Church, looks down on citizens moving across a pedestrian crossing. While almost all the citizens are walking according to the traffic regulations, a child stops in the middle of the pedestrian crossing to look up at Damiel. The film here contrasts the instrumentalized mode of seeing (in) the city, a "civic seeing" which is blind to everything except the regulation of circulation, with that of the curious child's mode of perception. The child stops moving, and can perceive the angel, but the child also sees the wound, the Kaiser Wilhelm Memorial Church (figure 1.1), much more dominant in the long shot of the angel.

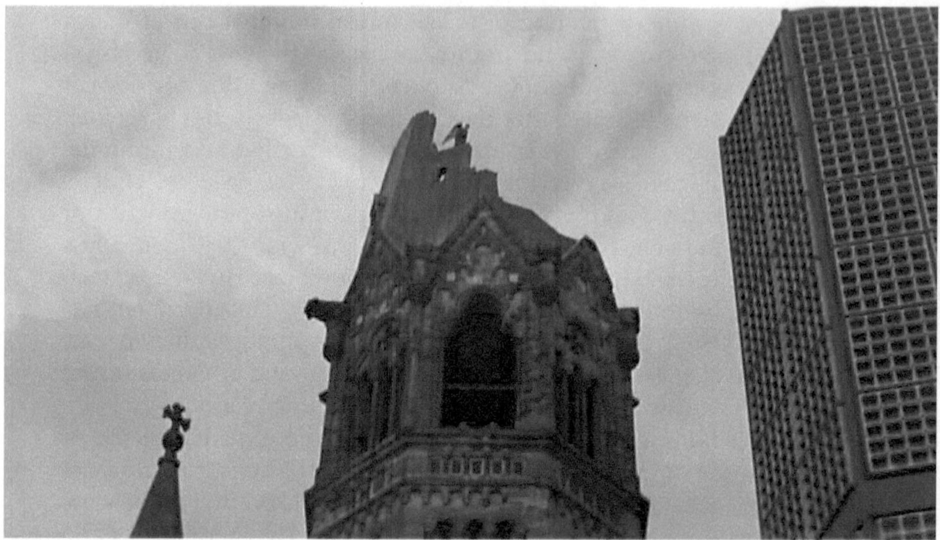

1.1 Still from Wim Wenders's *Himmel über Berlin* (*Wings of Desire*), 1987, showing the ruin of the Kaiser Wilhelm Memorial Church. Photo © and courtesy of Road Movies Filmproduktion.

Not only the child, but also the cinematic viewer, sees the "wound," and is invited to see, via the "age value" of the ruin, through the synchronic time of the city. It is of course debatable that the Kaiser Wilhelm Memorial Church "shows the history of the city better than any history book or document" (Wenders, *Act of Seeing* 98), but historical understanding is secondary to "age value." Importantly, right from the start, the film establishes a precondition of the museal gaze, one that is aligned with de Certeau: to see through the cityscape is to see through its reduction to a phenomenon of a utilitarian present, the means by which ever-present circulation can be regulated.

The "mobile mise-en-scène" (see Rectanus, in this volume) can thus be thought of as being constructed by the film in a contrast between two ways of encountering the cityscape: on the one hand, a form of civic seeing which may itself not be one of "visual mastery," but which is shaped by the logic of the synchronic organization of time, and, on the other, a gaze that performs a different form of perception, and therefore a different form of encounter with the material of the city. The dominant regime of seeing the city sees *only* the cityscape; the alternative regime of seeing the city which *Der Himmel über Berlin* proposes to its viewer is that which sees *through* the cityscape, by not seeing the cityscape as a framed object. Indeed, this strategy is manifest right from the start of the film, when the mobile camera (mimicking the film's angelic perspective) swoops down from above and passes *through* the walls of a tenement block to reveal the alienated lives of the citizens otherwise inaudible and invisible behind the facades of the cityscape.

Throughout, the film shows how the gaze of the vast majority of citizens is locked into the logic of the concept-city, most explicitly exemplified in the sequences showing them in their cars on the urban freeway whose construction, already inscribed into reconstruction plans in the immediate post-war period and then enacted from the 1950s onwards, was instrumental in the demolition of many old buildings. This "urban synchronic gaze" from the car is undone in sections that also demonstrate film's archiving function, and its potential for constructing a museal encounter. Through the use of archival footage that is montaged into a drive down the Potsdamer Strasse, this taxi journey becomes *also* a drive through the streets of Berlin towards the end of the Second World War. Wenders aligns the spectator's gaze with that of one of the film's figures, the angel Cassiel, who has a more complex relationship to time than that of the taxi driver, whose thoughts, which we hear, simply follow the logic of the synchronic city (he is, after all, a taxi driver). The live gaze of the cinematic spectator thus encounters the material object of film as an indexical record of a past that is conventionally invisible in a cityscape that has expunged past time. This form of filmic museal gaze is illustrated again in a sequence where Homer wanders across the empty space of Potsdamer Platz. As he wanders in a state of disorientation, the film montages colour images of the Platz presumably from the end of the Second World War. Homer's ability to see *through* time is used as a way of showing film's capacity to store past time, and re-present it at a later point.

The aforementioned drive down Potsdamer Strasse brings Cassiel to the former air-raid bunker which is being used as a location for *Der Himmel über Berlin*'s film-within-a-film, whose melodramatic appropriation of "Third Reich" history for a mass market forms another of the film's analogies with *Hiroshima Mon Amour*. If Resnais's film, in investigating Elle's story, formed the counterpoint to the "story of peace" which Elle was to make in Hiroshima, then Wenders's film, in following Peter Falk, who has come to play a role in this American production, constructs itself in an analogous way. As the "visitor to Berlin," Falk walks

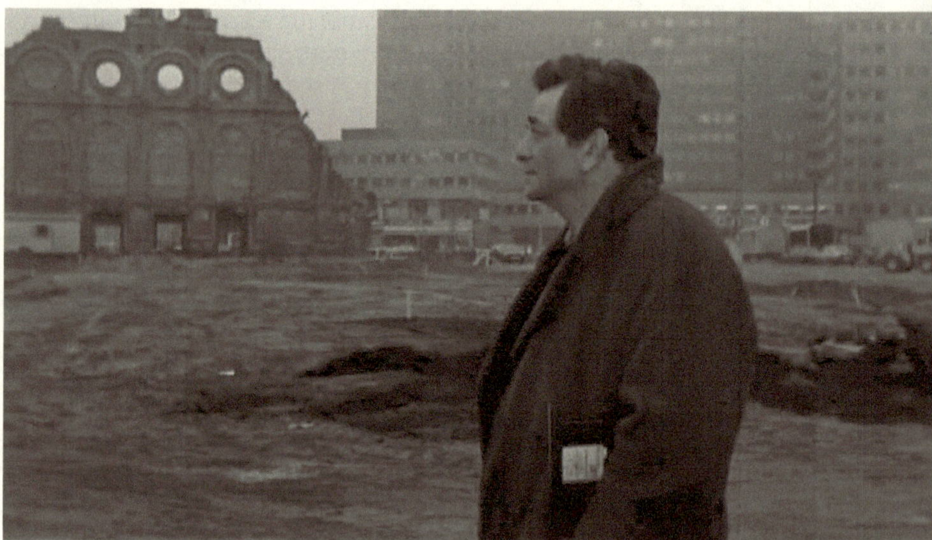

1.2 Still from Wim Wenders's *Himmel über Berlin* showing Peter Falk before the ruin of the Anhalter train station. Photo © and courtesy of Road Movies Filmproduktion.

through the city, also seeing *through* time. In one sequence the camera tracks Falk as he wanders across the vast empty space behind the ruin of the facade of the former Anhalter Bahnhof. The soundtrack allows us to hear Falk's inner monologue, which runs "spazieren, walking, looking and seeing," at which point he, and the camera, stop to look upon the ruin of the station "where the station stopped."[1] The cinematic museal gaze is again produced by a live gaze upon an opaque material object in which the spectator's gaze is aligned with that of a character. The special quality of Falk's "walking, looking and seeing" is established through a contrast with the Berliners who walk past him in the opposite direction. As Falk disappears from the shot, the Berliners wonder whether this figure is Columbo, illustrating their trained fascination with images from American television, as well as their obliviousness to the ruin. Yet the camera has stopped its tracking of Falk. The final shot is of the men aligned with the new building behind the ruin, which is still visible in the margins on the left-hand side of the frame (figure 1.2).

Here, Wenders makes use of depth-of-field to maintain the presence of the ruin even when the producer of the museal gaze, Falk, has disappeared from the shot. This recalls a sequence from Wenders's first feature-length film, *Summer in the City* (1970), which was set in Munich and Berlin, and already betrays his interest in vanishing buildings. *Summer in the City* is punctuated by a series of sequences that not only show but also embody movement through the city. In six separate extended tracking shots, Wenders engages with the view of the cityscape from a car. The film's seventh extended tracking shot then consists of the central character walking. The camera moves at the pace of the moving object. Yet the remarkable aspect of this sequence is that the object of our gaze is reversed in the sequence's conclusion. More radically even than in the Falk sequence in *Der Himmel über Berlin*, we thought the object of our attention was the walking protagonist, but in fact we realize that it was the building behind him for the duration of the shot. The camera allows the protagonist to disappear from the frame as it comes to a halt, and we are invited to contemplate the beautiful, but dilapidated building. Here, Wenders interrupts the conventional regime of cinematic seeing, which focuses on the movement of the body of the protagonist, and engages us in a form of museal gaze, a contemplation of the city through which he (and we) conventionally move without looking – crucially, the central character here is *also* not looking at the building. While there are parallels to the Falk/Anhalter sequence, perhaps the most striking thing is that Wenders actually reshot this sequence during the making of *Der Himmel über Berlin*. As Wenders remarks in his audio commentary to the DVD extras (itself a mini-museum to this "masterpiece" of film-making, which also suggests something of the contemporary musealization of the film that is enacted at Frank Werner's BMW-Welt, as discussed by Rectanus, in this volume), the building in the shot is Emil Fahrenkamp's Shell House, which at the time of filming (in both 1970 and 1986) was threatened with demolition. On the surface, the purpose of reshooting the sequence was to "preserve" the building one more time on celluloid. Yet Wenders also reshoots the mode of showing/seeing the building, the cinematic museal gaze that makes use of depth of field and tracking shots to induce the same temporal duration of the encounter with the material object in the spectator. In line with Bazinian film philosophy, and employing a Bazinian long take, Wenders uses film to construct a museal gaze that both records an indexical reality, and reveals that reality to the cinematic viewer.

Wenders's use of the mobile camera in the construction of the museal gaze in these sequences shows how cinema can elude the ossification of the material object through a haptic encounter with that object. The film shows that the present cityscape is inhabited by the past, even if that past is not always transparently visible, and also shows that through the encounter with those objects that bear a "register of reality," an alternative way of seeing the city, a museal gaze, can be redeemed.

Archiving "Ways of Seeing"

This kind of archiving of ways of seeing (of certain forms of gaze) is a central element in the museal encounters constructed by the film. Wenders's penchant for the cinephiliac reconstruction of sequences from the history of cinema is indulged not only in his archiving of his own way of seeing. I will draw out two example of this from the film.

In one scene, set in the film's one official "museum" (the Berlin State Library) we see Homer leafing through a book of photographs. Although there is nothing overt to indicate it, this book is August Sander's photographic collection *Citizens of the Twentieth Century*. When one turns to the book itself, one finds that while the majority of Sander's portraits date from the Weimar period of the 1920s, the ones Wenders chooses to show, and on which the camera lingers, are portraits of persecuted Jews from 1937 and 1938.

The ostensible self-evidence of the photographs is problematic, for the viewer is not privileged with the information about the subjects I have just provided, and therefore can only be expected to read the images in formal terms. What strikes the spectator about the images, perhaps, is that the subjects are looking directly into the camera in a rather unsettling manner. Again, the "innocent" viewer cannot know that this is different from the rest of the images of "persecuted Jews," whom Sander photographed in profile.

My suspicion is that this lack of information is Wenders's intention. The viewer cannot prejudge the individuals according to their "sociological" classification (the one which both the Nazi regime and Sander gave them). As a result, the viewer must treat them with the respect that Wenders believes Sander treated his subjects as a photographer-artist. This is a respect consonant with Wenders's conception of the art of seeing: such an art of seeing "rescues the existence of things" (*On Film* 159), or, as Sander, alluding to Rilke, himself described it in 1927: "Photography ... can render things with magnificent beauty but also with terrifying truthfulness ... We must be able to bear the sight of truth" (Sander 645–6).

Through the decontextualized manner in which he cites Sander's photography, Wenders evokes the memory of a particular way of seeing, in that Sander did not photograph the collective of which the individual is merely a functional unit, but invites the viewer to investigate the individuality of each photograph's subject. Such an interpretation of Sander's work, of course, is in line with Sander's own vision, and could well form part of Wenders's intention in recalling this past visual culture.

In the case of Sander's photography, film's museal gaze is a cinematic encounter with an earlier form of seeing objects, not as objects but as part of a more complex encounter. The encounter with former ways of seeing can also be read as an organizing principle behind some of the more allusive and elusive moments of filmic intertextuality in *Der Himmel über Berlin*. In one sequence, the camera tracks Damiel as he walks through a shopping arcade and then stops in front of a display window for electrical goods (television, cameras, and video recorders). Damiel, munching an apple, is captivated by a television screen, which at that moment is displaying the image of the actor Peter Falk. The image freezes, and is then replaced by a clock. Damiel checks his own watch, reminding us of his entrance into the regulation of "human" time, before he moves on.

This scene is a revisiting of the famous scene from Fritz Lang's *M* (1931), where M, played by Peter Lorre, munching an apple, stops in front of a metalware shop, attracted by the sheer number of knives displayed in the window (though Wenders, otherwise so keen to point out the references to the past in the film, omits to mention this in his audio guide to his museum-film). Wenders's film also becomes a display space for the archive of (his version of) film history. Once more, though, it is not simply the display of an object, but also an awareness that the object in its urban environment is subject to a certain regime of seeing. In Lang's film, as M stands before the window, devouring both the apple and the knives in a literal and visual sense, we are reminded, as Janet Ward writes, "how fundamentally the command of advertising on our psyches is based on the promise of gratification" (237), and the deadly way in which the display window fosters scopophilia and voyeurism in the denizen of the city. Lang's film, then, is a critical commentary on the "commercial forms of popular visual entertainment, which are said to lure the eye into civically unproductive forms of visual pleasure" ("Civic Seeing" 264).

In *Der Himmel über Berlin*, however, it is the moving image that has itself become commodified in the display window: and it is moving image technology, and American images and American TV (Columbo) that are for sale. Wenders's observation, in another essay, that "images once had as a primary purpose to show something, that primary purpose is becoming more and more the tendency to sell something" (*Act of Seeing* 96), implies that, as with Sander's photography, he displays past images (in his revisiting of Lang's *M*) not just to preserve a threatened object (in this case Lang's legacy), but to preserve and display a different regime of seeing: the images of Lang's films *show* us how images are being used to sell a mode of seeing. *Wings of Desire* invites us to see through time back to a different regime of seeing. The cinematic display of the past is thus, for Wenders, an act of showing, rather than selling, the past to the spectator. Again, the point of contrast would be the bunker in which the image of the National Socialist past is being framed to not show anything, but to be displayed for profit.

Such intertextuality can be read as a way of preserving a tradition, European traditions of ways of seeing versus a televisual way of seeing, but precisely not "pacifying" it. The intertextuality is not signposted, or framed in any way; its very surreptitiousness means that it does not rely on the recognition that this is an opaque object from the past.

Hotel Esplanade: "The City as Museum" and the Museal Encounter

If we follow the intertextual thread of *Hiroshima mon amour*, then the final melodramatic dialogue, framed in close-up, between the angel and the trapeze artist can be read as a reprise of the concluding dialogue between Elle and Lui. This dialogue is situated in the ruins of another threatened object of the Cold War era, the Hotel Esplanade. The Hotel Esplanade is a paradigmatic space in *Wings of Desire*, an interstitial space and time on the ultimate margin of West Berlin, the ruins of Potsdamer Platz where the concept-city has not yet imposed the regime of synchronic time. The scene in the Hotel Esplanade is not only, to my mind, a self-conscious pastiche of melodramatic narrative conclusions (see Rectanus in this volume), but also the culmination of the film's construction of a museal gaze, a way of encountering the city as the repository of past time. The materiality of the Esplanade is crucial in this regard.

Once again, Wenders makes use of a tracking shot as the camera follows Marion from the ballroom where Nick Cave and the Bad Seeds are about to perform "From Her to Eternity" and moves through the bar that is located to one side of it. As it does so, Wenders makes use of depth of field in order to record the material traces of the historic bar, but also mise-en-scène to track past a figure who reproduces, perhaps rather surreptitiously, Otto Dix's 1926 portrait of Sylvia von Harden.

This is most obvious in the position of the woman's arm and the cigarette and in the use of colours red and white reversed from the painting; it is, of course, Marion who is wearing von Harden's red.

Friedemann Kreuder, in his study of the Hotel Esplanade as a cultural-historical object, argues that the scene provides the "experience of one's own historicity" (36) in the Esplanade's atmosphere. In another formulation of the hapticality of the museal gaze, Kreuder argues that Wenders provides "an aesthetic experience of historical material, not in the sense of a critical-pessimistic judgment, but as a value-free perception, sensation, appreciation of shapes and colors" (36).

This mise-en-scène invites a museal gaze, the Esplanade is now a space in which the city's repository can be reactivated and put on display for the "live gaze" of the cinematic spectator. In the practically invisible presence of the past, the film precisely engages with the problem of musealization and the potential of the monument whose meaning is not foregrounded.

If one wishes to contextualize the Dix reference, then it would be possible to establish a parallel between this singular "close up" in Dix's oeuvre alongside the multi-panelled portraits of city life (such as Big City Triptych), and the "close-up" of the couple and the diptych that is the scene in the Esplanade. Such intertextuality is not (simply) a game for cinephiles (or connoisseurs) to play "spot the reference," but is part of a method throughout the film, whereby the museal encounter is staged in the film. The object is present within, but not ossified in, the frame. Wenders does not provide intentional signification, and in the absence of pacifying, pedagogical semantics, the object retains the potentiality of the material object.

Throughout the film Wenders cinematically frames the conditions under which the museal gaze can operate in the city. That gaze is, however, founded not on a singular and fixed spectorial vantage point ("Civic Seeing"), but mobilizes the medium of film to produce a "museal gaze" which dislocates the eye not only from its controlling position, but also from the "pace and speed of modernization" (Huyssen, *Twilight Memories* 255) and the synchronic organization of time that dominates in the city. Film can produce a hapticality that transcends the reification of the object, maintaining its opacity. It does not re*claim* the obsolescent object, as a subject appropriating an object, but can propose a way of engaging the non-musealized object, a moment of encounter which is simultaneously a moment of discovery and a moment of preservation.

The Museal Gaze in Berlin, 1979 to "Now"

The Hotel Esplanade is not just a film set. It is also a material part of the city and its past. Its recuperation as a fragment of urban memory, of an element in the city as repository/archive/museum, had begun in 1979, with the transformation of this "obsolete site" in the no-man's land of Potsdamer Platz into an installation space by the Italian graphic artist Antonio Recalcati and the stage director Klaus Michael Grüber. In his reading of this work, Friedemann Kreuder argues that they created a place for recollection for the viewer that allowed for numerous readings and induced the kind of association/recall/question-and-answer game that constructed anew a narrative/narratives out of extant knowledge, perceptions of the photographs, and products of the imagination (Kreuder 29).

For Kreuder, their installation became a "virtual storage facility" for reflections in which "no sense of certainty about the past," other than that there had been a past, could be gained (30). This is a formulation of the museal gaze that can be associated with the emergence of urban memory at this time in West and East Berlin – the expansion of the structures of the museum to the urban environment. We see the formation of the International Building Exhibition (IBA), the uncovering of the Topography of Terror, Raffael Rheinsberg's (pseudo-)archaeological investigations and exhibitions at the Anhalter Bahnhof, the preservation-reconstruction of certain areas of the Prenzlauer Berg and the Nikolaiviertel in East Berlin. The first high point of that wave were the civic celebrations for the 750th anniversary of the founding of Berlin, one of whose key elements was the *Mythos Berlin* exhibition, in which a material site, the Anhalter Bahnhof, became a kind of storage facility for an inventive exhibition engaging with the history of the city, without establishing a coherent historical narrative. A more extended analysis of the form of encounter with the past illustrated in these various constructions of the city as museum would allow the further elaboration of the museal gaze that we have identified at work in *Der Himmel über Berlin*.

The "aesthetic experience of historical material" has become one of the dominant paradigms of the display of the past in Berlin in the twenty years since unification, and is of course not a phenomenon limited to Berlin, as discussed by Rectanus in this volume. Indeed, Rectanus's concept of "refracted memory" can be fruitfully discussed in relation to the pseudo-museal installations of Christian Boltanski (such as "Missing House"), the many (re-)uses of the shell of the Palace of the Republic (most notably Lars Ramberg's "Zweifel"), and also in the more populist presentation of fragments of the Wall, S-Bahn memorabilia, and Weimar iconography at Potsdamer Platz, not to mention the translocation of the breakfast room of the Hotel Esplanade and its incorporation into the Sony Center (see Ward, "Globalization"), something in which Wenders himself played a leading role.

So significant in capturing the obsolescent in the formative years of the urban museal gaze, particularly in GDR cinema of the 1970s (see Ward, "Obsolescence"), the cinema has played only a minor role in this expansion of the museum into the urban environment, most notably in the documentary form of Jürgen Böttcher's *Die Mauer* (1991) and Thomas Schadt's *Berlin. Symphonie einer Grossstadt* (2002). It is only the more experimental forms of installation, following Hal Foster's observations on the archival in art, that have framed the museal gaze as something beyond the mere affirmation of the "memory value" of the material, drawing on informal archives but producing them as well, and underscoring the nature of all archival materials as "found yet constructed, factual yet fictive" (Foster 5). To take two examples, the unintended monument subjected to the museal gaze in Tacita Dean's installation film "Palast" and Lars Ramberg's ultimately multimedia project "Zweifel" is the obsolete Palace of the Republic.

Dean's film reflected both in its subject-matter and in its material on the question of obsolescence. Dean wrote about the decaying building:

> When the Palast der Republik was first opened in 1976, it was clad in white marble with 180 metres of windowed facade, triumphant in its transparent splendour ... There is now no trace of the white marble; the structure is raw wood and the windows are tarnished like dirty metal. It is as if the state is letting time make up its mind – letting entropy do the job and make the decision it is loathe to make. But the sore in the centre of the city is too public, and so a month ago, the wedding cake won and the Palast der Republik was condemned. The revivalists were triumphant. Soon Museum Island will be homogenized into stone white fakery and will no longer twinkle with a thousand setting suns. (Dean 95)

Dean's project, a ten-minute film, is a reflection on the status of the art object as "unintended monument" to film as a medium of preserving threatened objects at the time of celluloid's obsolescence, and in doing so it offers a haptic experience of historical material (both film and the building). In her commentary, Dean makes it clear that knowledge of the building's history was irrelevant to her approach to the object. Rather than simply an affirmation of Bazin's ontology of the photographic image (something evident in the photographic work of Sophie Calle's "The Detachment"), Dean's project is founded on a complex engagement with indexical materiality.

Yet, if film is still conceived as an index, and the spectator still situated in a conventional exhibition context in Dean's work, it is perhaps Lars Ramberg's project around the Palace of the Republic that draws out how the form of the "museal gaze" has developed on the margins of the frame of economic imperatives (see Rectanus in this volume). Ramberg's project was, like Christian Boltanski's "Missing House," a material intervention in the urban site, installing a series of letters facing west and spelling out "ZWEIFEL" ("Doubt") on the top of the now defunct palace. Beyond its playful engagement with the meaning of the building, like many of the other "Zwischennutzung" projects that took place within the Palast, "Zweifel" invited a tactile encounter with the building itself. Lifted out of the conventional tourist itinerary, visitors could stand on the Palast's roof, and move among the letters. "Zweifel" was temporally limited; it came to an end in 2005 (with the end of the "Zwischennutzung" initiative).

It lives on, however, in a form of digital archive, at www.palastdeszweifels.de. It could be argued that the material dimensions of the installation are now reduced to the visual spectacle of the photographs that document the installation's presence (and demolition) in the cityscape. Yet the visual is not necessarily a reduction; it poses instead a different set of problems, offering the opportunity to focus on the mechanisms by which the visual form of the cityscape becomes a projection surface for historical narratives. Rather than fetishizing the ruined Palast as a "obsolescent object" (an accusation that could be levelled at Dean's work), Ramberg reimagines his project as a form of "civic seeing" in terms of a hyperspatial navigation of the (im)material city centre in the "posturban" twenty-first century. Whereas, in the earlier era, the museal gaze was still formulated as a form of seeing that contrasted with distracting visual technologies within the museum space that is "the city as museum," in Ramberg's Internet project it is imbricated within it.

Ramberg's online exhibition can be read as a contemporary form of the Kaiserpanorama. The Imperial Panorama was the means of determining the "selectivity and rhythm of attentive response" (Crary 147) of the urban audience at the turn of the previous century: Ramberg's panorama is thus an ironic version of the urban training implicit in his panorama for the "Internet age." What Ramberg's online exhibition does exploit are the possibilities and limitations of such a form of displaying "the past," exploring questions and raising doubts about narrative linearity, legibility, and visibility, and as such it is a welcome commentary on the flood of Palast images that (over-)populate the Internet. The final date offered as a "hyperlink" on the front page, in a permanent state of becoming, is "now"; now, on 1 May 2012, when I screen-captured it, was the view from the webcam of the Deutsches Historisches Museum which showed Berlin's ever-ongoing antithesis to the value of the past: the circulation of traffic through the city centre, the timeless and time-coded, the punctual city as seen from the ostensibly secure vantage point of a historical museum.

NOTE

1 The object remains opaque; the communication of the full and complex history of the Anhalter Bahnhof, and how it ended up in this condition in 1987 is not the point. The same applies to other sites in the film that are invested with aura: the Kaiser Wilhelm Memorial Church (discussed above), the bunker where the film-within-the-film is being made, the Hotel Esplanade.

2 Refracted Memory: Museums, Film, and Visual Culture in Urban Space

MARK W. RECTANUS

Contemporary museums increasingly engage in, and construct, discursive and representational spaces outside the traditionally circumscribed boundaries of museum structures. In doing so, they create the potential for dialogic interactions with audiences, including acts of reflection, performance, and consumption. The construction of meta-narratives and discursive spaces outside the museum may also be considered in the context of historical shifts in the museum from private to public spaces, as Tony Bennett has shown, but also in terms of Bennett's notion of "civic seeing" ("Civic Seeing" 263–71). Bennett also underscores the historical relations and "tension between the museum as civic educator and the negative pull of distracted vision" through the "incorporation of television, video, touch-screen computer displays, and Imax theaters into museums [which] has undermined the distinction between museums and other forms of audiovisual culture" ("Civic Seeing" 275–6).[1] I would like to explore how "civic seeing" may also be employed to examine acts of seeing in spaces outside, or on the boundary zones, of museums, how the staging or framing of these spaces draws upon cinematic practices or discourses, and how the viewing experience contributes to the process of remembering as a form of refracted memory. (See Simon Ward's discussion above of "civic seeing" as it relates to urban space and *Der Himmel über Berlin*.)

This chapter will examine the representational and discursive spaces constructed by two cultural complexes in Munich: BMW Welt and BMW Museum and the Jewish Museum at St-Jakobs-Platz.[2] First, I will investigate how the notion of refracted memory relates to the representational space of BMW Welt, that is, how the architecture of Coop Himmelb(l)au and acts of viewing are situated as cinematic and performative experiences that intersect with the aesthetic and narrative strategies of Wim Wenders's film *Der Himmel über Berlin* (*Wings of Desire*, 1987), the musealization of cultural artefacts, and modes of seeing in the film. Second, I will examine the linkages between the BMW Welt and the BMW Museum which refract memory through the representation of present-futures and their musealization in a special exhibition, *Museums in the 21st Century*. Third, I will explore how the Jewish Museum Munich creates dialogic spaces on the boundary zones of the museum, which literally and metaphorically refract the visual experience of pedestrians and museum visitors through Sharone Lifschitz's project "Speaking Germany." In the context of my discussion, I employ the notion of refracted memory as a process that includes reflection but also the discontinuities and disjunctures of refracted images, that is, images that may alter or "deflect" the process of memory production in terms of how they structure the viewing experience or create an aperture for a more complex and textured engagement.[3]

Civic Seeing and the Mobile Mise-en-Scène

Before turning to an examination of these case studies, it is useful to consider the contexts in which discursive networks are constructed and how audience engagement may be staged. Urban landscapes are increasingly characterized by cultural complexes or cultural zones that have become an integral part of cultural consumption and marketing, for example, sites of cultural tourism or what John Urry has called "consuming places" (*Consuming* 150–1, 169). The competition among cities to garner cultural tourists has led to the segmentation of visitors according to target markets and categories of visitors, ranging from those who spontaneously explore cultural sites ("Entdecker" / "discoverers") to tourists who have specific destinations in mind and may possess more extensive knowledge of a cultural site ("Kenner" / "connoisseurs") (Schabbing 10).[4] Munich's Pinakotheken (Alte Pinakothek, Neue Pinakothek, Pinakothek der Moderne) and the Museum Brandhorst or Berlin's Museumsinsel (Museum Island) readily come to mind as examples of expanding museum complexes. Cultural zones also include theatres and multi-use complexes with restaurants and shopping – all of which become a part of urban event culture – and contribute to discursive networks on culture.

The emergence of cultural zones as an integral part of urban planning reflects competing discourses on urban cultural politics as well as interventions by museums and artists that foreground urban experience as a contested space.[5] These competing discourses on the representation of urban space also reveal the histories of the sites on which museums are constructed – histories which may invoke the musealization of the museum itself – understood as an archaeology of the museum's own past within the urban landscape. For example, public debates on the use of St-Jakobs-Platz in Munich became an integral part of urban planning over the course of decades and eventually resulted in the decision to construct the Jewish Museum, the new main synagogue (Ohel Jakob synagogue), and Jewish Community Centre on a site adjacent to the Film Museum and the City Museum (Bauer and Brenner 220–3; Rieger).

In his discussion of "civic seeing," Bennett underscores James Clifford's conceptualization of museums as "contact zones" where audiences are engaged in a dialogic process of interaction ("Civic Seeing" 279; Clifford 192). As Bennett observes, the dialogic context involves tensions between the museum's multiple and contested roles as a site for civic education and one for entertainment ("Civic Seeing" 276). Linda Hutcheon has argued that both dimensions are fused within the context of postmodern culture, that is, by appropriating aesthetic strategies of popular culture and simultaneously deconstructing them as critique (*Politics* 11).

From a historical perspective, civic seeing is closely linked to debates on cultural politics, the manner in which media culture positions viewers/spectators, and the destabilization of representation. As Gerhard Schulze has observed, the political and cultural movements of the 1960s and 1970s provided significant impetus for a democratization of cultural politics which shifted the roles of cultural institutions such as museums from being cultural arbiters of taste and distinction to having pedagogical functions and an appeal to more diverse audiences (500). In Germany, this shift was most apparent in urban cultural politics, epitomized by the title of Hilmar Hoffmann's book *Kultur für alle* (*Culture for Everyone*, 1984), which indicated a populist inflection in cultural politics during the 1970s and 1980s. This process reflected a simultaneous "de-verticalization" of culture that attempted to make high culture more accessible to wider audiences as well as validating the historical status of everyday culture as a critical dimension of the cultural heritage (Schulze 499–500). Yet, political mandates to democratize cultural institutions were largely implemented through market-oriented strategies that measured democratization in terms of increased audiences, through what Schulze has identified as "post-utopian cultural politics" (ibid.). The manner in which spectators were positioned, or how civic seeing was defined, was typified by debates over museum politics, for example, the museum being a site for blockbuster exhibitions as well as its expanded mandate for audience engagement and education programs (see Rectanus, "Globalization" 381–2). The rapid expansion of media culture during the 1960s and the proliferation of images fundamentally altered how spectatorship and (civic) seeing occurred, whether in the context of the individual or collective experience of viewing (television, film, exhibitions) or as part of event culture (e.g., rock concerts and classical music festivals).

Cinema played a crucial role in debates on culture and spectatorship by reframing the representation of everyday life and culture and destabilizing cinematic strategies of representation. The New Wave and New German Cinema fundamentally changed discourses on spectatorship through their use of strategies which undermined the viewing experience, for instance, the use of narrative intransitivity, estrangement, or multiple diegesis (Wollen). Thomas Elsaesser has underscored the contingency of spectatorship in the historical nexus of culture and politics in New German Cinema (151–202), drawing our attention to the individual and collective disjunctures of seeing. New German Cinema also provided an aperture for the representation of subjectivity, private lives, and those who were marginalized or "invisible." Rainer Werner Fassbinder's *Angst essen Seele auf* (*Fear Eats the Soul*, 1974) exemplifies one such cinematic intervention in discourses on migrant "guest workers." In particular, the film provides a critical intervention that challenges viewers to reflect upon the representation of those who are "invisible" in the media presentation of everyday life in Germany. While the deterritorialization and globalization of cinema have created and expanded trans-discursive spaces for image culture, they have also blurred the boundaries between television, cinema, and digital video, as well as the contexts of their reception. Moreover, globalization heightens the tensions between the museum's role in critical engagement ("civic educator") and in entertainment ("distracted vision") (Bennett, "Civic Seeing" 276–7).

While the BMW complex and the Jewish Museum at St-Jakobs-Platz are linked as sites of urban tourism and consumption, what is more revealing is how they construct sites for creating cultural meaning and knowledge through various modes of audience engagement, for example, through a "mobile mise-en-scène." The mobile mise-en-scène assumes visitors who are "mobile" both in terms of their physical movement across cultural zones throughout cities, but also with respect to their mobility across media (film, television, video, Internet), sites of cultural representation (museums, theatre, symphony, cinema), and their interconnected sites for consumption (in virtual and real spaces). In the context of my discussion, a mobile mise-en-scène may be understood in three dimensions: (1) aesthetic and curatorial strategies of audience engagement which draw on vocabularies of cinematic practice in order to create exhibition spaces or to stage events; (2) implicit references to shared (cinematic) experience embedded in visual culture; (3) the construction of meta-discourses (e.g., discourses on the museum itself) which engage audiences in processes of self-reflection and memory – both in terms of their interaction with the objects on display and with respect to their own awareness of how the viewing process creates cultural meaning.

Civic seeing intersects with the notion of a mobile mise-en-scène in terms of how cinema and museums position viewers and how they frame their respective subjects or objects through cinematic or curatorial strategies.[6] The (re-)negotiation of how we see (as part of the processes of museal and cinematic representation) is, in turn, related to an ethics of civic seeing and a politics of space. I will return to these issues later in the essay in the context of recent discussions on museum ethics which may inform a discussion of civic seeing.

The manner in which audiences participate in the process of viewing, reflecting, remembering, and creating meaning is, I will argue, simultaneously site-specific and trans-discursive.[7] That is, audiences may interact with cultural sites in different modes of engagement and viewing while drawing upon their own experience with other sites of memory-making or by communicating those experiences with other viewers, or, potentially, within communities (both virtual or real).[8] Both museums and corporations also engage in trans-discursive strategies, moving across media and engaging audiences at multiple sites. Moreover, the notion of a mobile mise-en-scène should be considered within the context of museums as sites for time-based art, site-specific art, and art in public spaces, as well as critical interventions which interrogate the relations among museums, corporate cultural politics, and the city. For example, the project *Dream City* – a cooperative venture by the Kunstraum München, Kunstverein München, Museum Villa Stuck, and the Siemens Kulturprogramm (deployed throughout Munich in 1999) – externalized institutional collaborations among museums and corporations in staging cultural interventions that attempt to create discursive spaces and networks across cityscapes. The nexus of artist-sponsor-museum was thematized, for example, in "Der ganz normale Luxus" ("The totally normal luxury," 1999), a work by artists Plamen Dejanov and Swetlana Heger which displayed a BMW Z-3 Roadster (donated by BMW) in front of the Kunstverein München (Kunstraum München 177–81, 277). The work simultaneously attempted to problematize the extent of corporate involvement in cultural institutions (staging the automobile on a platform including BMW advertisements in front of the Kunstverein), while recognizing the naturalization of product culture as part of everyday life – not unlike Warhol's staging of product culture in the museum itself – a boundary that had become an unproblematic part of the complicity of 1990s postmodern culture.

BMW Welt and BMW Museum

In 2007, BMW opened BMW Welt as the centrepiece of BMW's corporate representation in Munich and globally, but also as a site for increasing its engagement in the cultural landscape of the city. Designed by Coop Himmelb(l)au, BMW Welt provides a platform for visual and material consumption, event culture, performance, and exhibition, and was undoubtedly a response to event-based sites created by automotive competitors, for example, Volkswagen's Autostadt.[9] Within BMW Welt, visitors can view and sit in new BMW automobiles, pick up their new car, or watch other customers driving down the spiral ramp in their new cars, eat in multiple restaurants, shop for BMW merchandise, and view performances by motorcyclists in the open spaces of the structure (figure 2.1).

Visitors are engaged in acts of performative consumption through their interaction in and around the automobiles – becoming actors on a metaphorical stage who observe other visitors, and are observed by the spectators, as they drive away in their new vehicles.[10] As we will see, dimensions of cinematic staging become an integral part of the mobile mise-en-scène that frames audience engagement.

In his essay "Himmelblauer Wolkenbügel über München" ("Sky-blue cloud hanging over Munich,"), architect Frank Werner discusses the conceptual development of BMW Welt in the context of Coop Himmelb(l)au's past projects, including the proposal for a United Nations building in Geneva (Werner 7–15). More importantly, however, he underscores discourses on BMW Welt which foreground how the structure and its representation engage audiences in constructing meta-narratives on the sites of visual culture and memory. In the context of Werner's essay,

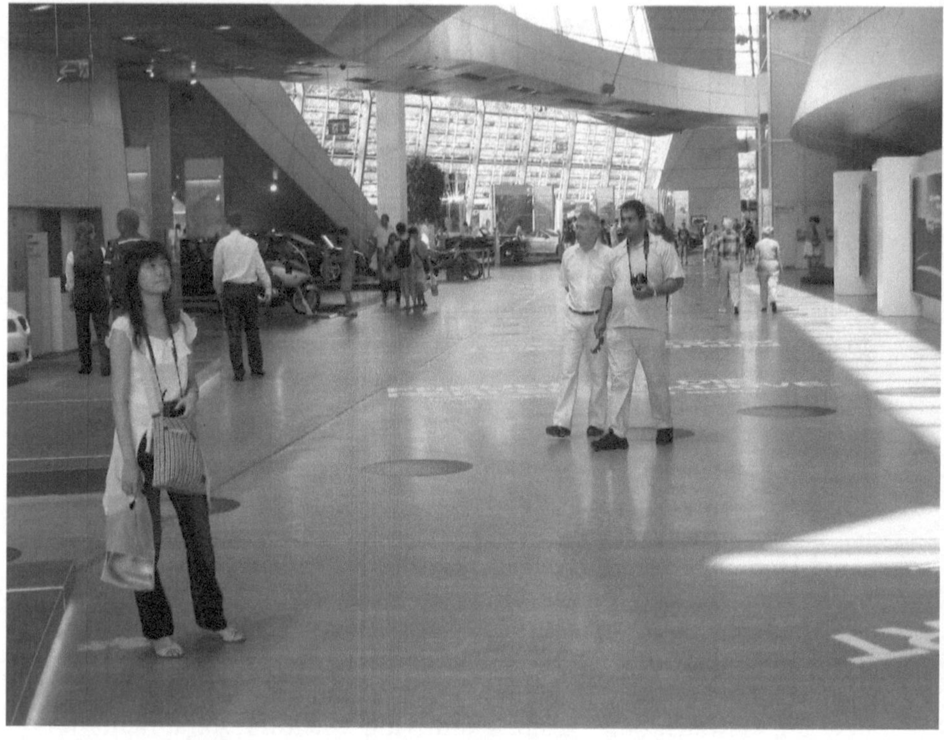

2.1 Staging the mobile mise-en-scène at BMW Welt. Photo by Mark W. Rectanus, 2007

this is articulated in two dimensions: the function of the building itself and its aesthetic mediation within visual culture. The former references the building's function as a multiple-use complex for audiences, while the latter addresses the production and mediation of visual culture and memory. Werner refers to the structure as "a real 'people's palace,' a secularized cathedral for night-lovers, well beyond any brand obsession. The glowing Utopias of the Expressionists in the early twentieth century have finally been realized here" (15). Werner observes that BMW Welt may eventually be open 24/7 and is free of charge, having attracted one million visitors during its first year (11). The notion of BMW Welt as a "peoples palace" simultaneously references the populist cultural politics of "Kultur für alle" (Hoffmann) – which fuses the notions of access and democratization with cultural consumption and entertainment – while invoking the cultural memory of the avant-garde's aestheticization of social projects.[11]

Werner's allusion to Expressionism and its utopias, or its dystopias, such as Fritz Lang's *Metropolis* (1927), also draws our attention to meta-narratives linking the aesthetics of the BMW Welt to cinema and visual culture. Werner identifies the narrative space of the BMW Welt as being divided into two primary zones which are composed structurally of an "earthly" and a "heavenly" zone. He argues that the cloud-like effect of the roof and the free-floating upper floor both reinforce the theatricality of the multipurpose space for events but also facilitate the central ramp on which customers descend via "a cascade of steps that would not feel out of place in Hollywood" (11). Throughout the essay, Werner draws further allusions to the narrative structure of BMW Welt, its cloud-like aesthetics, and cinema – referring to "a building oscillating between the emotional drama of a powerful image and the subversive undermining of that same image" (15).[12]

If, as Werner argues, BMW Welt foregrounds the aesthetics and exhibition strategies of cinema, then it is useful to examine cinematic projects which may intersect conceptually with the visual grammar and narratives created by BMW Welt. Although their narratives are quite different, both Wim Wenders's *Der Himmel über Berlin* and BMW Welt engage meta-narratives of popular culture. These include the role of the automobile and associated notions of mobility and stasis (e.g., when the angels Damiel and Cassiel share their experiences while sitting in a new BMW in the midst of the BMW showroom in Berlin).[13] Both the Peter Falk ("Columbo")[14] character and Damiel (who is mentored by Falk) assume a populist inflection – as a sort of "everyman" – which intersects with BMW Welt's promise of sensual gratification through a visit to the exhibition space. In the context of BMW's narrative, the cinematic "happy end" plays out in the promise of potential and future generations of car buyers.[15] However, for most visitors, achieving the "happy end" must be sublimated to the sensual experience of "the journey" rather than the end – a dimension that is also apparent in Wenders's film up until the end. Thus, the journey in the narrative structure of the film and the experiential space of BMW Welt is one not only of self-discovery but of realization and (deferred) gratification. In the film it is resolved in the creation of Damiel's attainment of "true love" and sensual gratification with the circus high-wire artist Marion,[16] while in BMW Welt it involves the promise of the automobile, its image, and the performance of mobility.

Werner's discursive framing of BMW Welt in terms of "cloud-like narratives" of architecture and "film-like narratives" (which structure visitor experience) intersects with the dialectics of aesthetic experience in Wenders's film (e.g., notions of spirituality versus sensuality). While I am not arguing that BMW Welt was literally modelled on *Der Himmel über Berlin,* I am suggesting that both projects intersect within the landscape of visual culture by drawing from meta-narratives that are instantiated in their respective responses to urban space, architecture, and visualization. In this sense, as part of the mobile mise-en-scène, they structure the experience of viewing within urban spaces which invokes forms of "civic seeing," for example, through the meta-narratives of populism which promise individual and collective fulfilment or gratification, but also through the process of creating what Andreas Huyssen refers to as present-pasts (1–29) – and as a link to imaginary futures promised by the present. (See also Simon Ward's discussion of *Der Himmel über Berlin.*)

Constructing present-pasts in *Der Himmel über Berlin* is also closely linked to the process of musealization on multiple levels – most notably through the musealization of the urban topography of the city of Berlin as a divided city, but also through the musealization of its cultural artefacts (e.g., the library), and multiple modes of (civic) seeing during the 1980s. For example, the film mediates seeing through the thoughts and reflections of its characters (including "everyday" Berliners) and by foregrounding the nexus of seeing, reflection (as part of the process of seeing), and the acts of everyday life, for instance, drinking coffee, driving, walking, and observing.

Musealization and memory production at the BMW complex are conceptually and structurally underscored through the representation of all three buildings (BMW Welt, BMW Museum, and the BMW Factory) in the company's promotional communication and via a pedestrian bridge that links BMW Welt with the BMW Museum.[17] BMW Welt, as the new centrepiece of the complex, shifts the focus of BMW's cultural zone from the representation and framing of present-pasts (in the BMW Museum) to present-futures (in BMW Welt), which are aligned with contemporary event culture and the promise of future gratification. Indeed, the BMW Museum simultaneously retains its museal status as a site for archiving and representing BMW automotive history while also embracing futuristic discourses that erase institutional links to the past, for example, by asserting that "contemporary museums have nothing in common with their predecessors of the nineteenth century."[18] Although the renovation of the BMW Museum has retained some exhibition space for the mediation of corporate history through the display of older vehicles, it has transformed the main exhibition space in the upward spiral (with its allusions to Frank Lloyd Wright's Guggenheim) into a site for special exhibitions with a focus on the present-future.[19] This was most apparent in the exhibition *Museums in the 21st Century*, based on an exhibition at the Art Centre Basel in 2005–6 organized by Suzanne Greub (2).[20]

"Museums in the 21st Century" reflects the globalization of museums while also examining how architecture situates museums within, and constructs, localized spaces – drawing on museum architecture on four continents during the first decade of the twenty-first century (Greub and Greub 3). Rather than attempting to interrogate what multiple visions of "the museum of the future" might mean, the exhibition confines itself largely to museum architecture during the first decade of the twenty-first century by displaying architectural models and building sites. Although the exhibition attempts to create linkages between the conceptual development of museum spaces, their environmental localization, and their global signification as cultural icons or centres, it does not explore the relations among the cultural politics of museum architecture, curatorial strategies of individual museums, or interactions with indigenous cultures.[21] Thus, visitors gain only a partial vision of "Museums in the 21st Century," primarily through the lens of architecture and meta-narratives on the museum as a global force defined by the image and branding of the building. The role of museum visitors or audiences seems to be lost – in terms of both the concept of the exhibition or the potential to engage visitors with the architectural models and photos on display.[22]

In many respects BMW Welt and the BMW Museum constitute parallel exhibition spaces with shifting emphases from present-pasts to present-futures. While the BMW Museum has retained its core collection of historical artefacts (automobiles) as part of the exhibition and museum space, they are employed as part of a larger narrative which provides continuity from histories of ownership (viewer identification with the BMW brand) to the promise of renewed fulfilment in the future acquisition of the brand and living in a "BMW world" (e.g., as mediated in the BMW Welt exhibition). Visitors can participate in communities of consumption on multiple levels, ranging from the purchase of BMW merchandise to identification with the BWW brand in media culture (advertising, product placement in films, e.g., the "Bond cars" in James

Bond films) or to the purchase of the automobile itself.[23] The bridge between the BMW Museum and BMW Welt reaffirms the legitimacy of the "world of BMW" as a global brand through its own musealization, that is, through the security of its status in history and its promise of the future. Yet, the brand's historical status must be constantly "updated" through an ongoing process of musealization that reaffirms its legitimacy. Thus, BMW Welt illustrates that, from an institutional perspective, there are strong links between musealization and legitimation.

BMW Welt and the BMW Museum operate in all three dimensions of the mobile mise-en-scène, that is, by using cinematic strategies of audience engagement through architecture and events (e.g., motorcyclists performing in the building), creating contexts for visitors' shared experience of the BWM brand (through shopping, viewing, and sitting in new automobiles), and by constructing new contexts for imagining both present-pasts and present-futures in terms of notions of mobility, innovation, experience, and exclusivity through the signage used in both exhibition spaces.[24] Although the musealization of present-pasts legitimizes and enables the imagination of present-futures, it is only possible by bracketing cultural memory, that is, competing discourses and narratives of mobility (e.g., critiques of automotive culture) that are absent or deflected within the discursive space of the complex.[25] Thus, musealization plays a critical role in refracting the memories of present-pasts to create (imaginary) present-futures.

Jewish Museum Munich: Sharone Lifschitz's "Speaking Germany"

I would now like to turn to another museum complex and cultural zone, located in Munich's city centre, which has emerged through the recent additions of the Jewish Museum Munich, the Ohel Jakob synagogue, and Jewish Community Centre to the complex of museums at St-Jakobs-Platz (i.e., the City Museum and Film Museum). A project titled "Speaking Germany" by Sharone Lifschitz draws our attention to how museum complexes and other cultural sites can become spaces for engaging pedestrians and museum visitors in reflections on culture and memory as modes of civic seeing. "Speaking Germany" was realized at the Jewish Museum and in multiple venues throughout the city and approaches the politics of space embedded in the location of the museum and the synagogue at St-Jakobs-Platz, as well as the communicative spaces that are shaped by other museums in Munich such as the Haus der Kunst.[26]

"Speaking Germany" documents Lifschitz's conversations with Germans who responded to her advertisement in German newspapers, which read: "Young Jewish woman visiting Germany would like to have a conversation about nothing in particular with anyone reading this." Lifschitz e-mailed with the respondents and subsequently travelled throughout Germany to meet and talk with many of them. These conversations and text fragments formed the basis of interventions, including billboards and posters at the train station, on public transportation, as well as a video in the exhibition space of the Jewish Museum, and a website (Bilski 70–1; Lifschitz 2011). The project provided a mobile mise-en-scène by engaging pedestrians through multiple media and contexts throughout Munich, including texts placed on a tram with different daily routes; ninety overhead texts on the subway system; a printing of 29,600 posters appearing in forty-eight different variations for museum visitors and placed on advertising towers; five complete advertising towers; and three bridge banners placed at major traffic intersections (Lifschitz).

In addition to the texts appearing on the exterior windows of the Jewish Museum beginning in March 2007, "Speaking Germany" was staged in Munich from December 2006 to 2007 in four thematic components, which appeared in chronological succession and provided a loose thematic organization to the e-mails and conversations, which appeared as excerpted texts: (1) *Aperitif* ("Some initial questions and assumptions"); (2) *Vorspeise/Starters* ("About the way we introduce ourselves to someone we have never met before"); (3) *Hauptgericht/Main Course* ("Conversations about nothing in particular and related topics"); (4) *One Last Drink* ("Goodbyes, afterthoughts and a few things that were almost left unsaid") (Bilski 71).

The texts of the conversations frequently form an ironic juxtaposition to the context of their placement, creating a tension between the text fragment and its context, such as a text in the subway which reads: "Are you a [female] tourist here or do you have other intentions?"[27] The "Speaking Germany" website shows a photo of a young woman seated below the text/sign on a subway car, drawing our attention to notions of tourism which underscore tensions between "locals" and "foreigners."

Text fragments also appear on the exterior windows of the Jewish Museum – windows that reflect the structure of the new Jewish synagogue adjacent to the museum. The texts simultaneously ask museum visitors to reflect upon the historical and representational space of the museum and synagogue at St-Jakobs-Platz while referencing the museum's own function within the cultural topography of tourism, for example, on the entry doorway window which reads "Grüß Gott" ("hello" or literally "God's greeting") – a common greeting in Bavaria. This self-reflective awareness of the Jewish Museum's own position within the urban landscape of Munich tourism, and with respect to other museums, is foregrounded by Lifschitz in a text fragment from a conversation reproduced on an exterior window: "Over there / is the Haus der Kunst … / a very large museum … / **Ha … Do you like it?** / No … no, because of / the history of the / building ... the part it / played in Nazi Germany" (emphasis in original). As curator Emily Bilski observes, "*Speaking Germany* addresses the issues that bind Germans and Jews, Germans and Israelis. The relationship is inescapable; the challenge is to transform its silence into an exchange that resonates, and to bring it out into the open" (71).

Placing the texts on the windows simultaneously externalizes the inside of the museum where visitors sit in the café (and view the visitors reading the texts on the windows outside of the museum) while reflecting the new synagogue and the City Museum – creating multiple planes of interpretive self-reflection upon which the viewing subject can read and interpret the texts. The texts on the museum's windows are more than simple reflections of the viewing subject. The viewer/reader, or photographer, becomes part of the object of viewing. Depending on the perspective or viewing angle, the time of day, and lighting from outside or inside the museum, the texts, the people, objects, and images inside and outside are layered, reflected, deflected, refracted, and transformed. As pedestrians engage in the process of seeing, reading, viewing, or reflecting, the experience becomes increasingly performative – moving from seeing to interpreting and reflecting, and to the production of memory (figure 2.2).

The notion of refracted memory allows for a productive realization of the fragmentary, nonlinear, and disjunctive impulses of memory production. Through this process of dialogic engagement among pedestrians, installations, and the windows of the museum, "Speaking Germany" and the Jewish Museum create an intervention which constructs and opens new spaces for civic seeing. Moreover, the creation of refracted memory through the layering of images, texts, and lighting – through a mobile mise-en-scène in urban landscapes – may also intersect with questions of how the viewing subject and the aesthetics of visualization in film are reconceptualized.[28]

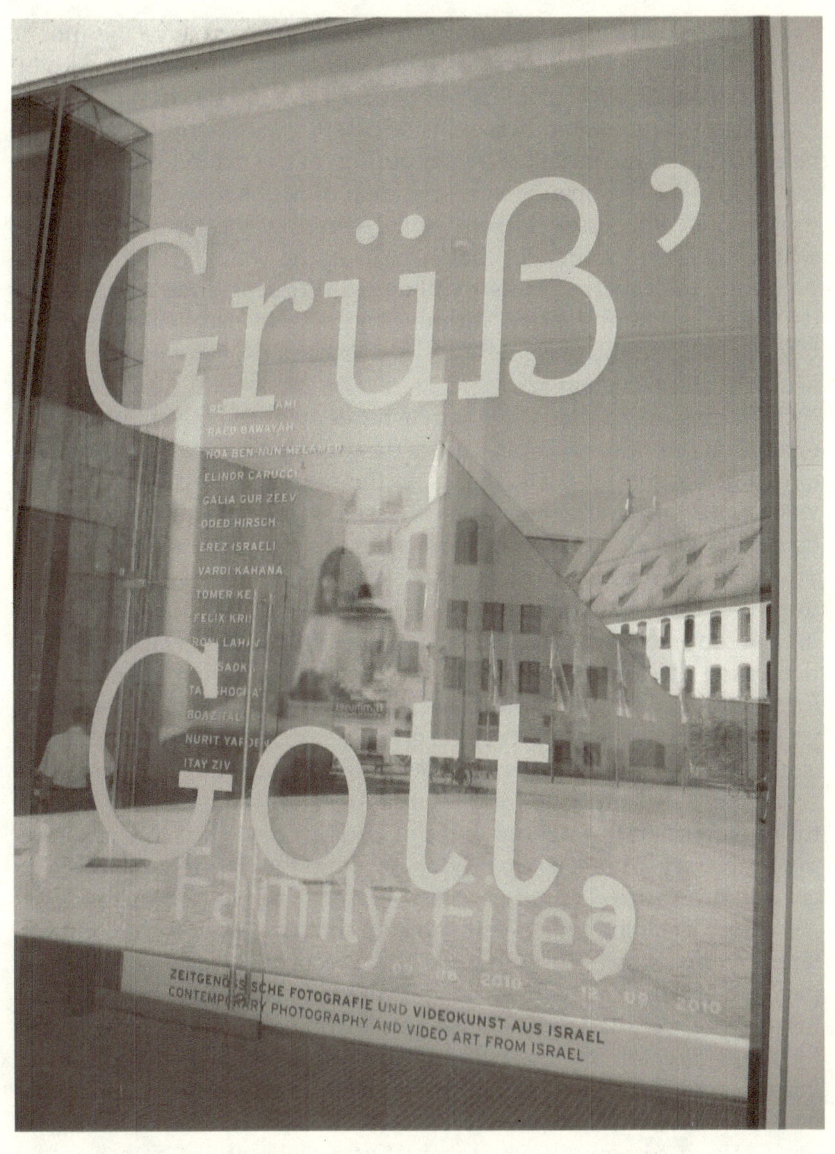

2.2 Jewish Museum Munich: Pedestrian Viewing "Speaking Germany." Photo by Mark W. Rectanus, 2007

The Jewish Museum has also foregrounded the role of the mobile visitor within the urban topography of Munich in its permanent exhibition *STIMMEN_ORTE_ZEITEN* (*VOICES_PLACES_TIMES*) by engaging visitors in an exploration of historical sites within the city that have been buried in the past. The audio portion of the exhibition is complemented by a large open area with a map of Munich on the floor. Visitors can move pedestal markers (signs) to various locations on the map, which are linked to images that appear on the wall: "This installation pinpoints the diverse places that have at different times been part of daily Jewish life in the city. Various aspects of Jewish history and culture, right up to the present day … are presented as an integral part of Munich" (Fleckenstein 32).

By linking urban sites with their histories of Jewish life in Munich, the exhibition provides multiple venues for engaging visitors in the process of exploring present-pasts, that is, in the permanent exhibition, in the windows which address passing pedestrians and museum visitors, and by creating an awareness of the sites beyond the museum boundaries. Thus, visitors are able to create their own mobile mise-en-scène within the exhibition by selecting sites of Jewish history and also envisioning present-pasts as they visit actual sites in the city. The musealization of the sites of Jewish life provides a context and point of departure for visitors to become more conscious of the process of constructing present-pasts through a process of civic seeing. In this case, civic seeing is informed by the pedagogical content of the museum exhibition, Lifschitz's installation (including interventions on the boundary zone of the museum and throughout the city), and by the visitors' own exploration of history and memory production from the critical perspective of civic engagement.

Notions of civic engagement and community are reinforced and fostered by the Jewish Museum through its website, blogs, and Facebook page, all of which provide an open forum for discussions, critique, and information on the Jewish Museum's exhibitions and events. Jewish Museum director Bernhard Purin regularly contributes to the blogs. Indeed, online discussions regarding recent exhibitions figure prominently into the museum's own representation. Purin frames the museum's role in community engagement as a "laboratory" rather than a "monument" by noting the limitations of visitors to receive or absorb large amounts of information during museum visits and, therefore, preferring to create multiple platforms and spaces for stimulating dialogue with audiences, i.e., "Dialogue Instead of Didactics" (Stock 89). Thus, the manner in which visitors are situated in the life of the museum itself (i.e., "dialogue vs. didactics"), the curatorial and administrative vision of the museum, and how the museum may construct informal or formal communities (both real and virtual) all play a pivotal role in terms of how we approach notions of civic seeing.

Conclusion

As part of urban cultural zones, museums reflect the deterritorialization of cultural discourses by engaging visitors in discursive networks outside traditionally circumscribed museum boundaries. The manner in which audience engagement is staged draws our attention to the intersection of museal and cinematic strategies and practices that are trans-discursive. While cultural complexes, such as BMW Welt and the BMW Museum participate to varying degrees as sites for consumption and events, that is, for "consuming places" (Urry, *Consuming*), I have suggested that installations and multimedia interventions such as "Speaking Germany" provide an aperture for engaging visitors in a dialogic process of critical reflection and memory production through the refraction of image and memory.[29] Moreover, civic seeing draws our attention to how museums situate visitors with respect to *communities of consumption and communities for critical engagement and dialogue* that increasingly communicate and act in real and virtual spaces – inside and outside museums, on their boundary zones, and throughout urban spaces.

The nexus of civic seeing and communities also provides an opportunity to explore the role of ethics, not only in terms of individual and collective notions of the "civic," but also with respect to museum ethics and the broader implications of musealization in visual culture. Janet Marstine has argued that a "new museum ethics discourse" should be based on "an understanding of the contingent nature of museum ethics in the twenty-first century – its relations with complex economic, social, political and technical forces and its fluid ever-shifting sensibility" (xxiii).[30] Marstine posits museum ethics as a social practice based on three paradigms of ethical engagement: "social responsibility, radical transparency and shared guardianship of heritage" (xxiv). Civic seeing as a form of social engagement and participation in shared communities is also reflected in what Suzanne MacLeod refers to as "an ethics of the built environment," which draws our attention to issues of sustainability and community as they relate to museum structures and their surrounding environments (381, 390). The iconography and visual impact of museum architecture – ranging from Frank Gehry's Guggenheim Museum Bilbao to Coop Himmelb(l)au's BMW Welt – underscore a politics of space and urban development that privilege cultural zones for entertainment and consumption. However, many contemporary museums function as sites for both entertainment and critical engagement, that is, as contested spaces for cultural representation and the production of culture (MacDonald and Fyfe 2). Thus, civic seeing is inextricably bound to a politics of space and how we critically engage our lived spaces through acts of viewing, seeing, and experiencing. Likewise, Wenders's *Der Himmel über Berlin* problematizes seeing and knowing (an epistemology of space) in the context of the divided city of Berlin and attempts to transcend or traverse the disjunctures of space through explorations of identity. Like the museum, cinema and visual culture provide a medial space not only for musealization but also for projects that interrogate the interrelations between seeing and knowing.

As Bennett points out, civic seeing in the context of the museum involves multiple forms of seeing, or what Kevin Hetherington refers to as "multiple optics rather than a singular trained one" ("Civic Seeing" 279; Hetherington). Moreover, seeing can be distorted or manipulated by the media and contexts in which we see, and through the complex process of seeing and interpreting, or making sense of what we see or assume we see. Nor can we always attribute certainty to what we see even if we are conscious of these issues (see discussion in Morris). The notion of refracted memory is informed by the complex process of seeing both in terms of its potential for discovery and creative memory-making and its ambiguities, disjunctures, and blurring of boundaries which limit the certainty of seeing and knowing. Both museal and cinematic practices make us aware of the fluidity and uncertainty of these boundaries through their aesthetics and objects of inquiry.

I would suggest that a critical dimension of civic seeing involves the process of *making the invisible visible*, in exhibition strategies and cinematic aesthetics, and through the dialogic engagement of individual and collective viewers in their own projects of critical reflection and memory. These projects go beyond the immediacy of acts of seeing or viewing by engaging all the senses in a complex reflection on experience.[31] Thus, competing notions or "multiple optics" of "civic seeing" may provide a productive point of departure for exploring how, and the extent to which, seeing, reflecting, visualizing, and memory become dialogic processes that are mutually informed by museums and cinematic aesthetics. In this sense, the intersections of museal and cinematic practices play a pivotal role in how complex, trans-discursive networks are constructed and contribute to cultural memory and the critical engagement of our lived spaces.

NOTES

1 Andreas Huyssen also refers to these tensions and their potential for audience engagement in "Escape from Amnesia: The Museum as Mass Medium," in *Twilight Memories* 13–35.

2 Also see my discussion of BMW Welt, BMW Museum, and the concept of a mobile mise-en-scène in "Moving Out: Museums, Mobility, and Urban Spaces," in the forthcoming volume *Museum Media*, ed. Michelle Henning.

3 Refraction also references both literally and figuratively the deflection of light and sound in visual media, calling attention to the aesthetic strategies of media production as well as the complex manner in which audiences are engaged in a dialogic process of creating memory through acts of seeing, observing, self-reflection, and refraction.

4 In their development of the notion of "educative leisure," Laurie Hanquinet and Mike Savage also propose a differentiated approach to how museum visitors conceptualize the museum experience, suggesting a range of subgroups that "connote the image of museums as educative leisure differently" (54).

5 Examples range from art in public places or site-specific interventions of time-based art (e.g., Christo and Jean-Claude's Wrapped Reichstag), to architecture as intervention (Daniel Libeskind's Jewish Museum Berlin), to cinematic events in urban spaces (e.g., open-air cinema at Munich's Königsplatz or the projection of the restored lost cut of Fritz Lang's *Metropolis* at the Brandenburg Gate in Berlin during the Berlinale in 2010).

6 While civic seeing is closely aligned with acts of *reception*, the mobile mise-en-scène references the aesthetics, discourses, and strategies of *production*. Although these two processes may be conceptualized as separate dimensions, they are linked through their common siting, e.g., to the site of the exhibition and/or museum.

7 While I am using Michel Foucault's notion of the trans-discursive as that which may refer to or transcend multiple discourses, I am also interested in the manner in which cinematic space and exhibition spaces mutually inform and construct discourses.

8 With respect to virtual communities and social networking, many museums have established an online presence in Facebook to expand audience engagement. See for example the statement of the Jewish Museum Munich on its Facebook site regarding its own engagement in culture which characterizes the museum as a laboratory that provides a forum for mediation, interpretation, and discussion.

9 See also corporate museums and event spaces designed for Mercedes and Porsche on their respective websites.

10 BMW Welt provides a locus of activity and representation which links the recently renovated BMW Museum, tours in the BMW factory, and the nearby Olympic park and stadium, as well as providing an anchor to Munich's northern corridor for event culture including the Allianz Arena.

11 The notion of the "people's palace" also references the changing function of public exhibitions and the transformation of exhibition spaces for consumption and artistic interventions.

12 Werner's reference to "film-like narrative structures" (15) draws our attention to a wide range of cinematic projects that reference urban spaces, in terms of both their foregrounding of locality as well as deterritorialization, ranging from Fritz Lang's *Metropolis* (1927), Walter Ruttmann's *Berlin. Die Sinfonie der Großstadt (Berlin. Symphony of a Metropolis)* (1927), to Wenders's *Der Himmel über Berlin* (1987) or Tom Tykwer's *Lola rennt (Run Lola Run)* (1998). Wenders, in particular, is attracted to interrogations of space, identity, and mobility, e.g., in *Summer in the City* (1971), *Alice in den Städten* (*Alice in the Cities*) (1974), and *Paris, Texas* (1984). With respect to the road film, see Kolker and Beicken 138–60, 161–7.

13 Kolker and Beicken implicitly reference notions of mobility and stasis in Wenders's (road) films. With regard to Damiel and Cassiel in the front seat of the BMW in the dealer's showroom they write: "This is a remarkable image for Wenders: a car, holding two male friends, but unable to move!" See Kolker and Beicken 152. The reflected and refracted light in this sequence which frames the characters also provides a metaphor for Damiel's own conflicted reflections on becoming human.

14 With respect to the role of the Peter Falk character, see Wenders's discussion of the development of this role in Wenders, "On Making It Up," 188–9.

15 Based on my own observation, a larger percentage of visitors to BMW Welt are young adults.

16 With respect to conservative, populist motifs in *Der Himmel über Berlin*, see also Kolker and Beicken's comments regarding the ending of the film and the trajectory of Wenders's films during the late 1980s: "At its worst, in

Wings of Desire and *Until the End of the World*, it appears as a mythologizing of romance, an apotheosis of the static, eternal couple, a home for the heart, a return to the simple life and good works. The movement of Wenders' films turns out, finally, to be a long drive toward stability and stasis" (165).

17 Drawing on the work of Bernard Tschumi, I have argued that the simultaneous attraction to the event and its undermining is a key dimension to contemporary event culture. See Rectanus, *Culture Incorporated* 134; Tschumi 255.

18 BMW emphasizes the function of contemporary museums as spaces for events with "attractive exhibitions" and the use of media to attract large audiences as part of urban marketing, noting that they serve as a "seismograph of a society's affluence and concept of culture." See BMW, "Die zweite Wechselausstellung."

19 The first special exhibition was titled *BMW Konzeptfahrzeuge*.

20 The exhibition subsequently traveled to museums throughout Europe and the United States, with future exhibitions in Latin America planned. See Greub and Greub 2.

21 The exhibition also does not attempt to interrogate how the multiple architectural concepts on display might relate to one another, other than through somewhat superficial conceptual groupings: "Museums in the fabric of the city," "Extensions to existing museums," "The solitaire – a building standing by itself," "Within the landscape – museums as part of nature." The thematic organization of the exhibition at the BMW Museum is different than in the catalogue, which groups the museums according to their respective architects. See Greub and Greub 2–3.

22 Although the visitor's experience in BMW Welt is one that situates audiences almost completely in terms of consumption and entertainment, it offers more space for individual interactions than the BMW Museum, which seems to revert to an older model of extensive texts with limited media (other than posters for the individual projects). This is a somewhat curious strategy given the overall technological orientation of the complex.

23 During 2001–2, BMW commissioned a series of short films by leading Hollywood directors, including John Frankenheimer and Tony Scott.

24 The use of signs in German and English to create a common experience of mobility – with links to notions of innovation, creativity, and exclusivity within BMW Welt and BMW Museum – is manifest throughout both exhibition spaces. Several examples of signage in BMW Welt include "High Performance: Der Inbegriff von Kraft und Exklusivität / The Epitome of Power and Exclusiveness" and "Motorsport: Siegeswille / Determined to Win." In the BMW Museum, words and phrases (alternating

in German and English) were painted onto the walkway walls of the renovated upward spiral and platforms of the museum (which provide space for special exhibitions), e.g., "Challenge"; "Klima"/"Climate"; "Natur"/"Nature"; "Umwelt"/"Environment"; "Fortschritt"/"Progress"; "Euphorie"/"Euphoria." The walkways and platforms housed automobiles in the original BMW Museum and now provide space for special exhibitions in the renovated museum.

25 Critical narratives of automotive culture such as notions of speed (no speed limits on some routes of the German Autobahn), automobile accidents, or a more nuanced interrogation of the automobile in everyday life, are missing in the exhibition spaces, nor is this an objective of the BMW Museum or BMW Welt. BMW is, however, aware of environmental issues related to automobile use and fuel consumption and has integrated these notions into the exhibition space of BMW Welt and BMW Museum.

26 Undoubtedly the Jewish Museum Munich is also part of cultural tourism at the St-Jakobs-Platz through its proximity to the Stadtmuseum (City Museum) and Filmmuseum (Film Museum), which is a subsidiary department of the City Museum. The Jewish Museum performs a productive function by at once engaging urban tourists in an exploration of local narratives and the sites of Jewish life, culture, and memory in Munich, while providing a counterpoint to urban discourses which foreground consumption and entertainment, e.g., the City Museum's exhibition on the 200th anniversary of the Oktoberfest ("Das Oktoberfest 1810–2010") during the summer of 2010.

27 "Sind Sie als Touristin hier, oder haben Sie noch andere Absichten?"

28 Here the visual grammar of cinema comes to mind, ranging from the representation of the image of self and self-image in the pathologies of urban life (e.g., in Fritz Lang's *M* as it may relate to notions of civic seeing – including the collective response to the murderer), to the use of texts and voice-over texts (e.g., Peter Handke's text in *Der Himmel über Berlin*).

29 In terms of how the process of experiencing exhibitions is situated, Michelle Henning writes: "It is worth asking what exhibitionary forms would be adequate to an exhibition practice which did not set out to control or shape visitor experience in order to inculcate certain values, but instead to connect with the lived experience of visitors on a sensory as well as intellectual level." See *Museums, Media* 98.

30 See, for example, discussions regarding the broader definitions and implications of museum ethics in Marstine xxiii.

31 Bennett refers to "pluri-directional civic exchanges that engage a broader range of the visitors' senses" ("Civic Seeing" 279). With regard to the sensual aspects of everyday life in *Der Himmel über Berlin*, see Wenders, "An Attempted Description" 74, 82.

3 Nikolaus Geyrhalter's *Unser täglich Brot*: Preservation, the Food Industry, and the Interrogation of Visual Evidence

ALICE KUZNIAR

Scholars such as John Berger, Randy Malamud, and Jonathan Burt have addressed the "relationship between the animal as a visual image and the technology that produces this image" (Burt, "The Illumination of the Animal Kingdom" 269), specifically in relation to the spectacle of animals within zoos, the live equivalent of the natural history museum. They have argued that the increased visibility of the animal in the zoo, on National Geographic programming, and in Disney films directly relates to the effacement, even disappearance of the animal in the industrial and, now, post-industrial, technologized world. As Berger writes, "Zoos, realistic animal toys, and the widespread commercial diffusion of animal imagery all began as animals started to be withdrawn from daily life" (260). Berger, Malamud, and Burt are joined by animal historians such as Harriet Ritvo, who proposes that the rise of the zoo in Victorian England puts colonial conquest on display.

I would like to expand on this notion of the disappearance of the animal from everyday life in capitalist, consumerist society, similarly resulting in its preservation or musealization in a different, displaced realm. The vanishing referred to by Berger, Malamud, and Burt pertains as well to the mechanization and mass production of the food industry: we no longer live in close proximity to the farm animals, indeed also the crops, that feed us; farms are often in foreign countries; animals are locked in pens and cages and often never see the light of day; we are never witness to their slaughter, dressing, and rendering; the vast distances of source from consumption also entail an extensive technology of preservation. However much both the zoo and the slaughterhouse correlate to the disappearance of the animal in our everyday life, though, the huge difference between them is that rather than being put on display as in the zoo, animals in slaughterhouses are sequestered out of sight and sound. What happens then in essay films that exhibit what occurs in the abattoir and on the factory farm? If we can say that everything in our lives has been photographed and mass-circulated, one of the very few areas that have not been captured by the camera are the places our daily food comes from. The 2005 documentary by Austrian filmmaker Nikolaus Geyrhalter *Unser täglich Brot* (*Our Daily Bread*) engages precisely that taboo topic.

Slavoj Žižek interrogates "such a blindness, such a violent exclusionary gesture of refusing to see, such a disavowal of reality" in relation to "animals slaughtered for our consumption[.] Who among us would be able to continue eating pork chops after visiting a factory farm in which pigs are half-blind and cannot even properly walk, but are just fattened to be killed?" (52–3). Geyrhalter's film engages complexly with this dilemma of providing documentary evidence about what occurs in the raising and growing of the food we eat. He shoots at various locations in Europe where animals are bred, kept, and slaughtered as well as at mammoth farms and gigantic greenhouses where monocrops are grown and packaged for mass consumption. Geyrhalter's long takes with a stationary camera lend not only a photographic impression to *Unser täglich Brot* but also a distancing from events, both of which are evocative of a kind of musealization. The cinematic apparatus puts the object on visual display at cold remove from the spectator. Reinforcing the dispassionateness with which he presents this documentary footage, Geyrhalter refuses to direct the audience's viewing by adding a voice-over commentary. The result is that the audience is left to ponder what it has witnessed, what has been excluded from view in the editing process, and, above all, what the affective response, if any, should be to this sang-froid presentation which runs counter, say, to a PETA exposé and the visceral response it elicits. In other words, the audience is led to ask whether to witness the evidence Geyrhalter provides paradoxically means to participate in the "violent exclusionary gesture of refusing to see" (52–3) that Žižek regards as operative in the consumption of factory-farmed meat.

To put it yet a different way, the processes of recording and then putting in the public eye coalesce uncomfortably for the spectator of *Unser täglich Brot* with a form of disavowal, refusal to see, and forgetting. As much as it collects sublime images from mass-scale factory farming, resulting in their musealization, this film contravenes the act of memorialization. The custodial task is usually thought in terms of sustaining, preserving, sheltering, safeguarding, and upholding. Here, though, it seems that Geyrhalter's act of preservation wants to resist a vocal, activist defence and protection, in this case on behalf of animals. If justice is arguably premised on the acknowledgment of the singularity of an individual's case, is justice possible for the single animal when it is not only treated as a cog in the Fordization of meat production but also presented as such by Geyrhalter's camera? Do the long takes and the long shots, together with the absence of vocal protest, serve to mimic the technologization at work in this industry? In other words, the question *Unser täglich Brot* raises is whether it is complicit with or critical of this erasure: with its self-conscious deployment of the cinematic apparatus that refuses the signature of the body does it mimic its subject matter – the hegemony of technology over life? Ultimately, do Geyrhalter's choices bracket out protest against the industry, indeed, even any form of affective involvement?[1] These are questions that lie at the heart of contemporary visual culture; they interrogate what visual evidence means today, especially in its documentary form, and what the pedagogical and ethical potential of such evidence could and should be.

The opening sequence of *Unser täglich Brot* is exemplary for the rest of the film: before the title appears, a slow tracking shot takes the viewer down an endless row of pork carcasses strung upside down, as a worker mechanically walks down the aisle spraying the floor, his back to the viewer. Not only in this carefully composed shot are the pigs converted into symmetrical white forms architecturally lined up en masse, but the worker too is presented impersonally. His function is to preserve hygiene, in other words, to remove blood – the trace of life. The film then ends with the gleaming equipment in a cattle abattoir being washed down with a white soapy solution, as if this locale were not a place of death and as if the entire industrialized food complex whitewashes its killing. Indeed, the film demonstrates the processes of preservation, and not only in the case of the meat held in cold storage rooms: we also see vast fields and gigantic hothouses being sprayed with fungicides and pesticides to prevent decay. At first I was tempted to call the musealization at work in *Unser täglich Brot* "death on display," but then realized that we see very little of the killing of animals: the musealization here is indeed more akin to a process of embalming, of preserving. The animal corpse drained of its blood resembles more the product of the taxidermist than something destined to be eaten. The modern food industry, whether through the abattoir or hothouse, wishes to remove death and spoilage to produce a clinically perfect product.

Of course, the metaphor of preservation is fundamentally ambiguous to the point of being outright paradoxical. To preserve means to keep alive and to conserve. It connotes saving, sheltering, protection, defence, safeguarding, or a custodianism. This form of salvaging is related to salvation. When one speaks of musealization as preservation usually this set of associations is evoked. But preservation in Geyrhalter's film suggests less this conserving of life than its killing. He records the process of death in the abattoir, followed by the cold storage of the carcasses. Preservation as refrigeration, as the opening sequence of the film indicates, comes into conflict with the function of the documentary film to conserve and display. Moreover, the mass scale on which the production of food occurs – and which Geyrhalter records – suggests that much of this food will be destined not for consumption but for waste. In other terms, the metaphor of preservation suggests here less retention than the disposal of food. Indeed, the final image of the clean, gleaming halls of the abattoir suggests that life itself has been disposed of.

My point here is not to suggest that Geyrhalter unwittingly falls into reproducing the technological impartiality of the industry he documents. On the contrary, if documentary at its core is about recording and preservation, then what he has created is a meta-documentary, that is to say, a reflection on how to document preservation itself. As the following paragraphs will detail, Geyrhalter is intensely aware of the choices in cinematography, sound, and montage that he makes while putting images to screen.

Cold Storage, or, the Techniques of Preservation

First and foremost, with his insistently stationary camera, Geyrhalter conspicuously refrains from using the handheld camera which has become synonymous if not with the documentary genre today, then at least with the reality effect of *cinéma vérité*. The resulting impression is that of an impartial, impersonalized camera that bears no trace of the movement of the arm holding it. By resolutely not panning Geyrhalter also refuses to suture the spectator into the flow of images: he or she is instead confined to concentrating on the movement that occurs inside the frame. This control makes it impossible for the viewer to see what transpires outside the frame – as if Geyrhalter were commenting on our lack of access to what occurs in this industry or, which is another matter, our willed blindness to it. Enhancing this sense of not being able to see, Geyrhalter also keeps the camera at a studied distance from the object he

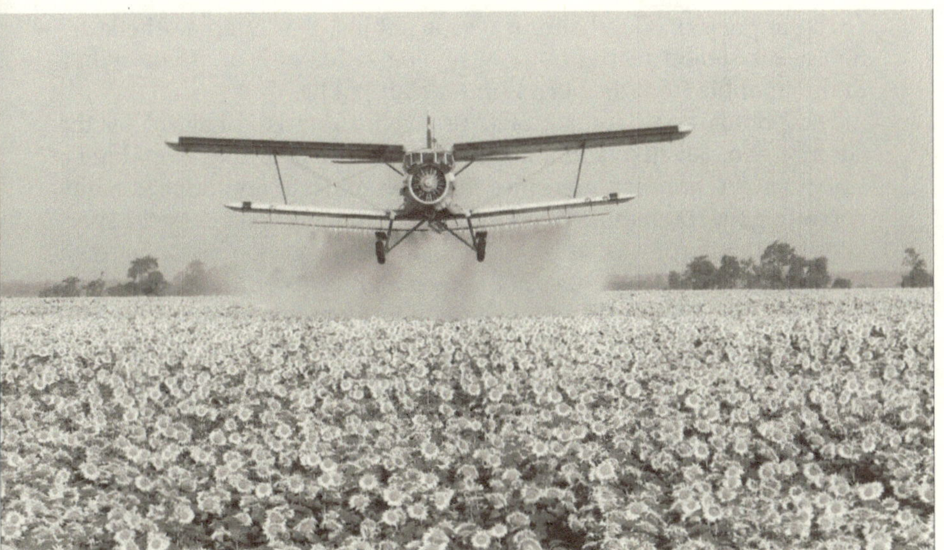

3.1 Flieger (crop duster). *Unser täglich Brot*. Dir. Nikolaus Geyrhalter, Mongrel Media, 2005. © Nikolaus Geyrhalter Filmproduktion

photographs. Very often he uses this technique to capture the immense scale of the farming, usually outdoors in sprawling monocrop farms. But when used indoors as well, this technique means the refusal to cut to a close-up to gratify the curiosity of the spectator; he resists creating the illusion of seeing more deeply into the scenes he depicts. Finally, the monotony of the repetitious actions performed within any given shot contributes as well to a sense of a non-registering of what one sees.

Instead, Geyrhalter trains one's eye on the absolute symmetrical framing in his shots or on the saturated colours, intensified by the bright, artificial lighting of the factories or their gleaming white wall tiles. Geyrhalter here subscribes to a Bauhaus aesthetic of purity. We are left with the impression not just of the director's fastidious eye, but of the order and regimentation of the food industry, in which mould, weeds, dirt, and even death are not permitted. In one scene, for instance, we see a field of sunflowers, a seemingly idyllic panorama until a beautifully matched yellow plane flies overhead to blanket them in pesticide (figure 3.1).

The impression Geyrhalter leaves is not just that of an aestheticization of his subject matter but a technologization of it or, if you will, a draining of life from the very stuff (or staff!) of life.

The photographic impact of *Unser täglich Brot* is enhanced by the absence of a narrative and a documentary voice-over that would tell a story,[2] an absence that intensifies the sense of death and impersonality pervading the mechanized food industry. Without a voice-over the spectator has to interpret what is occurring in the images on his or her own For instance, the viewer does not immediately register that in one scene the repetitive action of a female worker in a poultry factory is the debeaking of chicks – a process necessary so that, in the impossibly close, confined quarters where the chickens are kept, whether in battery cages or in a massive grower house, they do not start to attack each other. But without knowledge of this practice and the reasons for it, the mutilation of the chicks would not be obvious. In this scene, as in others, instead of a voice-over we hear the low hum or rhythmic clicking of machinery, but even that is muted, as are the quick, short cries of the chicks.

The quick cuts to radically different scenes, characteristic of the editing style of *Unser täglich Brot*, also lead to a disorientation of the viewer and compound the absence of a narrative thrust. These rapid cuts, together with the stationary camera that refuses to give a sense of surrounding space, suggest that the hothouses or poultry factories could be located anywhere. Although the viewer becomes through the long takes familiar with the interiors of these specific spaces, they offer no sense of extended or continuous space surrounding them or their geographical location. Only insofar as one would notice in the credits that the film was shot over the span of two years would one suspect that Geyrhalter had travelled extensively throughout Europe to set up his camera. Likewise the sense of time passing is distorted. The film depicts an eternal, ongoing present, whereby seasons function merely as markers in the industrial time clock.

What substitutes for geographical location is the sense of the geographical extent of the industrialized farming. Monocrops stretch as far as the eye can see. Hothouses growing peppers, tomatoes, and cucumbers are vast cathedrals of light. By night they cast extensive light pollution as they tinge the sky orange for miles around. Greenhouses extend endlessly through a flat countryside. Salt mines form gigantic underground caverns. A chicken warehouse seems interminable. With the long takes, the viewer would be left with a sense of boredom and monotony, were it not for being at the same time held captive by this immeasurable industrial sublime.

The spraying of the herbicides or fungicides in these hothouses and fields occurs largely without human assistance. Unmanned mammoth machinery performs these operations. The preservation and sustenance of life entails cold mechanization and technologization, both diegetically and, in Geyrhalter's awareness of his own cinematic choices, meta-diegetically speaking. One sequence, for instance, is composed of two shots: first of a vast stubbly field with wind turbines, into which an immense harvester appears. Potatoes being reaped are next, but with no human being shown at the wheel. In another sequence, we see a tractor shake a fruit tree, another machine scoops up its fruit, cut to large vats with the fruit floating in a chemical preservative brine. Human hands barely touch the product. Most shots of the animals show them, too, without interaction with a human being. Cows are milked by machines, to which they are brought by a conveyor belt. Close to the start of the film a small sliding door opens to a window through which someone peers at chicks in tight cages, the *pane* marking the separation between human and animal and across which animal *pain* is not transferred. In another scene workers in white coats sit at computer terminals while in the background, again on the other side of a window, bulls are brought to collect their semen for artificial insemination.

When human beings do appear, they are rendered unidentifiable in white suits, gloves, boots, and masks that protect them from the poisons. The workers in the factories are also dressed in identical white scrubs, as if they were scientists or doctors working in clinical impunity in a laboratory. At times Geyrhalter will train his camera on one of these workers, alone, meditatively taking a break from her duties while eating a sandwich. Melancholy silently pervades these scenes as well. When the workers do speak with each other, no subtitles appear to translate their dialogue, which is in any case so muted that it cannot be understood. The result is that, again, we do not know the provenance of the food we eat or who actually harvests it; the anonymous workers of the food industry are cogs in its machine. Furthermore, except in one instance, the workers are not of African descent, contributing to the sense that what we are witnessing is a clinical, all-white environment. The issues migratory or immigrant workers face in the farm industry, such as injuries, exposure to pesticides, or substandard living quarters, are made to seem non-existent.

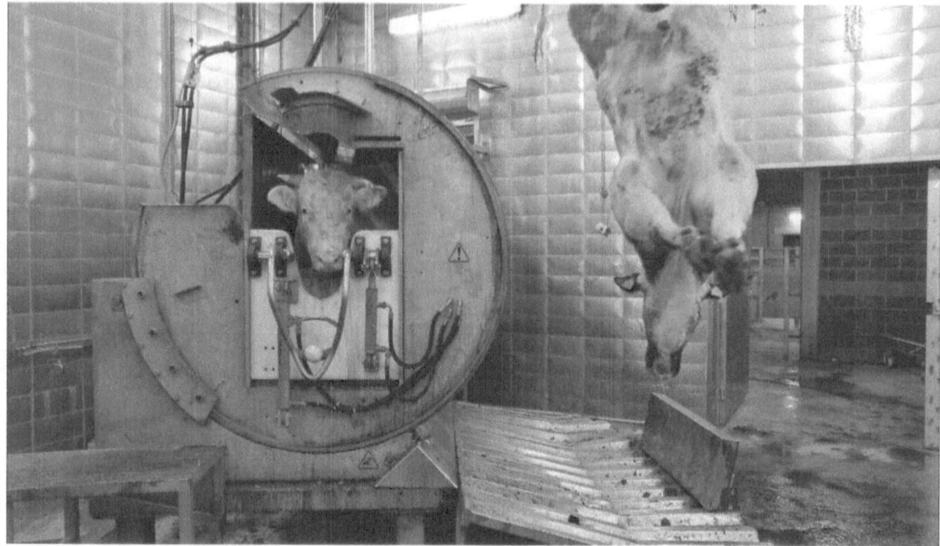

3.2 Schlachtbank (Slaughter House). *Unser täglich Brot*. Dir. Nikolaus Geyrhalter, Mongrel Media, 2005. © Nikolaus Geyrhalter Filmproduktion

The absence of the human being in Geyrhalter's post-human art is mirrored by the absence of animal life. Curiously for a film about where our daily sustenance comes from, there are hardly any scenes of the actual slaughter and struggle of the animal. One exception, if it can be taken as such, occurs in a long shot, that is, at a distance from the events being depicted, as a cow resists as she is led into a container where she is stunned; the tank then turns the carcass around to empty it onto a conveyer belt (figure 3.2).

There is no close-up of the cow's face or body. Moreover, she is followed directly by another cow in an assembly-line production suggestive of Derrida's critique of the undifferentiated term of the "animot" (*The Animal* 41), his neologism to signify the confinement of the pluralistic "animaux" to the singular word: "The animal is a word, it is an appellation that men have instituted, a name they have given themselves the right and the authority to give to the living other" (23). In addition, in Geyrhalter's film there are scenes neither of cattle grazing outdoors nor of chickens in a barnyard. In an earlier sequence, for instance, cattle are penned within an extensive, mausoleum-like complex where their feed (be it hay or corn – it is difficult to determine which) is sprayed violently at them through a large chute.

It is crucial that the sequence of the stunning of the cow appears towards the end of the film, almost as its anti-climatic culmination. Jessica Carey has astutely observed that "the act of stunning purges both the perceived threat posed by animal consciousness, and the necessity to interrogate any of the possible implications of animal consciousness … After stunning, there is only the calm dispatch of pulsating biology left to carry out" (33–4). Thus, for Geyrhalter to focus on the act of stunning the cow means to reinforce this lack of ethical confrontation with the question of whether the cow might anticipate the slaughter awaiting it. With stunning, the animal is treated, under the auspices of a merciful killing, as if it didn't possess a consciousness or foreboding of death.[3] To pursue even further the implications of stunning, what Geyrhalter accomplishes with his resolutely distant camera that refuses to cut to a close-up of the cow is paradoxically a "stunning" of the spectator. We, too, are anaesthetized as if prevented from the surprise of its death. We are "stunned," but not in the sense of being shocked into disbelief or outrage: our metaphorical loss of consciousness is simultaneously a loss of conscience. On the one hand, Geyrhalter's cinematography and editing thus propose to desensitize us to death. Yet on the other hand, this interpretation of "stunning," paralleling that of the cow, entails quite the opposite of immunization: we are actually not immune from the procedures affecting the animals. Despite all the precautions against spoilage, animal being infects/affects us.[4]

Corresponding to discourse of protection, immunization, and insurance against risk, the lack of messiness in animal husbandry reinforces the message of the film that the food industry maximizes capitalist efficiency. Whether in the scene shot from the observation booth where the bull is led to the cow only to collect his semen, in the shock of witnessing the stunning and sudden collapse of the cow, or in the opening shot of the pork carcasses strung up symmetrically without a trace of blood, the impression Geyrhalter leaves is of an ultra-efficient, sterile environment – from conception to death and beyond. The stress on cleanliness and hence preservation makes it seem as if, even in its production, food is as unsoiled and hygienic as when it is presented in the supermarket. As Bob Torres confirms in *Making a Killing,* "While it is certainly the case that animal exploitation could exist without capitalism, the structure and nature of contemporary capital has deepened, extended, and worsened our domination over animals and the natural world" (11). The other dimension to a capitalist, mechanized efficiency that *Unser täglich Brot* underscores is that this industry is disaggregated into multiple operations. As noted previously, the quick cuts to different scenes mean that the film offers no sense of geographical or temporal orientation, for instance, the seasonal growth pattern of a certain crop or of the succession of vehicles, pens, and corridors that cattle are led through. Even the de-assembly line their carcasses follow is not retraced by Geyrhalter: to repeat, instead he stresses the disconnectedness of the operational stages in the ultra-mechanized, ultra-sanitary environment of the manufacturing of food on a large scale.

Archiving Scenes of Consumption and Death: Art after Auschwitz

With its slide-show-like presentation of crop engineering and meat production *Unser täglich Brot* archives its subject matter neutrally. Its viewer can be compared to a visitor in a museum who is invited to distanced, clinical, educated observation but not to reflection on his or her personal connection to the visual documents. The quiet succession of snapshots encourages a response that is likewise muted – a response ushering in the sense of a routinized, dulled viewing that mirrors the routinization of "our daily lives" in capitalist economies. The kind of bland consumerism of visual evidence promoted here resembles a consumption of food devoid of nourishment. The food industry, Geyrhalter seems to suggest, is less about eating than about the clinical manufacturing and assembly of products, destined for supermarket shelves where the emphasis is not on eating for sustenance and health but on the satisfaction of shopping, regardless whether one buys groceries at Loblaws or Whole Foods. His documentary emphasizes visuality, above all, in its use of saturated colours and aesthetic framing, rather than the smells, taste, or touch of food that close-up shots might evoke.

This ultra-efficient expenditure pertains not only to the buying (and much less to the ingestion) of food but also to the disposal of its waste. Zygmunt Bauman had noted that "we dispose of leftovers in the most radical and effective way: we make them invisible by not looking and unthinkable by not thinking" (27). According to this logic of efficiency and disavowal, the cow, pig, or lamb is not only destined to become leftovers on the plate of a society that overeats, but is already treated as waste or refuse from the very start insofar as its living conditions as well as its death are rendered "invisible by [humans] not looking and unthinkable by not thinking." If the museum preserves what would otherwise remain invisible and unarchived, then Geyrhalter's film participates in a musealization to the extent that it documents this hidden capitalist logic of efficiency, immunization, and removal of waste.

Boris Groys has suggestively written: "The most consistent form of consumption is ... general annihilation – the definitive use of all things. Death is an ideal consumer because it consumes everything; only for death is it true that anything goes ... Now the history of art, as is well-known, begins as the archiving of death – through the erection of burial places, pyramids and museums. Art consumes death – it consumes consumption – and at the same time archives this consumption" (59). If this is the case, then *Unser täglich Brot* arguably portrays the ultimate museum: it not only preserves the preservation process, it archives death, and it does so in a way that self-consciously points to techniques of preservation. Groys goes on to say: "Present-day art ... devotes itself to the subject of mass consumption, begins to collect and to archive precisely that which is the first thing to be annihilated and rejected by consumption and thrown into the rubbish. Andy Warhol was primarily interested in packaging, container and posters – all those things first removed from a purchase and thrown away" (59). Much like Andy Warhol's rendition of, say, the Campbell Soup Can, Geyrhalter critically reflects on the capitalist management of consumption. The simple difference from Warhol, however, making Geyrhalter's approach unique, is that his film intentionally, and actually quite surprisingly, does not deal with advertising or packaging. In consumer culture, the public is presented with the advertising and display of an item to purchase, not its production process, hidden from view, especially in the case of food. Whereas Warhol treats the former, Geyrhalter exposes the latter. In terms of Groys's comment, though, what *Unser täglich Brot* accomplishes is to train our eye not just on how this food is produced and preserved within the capitalist economy but on the very process of selectioning out and removing waste – blood, beaks, bad fruit. As the final image intimates, all that is left is the gleaming, empty factory, washed down at the end of the day.

Alongside Warhol, Geyrhalter merits comparison to contemporary artists. His emotional distance evokes the postmodern taxidermist installations of Mark Dion and Damien Hirst, which can be termed post-traumatic, not in the sense that they register a former traumatic experience but that their work seems to be located beyond any registering of animal suffering or response to it. Like Geyrhalter, they resist relationality to the animal, especially responses of pity or compassion.

In this sense, these postmodern artists – in installations radically different from the visceral images of animal suffering that PETA publicizes – de-politicize the human (or is it rather inhumane?) relation to the animal. For comparison and at the other end of the postmodern spectrum are the drawings by the animal rights activist Sue Coe.[5] Steve Baker, for one, criticizes her drawings in that they "constantly risk being drawn close to a stylistic sentimentality in order to express the artist's moral and political outrage" (178). In order to be taken seriously, Baker opines, she needs to devise "animal representations which might be acknowledged, with some degree of reliability, as *being* ethically responsible without *looking* aesthetically sentimental" (178–9). In a subchapter on Sue Coe in his book *What Is Posthumanism?* Cary Wolfe asks with the same intent: "How can the looking back of the animal – and the ethical call harbored by that look – be disengaged from the humanism for which the face (and faciality generally) is perhaps the fundamental figure?" (148).

The problem that Hirst, Dion, and Geyrhalter, as well as Wolfe and Baker, inadvertently raise, is where is the animal in posthumanism?[6] The question is a paradoxical one because posthumanist theory is closely intertwined with animal studies. With the posthumanist bent of animal studies, are its scholars then tacitly participating in what Derrida singles out as an assault on compassion? "War," he writes, "is waged over the matter of pity" (*The Animal* 29). How can "ethical responsibility" possibly exclude pity and "facialality," too easily being read by the above scholars and artists as "sentimentality"? How, in other words, are the arts and humanities to respond ethically and efficaciously to the vast suffering and waste of animal life and to environmental degradation in the second decade of the twenty-first century?[7] How are they able to articulate the mourning and testimony needed to cope with this trauma? Specifically, with regards to Geyrhalter's film, how is the viewer to respond to the assembly-line factory production of food that erases and normalizes animal suffering, even though it takes this viewer behind the scenes? As Josef Lederle asks of this film, can one present something as beautiful that one doesn't sense as beautiful?[8] Or is the very distancing that Geyrhalter replicates and mimics via his own use of the technological apparatus of the camera the actual point of his film? Does not the apparent absence of a cultural critique, for instance, in a voice-over, demonstrate precisely the dilemma – the impossibility of affect and protest in a technological era?

The other side of the coin – and here Geyrhalter is very different from the sensationalism of either Coe or Hirst – is that unlike his fellow artists he resists in his art playing upon the power of the spectacle. If slaughterhouses are indeed kept sequestered from view, then to display them in *Unser täglich Brot* paradoxically does *not* mean to gratify voyeurism, for the film consistently refrains from granting the viewer the cut he or she desires to a closer look. Thus, it could be argued that Geyrhalter here responds to the larger culture of violence to which visual media, whether in television news programming, video games, or Hollywood blockbusters, contribute and shape. On the one hand, the shocking quality of *Unser täglich Brot* is thus that it resists hitting us with violent images of animal death, images that would otherwise remind us of a sacrificial aspect to creaturely submission to the knife. On the other hand, does this very resistance to violence mimic the impartiality of the industry to the violence it commits? Although the images we see on Geyrhalter's screen may be new and unseen before, the cold affect, combined with aesthetic splendour, with which they are presented, suggests that there is actually nothing new about them that should startle us; in other words, that we live in a condition where we even fail to perceive the violence.

How, though, does the routinized viewing that fails to register violence interact with the sublimity of the scale of farming that Geyrhalter is so well able to record? The religious dimension resonant in the title *Unser täglich Brot* is clearly ironic, for with mechanized mass food production the relationship of the consumer to the source of his or her daily bread is severed and taken for granted. Its provenance is no longer God, supplicated to in the Lord's Prayer, but acres of genetically modified foods. Thanks be to Monsanto! Moreover, Geyrhalter's title seems to give human beings the temerity to ask God to forgive their trespasses, their sacrilege against nature. If there is a ritualistic aspect in the film, it would reside solely in the repetitive, automated motions documented by the long takes, not in the taking of animal life that could be seen as sacrificial. The routine becomes sublime or, better yet, technologically sublime. But at what cost to the animal?

Heidegger has infamously written: "Agriculture is now a mechanized food industry. As for its essence, it is the same thing as the manufacture of corpses in the gas chambers and the death camps, the same thing as the blockades and the reduction of countries to famine, the same thing as the manufacture of hydrogen bombs" (qtd in Levinas 487). In commenting on this passage, Levinas writes: "This stylistic turn of phrase, this analogy, this progression, are beyond commentary" (487). The problem with Heidegger's statement, as Levinas suggests, is its facile lining up of analogies: not only is each of these respective atrocities "unspeakable" but their comparison is as well. But is the comparison of the mechanized slaughterhouse to Auschwitz therefore beyond commentary? Even though both atrocities are incommensurably different, a purpose can be argued for investigating where the similarities lie in order to make recognizable the condition of factory farm animals today. Sue Coe takes recourse to Adorno when she inscribes his words on a 2009 woodcut: "Auschwitz begins whenever someone looks at a slaughterhouse and thinks they are only animals."[9] Derrida writes: "It will therefore be necessary to reduce, little by little, the conditions of violence and cruelty toward animals, and, to that end, to modify, on a large historical scale, the conditions of breeding, slaughter, treatment en masse, and of what I hesitate (only in order not to abuse the inevitable associations) to call a *genocide*, in a situation where, in fact, the word would not be so inappropriate" (*For What Tomorrow* 73).[10] Finally, none other than Isaac Bashevis Singer has termed the factory farm an "eternal Treblinka" (see Patterson). For the Nazis the death camps were not considered exceptional institutions; murder could be committed as if it were an everyday, commonplace occurrence. The assembly-line mass slaughter of animals, too, is considered unexceptional; but in contrast to the normalized mass killing in Auschwitz, the industrialized meat industry today has yet to be acknowledged as horrendous by society at large. What, then, is the ethical space in which we can live knowing of this "eternal Treblinka"? What do mortality and morality mean in the wake of it? And how is contemporary art to express its ethical obligation? To put the problem in terms that this volume raises: academic discourse has amply theorized how to commemorate the victims of the Holocaust. But it has yet to address how to memorialize the life sacrificed in the factory farm.

Although I shy away from addressing the gravity of the comparison Singer and others make, the above questions remain to be posed to Geyrhalter precisely because of their notable absence. Or, another way of framing the relation between ethics and aesthetics would be to inquire into the purpose and characterization of art after Auschwitz. Adorno writes: "To survive reality at its most extreme and grim artworks that do not want to sell themselves as consolation must equate themselves with that reality. Radical art today is synonymous with dark art; its primary color is black" (*Aesthetic Theory* 39). He then notes "the impoverishment of means entailed by the ideal of blackness" (40). Sue Coe's preference for the heavy dark line of her pencil and the predominance of a black palette contrasts with Geyrhalter's saturated colours and bright white lighting in the factories or the artificial sunlight in the hothouses. Preferring newspapers to magazines to display her work, Coe writes, "I love the immediacy, the urgency, and the way everything is a little smudgy" (Sherrill, D1).[11] In Geyrhalter, by contrast, one finds a clinical impunity that mirrors the cleanliness of the lifeless factory. Yet although we can line up these dichotomies among Coe, Adorno, and Singer, on the one hand, and posthumanist artists such as Geyrhalter and Hirst, on the other, what Coe, Hirst, and Geyrhalter share in their post-Auschwitz art is an interest in the postmodern sublime and an allegorical discourse that shows in images what defies interpretation.

Melancholia and Musealization

This defying of interpretation and the fall into silence explain why the process of musealization is attempted in the first place, namely, to counteract forgetting. Yet because this attempt is ultimately unsuccessful, it creates a melancholic relation to the past. Thus, worth pursing here is the dialectical relationship between melancholia and musealization. The melancholic individual wishes to preserve or cling to the lost object, according to Nicolas Abraham and Maria Torok, to entomb it away in the self. Melancholy thus differs, according to Freud, from mourning in that it refuses to acknowledge the loss. On the one hand, the result for the depressive subject can be the fall into muteness: words can seem extinguished of meaning, absurd, and delayed. On the other hand, according to Julia Kristeva in *Black Sun: Depression and Melancholia*, a heightened aestheticization can compensate for the loss and disavow it: "Beauty is consubstantial with [artifice]. Like feminine finery concealing stubborn depressions, beauty emerges as the admirable face of loss" (99).

As amply demonstrated above, *Unser täglich Brot* exhibits both this aestheticization and the muteness that result from the musealization and technologization of animal life and death. The film desensitizes the viewer through its own dispassionate use of technology – its peculiar use of sound, cinematography, and editing that are disconcertingly unusual for the documentary genre. The horror of the automatized processing of chickens and breeding of cattle, and, of course, their slaughter, is thereby both kept in abeyance yet also enhanced: the viewer is made doubly aware of the mechanization of how animals are treated – how they are rendered on camera and rendered in the abattoir.[12] On the one hand, European viewers can see what is usually kept out of sight – how their food is mass produced. On the other hand, what the spectator watches is so removed from life that precisely the invisibility against which such a documentary militates is reasserted. Disavowal of loss, in other words, a cognitive dissonance, somehow lies at the heart of musealization because it utilizes and preserves this loss – "I know very well that there is a loss of life, but …" With respect to the animal, this disavowal, even foreclosure, of death, operates every time we eat meat, resulting in a melancholic relationship to the animal. It is also a melancholic, constantly disavowed relationship to contemporary technologized lives distanced from contact with nature.

The melancholic classically cannot articulate what the loss is from which he or she suffers. This inability to grasp and communicate is what links melancholy to the sublime. The mind is overwhelmed and cannot maintain a human relation to what it perceives. Thus, in *Unser täglich Brot* despite the sublimity of the extent of the massive factory farming, which is enhanced by the corridors and caverns captured by Geyrhalter's minimalism, the world he depicts is still unavailable to comprehension. Nor can Geyrhalter in his wordless melancholy offer any commentary to his beautiful pictures. Everything is in place, in its place, and not off centre – and yet it cannot be grasped and interpreted. Moreover, as Geyrhalter's still camera endows his film with a sense of the photographic, it is perforce – at least according to André Bazin and Susan Sontag – associated with death. Sontag, for instance, wrote that "photography is an elegiac art, a twilight art" (*On Photography* 15).[13] With its photographic qualities *Unser täglich Brot* is tinged with an aestheticized melancholy, indeed with what Sontag elsewhere called the "sign of Saturn," the melancholy of the collector (*Under the Sign of Saturn* 120).

Sontag also wrote that "to take a picture is to have an interest in things as they are, in the status quo remaining unchanged … to be in complicity with whatever makes a subject interesting, worth photographing – including, when that is the interest, another person's pain or misfortune" (*On Photography* 12). Sontag, of course, was intensely suspicious of the documentary photograph for its resistance to political efficacy. She wrote: "To possess the world in the form of images is, precisely, to re-experience the unreality and remoteness of the real" (*On Photography* 164). Geyrhalter's film presents the same dilemma in that, although it can be read as a protest against the food industry, its melancholy and sublimity are complicit with the status quo and create a sense of inevitability and powerlessness. He shows the typical, and as such it is not revealing. And although his is a documentary about the ordinary, daily production of food, its images are remote and surreal in their ultra-cleanliness. It is disturbingly as if the images he exposes are merely props for his stylized film. The result is that, just like the camera, the viewer is paralysed. Or is it not so much that the viewer as an individual is paralysed, but that Geyrhalter is able to mirror through his use of the cinematic apparatus how our society as a whole is anesthetized? Whether or not Geyrhalter is critical of the industry he dissects, *Unser täglich Brot* is fundamentally about the way we see in an era of the hegemony of visual culture, namely, disengaged from the spectacle, all while taking in the sublimity of it. One could argue that Geyrhalter encourages the viewer to react precisely because the film does not: it elicits affect in the viewer even in its very absence. But his artful techniques of preservation, however self-conscious and brilliantly deconstructive, do manipulate the viewer into a lethargy and melancholy. In short, the more he shows, the less we know and want to know, for the killing of animals and the natural environment sustain our daily lives.

NOTES

1 See Pichler's similar analysis of this contradiction: "Geyrhalter's rigorous aesthetic, which in itself might be free of a valuation, still leads to an ethical moment: the recognition that this mode of production is a mirror of our society, and that we as consumers are automatically implicated in the internal logic of this system. Nevertheless, Geyrhalter consistently refuses to comment or to offer any solution or even an evaluation" (278).

2 In his pulling back from voice-over commentary, Geyrhalter resembles his fellow Austrian documentarian Ulrich Seidel, though the pristine composition of Geyrhalter's work is vastly different from the scrappiness of Seidel's work and lacks the latter's voyeuristic interest in his subject matter.

3 See also the discussion of how stunning displaces "the charge of killing from the act of slaughter" in Shukin (159). Burt also investigates stunning in his essay "The Illumination of the Animal Kingdom."

4 To take the bio(political) metaphor even further, the meat contaminates us in our very consumption of it – we too consume to our detriment the antibiotics and hormones fed to the farm animals.

5 Sue Coe (1951–) is a contemporary artist of the printed page whose illustrations have appeared on the covers of *The New Yorker* and *The Nation*. *Dead Meat* (1996), a visual and written account of Coe's infiltration of

numerous slaughterhouses with a foreword by *The Nation*'s Alexander Cockburn, exposes the meat industry's treatment of animals and workers. In *Sheep of Fools: A Song Cycle for Five Voices* (2005), she turns to the children's illustrated book format to depict the massive shipment of live sheep under horrific conditions from Australia and New Zealand to their destination for slaughter. Although her work is represented by the Galerie St. Etienne (known for its showings of prints by German Expressionist artists), she refuses to participate in the high financial stakes of the art world. Her pieces are intentionally affordable so as to reach a wide audience and are auctioned off to support animal welfare causes.

6 See my article "Where is the Animal after Posthumanism?"

7 Here Geyrhalter merits contrastive comparison to documentaries that operate as educative exposés of the global implications of the food industry for the environment, *Fast Food Nation* (Richard Linklater, 2006) and *We Feed the World* (Erwin Wagenhofer, 2005), to give just two examples.

8 "Kann man, darf man etwas als schön zeigen, das man nicht als schön empfindet?" (8).

9 Coe writes reluctantly in *Dead Meat*: "The Holocaust keeps coming into my mind, which annoys the hell out of me. I see this reference in so many animal rights magazines. Is this the comforting measuring rod by which all horrors are evaluated? My annoyance is exacerbated by the fact that the suffering I am witnessing now cannot exist on its own, it has to fall into the hierarchy of a 'lesser animal suffering' ... Twenty million murdered humans deserve to be more than a reference point. I am annoyed that I don't have more power in communicating what I've seen apart from stuttering: 'It's like the Holocaust'" (72).

10 See also *The Animal That Therefore I Am* (80).

11 Donald Kuspit refers to the "abysmal abstract blackness of her space, and the way her scenes tend to exist as snatches of representation which seem about to sink into the blackness as if into quicksand" (179).

12 On the play between "rendering" as representation and the use of animal byproducts, see Shukin.

13 Bazin writes: "If the plastic arts were put under psychoanalysis, the practice of embalming the dead might turn out to be a fundamental factor in their creation" (9).

4 The Concealed Curator: Constructed Authenticity in Uli Edel's *Der Baader-Meinhof Komplex*

CATRIONA FIRTH

Our view of the past is by necessity a mediated one – we cannot experience directly that which is no longer present. We rely instead on written, visual, and audio mediations to form our individual and collective memories of historical events. The logic of this potentially infinite "remediation" of the past insists that "there was never a past prior to mediation; all mediations are remediations, in that mediation of the real is always a mediation of another mediation" (Grusin 18). As the principal, and often, only gateway to the past, remediated memories stand at the heart of collective remembering: "When we look at the emergence and 'life' of memory sites, it becomes clear that these are based on repeated media representations, on a host of remediated versions of the past ... which create, stabilize and consolidate, but then also critically reflect upon and renew these sites" (Erll and Rigney 5).

Each remediated instance brings something specific to the table of historical remembering, serving up for consumption its own version of the past, determined in part by the properties of the medium itself. To comprehend collective memory, then, we must consider the diverse ways in which contemporary media musealize the past and turn bygone events into consumable products for the present.

Film adaptations offer a particularly vivid example of remediation in action. The transfer from the verbal medium of literature to the audio-visual experience of film lays bare the unique contribution of each form to the construction of memory, shaped by qualities inherent in the medium and by the recipient's horizons of expectation. Especially in those cases where book and film carry the same name, and hence operate under certain shared expectations, a comparative study of adaptation promises to shed light on the impact that medium-specific properties exert on the dynamics of remembering, whether technological, ontological, or generic. Furthermore, when dealing with historical accounts and the memorialization of the past, we may also consider the ways in which both film and literature borrow from representational strategies associated with the museum. In the museal space, artefacts are selected from an archive, arranged in a specific order and presented to the visitor in a particular way. Each step of this process is implicated in wider signifying practices that attribute meaning and value to the past. This chapter argues that historical writing and filmmaking operate in a similar manner. Film in particular selects from an almost infinite combination of possible shots, edits them into coherent scenes in post-production and presents them to the viewer in a certain style or genre. In both film and the museum, the production of historical meaning involves countless agents (including producers, cinematographers, editors, and actors in film; or experts, subject specialists, and front-of-house staff in the museum), whose work is frequently subsumed under the name of the director/curator. It is this metonymically empowered figure who controls what the viewer/visitor sees, understands, and interprets, and it is she who determines the degree to which historical representation may be questioned, challenged, and revised.

My analysis focuses on Uli Edel and Bernd Eichinger's adaptation of Stefan Aust's monumental work on left-wing German terrorism, *Der Baader-Meinhof Komplex* (*The Baader Meinhof Complex*, 2008), as an intricate process of musealization. In both works, the selection, arrangement, and aesthetic presentation of recent historical events play a crucial role in constructing collective memories of the "Red Army Faction." The RAF or Baader-Meinhof group, as it was named after two of its founding members, was Germany's most prominent extreme left-wing terrorist organization, which came into being with the liberation by force of Andreas Baader in May 1970. Although the group existed officially until 1998, it was most (in)famous in the 1970s before the suicides of its leading members in the Stammheim prison on 18 October 1977. At its peak, the RAF was responsible for numerous bombings, in particular of US institutions, along with several bank robberies, kidnappings, and murders.[1] From the media furore surrounding the release of *Der Baader-Meinhof Komplex* and the public outrage following ex-terrorist Christian Klar's successful appeal for clemency, it is apparent that the wounds of the German Autumn have yet to heal. Serving as a "projection screen for demonization, idealization, for an absent reckoning with the Federal Republic" (Blumenstein 16),[2] the RAF continues to divide public opinion to this day. As Butz Peters notes wryly, "Whether we like it or not, the history of the RAF is part of the history of the Federal Republic" (9).[3]

Examining the film's dynamics of remembering, this study situates *Der Baader-Meinhof Komplex* within the new wave of "heritage films" that has swept through German cinema in the past decade (Cooke, *Contemporary* 100). International blockbusters such as *Der Untergang* (*Downfall*, 2004) or *Das Leben der Anderen* (*The Lives of Others*) present the past as "a spectacular museum to be consumed by the present-day spectator" (Cooke 101), and attempt to recreate in painstakingly faithful detail the past worlds in which their protagonists operate. As Cooke notes, the question of authenticity is central to heritage cinema and the way it is marketed internationally (100). Posters, trailers, and numerous interviews propagate the films' claims to present the past "as it really was" and draw attention to the elaborate research process that inevitably precedes their cinematic production. Yet I would argue that the mode of authenticity propagated by the filmmaker-curators is at odds with that actually present in the heritage film. Whilst the films' aggressive marketing campaigns relentlessly emphasize their fidelity to an inconceivably broad range of documentary sources, the films themselves create "authenticity" in a very different manner, one based on affect and sensation rather than objective intellectual rationalism. The discrepancy between an allegedly documentary authenticity and the intensely "real" experience of the past offered in *Der Baader-Meinhof Komplex*, I will argue, sets into relief the troubled relationship between the popular heritage film and perhaps more intellectual conceptions of history. This chapter will compare the authenticating discourses employed by the blockbuster feature film to its literary source and consider to what extent the filmic medium offers a more widely accessible alternative to more "serious" and ostensibly objective (written) historical discourses.

Authenticity

Historical representation in any form or medium raises pressing questions about authenticity. Yet authenticity is not a pre-existent quality that a work may "possess"; it must first be created and crafted within the text, where it thus emerges as the complex product of various discourses and narrative strategies. Authenticity, therefore, is not a homogeneous and uniform entity, but rather dazzles in its flexibility and diversity. "Authentic" in its almost infinite malleability can describe the taste of beer, a museum artefact, or a historical narrative, gilding each with the prestige of originality and veracity. Authenticity has become an indication of quality and gravitas and functions in the world of media as "a magic word that marks the borders between cheap tat and true value which are audible and comprehensible to all" (Schlanstein 206).[4] It has been argued since Walter Benjamin that with the advent and proliferation of the digital media, the modern subject's desire for authenticity has increased dramatically, becoming an almost "universal longing" (Todd xiv).

In a recent volume on "fictions of authenticity," Ulrike Eva Pirker and Mark Rüdiger identify two seemingly opposed modes of authenticity. On the one hand, the "testimonial mode" constructs authenticity through sources, witnesses, artefacts, and auratic locations which evoke "the suggestion of an original, a relic from the past, whose effect seems to emanate from its own historical authenticity" (Pirker and Rüdiger 17).[5] The "experiential mode," on the other hand, relies less on the actual origin of historical artefacts than on "evoking an 'authentic feeling,' a contemporary mood or atmosphere by approximating the original or creating a plausible or typical past" (ibid.).[6] Whilst the former is bound to genuine objects, documents, and witnesses, the latter may circumvent thorny issues of provenance and reliability by the sheer sensational force of its evocation. In a museal context, testimonial authenticity relies heavily on labelling and presentation to legitimate its sources, with the curator acting as a guarantor of authenticity through his or her expertise. Conversely, the experiential mode depends on an immediacy of experience, rendering the curator not merely superfluous but, in fact, obstructive to the production of authenticity. The curator who chooses to focus on testimonial authenticity may be regarded as operating on similar ground to that of the traditional historian. Where the historian looks to footnotes and references to verified documents to authenticate her discourse, the curator foregrounds the proof of provenance and process of verification to support her authority. Unlike the historian, however, the curator's claim to authenticity lies ultimately in the curated objects themselves, which take precedence over the curator's narrative. As Stephan Jaeger notes elsewhere in this volume, "objects convey far more historical aura than the visitor experiences through simulated history" (147).

Even at first glance, these categories sit comfortably with a medium-specific analysis of authenticity in *Der Baader-Meinhof Komplex.*

On the one hand, the book insistently invokes a testimonial form of authenticity. Aust dazzles his readers with an almost overwhelming abundance of facts, historical detail, and conventional documentary sources, and repeatedly lays bare his role as curator. The book's preface provides a first-person blow-by-blow account of his research process: "I carried out interviews, collected and viewed about sixty metres of files, through which I attempted to reconstruct the history of the 'Baader-Meinhof group'" (Aust 13).[7] Conversely, the film's emotionally engaging, high-speed narrative offers the viewer an intense "experience" of history that focuses on sensory stimulation and affective implication. Accordingly, Edel and Eichinger strive to conceal their curatorial role in an effort "to place the spectator right in the middle of events" (Bernd Eichinger, quoted in Eichinger 12).[8] The following comparative analysis of the musealization process seeks to reveal a shift from testimonial authenticity to its experiential counterpart, and to explore the thorny issue of medium specificity. This step-by-step examination of the selection, arrangement, and presentation processes will ask whether there is such a thing as "filmic authenticity" and, if so, how it differs from the construction and reception of authenticity in written texts.

Selection

The process of selection is a necessary prerequisite for representation in museums, film, and written histories. However, as Peter Vergo points out, "the criteria for the selection or rejection of the material for an exhibition are neither random nor arbitrary – on the contrary, they are based on an underlying though usually unspoken sense of purpose" (46). In the case of Aust's book, the selected material is constituted primarily by written and oral testimonies and visual artefacts, in particular photographs. In material terms, this pool is supplemented in the film by a series of "original artefacts" ranging from iconic items of clothing to archive television footage. Furthermore, the process of selection is doubled in the adaptation. Not only does it extract from Aust's book the salient details and exciting events that make up its narrative, it returns also to the source of Aust's work: the real-life events, documents, and artefacts. Indeed, it may be pertinent to ask in what sense the film in fact constitutes an adaptation of Aust's book. I would argue that this designation in itself fulfils an authenticating function. In presenting the film as an adaptation of Aust's text, Edel and Eichinger not only efface their own creative role but install in its place a documentary source imbued with all the authority of a "standard work."[9] The film's authentication process, it would appear, begins even at the most foundational level.

Aust: The Self-Reflexive Curator

From the outset, Aust demonstrates an awareness of the power and authority of the curator and explicitly addresses his problematic role, stressing that "I avoided judgment as far as possible. However, the selection, emphasis, and composition of the material are my subjective decision" (15).[10] Aust is also keen to point out where sources may be missing, such as letters belonging to leading terrorist, Gudrun Ensslin (815), or the original recordings of conversations between Ulrike Meinhof and her lawyer (41). Where information has been withheld from him by the authorities, he openly addresses this issue and draws attention to their secrecy, commenting that "some of the meetings were held in secret – food for speculation" (Aust 854).[11] The process of gathering sources and the challenges it poses to the curator are thus laid bare.

At the same time, however, Aust frequently delegates the responsibility of selection to state institutions and questions their reasons for withholding potentially significant documents. This is most apparent in his criticism of official reports on the controversial night in Stammheim, when Baader, Ensslin, and Jan-Carl Raspe are believed to have committed suicide. Aust regards the secrecy surrounding the police investigation as the main source for the RAF's popular mythologization and suggests that "the majority of the speculations would possibly not even have arisen had the examination been more thorough and the investigators less biased" (854).[12] The heavily implied suspicion of foul play that emerges thus appears as an inevitable conclusion forced upon the writer by the authorities' stubborn secrecy. Brushing over his subjective interpretation of the limited sources, Aust emerges as a visible and responsible curator whose hands are unfortunately tied by bureaucratic obstinacy with potentially sinister motives.

This impression is reinforced by the book's claim to comprehensiveness. Its cover proudly proclaims that it is "completely updated" and it appears that no element is too small to escape the notice of its meticulous curator. The reader is bombarded with seemingly superfluous details, such as the precise inventory of the prisoners' cells: "On his four shelves Baader had 974 books and 75 LPs. A mouth harmonica, an

'Olivetti' typewriter, a box of 'Pelican' watercolours, two pairs of sunglasses, hairspray, eye-shadow, two fur coats, an electric alarm clock with batteries, a record player with amplifier and speakers" (Aust 659).[13] This inventory suggests a striving for the greatest possible accuracy, and inspires confidence in Aust's curatorial competence.

More significantly, the book appears equally generous in its selection of witness accounts, treating the reader to a vast array of conflicting testimonies. Thus, ex-terrorist Peter Jürgen Boock's claim that the RAF had not imprisoned their hostage in a wardrobe is juxtaposed with a police report that identifies samples of the victim's hair inside the closet (Aust 657). Aust's refusal to comment on either of the sources is testimony to his desire to present an unbiased account, although the reader is nevertheless likely to attribute greater credibility to the police account than to that of a terrorist implicated in the events. All the same, the reader believes herself to be in full command of a wide range of facts from which she may make an informed evaluation of past events.

Indeed, Aust almost requires this of the reader through his frequent and extended use of the interrogative mode. The reader is repeatedly called upon to join together the pieces of the jigsaw or draw conclusions from numerous contradictory sources. In a chapter on the RAF's relationship with Palestinian organizations, Aust asks: "Was the whole operation perhaps linked to the secret services of which even the RAF members themselves were unaware? Was not the Yemeni secret service that inspected the training camp completely in the hands of the Stasi?" (730).[14]

These questions render Aust visible to the reader and include her in the meaning-making process. She is encouraged to continue his investigative work in order to get closer to the truth of an as yet unresolved historical mystery.[15]

Aust's role here is reminiscent of Mieke Bal's ideal curator, who is prepared to "relinquish his monopoly over that first-person position, exchange it with the second person and at the very least show his own subjectivity, his own hand, let the 'you' speak back" (*Double Exposures* 159). Bal conceives of the museum as a communicative act of exposition with a first-person exposing agent (the curator), a second-person recipient (the visitor), and a third-person object of discourse (historical events or museum objects). Referring to Emile Benveniste's theory of discourse, Bal stresses that communication depends on the reversibility of the first- and second- person positions, which may occur only if the first-person curator is perceptibly present: "If that presence is visible, then the address to the 'you' who is asked to accept the constative statement is also visible as what it is: a speech act of authority. This authority can then be either accepted or rejected" (157). By revealing his selecting hand, Aust opens up multiple interpretations and bestows upon the reader the power to accept or reject his version of events. Whilst their almost rhetorical nature renders these questions more coercive than they first appear, Aust's willingness to put himself on display and lay bare the act of selection is apparent.

Edel/Eichinger: Sly Selectors

The cinematic curator is far less conspicuous and the film's selection process is at once more radical and less discernible. The book's multi-perspectival approach is whittled down in adaptation to a single point-of-view, which assumes an air of authenticity and authority. For example, the question of Ulrike Meinhof's role in the bombing of the Springer newspaper offices remains unclear in the book. The bombs, which went off on 19 May 1972 and injured seventeen employees, were the source of great controversy among left-wing radicals, and the RAF publically and unequivocally condemned this attack against civilians. On the one hand, Aust mentions police reports that support claims of her involvement (525), yet a few pages later we are offered a contradictory statement by RAF member Brigitte Mohnhaupt, who rejects this theory and stresses the unity of the group (554). The book makes no attempts to reconcile these conflicting accounts, even though it identifies this information as crucial in understanding Meinhof's relationship to the group and her gradual psychological breakdown (525).

The film, however, leaves no such room for ambiguity. Its account of events depicts Meinhof, in disguise, standing outside a telephone booth from which an unidentified man issues a bomb warning. Wearing a blond wig and a decidedly bourgeois two-piece suit, Meinhof gazes intently at the top left of the screen, displaying obvious signs of anxiety, which are heightened as it becomes clear that their warning is not going to be heeded. In inviting the viewer to recognize Meinhof through her camouflage, the film provides her with an illusory sense of epistemological mastery and she gains pleasure from her perceived ability to "see through" Meinhof's disguise. The spectator is coerced into accepting the film's selective version of events, since to challenge the veracity of the depiction would be to deny her own visual competence. The viewer thus assumes the position of passive witness to Meinhof's presence (and guilt), confirming Rainer

Wirtz's assertion that recent historical films "evidently intend to render the spectator an eye-witness to the events ... We are the new eye-witnesses, we allow ourselves to be gripped, touched and even as professional historians we say: that's how it was" (200).[16]

In this instance, the ontological assumptions associated with cinema reinforce the film's authoritative view of history. Although long discredited by semiotic and psychoanalytic approaches to film, Bazin's conception of film as a transparent medium lives on as a central illusion within the cinematic apparatus. Whilst theoreticians such as Christian Metz may have transformed Bazin's "window-on-the-world" into a Lacanian mirror, classical feature film continues to draw its representational power from a careful concealment of the medium itself. Speaking of the photographic image, Barthes notes that "whatever it grants to vision and whatever its manner, a photograph is always invisible: it is not it that we see" (*Camera Lucida* 6). Ignoring the medium to grasp at its object, the viewer enters into a Freudian act of disavowal – the "I know that ... but even so" experience which allows her to simultaneously recognize and deny the fictionality of the image – more commonly referred to as the "willing suspension of disbelief."

Vivian Sobchack equally notes the viewer's double occupation of the cinematic space both as an external recipient of what the "other," the filmmaker, sees, and as an active spectator in the "here, where we see" (10). In this scene, the second experiential mode of spectatorship overpowers our awareness of the other as the source of the gaze. Crosscutting between the office workers, the telephone operators who refuse to react to the bomb threat, and an increasingly agitated Meinhof, the film creates an intense atmosphere of suspense. This tension acts forcefully upon the viewer, demanding from her a visceral, physical response, a powerfully felt desire for satisfactory resolution. Alison Landsberg has argued that "affect might usefully complement cognition in the acquisition of knowledge about traumatic events of the past" (*Prosthetic Memory* 113). Here, however, the stressful experience of the filmic moment is called upon to replace consciously acquired knowledge, as emotion overrides the viewer's cognitive response to the cinematic assertion of Meinhof's guilt. Although aware at one level that *Der Baader-Meinhof Komplex* is a fictionalized historical narrative, she chooses to believe in its version of events, even when presented with no evidence save that of her own "witnessing." Following Landsberg, we may say that the spectator has been implanted with a "prosthetic memory" of the Springer bombings, whereby she "does not simply apprehend a historical narrative but takes on a more personal, deeply felt memory of a past event through which he or she did not live" (2). We do not *know* that Meinhof was responsible for the bombing, but we certainly *feel* that she was.

The spectator is thus presented with a selective view of history, offered up as the definitive, "authentic" story. Aleida Assmann identifies the potential danger inherent in a narrativized and fictionalized representation of the past, which replaces the "might-have-been" with a definitive "that's exactly how it was" (*Geschichte* 163). By obscuring the curator's role in selecting those events and perspectives that constitute the cinematic narrative, the film places its version of history beyond the reach of critical scrutiny. The curator-filmmaker's invisibility "cuts the dialogue short and precludes the performance of a range of speech acts, such as affirmative ones, but also, amongst many others, interrogative, mandatory, and prohibitive ones" (Bal, "Exposing the Public" 529). Unlike her reading counterpart, the spectator of *Der Baader-Meinhof Komplex* is thus excluded from the process of meaning-making. All the time believing herself to be an active participant, she is rendered the passive recipient of an authoritatively formulated version of history, one which definitively lays the blame on Ulrike Meinhof's shoulders.

Arrangement

Once selection has taken place, the chosen artefacts (or in Aust's case, facts, details, opinions, etc.) must be arranged into a coherent display, which endows these diverse objects with a sense of significance. Henrietta Lidchi speaks of the "poetics of exhibition" to describe "the practice of producing meaning through the internal ordering and conjugation of the separate but related components of an exhibition" (168). The two versions of *Der Baader-Meinhof Komplex* vary only slightly in their actual ordering, since both follow a roughly linear chronology that begins with the student protests in 1967 and concludes with the Stammheim suicides and Schleyer's murder in 1977. Yet their "poetics" differ greatly in rhythm and emphasis. Whilst Aust frequently pauses or rewinds the narrative to provide supplementary information, the film's fast-paced storytelling bears witness to Eichinger's assertion that "a narrator should never press the stop button" (113).[17] The following section will consider how Eichinger's rejection of obvious curatorial intervention manifests itself in the film's (re)arrangement of events and how this impacts on the process of historical signification.

Aust as Tour Guide

Stefan Aust repeatedly interrupts the flow of his narrative and demands from the reader an active engagement with the book's historical exhibits. Cross-referencing, for example, disrupts the narrative and forces the reader to retrace her steps (Aust 863). Rather than following a gradually unfolding story with a clear sense of direction, the reader is called upon to leap back and forward and weave a complex web of associations and connections.[18] Her immersion in narrative events is further challenged by the frequent incursion of dry, dull facts into otherwise exciting or scintillating passages. In particular, the meticulous records of the Stammheim night reports, which frequently consist only of the time, date, and "no incidents," are a very literal manifestation of "nothing happening." At one point, Aust cites verbatim over two pages the reports of one night in which nothing interesting at all occurs, repeating like a tedious mantra the unspectacular information "checks carried out" (755–6).

Despite its chronological ordering and potentially sensationalist subject matter, the book does not permit the reader to engross herself in the narrative; there is no danger of her being swept away by the excitement of the story. In this sense, Aust's book approaches the Barthesian "writerly text," in which the reader takes an active role in the construction of meaning and is "no longer a consumer, but a producer of the text" (Barthes, *S/Z* 4). The writerly text, Barthes argues, encourages a slow, reflexive form of reading and a dynamic interaction with the text and its multiple meanings. It is not a finished text with a clear beginning, middle, and end. Its meanings are not fixed, but must be reconstructed by the reader, who pauses and reflects at regular intervals. This mode of reading is facilitated greatly by the text's fragmented structure. Far from producing a freely flowing narrative, Aust's work is heavily partitioned into over three hundred segments with an average length of three pages. The reader's experience is thus comparable to that of the museum visitor participating in a guided tour. While Aust clearly directs her attention towards specific facts and details and gently leads her forward in a regulated order, she is also encouraged to stop and examine the historical objects (or possibly return to earlier exhibits) and reflect upon their significance within the historical narrative. Narrative interruption thus thrusts the curator into the foreground as the hand that stops the reader's progression and offers an opportunity for questions.

Cinematic Sensations

By contrast, the spectator is treated to an "experience ride" of the sort often found in heritage museums. These "Disney-style dark rides" lead visitors through the past "as it really was," recreating its sights, sounds, and smells "to give visitors an emotive impression of what a typical day ... was like" (McIntosh and Prentice 80). In Barthesian terms, the adaptation can be said to encourage a more "readerly" approach, in which the spectator is "plunged into a kind of idleness" by a forward-driven, classically linear narrative (Barthes *S/Z* 4). Edel and Eichinger arrange the selected scenes and events into a thriller-based narrative of suspense which asks "What happened next?" rather than "Why did that happen?" The viewer is locked into an automated carriage and whizzed through the "past." She can sit back, enjoy the ride and the authentic sensations it offers, but she cannot pose questions to her guide, nor alight before the end.[19]

While Aust's book dwells on names, dates, and statistics, historical detail is subordinated in the film to the intense experience of the action-packed narrative. This is evident in a key moment in the film's narrative: the anti-Shah protests on 2 June 1967, which were repressed brutally by the police and ended in the death of student Benno Ohnesorg. Aust's depiction of events provides the reader with key details, such as exact times, locations, and the degree to which police action had been predetermined (80). Although by no means unemotional – Aust describes the police response as "the most brutal bludgeoning experienced in Berlin since the war" (79)[20] – his attention to detail forces the reader, even at this very tense moment, to consider the "facts."

The spectator, however, is thrown headlong into the events by a fast-cut montage of intense shots depicting police brutality and mass panic.[21] Frequently switching between different perspectives, cutting from high to low angles, from close-up to wide shots, this sequence disorients the viewer and creates an almost unbearable tension. Dramatic music and dusky lighting further contribute to the spectator's sense of unease as she is plunged into the action. This experiential immersion finds its ultimate expression in the water-cannon shot, where a powerful blast of water is directed straight at the camera and, thus, at the viewer. This shot should, in fact, draw attention to the presence of the lens and the constructedness of the spectacle; after all, the spectator does not actually get soaked. However, the compression of events into a single montage creates an intense sense of excitement, which solicits from the viewer a visceral rather than a rational response. Martin Rubin suggests that "in a thriller it is as if we give ourselves up to be captured, carried away, in order to be thrilled, to receive a series of sharp sensations" (7).

These sensations suture over the potentially disruptive presence of the camera as a barrier between us and the depicted action. Swept away by the scene's sensory intensity, the spectator is in no position to recognize the arranging hand of the filmmaker-curator. Thus, she is drawn into an experiential mode of authenticity, feeling that she "really was there." Persuasive to the point of coercive, these scenes demonstrate that the experiential mode elicits and exploits a sensory response in order to assert its authoritative interpretation of history. Emotionally and sensorially engaged in the narrative, the spectator unquestioningly identifies with the assailed students, with whose perspective she is visually aligned. Although the book shows an undeniable bias in favour of the students, the reader is encouraged to arrive at her condemnation of the police through rational judgment and by assessing the facts spread before her. When presented by a visible curator, these issues are opened up for discussion and the reader may plausibly choose to reject Aust's depiction of events. The absence of the cinematic curator, however, precludes the possibility of dialogue and debate, demanding instead an immediate identification with the protesters.

Presentation

Finally we arrive at the issue of presentation: how are the historical objects, source materials, and documentary "evidence" displayed? This element of the curatorial process is most often associated with the act of labelling or providing an accompanying text, which explains the provenance, significance, and context of the object. It is here that the hand of the curator is at its most apparent and it is in this final act that she may lay bare her role in the creation of historical meaning. While this intervention assumes various forms in the book, it is most striking in Aust's labelling of the numerous photographs which illustrate his text. Set below the images, these captions follow a fixed structure: first, we are provided with the bare facts, including the date, location, occasion, and persons in the photograph. These facts are followed by a more subjective comment, either a snappy, journalistic phrase, such as "Ulrike Meinhof (1952): Boogie-Woogie and Morality" (Aust 46), or a quotation extracted from the respective chapter: "Meinhof's forged driver's license: 'Please stay here'" (Aust 227).[22] These captions reveal the presence and (subjective) expositionary discourse of the images' curator. In particular, the journalistic comments remind the reader of Aust's professional credentials as former editor-in-chief of *Der Spiegel* and attach a well-known face to the potentially anonymous curator. Here, as elsewhere, Aust functions as guarantor of authenticity, using the authority gained through association with Germany's leading newsmagazine to support his explicit comments on the book's photographic sources.

The Concealed Curator

While the objects curated in Aust's book are on the whole written documents and photographs, the filmic version has at its disposal a far greater range of original artefacts. Vintage 1970s clothing, real filming locations, and original copies of newspapers and magazines abound in the film and are summoned to create a sense of authenticity. Attention is repeatedly drawn to these items as the otherwise rapid camera lingers on the objects like the spotlight on a prize exhibit, lest the viewer overlook the film's extraordinary attention to detail. In the DVD's "Making of" bonus material, the filmmakers are at pains to impress upon the viewer the great efforts undertaken in order to create an authentic environment. Indeed, in referring to the use of the original Stammheim courtroom, Eichinger goes so far as to claim that "the fact that we were able to shoot here gives me a sure sense that we couldn't be more authentic" ("History in the Making"). These objects and auratic locations inevitably recall the testimonial mode of authenticity, which harnesses the "authority of the object" to convince the recipient of the validity of its historical representation (Pirker and Rüdiger 17).

Closer analysis of the film's authenticity discourse, however, suggests a greater proximity between testimonial and experiential modes than has previously been argued. When collected in such abundance and presented in a vivid manner, the testimonial objects may evoke an "authentic feeling, a contemporary mood or atmosphere," that is, an experiential form of authenticity. The use of colour film, along with the transfer from static photography to the moving image of cinema, intensifies the experiential aspect. Many of the objects are in themselves doubly remediated, since, for most viewers, they evoke not personal memories of the original events but the media images that make up a vast collective pictorial memory.[23] We are provided, for example, with replicas of now iconic images, such as the mortally injured Ohnesorg or

Baader and Ensslin at their trial for arson in 1968. The film tailors these infamous images to fit modern-day expectations of news reports, appealing to a younger generation for whom the original black-and-white photographs connote a history far removed from the present. This unobtrusive making present of the past encourages the spectator to experience the 1960s and 1970s not as detached, distant history but as events assimilable to her own experience, as a "potential self-image of contemporary producers and consumers" (M. Zimmermann 144).[24] The intense concentration of auratic locations and original artefacts immerses the viewer in a specific atmosphere marked as authentic. Testimonial and experiential modes of authenticity are in no way mutually exclusive in *Der Baader-Meinhof Komplex* but rather complement and augment each other.

The filmmaker-curator, however, remains an invisible figure in the presentation of these iconic images. That these visual artefacts are not labelled must be put down to simple generic conventions: this is not a documentary but a feature film. However, there is one aspect of presentation that cannot be so easily explained by any constraints of the genre. At various points in the film, archival television footage, most often from the daily news program *Tagesschau*, is incorporated into the narrative. Unlike the artefacts explored above, however, these archival images do not operate at the intersection between testimonial and experiential authenticity. Rather, they represent a deliberate and concerted attempt by the filmmakers to efface their testimonial aspect and transform their presence into pure experience. Sequences including original footage follow a distinct pattern. Initially, the newsreel image is presented full-screen, appearing to the spectator as it would have been seen by its contemporary viewers. This switch in ontological level from re-enacted drama to original images of real events could potentially disrupt the viewer's immersion in the fiction, exposing the illusory nature of its purported reality. But this crack in the narrative is quickly papered over. In almost every instance, the full-screen archival film sequences are followed by a subsequent shot of the same footage, now framed by a television, as the camera zooms out to reveal intradiegetic characters watching the screen. The footage thus appears to be diegetically motivated and is sutured into the same ontological level as the main storyline. The mediating presence of the curator, who has selected the archival material and placed it within a carefully crafted narrative arrangement, is entirely obscured by the attempt to preserve the narrative coherence of the fiction.

The transition from testimonial to experiential authenticity results in a problematic blurring of fact and fiction. On several occasions, the framed television images, although replicating exactly those previously shown full-screen, are, in fact, re-enactments, where real-life protagonists are replaced by their fictional counterparts, as portrayed by the film's star-studded cast. The striking resemblance the actors bear to the historical figures, frequently remarked upon in the press,[25] makes it almost impossible for the viewer to distinguish between student leader and leftist hero Rudi Dutschke and actor Sebastian Blomberg, for instance. This ontological blurring is even more crudely apparent in the film's depiction of the hijacking of the Lufthansa airplane, *Landshut*. For obvious reasons, documentary footage of this incident does not exist. Rather than filming these scenes from scratch, however, Edel and Eichinger incorporate re-enacted scenes from Heinrich Breloer's 1997 film *Todesspiel*. The grainy quality of these clips and their own authentic feel render them indistinguishable from real archival footage to all but the most informed spectator. With no indication to the contrary, the viewer is encouraged to regard these sequences as documentary evidence on the same ontological level as the *Tagesschau* clips. Authenticity is generated here not by the insertion of real artefacts, but by our belief in their reality – "it is not about the historically authentic in the sense of scholarly reconstruction but about the creation of a successful illusion of authenticity" (M. Zimmermann 144).[26] Experiential authenticity, like the classical cinematic experience itself, finds its foundation in illusion, in its ability to recreate as plausibly as possible the world which it purports to depict.

History or Heritage?

The experiential authenticity of *Der Baader-Meinhof Komplex*, then, engages the viewer in an affective and physical relationship with Germany's terrorist past, which is musealized and commodified for easy consumption. Swept away by the turbulent and exciting events, she does not (and cannot) stop to question the film's historical perspective thrust upon her by the invisible cinematic curator. But is this experience necessarily problematic? In David Lowenthal's terms, Aust's book may be said to provide us with "history," while the film promotes a sense of "heritage." History "seeks to convince by truth," while heritage "exaggerates and omits, candidly invents and frankly forgets, and thrives on ignorance and error" (Lowenthal 121). The latter draws its strength from a collective faith in the veracity of its claims; it is "not erudition but catechism: what counts is not checkable fact but credulous allegiance" (121). Lowenthal further warns us that "to vilify heritage as biased is futile: bias is the main point of heritage ... it is its essential purpose" (122). Is it not, in fact, this partiality that allows our intense identification with the film's protagonists, encouraging us to invest emotionally in this chapter of German history? After all, as Landsberg points out, "commodification makes ideas and images available to people who reside in different places and have different backgrounds, races, ethnicities and classes" (18). Public reaction to the film appears to confirm that memory, when packaged in a tangible and emotionally accessible form, can extend beyond those who actively lived through the events remembered. An article in *Stern* magazine charting teenagers' responses to the film revealed an overwhelming sense of active involvement in the events depicted and concluded that "history lessons as popcorn cinema work" (Buchner).[27] Eichinger's film, it would seem, opens up the history of the RAF to a younger generation otherwise cut off from this not-so-distant past and in doing so encourages them to delve further into Germany's violent revolutionary tradition.[28]

However, Lowenthal also informs us that "heritage diverges from history not in *being* biased but in its attitude toward bias" (122), which it embraces and displays rather than conceals. Not so *Der Baader-Meinhof Komplex*, which consistently sweeps its subjectivity under the carpet both inside and outside the filmic text, operating "under the guise of an impartial historical chronicle with a veracious claim to reality" (Homewood 135). Constantin's aggressive marketing bombarded the potential spectator with claims to testimonial, "historical" authenticity: the filmmakers' painstaking attention to detail, their comprehensive research, and dedication to providing the full picture. In fact, the film's official website offers comprehensive teaching materials, which combine a history of left-wing terrorism in Germany with information on the filming process. Here again, documentary sources take centre stage with the claim that Aust's book, supplemented by additional primary sources, guarantee that the film "reconstructs the historical course of events in as accurate and detailed a manner as the non-fictional book" (Conrad 10).[29] Cinematic sensations and the "force of the fictional narrative," we are told, strengthen the film's documentary claims that "what is told here is authentic" (Conrad 8).[30] It is precisely this blurring of history and heritage, testimonial and experiential authenticity, that is troubling. In claiming to present a comprehensive and factually accurate history, the film conceals its dependency on the biased affective appeal of heritage cinema. As heritage, it must be conceded, *Der Baader-Meinhof Komplex* excels; as history, however, it appals.

NOTES

1 For a comprehensive history of the RAF that locates the group within wider left-wing radicalism, see Kraushaar, vol. 1.
2 "Projektionsfläche für Feindbilder, Idealisierungen, für eine fehlende Auseinandersetzung mit der Bundesrepublik."
3 "ob es uns gefällt oder nicht, die Geschichte der RAF ist ein Teil der Geschichte der Bundesrepublik."
4 "ein Zauberwort, das für jeden hörbar und nachvollziehbar die Grenzen zwischen billigem Tand und echten Werten markiert."
5 "die Suggestion eines Originalen, eines Relikts aus der Vergangenheit, das durch seine historische Echtheit selbst zu wirken scheint."
6 "das Evozieren eines 'authentischen Gefühls,' Zeitstimmung oder – atmosphäre durch Annäherung an das Original oder Erzeugung einer plausiblen beziehungsweise typischen Vergangenheit."
7 "Ich führte Interviews, sammelte und sichtete etwa sechzig laufende Meter Akten und versuchte, daraus die Geschichte der 'Baader-Meinhof Gruppe' … zu rekonstruieren."
8 "den Zuschauer mitten ins Geschehen zu versetzen."
9 This is the term frequently used to describe Aust's seminal text.
10 "Wertung habe ich möglichst vermieden. Dennoch ist die Auswahl des Materials, die Gewichtung, die Zusammenstellung meine subjektive Entscheidung."
11 "Einige der Sitzungen waren geheim – Futter für Mutmaßungen."
12 "ein Großteil der Spekulationen über die Todesnacht von Stammhein [wäre] bei gründlicher Untersuchung, bei weniger Voreingenommenheit der Ermittler möglicherweise gar nicht erst entstanden."
13 "Baader hatte in seinen vier Regalen 974 Bücher und 75 Langspielplatten. Eine Mundharmonika, eine Schreibmaschine 'Olivetti,' einen Kasten Wasserfarben 'Pelikan,' zwei Sonnenbrillen, Haarspray, Lidschatten, zwei Pelzmäntel, einen Elektrowecker mit Batterien, einen Plattenspieler mit Verstärker und Lautsprecherboxen."
14 "Hatte die ganze Operation vielleicht einen geheimdienstlichen 'Ast,' den die Akteure der RAF selbst nicht kannten? War nicht der jemenitische Geheimdienst, der auch das Ausbildungslager kontrollierte, voll in der Hand des DDR-Geheimdienstes?"

15 The exact nature and extent of GDR cooperation with West German terrorists has not yet been fully investigated and remains a "hidden history" (Henze 180). For a controversial but detailed analysis, see Müller and Kanonenberg.

16 "legen es offenbar darauf an, den Zuschauer zum Augenzeugen des Ereignisses zu machen ... Die neuen Augenzeugen sind wir, wir lassen uns ergreifen, anrühren und sagen selbst als professionelle Historiker: So war's."

17 "Man darf als Erzähler niemals auf die Stopptaste drücken."

18 These disruptions also validate the book's authenticity; in referring back to previous sections, Aust effectively cites the book itself as a reliable source on the same epistemological footing as original documents, police statements, and court records.

19 McIntosh and Prentice describe the experience ride as a "managerial setting," drawing attention to the curator's level of control over the visitor (80).

20 "die brutalste Knüppelei ..., die man bis dahin im Nachkriegsberlin erlebt hatte"

21 In his analysis of documentary films and museums, Stephan Jaeger contrasts "speed and progress" with "the contemplation and slowness that a museum could provide" (Jaeger 176).

22 "Gefälschter Führerschein von Ulrike Meinhof: 'Bitte bleiben Sie hier.'"

23 Pirker and Rüdiger note that the insertion of familiar images provides the viewer with important "Anknüpfungspunkte" (associations) that allow her to relate more personally to the historical events (21).

24 "potentielles Selbstbild der zeitgenössichen Produzenten und Konsumenten."

25 The *Süddeutsche Zeitung* comments on their "verblüffende Ähnlichkeit" (Stendel), while another website describes the actors as "verstörend ähnlich" ("Die Darsteller im *Baader-Meinhof-Komplex*").

26 "es geht mithin nicht um das historisch Authentische im Sinne wissenschaftlicher Rekonstruktion, sondern um die Erzeugung einer möglichst gelungenen Illusion von Authentizität."

27 "Geschichtsunterricht als Popcorn-Kino funktioniert also."

28 Cooke notes that "the recent wave of heritage films ... provides, it would seem, a far more immediate and accessible *experience* of history than is to be found in earlier films" (113).

29 "rekonstruiert, ähnlich dem Sachbuch, den historischen Lauf der Dinge so detailgenau wie möglich."

30 "Was hier erzählt wird, ist authentisch."

5 Remembering and Historicizing Socialism: The Private and Amateur Musealization of East Germany's Everyday Life

ANNE WINKLER

Whilst the reality of life under socialist rule severely undermined official socialist propaganda during the GDR, the tables have now turned, and instead today's official image of socialism undermines the reality East Germans remember.

Anna Saunders[1]

The musealization of East German everyday life takes place largely on the margins, outside of dominant institutions. Throughout the former East Germany, retirees, unemployed men and women, novice entrepreneurs, and passionate collectors have for the past twenty years established museums displaying material traces of life under socialism. These exhibits have many names besides "DDR Museum" (Museum of the German Democratic Republic – GDR Museum), although colloquially they are often referred to by this term. Their number is difficult to estimate; new ones continue to be established, some have ceased to exist, and others are private collections that open their doors to the public only occasionally. I am aware of twelve to sixteen that are in operation today, depending on the inclusion criteria.[2]

The museums' owners are typically amateurs, having neither formal curatorial training nor prior museum experience. The museums receive little or no government funding, many struggle to survive financially, and all rely on similar, rudimentary representational strategies. These approaches include classificatory displays, or what Barbara Kirshenblatt-Gimblett calls "in-context displays" (3), such as televisions of various models in a room or coins and award plaques in a display case in a hallway. Their hallmark are mimetic "in-situ displays"

(Kirshenblatt-Gimblett 3) that attempt to simulate the lived past as closely and completely as possible. Recreated living rooms, kitchens, laundry rooms, bedrooms, and even institutional spaces, such as school classrooms, day-care rooms, and offices, are examples of this exhibition technique. While vitrines hold the in-context displays of small items, such as coins and toy cars, frequently only a rope separates the visitor from the objects and mimetic displays. In some cases, there are no barriers at all. Simple interpretive strategies also define GDR museums. Although some descriptive signage does exist – and in the case of the *Olle DDR*[3] exhibit in the Thuringian town of Apolda, an audio recording guides the visitor – didactic panels that reflect conceptual frameworks are largely absent. Moreover, typically professional conservation and research does not take place at the museums, which means that, according to definitions by such organizations as the International Council of Museums, these sites fail to classify as museums.[4]

Despite the overall amateur character of GDR museums, their number and similarity in form and content begin to suggest that they must be understood within the wider context of dominant ideas about Germany's socialist past. The analysis I present below, which is based on extensive field research, locates these sites firmly within the struggle over the meaning of history and memory. I argue that, as a group, GDR museums point to an exciting democratization of traditionally privileged representational practices. Here, individuals and small groups establish frameworks for the exploration of the quotidian past, aiming to access experiential knowledge through the display of objects, ones that hegemonic discourses cannot, fail, or refuse to address. Indeed, they put into question not only the authoritative and legitimizing status of other museums that represent the East German past but also of museums as institutions more broadly.

The exhibits also point to what Andreas Huyssen describes as the contemporary "fundamental disturbance not just of the relationship between history as objective and scientific, and memory as subjective and personal, but of history itself and its promises" (*Present Pasts* 2). GDR museums offer themselves to the visitors unapologetically as DIY "for the people by the people" sites that attempt to salvage and reanimate the past by taming the fringe, all the things and memories that have little room elsewhere in such a concentrated, visceral, and approachable manner. Their visitor logs suggest that going to the museum entails processes of identity affirmation, particularly for Easterners with memories of living in the East. Unlike other, state-funded museums that highlight resistance and opposition to the totalitarian East German regime, the popular musealization of the GDR refuses to let these categories be the only interpretive lens through which to examine the past.

The empirical foundation for this essay are four research trips to Germany between March 2008 and July 2013, during which I visited twelve GDR museums and interviewed museum professionals as well as visitors. When discussing amateur and private GDR museums as a group, my observations exclude Berlin's DDR Museum, the DDR-Geschichtsmuseum im Dokumentationszentrum Perleberg, the Eisenhüttenstadt Dokumentationszentrum Alltagskultur der DDR (DOK), and the Wittenberg Haus der Geschichte. While in subject these museums overlap significantly with the sites in which I am particularly interested here, several characteristics set them apart. Berlin's DDR Museum, the best marketed and by all appearances the most successful of the GDR museums, employs trained staff, including renowned museologists and historians, such as Stefan Wolle. The fact that it has been twice nominated for the European Museum of the Year Award also points to the high quality of this professionally curated exhibition. While other GDR museums are located in small cities and towns – many not easily accessible to domestic and foreign visitors – the Berlin museum is located in a tourist hotspot on the banks of the Spree River near Museum Island and in walking distance to the Alexanderplatz. A more subjective reason for why the Berlin museum does not fit is that when asked to reflect on the work of similar sites, curators/owners of popular GDR museums agreed that the Berlin DDR Museum "does not get it right." They objected to a Westerner having initiated the project as a business venture, the presence of insufficient exhibit objects, in both kind and number, and the wrong overall feeling. Although the curators/owners did not specify the latter, I would like to suggest that this sentiment of "not feeling right" likely stems in part from the museum's professional character, which with its polished displays, interpretive signage, and overall concept has the effect of distancing the visitor from the subject matter.

The analysis I present here also does not apply well to the Perleberg museum, neither in exhibit content nor from the perspective of the motivation of its founders, a retired Lutheran minister and his wife. For example, the owner/curator Hans-Peter Freimark described in his interview with me that the displays focusing on everyday life are not the main purpose of the museum, but rather that they serve to give "people space to breathe and recover from the material evidence of an oppressive system." Moreover, he offers detailed guided tours to as many visitors as possible in order to explain the museum's intention of highlighting the atrocities and injustices that took place under the GDR regime. At the DOK in Eisenhüttenstadt, historian and professional museologist Andreas Ludwig employs strategies that artistically and skilfully walk the tightrope between condemning and condoning the GDR, a topic that I have discussed elsewhere ("Kept Things") due to limited space here, although I will refer to it for comparative purposes to highlight specific characteristics of private and amateur museums. The Wittenberg museum takes visitors on guided tours through mimetic displays in the form of period rooms that historians created.

This essay offers an interrogation of the private and amateur musealization of East Germany's everyday life that, although in most cases pointing to repressive elements of the GDR regime, refuses the interpretive primacy of totalitarianism. Despite the significant potential of this narrative to illuminate contemporary cultural practices relating to the construction of memory and historical knowledge, this topic has received little focused attention in the academic literature. Therefore, this analysis, in conjunction with the chapter by Jonathan Bach in this volume, stands as an invitation to a scholarly conversation about popular museums dedicated to East Germany and the broader mechanisms by which the past moves forward. A description of the political and cultural context in which these museums emerged and continue to thrive situates the subsequent discussion. The detailed examination begins with an exploration of the unique visitor–museum relationship that unfolds at these sites. Second, I investigate possible reasons for why interpretive texts are nearly absent in GDR museums. A discussion on the centrality of materiality and the significance of embodied museum-going further underline the distinctive approach these museums take in their representation of East Germany's socialist past.

Political and Cultural Context

The idea of the GDR museum began at a particular juncture, one that defines the museums' practices and reflects contemporary political circumstances within Germany, part of which arose from the rapid collapse of the GDR in 1989 and the unexpected and swift unification of Germany in 1990. Moreover, these museums must be understood as a symptom of what Huyssen describes as the crisis of temporality and the double movement of collective amnesia and obsession with memory. Borrowing from Huyssen, the GDR museum in this context emerges as "an attempt to slow down information processing, to resist the dissolution of time … to claim some anchoring space in a world of puzzling and often threatening heterogeneity, non-synchronicity and information overload" (*Twilight Memories* 7). The musealization of the GDR can also be understood as a cultural process of compensation, for, as Hermann Lübbe suggests, "through a progressive musealization we compensate for the burdensome experience of a loss of cultural familiarity brought about by change" (qtd in Korff, "Popularisierung" 268). Borrowing Beier-de Haan's words, in addition to attempting to find grounding and address this sense of a disappearing world, GDR museums attract visitors because like other "historical exhibitions [they] serve at the same time to restore shared memory" (196). Moreover, the popular musealization of East Germany exemplifies the processes that John Urry argues shape museums in contemporary societies, societies that he defines as disjointed, sped up, hybridized, and fractured. For him, these characteristics culminate in a changing hierarchy of modes of remembering in that they "undermine many auratic and authoritative traditions such that there is no remaining single, autonomous essence" ("How Societies Remember" 62). Simultaneously, "there is the proliferation of many new heritage sites, which are often started and run by enthusiasts who contest once-dominant traditions" (62). Although Urry speaks to British heritage museums, I would like to suggest that these processes apply similarly to GDR museums because these sites challenge hegemonic musealizations of East Germany by not conforming to dominant representational strategies and conceptual frameworks. In addition, as I have already established, amateur curators and collectors own and operate these museums rather than trained museologists. GDR museums emerged within the context of the processes and changing hierarchy of modes of remembering that Urry describes, while their operation also exemplifies, propels, and develops them further.

To specify this broad description of how the popular musealization of East Germany fits within broader cultural trends, I now examine the overarching interpretative position GDR museums take in their representation of everyday life. I would like to suggest that the overall orientation of the GDR museum might be summarized best by the phrase "Nicht alles war schlecht" ("Not everything was bad"), words that gain poignancy in reference to what I consider its opposite, "Es gibt kein richtiges Leben im falschen" ("Wrong life cannot be lived rightly"). These expressions correspond to diametrically opposed interpretations of the GDR. The latter, "Wrong life cannot be lived rightly," a quotation from Theodor W. Adorno's *Minima Moralia* (39), is now an adage that in the context of discussions about East Germany refers to the mechanisms of dictatorship permeating and shaping all areas of life. To illustrate, in Christa Wolf's novel *Stadt der Engel oder The Overcoat of Dr. Freud* (City of Angels or The Overcoat of Dr. Freud, 2010), the protagonist reflects on a presentation entitled "Es gibt kein richtiges Leben im falschen" that explores how writers in East Germany had not been able to live a meaningful life (70).

"Nicht alles war schlecht," the phrase that summarizes the overall message of GDR museums, rejects dictatorship as prime and sole explanatory framework. Simultaneously, it refuses a direct comparison between National Socialism and East German socialism. Instead, these words imply an insistence on valid, real past lives lived by locating the mundane everyday greatly outside of the purview of state politics. This position has consequences for the relationship between the GDR museum and other history- and memory-making agents. For example, private and amateur museums are largely excluded from taking part in public and scholarly discussions on the musealization of the GDR. When the Stadtgeschichtliches Museum Leipzig (Historical Museum of the City of Leipzig) and the Bundesstiftung zur Aufarbeitung der SED Diktatur (Federal Foundation for the Reconciliation of the SED Dictatorship) organized a three-day conference in June 2010 entitled "Die Musealisierung der DDR: Wege, Möglichkeiten und Grenzen der Darstellung von Zeitgeschichte in Stadt- und regionalgeschichtlichen Museen" ("The Musealization of the GDR: Ways, Possibilities, and Limits in the Representation of Contemporary History in City and Regional History Museums"), none of the twenty-seven scholar and practitioner speakers represented amateur and private GDR museums. Their absence seems peculiar in the context of the five-sentence summary statement describing the conference topic:

> For city and regional history museums, the scientifically based collection, preservation, and documentation of objects from GDR history hold a great potential. This has been little used until now. At the same time, the increasing number of privately run, commercial GDR museums suggests a public interest in this topic. The conference takes this circumstance as starting point. Various dimensions of the musealization of the GDR will be discussed, as will the possibilities and limits of the representation and

> communication of contemporary history in the museum. (Stadtgeschichtliches Museum Leipzig)[5]

In other words, the conference organizers and participants recognize the popularity of representations of everyday life in GDR museums, but are unwilling to consult and collaborate with those who run and own them. This refusal to work together relates to hegemonic discourses on the historical significance of the GDR, which federal government funding structures exemplify, that attempt to shape and stabilize the past. For example, the *Gedenkstättenkonzeption* (Conceptualization for Historical Sites) that the German federal government put into place in 2008 outlines funding guidelines for the musealization and memorialization of the Nazi era and the East German past. I quote one section of the document extensively for it provides a concrete example of both museum funding and the federal government's position on the historicization of the GDR. The text signifies hegemonic strategizing that works unrelentingly at shaping a singular interpretive framework, one that leaves little room for nuance and the presence of diverse voices:

> Everyday life in the GDR is taken into consideration to prevent a romanticization and trivialization of the dictatorship of the Socialist Unity Party (SED) of Germany and to decisively work against all kinds of nostalgia for the East. For this purpose everyday life must by necessity be placed in the context of the dictatorship. It must be made clear that people in the GDR were subject to extensive control by the state and were exposed to intense pressure to assimilate, while the dictatorship also derived its power from the collaboration of the general public. The instruments and mechanisms that the SED employed to ideologically penetrate the entire society and the life of people in all domains should be identified – from nursery school to grade school and from university to working world and recreational activities. At the same time, it must be documented how and where people in the GDR attempted to remove themselves from the pull of the Party. (Deutscher Bundestag 9)[6]

These guidelines in effect block any funding for the musealization of the everyday outside of the context of dictatorship, both directly through the federal government and other agencies that use them as a model. Particularly troubling is the vilification of the general public as perpetrators of undefined crimes. Moreover, the framework, which reflects a dominant discourse, declares that all museal engagement with East German everyday life outside of the context of dictatorship is nostalgic in the pejorative sense of romanticized longing. Some scholars counter the negative connotation of this type of nostalgia, or "Ostalgie" (nostalgia for the East), as they theorize its deeper socio-cultural significance. For example, Paul Cooke places the origin of "Ostalgie" in a collective sense of loss and dislocation that resulted from the unequal merging of two cultures (Cooke, "*Ostalgie*'s" and "Surfing"). With her term "reflective nostalgia," Svetlana Boym explores the contradictory character of the phenomenon. Here, nostalgia "can be ironic and humorous. It reveals that longing and critical thinking are not opposed to one another, as affective memories do not absolve one from compassion, judgment or critical reflection" (59). Dominik Bartmanski describes "Ostalgie" as the practice that assists memory processes, linking the past and the present instead of lingering uncritically in a bygone era. For him, "nostalgic icons are successful because they play the cultural role of mnemonic bridges *to* rather than tokens of longing *for* the failed communist past" (213). I have also undertaken a close reading of "Ostalgie"-related material culture to point to the limits of nostalgia as an interpretive category, particularly in the absence of detailed analyses of specific practices ("Not Everything").

Private and amateur museums dedicated to the GDR emerged despite, and at the same time because of, the socio-economic and political climate of the post-unification years. As a group, their undertaking speaks to this context, in part by subverting dominant representational practices. For example, unlike most museums, they enact a uniquely intimate visitor–museum relationship, a topic to which I turn now.

The GDR Museum and Its Publics

It is difficult to access information on the types of visitors the GDR museum attracts and what experiences they have. Henrietta Riegel points out that museums are sites that are intimately involved in the accumulation of social and cultural capital. Museum-goers "look to museums as the arbiters of 'high class' taste, a source to be relied upon when it comes to matters of culture" (87). Yet, GDR museums do not exude the kind of authority that underlies such a role, which suggests that the groups of people who traditionally seek out museums are unlikely to deem the GDR museum appealing. A more direct approach to accessing visitor experience is to interview them. However, during my fieldwork I found it difficult to initiate conversations and when I did, people were generally unwilling or unable to articulate what had brought them to the museum and what they thought of the exhibits. I suspect that the museums' tendency to elicit memory, both cultural and personal, and their political ambiguity may have contributed to this challenge. Guestbooks could potentially also provide insights, but they typically indicate only broad impressions. For example, Susan Crane notes that although she is an "inveterate reader of museums guest books, … generally, one finds school groups' scribbles and drawings, inscriptions of names and hometowns, often only single words of approval or disapproval" (45). I too encountered this absence of detailed and thoughtful reflection in the dozens of guest books that I analysed. Yet, a general pattern did emerge. The ubiquity of phrases such as "It was nice to be reminded of everything"[7] and statements such as "This was our favorite exhibit so far. One finds memories from every arena. Thank you for this nice exhibit and continued success"[8] suggest that many visitors are former East Germans and that for them the museum functions as a site of memory that evokes processes of identity affirmation.

When I asked who their visitors were, curators/owners echoed these comments. They thought that most of them were former Eastern Germans and their friends and family. Requesting that they state how they knew this to be true, several replied that easterners stay much longer than westerners because they linger in front of displays and begin to reminisce. The processes of memory that unfold at these sites indicate that the museum–visitor relationship operates differently at GDR museums than at most other museums. As Crane points out in reference to mainstream museums: "Visitors are interlocutors without discussion partners in the museal conversation: they usually have only objects and text to respond to, rarely curators, historians, or experts" (48). Within the context of the popular musealization of East Germany, the role boundaries between those who look at displays and those who create them are blurred, which brings with it lively exchanges among those involved.

The curators/owners of GDR museums aim to capture a way of life, one with which they are intimately familiar. Memory, and the *sense* that something is presented correctly or incorrectly, guides the curatorial process. Several curator/owners commented in interviews that their personal experience of living in the former East informed how they shape the museum. At the same time, they are never alone in determining what is on display and how because the making of the exhibits involves dynamic, collective and democratic processes. Employees, volunteers, visitors, other museum owners/curators, friends and family members play the role of expert consultants as they serve as sources of ideas and the correction of existing displays. They might even contribute objects to create more "authentic" exhibits. For example, Frau Müller, the curator/owner of the Gelenau DDR museum recounted in her conversation with me a visit by her counterpart from the Pirna DDR museum, Herr Kaden. He noticed that the ceramic Mitropa[9] cups did not fit into her kindergarten display and consequently supplied her with authentically peppermint-tea-stained plastic cups, which both deemed more appropriate. Not only those directly involved in running GDR museums contribute to other museum exhibits. The museums that opened in the ten to fifteen years following the fall of the Wall relied almost exclusively on donations for their displays.[10] Several visitors pointed me towards items such as a toaster, schoolbooks, and toys they had given to the museum. They explained to me that although the items were out of use in their homes, they were connected to their East German biographies, which had no relevance in contemporary Germany and yet deserved to be preserved. By handing over their belongings to the museum, they sought to participate in what André Malraux describes as the "museum effect," a process whereby the very placement of the object within the museum creates its importance and validity. The donation of items by individuals to the exhibit also suggests why visitors lay claim to authorship in the curatorial process and why they may be attracted to the GDR museum. In fact, many visitors may feel like their involvement makes the museum theirs, through the donation of objects, the advice they give, the great familiarity they have with all objects, or because they bring them to life when they visit and reminisce about life in East Germany.

The overlap in roles between those who curate and those who visit the GDR museum begins to indicate the ways in which this type of site operates differently than most mainstream museums. A consideration of interpretive texts further underlines their particular approach to representing the past.

Where Are the Words?

Unlike most art, historical, and other exhibitions, GDR museums present few text panels and labels that would orient visitors to the overall aims of the museum, interpret artefacts through defined conceptual lenses, or indicate precisely what is on display. Pragmatic reasons for this absence include a lack of clearly formulated frameworks for the exhibits that would guide the texts' content as well as limited financial resources and professional capacities to create them. I would like to suggest that a further reason for this absence is that they would undermine the aims and raison d'être of the museums. Riegel's report of a visitor study of a historical exhibit that purposely had no textual guides illustrates this point. The project she reflects upon recreated scenes that exemplified life immediately following the Second World War and included a bombed-out cellar and a room that demonstrated the living conditions of displaced people. Riegel argues that the absence of textual framings contributed to the great discomfort that many older visitors experienced as they were confronted with a part of their biography to which they had not attended for a long time. Visitors commented that they "felt too 'close' to the exhibit, that it brought back a whole host of unpleasant memories" (Riegel 87). While in Riegel's example the evocative power of the displays was problematic for those who found that their life was on display in a way that prohibited disengagement, this potential to unleash memory is precisely the objective of the GDR museum, for it functions, at least in this historical moment, predominantly as a site of memory. Visitors' memories can be accessed and formed unmediated by texts that prescribe or at least narrow the meaning of the objects and environments the visitor encounters.

The third, connected factor that could explain the near absence of labelling is that text concretizes meaning. Not unlike a caption of a press photograph, words that accompany the objects narrow interpretive possibilities. Paraphrasing Roland Barthes, though recognizing the profound epistemological difference between press photographs and objects in museums, "it is not the [object] which comes to elucidate or 'realize' the text, but the latter which comes to sublimate, patheticize or rationalize the [object]" (*Image* 25). The power of the text to (re)define meaning poses a great difficulty in the context of the GDR museum, for it would require its authors to put forth a political stance on the past. The majority of these sites claim explicitly that they operate outside of the political realm because they merely *display* the everyday and thereby neither condone nor condemn East Germany's political system. This position appears to narrow the "political" to pertain only to statements on the overt workings of the state and its agents rather than the ordinary life of ordinary people. At the same time, conversations with some museum visitors and curators/owners suggest that they are acutely aware of the political nature of the museums' endeavour and the fact that their projects operate outside of dominant discourses, even threatening hegemonic efforts of writing the East German past. For example, during interviews, one museum owner and several museum visitors did not wish to be identified, either by divulging their last names or consenting to a recorded interview. Another museum owner/curator insisted on meeting in a public space. Once we arrived at the agreed upon café, she chose a table far removed from any other customers and spoke only in a whisper, as though she was afraid someone could overhear our conversation.

The claim of apoliticality is particularly curious given the pervasiveness in the GDR of the doctrine that all realms of life are political. I would like to suggest that such a self-description on part of the museums involves an extraction from the difficult project of representing the East German past in ways that simultaneously recognize its repressive character and leave room for accounts of individual and group accomplishments or simply valid, worthy lives lived. While the majority of GDR museums do reference repressive elements of the socialist regime, they do so in an unfocused manner or as an aside.

Yet another possible reason for the dearth of textual interpretation in the GDR museum is that it is clear to visitors what they are seeing, regardless of background: a living room, a kitchen, a television – all objects of everyday life – do not require a statement on what they are because their significance appears self-evident. Nonetheless, the problem arises of how objects constitute meaning. Reflecting on broader trends, Gottfried Korff observes that many of the museums founded since the 1970s are dedicated to the preservation and presentation of *Alltagskultur* (everyday culture), a development he describes as the "musealization of the popular" (12). Within this context, Korff warns of the "auratization of the banal," wherein popular objects and objects of everyday life operate out of contexts, concluding that "with a hairnet, a cheese slicer and sausage stuffing device ... one cannot represent the history of social movements and historical transformations" (13).[11] Given this critique, he argues for connecting these objects of everyday life to larger socio-cultural and political developments to produce meaningful historical engagements.

This situating of the everyday object within a bigger picture does occur in government-funded museums where East German *Alltagskultur* exemplifies elements of a dictatorship. However, the existence of GDR museums suggests that this approach alienates many former East

Germans. Thus, questions arise about the possibility of musealizing everyday life in a way that reflects and respects peoples' experiences, remains highly evocative in terms of memory and recall while providing a sense of macro-historical trends and transformation. I suggest that the DOK in Eisenhüttenstadt has made these links and could serve as a model for popular musealization attempts that aim to contextualize *Alltagskultur* historically.

Like other GDR museums, the DOK is concerned with the material traces of East Germany's everyday life. However, unlike them, various levels of governments funded it until 2012 and professional staff supported its director, a trained historian and museologist, all of which contributed to the possibility of putting in place innovative representational strategies. The first display of the permanent exhibit which was installed until 2012 and was entitled "40 Years – 40 Objects," featured a room filled with glass boxes stacked one on top of another forming a cube. Each box contained one to three objects and had affixed to it a label that first stated the year to which it spoke and second related the object to the history of the GDR in one or two sentences. Notably, the boxes were not grouped chronologically, which reflected the curators' awareness that such an arrangement is nonsensical given the shape of the display, while also acknowledging and working within the limitations of it serving merely as a synoptical device. Nonetheless, the display spatially and organizationally harnessed historical change, providing an overview of social, political, cultural, and economic transformations in a tangible manner. Four examples from the display provide a sense of the range of themes. A travel bag accompanied by the words "Minimum holiday time is increased to 15 days" marked the year 1967. The 1952 box contained a hairdryer. Its text read "Married women receive a paid domestic work day once a month." A map of Prague and the text "More and more GDR citizens flee via West Germany's Prague embassy and Hungary" stood in for the year 1989. In 1978, the song "Am Fenster" [At the Window] by the rock group City is described as the best song of the year, an event that an album cover of the band signified. Although the limitations of forty objects and their captions standing in for forty years of a nation and its people are considerable, this display hints at the complex political, cultural, and economic transformation that took place in the forty-year history of the GDR, the range of which GDR museums do not tackle.

At the same time, simply providing words to connect objects to larger historical trends, which the DOK did in its "40 Years – 40

Objects" display, may not overcome fundamental problems in historical representation that lie with the objects themselves. Urry suggests that artefactual history "partly obscures the social relations and struggles which underlay that past" (52). For example, the simulation of a past that GDR museums offer their visitors creates powerful and persuasive, but also deceitful and dishonest, exhibitions, not unlike mimetic displays in other museums. Although the aim of this type of display is in large part that of Easterners recognizing themselves, this approach is reductive not only in its oversimplification of the complex realities of the past but also in its inability to approximate how people actually lived. Because the aim of the GDR museum is to display the essence of everyday life and many involved in its project have to agree on its contents' typicality, any object that has unique qualities – such as inherited antiques, original art and crafts, and most goods produced outside of the GDR – is amiss. Yet, as Milena Veenis observes, East Germans fetishized goods from elsewhere. For example, they "proudly displayed empty cans of Coca Cola in their living-room cabinets as visible emblem of western consumer society" (490). I would like to suggest that more problematic yet is that mimetic representations such as these effectively wipe out all socio-cultural difference, such as those relating to gender, sexuality, age, religion, ethnicity, and regionality, thereby replicating the socialist doctrine of the equality of all. Other types of GDR museum displays also largely fail to account for these types of differences. While visitors may engage in diverse readings, the reduction of the East German object world to the agreed upon or a perceived essential, which in this constellation seems particularly narrow, raises questions about what type of things and ideas move from past to future. A reduction of the past may be inevitable as its traces project themselves forward. However, if the GDR museum is understood as putting on display that which is left out in dominant representations, an analysis of what it leaves out must also take place. Despite these limitations, East German artefacts have an enormous potential to connect museum visitors to the past, the topic with which the next section occupies itself.

The Thingness of Things

As I noted in the introduction, GDR museums offer up the past primarily by way of objects; the exhibits' narrative usually relies exclusively on things arranged in situ, or categorically, rather than on ideas.

The organizing principles are the objects themselves and the notion that they bore witness to everyday life in East Germany. Many of the GDR museums seem to be spilling over with things and the majority of the owner/curators mentioned in my conversations with them that their archives contain many more displayable items. Combined, the museums evoke the sense that if those in charge had available to them the pertinent resources, the entire material culture of the GDR would be on display, impossible as that may be, and only the lack of resources such as space, time, and money impede this project. Although likely not intended, the abundance of things counters the hegemonic interpretation of East Germany as an economy of scarcity.

The thingness of the objects on display in the GDR museums plays a key role in their operation and in the practices people enact at these sites. I would like to suggest that, in fact, materiality, and its relationship to memory, is a key reason for why they exist, a topic this section explores.

The phrase "objects cannot speak for themselves" (Alfrey and Putnam 187) has almost an axiomatic quality. For example, Eilean Hooper-Greenhill states, "Individual objects have shifting and ambiguous relationships to meaning. Being themselves mute, their significance is open to interpretation" (*Museums and the Interpretation* 3). Yet, the emphasis on the primacy of human interpretation does not fully take into account the factuality of objects, particularly in reference to the accessibility of the past within the contemporary context. Korff writes: "The importance of things is grounded in their materiality, permanence, visibility, and concreteness. This materiality is an important facet of the creation of a sense of history and appears to be part of an overall social dynamic in a time of the transitory and the fugitive" ("Popularisierung" 268). This unique relationship between objects and the past, one that occurs beyond interpretation and is grounded in the thingness of things, arises from the lifelessness of objects. In Susan M. Pearce's words, the object "which carries meaning is able to do so because, unlike we ourselves who must die, it bears an 'eternal' relationship to the receding past, and it is this that we experience as the power of the 'actual object'" (25). From this argument follows the conclusion that although human beings bring meaning to objects, it is the object that carries more weight in this relationship. As Pearce puts it, "The meaning of the object lies not wholly in the piece itself, nor wholly in its realization, but somewhere between the two ... The balance is held by the object itself, with its tangible and factual content" (26–7). In an era in which museums place greater emphasis on conceptual frameworks than objects, it is striking how object-bound GDR museums are.

Igor Kopytoff ("Cultural Biography") applies to the process of commodification the notion of the biography of things, that is, the idea that an object has a complex, variable, and sometimes contradictory life story. He is interested in how things become (un)fit for exchange as they move between singularity and commodity. Considering the "biography of things" in the context of GDR museums illuminates why GDR museums are object-centred. Items on display at these sites began their life outside of a collection. Although their biographies vary as much as that of individual human beings, I would like to suggest a generalized life story. The objects now located and framed through the museum were manufactured in a collectively owned plant by union members under the directive of a central economic plan. As commodities they were sold and made their way into homes and institutions. Before becoming museum artefacts, many made a stop at sites of refuse, such as cellars, attics, and often the literal rubbish heap. While this biographical outline might not be unusual, the scale and speed at which financial and use value fluctuated between objects being part of everyday life and display items in the museum is astonishing. With monetary union in 1990, the material possessions of an entire nation with 17 million citizens became outdated and undesirable overnight, which brought with it their rapid expulsion from homes and other settings. Almost simultaneously, collecting and placing these items into museums began.

Considering this particular biography of items that are now on display in GDR museums provides a starting point for examining the mechanisms that connect objects, interpretation, and memory. The content of the GDR museums that I have visited and my interviews with their owners/curators suggest that one of the museums' primary aims is to put on display not only the mundane but also the typical. They seek to bring together the material traces of the average person's past, things that all those who lived consciously in the GDR would recognize. The DDR museum in Apolda near Erfurt in Thuringia epitomizes this pursuit of the typical. Here, an extensive mimetic display that encompasses an entire apartment is entitled "Familie Jedermann" ("The Everyman Family"). At a site such as this, multiple factors relating to the culture and politics of post-socialism converge. One pertains to manufactured materiality taking a central role in the processes and practices of remembering. Examining the relationship between materiality and memory, Alan Radley argues:

> Remembering is something which occurs in a world of things, as well as words, and ... artefacts play a central role in the memories of cultures and individuals ... In the very variability of objects, in the ordinariness of their consumption and in the sensory richness of relationships people enjoy through them, they are fitted to be later re-framed as material images for reflection and recall. (57)

I would also assert that the unchanging design of East German consumer goods over the course of decades, or what Paul Betts calls an "aesthetics of sameness," amplifies this role of objects in recall (754). Moreover, according to Daphne Berdahl, this characteristic renders them "particularly effective *lieux de mémoire*" ("Expressions of Experience" 163). Thus, in the context of GDR museums, assemblages of consumer goods function as environments of memory. Visitors are invited to remember their past and, more specifically, to access and (re) formulate their experiential memory. The visitor sees a living room, recognizes a couch that she or someone she knows owned, and begins to reminisce about life in East Germany. Reflecting on a past exhibit at the DOK that employed mimetic displays extensively, Berdahl describes this process as follows: "The display items elicit what the exhibit organizers describe as an 'Aha effect,' a reaction that connects personal biographies to collective memory as visitors recognize and tell stories about familiar but forgotten cultural objects" ("Expressions of Experience" 163).

To specify the discussion on the link between materiality and memory further, I now return to the beginning of the biography of the museum artefact, that of industrial production. My fieldwork suggests that one of the dominant discourses operating in amateur and private GDR museums is that despite the limitations that the socialist system placed upon individuals, East Germans led valid and productive lives. They were agents who knew how to help themselves in difficult situations and who made things, something Berdahl has taken up in the context of theorizing *Ostalgie* (nostalgia for the East) as "mourning for production" ("'(N)ostalgie' for the Present" 198). She suggests that nostalgia for the former East, and particularly its articulation through *Ostprodukte* (products of the East) relates to Easterners' loss of identity due to their fundamentally altered relationship to products and the processes of production in the transition to capitalism. The idea of "mourning for production" highlights the fact that GDR museums are not concerned merely with putting the past on display. Rather, they interpret the present and past in relationship with one another;

historical knowledge and cultural memory emerge as serving the needs of the present. These needs are entangled with contemporary realities of post-socialism, which social, economic, cultural, and political differences and inequalities between eastern and western Germany partially define. At the same time, the museums also speak to the more global process of deindustrialization in the Western world.

"Mourning for production" articulates itself in several connected registers in GDR museums, three of which emerged as dominant themes in my field research. First, the museum narratives *assert productive capacities and capabilities in the industrial realm*. The objects on display and the stories curators/owners tell about them centre on East Germany as a nation that manufactured consumer goods and workers who produced them. The most extreme example of this assertion is the now closed Erfurt GDR museum, which displayed only consumer goods produced in the region, as opposed to East Germany as a whole. As is the case for all GDR museums, the vast majority of the plants from which the museum pieces came no longer operate. The assertion of productive capacities and capabilities tells the story of East Germans producing things and the high rate of unemployment that became an unexpected reality in the early post-unification years when many factories became obsolete and closed their doors.

A second and connected dimension of "mourning for production" consists of the museums' establishing a *relationship between the product and producers of the East with consumers of the West*. Curators and signage point out that many of the objects on display in GDR museums, including furniture and small household appliances, were manufactured in the East, exported to the West, and consumed by Westerners who were unaware of their origin. The story of a successful and well-functioning industrialized nation that the museums tell contradicts and rejects dominant discourses that classify East Germany as a failed economy, primarily in the realm of industrial production. In this case, "mourning for production" extends itself from the actual producing of things that involve individual producers to the GDR as a nation in relationship to the Federal Republic of Germany (FRG). Moreover, these narratives are inextricably tied to the idea that the easterner occupies a second-class status within the unified Germany.

In a third register, GDR museums express a "mourning for production" by *asserting agency beyond the walls of factories*. While curators/owners speak of the high quality of manufactured goods, they also acknowledge the limitations of the East German centrally planned economy. The museums construct narratives of East Germans as knowing how to be resourceful in the face of consumer good shortages, thereby rejecting discourses that characterize Easterners as lacking self-motivation and an entrepreneurial spirit. East Germans emerge as having been creative and clever problem solvers, qualities that dominant discourses seemingly fail to recognize or undervalue. While this dimension of "mourning for production" focuses on the DIY culture of the GDR, I would like to suggest that it also mourns the now outdated bricolage approach to making everyday life work.

While I have unpacked Berdahl's notion of mourning for production in light of my research to show a mechanism for how objects provoke memories and tie the past to the present, this exploration has sidelined the idea that the power of the object lies in its materiality and in our ability to encounter it sensuously.

Embodied Visiting

During our interview, the director of one of the federal-government-sponsored museums lamented what he perceived to be a disrespect for objects that takes place in GDR museums, for these museums care too little about conservatorial matters by letting visitors touch their exhibits and thereby fail to protect them from unnecessary decay. I would like to suggest that it is precisely the embodied encounter, this ability to feel things, that sets apart the GDR museum from other museal engagements with East German everyday life.

Unlike most typical museums where the sense of vision dominates as the mode of engagement (Riegel 83–104), the GDR museum animates its visitor through many, if not all five, methods of perception: hearing, sight, touch, smell, and taste. It expresses itself in such ways as being able to procure typical East German food, sitting in Trabant cars, being able to open kitchen cupboards and drawers, sitting on sofas in recreated living rooms, and being invited to feel the texture of polyester housecoats and uniforms. The sensory dimensions of museum experiences arise not only because owners/curators create them intentionally. Rather, the lack of vitrines and other means of distancing observer and observed invite sensuous engagement. Moreover, olfactory encounters are more likely to be accidental than purposely constructed. For example, mimetic displays of grocery stores and laundry rooms invariably include cleaning products. For the purpose of authenticity, these types of display items often still hold their original content. However, decaying packaging lets seep out what they hold.

In addition to the absence of much overt interpretation by means such as text, the sensory experiences that GDR museums afford the visitor are tied inextricably to the memory-related processes that unfold at these sites. As Elizabeth A. Ten Dyke observes: "After the *Wende* the physical environment in eastern Germany, including its sights, sounds and smells, underwent a radical transformation" (166). More specifically, she describes how, with the demise of the GDR, East Germans found themselves suddenly in an environment in which their memories of habitual practices, daily routine, and customs of speech which had ruled their everyday lives, had become entirely irrelevant. She argues that this "rupture of memory" (166) was the basis of the existentialist crisis of disorientation that many former East Germans experienced after the fall of the Wall. Ten Dyke writes: "The future was irrevocably transformed; its relationship to the past severed. East Germans were cast adrift in an utterly foreign present; they were strangers in their own land. As a result it was as if East Germans had lost their memories" (166). The sensory landscape that the museum offers animates these memories; the sites signify that memories are not lost. The sensory possibilities invite visitors to perform the GDR. The spaces provoke those with and without personal memory of living in the East to imagine their lives as East German. Possibilities of enacting East Germanness include sitting in a living room where the coffee table is set for an afternoon of "Kaffee und Kuchen" ("coffee and cake") and the television is broadcasting an episode of "Der schwarze Kanal,"[12] eating Soljanka soup, or simply sitting at a desk in a classroom and looking through schoolbooks. For those who lived in East Germany, these embodied practices can evoke memories that seemed to be forgotten. The sensory landscape that GDR museums offer intentionally and inadvertently also offers visitors without direct knowledge of the GDR what few other historical museums do: the smell, taste, touch, and sound of the past.

Conclusion

This essay has argued that amateur and private GDR museums operate as a distinctive site of cultural practice that emerged in the context of a caesura in German history, a transformation whose aftershocks continue to be felt. Their construction of the past relies significantly on accessing memories of life under socialism. Manifesting a struggle over the kind of history that is carried forward, the museums respond to and reject hegemonic discourses on everyday life in East Germany. The intimate relationship between the museums and their publics, which GDR museums enact, entail democratic curatorial processes that are uncommon in mainstream musealization efforts. Although the near absence of interpretative texts at most sites could be understood as reflecting amateurism, I have suggested that this characteristic plays an integral part in the memory work that the GDR museum affords its visitors. Moreover, the prominence of objects, particularly industrially produced ones, relates to their capacity to affirm an East German identity. The sensuous encounter with the past, even if often accidental, leads visitors to perform the GDR, a topic which Jonathan Bach specifies further in the next chapter as he discusses museums' "strategies of authenticity."

Emphasizing what engages, seems to work well, and operates uniquely, this essay has provided a relatively generous reading of the GDR museum. Although this type of museum represents and hints at that which is forgotten or refused elsewhere, it too omits and distorts. In addition to displaying a limited range of artefacts, it accounts poorly for social, economic, political, and cultural transformation that occurred over the course of the entire existence of the GDR. Materially, it offers most frequently those artefacts that have been readily available and affordable. In addition, mimetic displays tend to represent the material cultural landscape of the later years of the nation. Reasons for the ubiquity of artefacts from the nineteen eighties include that more of the material traces of the recent past survive and that visitors may want to see what they remember best. Moreover, constructing content that speaks to different periods within the history of East Germany, such as contrasting the eras of Walter Ulbricht's and Erich Honecker's rule, exceeds the professional and financial capabilities of private and amateur museums. Despite these limitations, popular museums that dedicate themselves to the history of East Germany raise significant questions about the possibility of joining together museal narratives that simultaneously address repression and resistance while representing everyday life in such a way that it respects and recognizes the experiences of most or all East Germans. What is at stake is how diverse the voices of the past can be as they move forward in time.

NOTES

1 Saunders (4–5)

2 Currently in operation are GDR museums in Apolda, Burg, Gelenau, Kusey, Langenweddingen, Malchow, Mühltroff, Klettenberg, Pirna,

Radebeul, Thale, and Tutow. Also included could be museums in Berlin, Perleberg, Eisenhüttenstadt, and Wittenberg. Although both groups of museums put on display material traces of the everyday, their approach to the subject matter differ significantly. During my research trips to Germany, people repeatedly told me about small collections of East German everyday objects in various locations. One example is a private, one-room collection in Dummerstorf, Mecklenburg–Western Pomerania, that is open to the public on special occasions. I heard of many others, but was unable to confirm their existence.

3 "Oll" is a Low German colloquial expression that means old but has pejorative meanings such as stupid and dense.

4 "A museum is a *non-profit*, permanent institution in the service of society and its development, open to the public, which acquires, *conserves*, *researches*, communicates and exhibits the tangible and intangible heritage of humanity and its environment for the purposes of education, study and enjoyment." Emphases added. International Council of Museums. http://icom.museum/the-vision/museum-definition/.

5 Unless otherwise indicated, all translations are mine. "Die wissenschaftlich fundierte Sammlung, Bewahrung und Dokumentation von Objekten der DDR-Geschichte birgt für stadt- und regionalgeschichtliche Museen ein großes Potential. Dieses wird bislang jedoch nur selten genutzt. Zugleich verweist die steigende Zahl privat betriebener, kommerzieller DDR-Museen auf das öffentliche Interesse an diesem Thema. Diese Situation nimmt die Tagung als Ausgangspunkt. Diskutiert werden die verschiedenen Dimensionen der Musealisierung der DDR sowie die Möglichkeiten und Grenzen der Darstellung und Vermittlung von Zeitgeschichte im Museum."

6 "Das Alltagsleben in der DDR wird berücksicht, um eine Verklärung und Verharmlosung der SED-Diktatur und jeder "Ostalgie" entschieden entgegenzuwirken. Dazu ist das alltägliche Leben notwendigerweise im Kontext der Diktatur darzustellen. Es muss deutlich werden, dass die Menschen in der DDR einer umfassenden staatlichen Kontrolle unterlagen und einem massiven Anpassungsdruck ausgesetzt waren, ebenso wie die Diktatur ihre Macht auch aus der Mitmachbereitschaft der Gesellschaft schöpfte. Die Instrumente und Mechanismen, derer sich die SED bediente, um die gesamte Gesellschaft und das Leben der Menschen in all seinen Bereichen ideologisch zu durchdringen, sollen benannt werden – von der Kinderkrippe über die Schule und die Universität bis hin zur Arbeitswelt und zur Freizeitgestaltung. Zugleich muss dokumentiert werden, wie und wo sich Menschen in der DDR dem Zugriff der Partei zu entziehen suchten."

7 "Es war schön, an alles erinnert zu werden."

8 "Dies war bis jetzt unsere Lieblingsaustellung. Man findet aus jedem Lebensbereich Erinnerungen. Danke für diese schöne Ausstellung und weiterhin Erfolg."

9 Mitropa, a catering and restaurant business, was founded in 1916 and operated as one of the only stock companies in East Germany.

10 In recent years, "Made in the GDR" products have become more rare and consequently have gained in value. Museums now must often purchase potential display items or exchange them for objects they already have in their archives.

11 "Mit dem Haarnetz, Käsehobel und Wurststopfapparat ... ist keine Bewegungsgeschichte und Geschichtsbewegung darzustellen."

12 *Der schwarze Kanal* [The Black Channel] was a weekly political propaganda program that was broadcast on East German television between 1960 and 1989.

6 Object Lessons: Visuality and Tactility in Museums of the Socialist Everyday

JONATHAN BACH

Museums, by dint of their social role and implied authority, operate as symbolic spaces mediating the border between living and dead worlds. Ethnographic museums in particular embody the tension between offering a space where objects "go to die" and where the past is "kept alive." This tension is particularly acute when a museum's artefacts are from the recent past, and when the objects in question conjure controversy. This chapter looks at this tension in private museums of everyday life *(Alltag)* in the former German Democratic Republic (GDR), referred to here as GDR *Alltag* museums. As Anne Winkler argues above, these museums are sites of cultural practice that actively contest the German memory landscape through questioning the widespread isomorphism of the socialist everyday with its ideological context. This contestation brings with it a set of representational challenges for these private museums, which, as she shows, rely heavily on object-focused amateur exhibits to stake their claim to "authentic" representation of the socialist past. This chapter focuses on the representational strategies that emerge through these museums' exhibits, exploring how historical knowledge is constructed out of an interactive process that mediates the boundaries of dead objects and living memory.

As the memory of the *annus mirabilis* of 1989/90 fades, the changing discourse over how to treat the socialist legacy becomes central to our emergent understanding of German history and identity today. The museums under discussion are an active part of the discursive construction of unified Germany one generation after the reunification of 1990. Their presentation of everyday objects lies at the heart of a divisive discourse over the trivialization of the communist past and the museums' immersion in and evasion of this discourse

(Winkler, this volume). We turn first to the phenomenon of the GDR *Alltag* museums and how their modes of display open them to critique. This sets the stage for exploring a post-socialist synaesthesia where sight, touch, and other senses are deployed to revalue objects that have been made "unworthy" of musealization. This re-valuation is accomplished through a privileging of authenticity that relies on strategies of visuality, tactility, and intimacy.

Transitional Objects

Into the Museum

GDR *Alltag* museums form a kind of parallel private world juxtaposed with state-sanctioned representations of Cold War German history. In the former East Germany today there are, more than two decades after 1989, at least twenty-three private museums devoted to everyday life under socialism. They range from little more than overcrowded basements run by retired individuals to large commercial operations with a side business in GDR-nostalgia products. These museums seek to consciously expand, subvert, supplement, and sometimes openly oppose what they perceive as dominant state narratives about East Germany as expressed in the few state-sponsored museums dedicated to recent history, above all the German Historical Museum in Berlin, the House of History (*Haus der Geschichte*) in Bonn, and its branch in Leipzig, the Forum for Contemporary History (*Zeitgeschichtliches Forum*).

The state-supported museums have been criticized for emphasizing the themes of repression and resistance in their portrayal of the former East, constructing a narrative that apotheosizes East Germany's indigenous revolution against a background of inexorable decline.[1] The private museums are, in contrast, concerned by and large "not with the overly common portrayal of the GDR and its mechanism of repression," as a concept paper for the GDR museum *Zeitreise* in Radebeul put it, but with "real" life. With the notable exceptions of the larger museums in Berlin, Eisenhüttenstadt, and Radebeul (near Dresden), the GDR *Alltag* museums often take the form of personal shrine, usually presided over by a charismatic individual, with little clear plan for the disposition of the artefacts after the museum is closed. In the context of the transition from socialism to capitalism and democracy, these shrine-style museums are literally transitional, their existence tied to the biography and biology of their founders, nearly all of whom came of age during the Cold War and whose relation to the objects displayed is visceral and intimate.

The museums' collections are a material instantiation of a hodge-podge collective memory – large numbers of everyday-life objects from the GDR era, primarily from the 1970s and 1980s. The collections are presented as a thematic assemblage interspersed with dioramas: Rooms or walls are devoted to species of objects (clocks, toys, typewriters, etc.) or events (school, home, vacation), more or less ordered, sometimes labelled, more often not, sometimes protected behind glass, sometimes explicitly available to be picked up and held. Dioramas range from kitsch to serious recreations, such as in Apolda, where mannequins complete the frozen image of a meticulous schoolroom or a dentist's office.

The objects overwhelmingly represent products that after 1989 became culturally obsolete while remaining functional. Trash in the early 1990s overflowed with the daily objects of sixteen million people that were "indiscriminately tossed overboard like ballast," as a stunned Westerner put it after exploring the East Berlin landscape. "From work brigade books and Party insignia to coming of age gifts and many other things," he remarked, ex-GDR citizens "could not get rid of their everyday stuff fast enough" (Rundbrief 3: 9).[2] The first museums grew out of this landscape, driven by avid collectors on personal salvage missions to collect as much of the past as possible in a "brutal and unsystematic" (as one collector put it) operation to rescue the Eastern everyday – and the collectors' own life experiences – from the fringes where it was consigned after 1989 (Rundbrief 5: 7).[3]

Aura and Error: Memory and the Unmemorable Object

While most of these collections use the word "museum" in their name or description, few of these institutions seek de jure designation as such (with the exception of Eisenhüttenstadt). Since the form of exhibits, as the Radebeul director put it, is generally viewed by the state as "unmuseum-like" (*nicht museumsgerecht*), there is little effort to abide by international norms (known as ICOM standards), especially regarding cataloguing and preservation of material (Stephan). Yet precisely because they de facto present themselves as museums and, importantly, are regarded colloquially as such, they find themselves subject to significant criticism from professional curators and historians.

A notable example is Martin Sabrow, of the Institute for Contemporary History in Potsdam and former chair of the second Federal Experts

Commission dealing with the historical legacies of the SED dictatorship. He is a strong advocate for the inclusion of the everyday in the field of history, and precisely for this reason is deeply troubled by what he sees as dangerous deficiencies in private GDR *Alltag* museums. Speaking at a 2008 colloquium on the second anniversary of the GDR Museum Berlin, Sabrow spoke frankly to his hosts, presenting a critique widely shared among professional historians and curators ("DDR-Alltag im Museum" 12). Above all, the objects in the museum are not being properly treated, from their intake, cataloguing, and storage through to their display (12). He was especially concerned by their availability to be touched by the viewers (12). Further, the exhibits lack critical distance and are too affirmative of life in the GDR (12). This problematic affirmation is only intensified by the museum's explicit focus on experience and feeling, which works to inhibit reflection, with the effect that the everyday becomes separated from dictatorship (12). Accordingly, by encouraging a good feeling (*das Wohlfühlen*), the museum effectively crosses the line into entertainment. All of this creates a high risk for trivialization (*Verharmlosung*) of the GDR past with implications for subtly undermining the legitimacy of democracy in united Germany (12). The museum's aura, Sabrow concludes, needs correction to avoid what he saw as its current, decontextualized, "amusement park of everydayness" (12).[4]

Sabrow's critique echoes a more general one of museums of everyday culture, as presented by Gottfried Korff, who argues that, while the everyday, heritage, and popular culture made sense in years past, today these are "likely a false strategy because they encourage not only the devaluation of everyday culture but of museum-work itself ... [Today] we require not only the turn towards small worlds but – increasingly – the recollection of grand structures, questions, and legacies" (*Museumsdinge* 136).[5] In light of critiques such as Korff's and Sabrow's, the GDR *Alltag* museums appear problematic, from a generally poor attitude towards history – what Korff would call a "banal lust for relicts" (*banaler Reliktbegier*) at the expense of the "grand structures" (ibid.) – to their claims to be a "museum," to their perceived apologia for a dictatorship. At stake, thus, in the seemingly innocent stacks of plastic eggcups, Mitropa menus, furniture units, cameras, and children's toys, is the ability of a democratic society to maintain its professional and critical standards, tied closely with the ability of the name "museum" itself to retain, as Susan Crane once put it, its "trustworthiness ... as a memory institution" (45).

The critique of GDR museums as trivializing the past to the point of apology for dictatorship, however, draws us precisely to the challenge of representing shared experiences that are simultaneously "banal" and "political." Representing the everyday under the least political of circumstances is a difficult task, since the very act of presenting something "normal" in the sacral context of a museum makes the normal exceptional by its very elevation to museal status. This task is made exponentially more complex in cases such as the GDR's, where the rapid disappearance of a regime turns lived memory and academic history into simultaneous occurrences. Michael Baxandall once wrote about the three types of agents involved in a museum: makers of objects, exhibitors of objects, and viewers of exhibited, made objects (36). In the case of the GDR museums the same person could inhabit all three positions.

Being subject and object of the exhibit is common enough when contemporary popular culture is on display, especially in the form of everyday objects, but there is a twist to the GDR *Alltag* museums. While state socialism doggedly campaigned to demystify the everyday from what it saw as the false consciousness of commodity fetishism, it ended up re-enchanting the very objects by investing them with the magic of the state. While in the West everyday life is often celebrated as a sphere of resistance, this was only true in limited respects in the GDR, given how, under state socialism, everyday life existed not in opposition to ideological life but as "a fundamental site of ideological intervention" (Reid and Crowley 7).

When GDR museums are often accused of trivializing the past (*Verharmlosung*), they tend to react defensively, as when the Radebeul director claimed adamantly in an interview with me that "Stasi and persecution are not important in the sphere of the everyday" (Stephan).[6] The museums try to escape the cycle of accusation and defensiveness over trivialization. To understand how they do this requires us to slightly shift the axis of the debate, in Nikolai Vukov's formulation, from a struggle between memory and forgetting to the struggle between memory and representation. Vukov suggests the concept of the "unmemorable" to describe this "fighting ground" between memory and representation. The "unmemorable" refers at one level to the everyday – hence banal – aspects of life, but the term signals conflicts over the "worthiness" of remembering. Vukov differentiates this from repression of memory due to trauma: the "unmemorable" is a category of worth, and the exploration of the memory of the "unmemorable" is thus an exploration of how memory is given or deprived of value.

In trying to represent what the GDR was "really" like, the GDR *Alltag* museums thus face a common representational challenge: How is the "unmemorable" made "memorable"? How is value (worth) created through the representation of the past, especially when that past concerns the everyday? How, in this context, do these museums work to represent the GDR as lived experience? How is East German identity expressed across space and time?

Strategies of Authenticity

Objects, Intimacy, and Tactility

In the GDR *Alltag* museums, authenticity, the stock in trade for presenting life "as it really was," becomes the primary strategy for representing the unmemorable. The aura of authenticity, more than any other element, gives the museums their edge and draws visitors. Authenticity operates as a form of trust that puts people at ease with objects, from the reassuringly amateurish nature of the more homespun exhibits to the sleekly designed GDR Museum Berlin, where, as the research director put it, "we produce authenticity" (Wolle). One of the directors of a provincial museum explained that people donate to his exhibit because they trust him personally, and they come to the museum because they can trust the authenticity of the objects and the non-judgmental context of their display (Freimark).

Because the objects bear the legacy of ideology along with their aura of familiarity, they gain their viewers' trust initially by being embedded in a narrative that claims to remove the objects from the realm of politics. Because the *everydayness* of the objects becomes the signifier of authenticity, the museums have a compelling interest in the very opposite of what Sabrow and other critics deem responsible: decoupling the objects from ideology. Political neutrality is, in Sabrow's critique, impossible, yet it is precisely what many of the museums strive for: "We want to remember, not to provoke" is the motto of the museum in Langenweddingen and the first item on its promotional material (*Ostalgie-Kabinett*).[7] As Maya Nadkarni and Olga Shevchenko note, it is precisely this "non-partisan quality of memory [that] lends an aura of objectivity" (506). The GDR *Alltag* museums' message is that *other* museums (i.e., the state-supported ones) are "political," and therefore are not "authentic." Authenticity is not expressed through fidelity to objects, but through being apolitical, or more precisely anti-political.

Political objects themselves are not entirely absent in displays, but are often deployed as background context: at times atmospheric (as with slogan banners, songs, and newspaper headlines), other times as a counterpoint to the anti-political niche society of everyday life (as with images of mass demonstrations), or as extensions of politics into everyday life (as with displays of objects from the Pioneers or Free German Youth movements, pins, or awards).

In this context the objects play a special role in indexing authenticity. Authenticity speaks above all through the objects, or perhaps more precisely, the objects are presented as speaking for themselves – the objects as bearers of objectivity. They speak for themselves, ironically, by speaking for others: for other persons from a bygone era, but also for other objects. Their authenticity is confirmed by viewers' familiarity and a form of common sense that knows that there is a surfeit of objects. This functions as reassuring – there is safety in numbers. Visitors are quickly struck by the scale of *Alltag* museums' exhibits, which themselves represent only a fraction of the objects that the directors eagerly tell you they have stored away in garages, barns, basements, and warehouses. The numbers are an important part of the strategy of authenticity, as when the museum in Apolda proudly advertises over 12,000 objects, as if to convey both the scale of the lost past and the comprehensiveness, and hence authenticity, of the collection (Olle DDR).

The sheer plenitude of excess products and ephemera from the GDR allows them to accrue the status of original, even when – or precisely because – there is no systematic means of verifying their provenance. This is fitting for the material culture of a society where collectivization achieved efficiency in mass production, where individual taste was subordinated to social norms, and the material world was designed to align the individual with the mass. An object is thus on display not because it is unique, but because it indexes all other objects of its type. The often "unprofessional" form of exhibit – walls of televisions, or rows of sewing machines, what might be called the aesthetics of the pile – is important here, because it downplays the originality of the object and inserts it into a concentrated version of the GDR everyday, when people would encounter these objects in each other's homes or offices.

Accordingly, objects appear as generic and disconnected from their actual owners or personal stories. Objects on display are almost never linked to a particular narrative; rather, the point of displaying the object is less to relate someone *else's* personal story than to trigger memories of the *viewer's* personal story, or to trigger their asking of others (such as children asking parents). This makes the museums primarily author-centred rather than "witness centred," with no reliance on filmed interviews or documentaries, and only occasional commentary from staff members who are GDR contemporaries, when available. Wandering among the cornucopia of authentic objects, visitors are left to generate their own narratives, a type of self-narration that accompanies self-curation. This works, in different ways, for both Westerners and Easterners, who often exclaim "my mother had that!" or "I remember standing in line for those" or "I saw that on visits to my relatives." These parallel narratives across East and West are inadvertently produced by the film-still-like quality of the many dioramic presentations that highlight the objects almost as if they were archaic advertisements for a shared post-war modernity. The common lack of specific labelling lends many objects an auratic air that makes them differently legible for Eastern and Western viewers.

Ironically, the very anonymity of the objects enhances an experience of intimacy. Intimacy lies in the very things that the professional historians and curators criticize – the open display of objects as if they were in someone's house rather than a museum, the ability or explicit invitation to touch the objects, tours by "real" former East Germans who are not professional museum workers. Some of the displays in particular strive for authenticity through intimacy – underwear drying on a clothesline, plates piled up pell-mell in a kitchen, toys left in mid-play. Sometimes these appear as frozen tableaus behind a thin cord asking visitors to stay back. Others, such as the lovingly recreated full-scale apartments spanning four decades in Lutherstadt Wittenberg's "House of History," invite you to sit on the couch and watch TV, grab a book from the bookcase, and all but take a beer from the refrigerator.

While there is an air of respect for the absent hosts in Wittenberg, the GDR Museum Berlin takes intimacy further, allowing visitors to feel like a nosy guest, an intruder, or a ghost in someone else's house. In this most commercial of the GDR *Alltag* museums, wardrobes can be opened, kitchen utensils and bath items handled, magazines leafed through, couches sat on, telephones talked on, and so on. Visitors can try on clothes, literally inhabiting the Other who, perhaps by design, looks a lot like a slightly retro self. In this fashion, the tactile enters into engagement with the intimate.

The GDR museum in Berlin is atypical among the *Alltag* museums in that it is founded and run largely by West Germans and is the most commercially successful and visible of the nearly two dozen *Alltag* museums, with over one-and-a-half million visitors in the first five years of its existence (2006–11) (DDR Museum, Statistiken). The motto of the museum is "History to Touch: See, Feel, Experience" and it describes itself as a museum to "*be-greifen*" (to grasp). As the press spokesperson for the museum put it upon the opening of the expanded exhibit in 2010, "Visitors should just go right ahead and touch everything, any exhibit that comes between their fingers, actively and curiously. As a Berliner I would say 'don't be shy! Grab those hamburgers' or in this case 'grab those exhibits'" (Museumsnews)![8] Or as the official English promotional material states, "Everything waits to be touched and experienced: Open the drawers and closets, rummage through them and discover" (DDR Museum Berlin)!

Touch blurs the border of self and other, and invoking tactility in the museum is, consciously or not, another way of generating trust, and thereby shoring up the experience of intimacy and authenticity that makes it possible to represent the unmemorable. Tactility also attracts because it is something denied in the modern privileging, and subsequent reduction, of apprehension to the visual. Tactility is not always considered a positive quality: Marshall McLuhan, in his analysis of tactility and technology in the media, considered it to have a numbing effect (44–7). Following Walter Benjamin's use of the term in connection with the optical unconscious, tactility is thought of as allowing for the experience of the new in the early stages of encounter with a medium ("Work of Art" 117–20). For McLuhan this means, especially with the rise of television, the dominance of a new de-sensitizing, anaesthetic effect caused by exposure to media with its "daily sessions of synaesthesia ... that wash about the great visual structure of Abstract Individual Man" (315).[9] But what we see in the Berlin GDR museum is a different employment of the *synaesthetic*, where one modality of experience, for example touch, calls for another, for example sound, or smell. Unlike with the analyses of Benjamin or McLuhan, we find less the optical unconscious being prepped for a new medium than a deployment of multi-sensory experiences in the service of creating memory value.

Visuality, Sensory Experience, and Post-Socialist Synaesthesia

Particularly in the Berlin GDR museum, but increasingly in the smaller, less commercial *Alltag* museums, multi-sensory experiences are a central feature of the experience of the "real" GDR, combining the strategies of intimacy and tactility. The GDR Museum Berlin claims to be "one of the most interactive museums in the world," a distinction that helped it be nominated for the European Museum of the Year Award in 2008 (Pressemitteilung). This is in part, as the research director explained to me, "a response to the virtualization of the world," but also, he noted, because they are attempting to create an anchor for a "rudderless sense of memory of the GDR that combines colour, taste, history as fantasy and history as personal trauma" (Wolle). In this phantasmagoria, film, sound, and interactive media appear in the *Alltag* exhibits as privileged sensory experiences that contribute to the post-socialist synaesthesia.

While these museums do not use eyewitness interviews or documentaries looking back at the GDR, film and video are deployed in three primary ways. First, actual footage is often used to create a sense of authenticity by putting the visitor in the position, respectively, of voyeur, spectator, and addressee. In the position of a voyeur, visitors to the Berlin museum can watch loops of demonstrations or street scenes observed through the lens of footage from Stasi security cameras. As spectator, visitors in many of the museums can watch snippets of GDR television, such as a loop of news on *Aktuelle Kamera*, or, as in the Berlin museum, see short movies in a small cinema recreated to showcase both GDR-era technology and period films, with a huge functioning projector taken from the State Council, as large as a boiler, placed as an object d'art behind the seats.

Most cinematic and television images are shown to ironic or humorous effect, such as old talk shows, political congresses, *Sandmann* cartoons, or dated anchormen on old news broadcasts. Yet at times the footage shifts from an amusing background to placing the visitor in the role of addressee, as in Perleberg, where a looped segment from the propaganda show *Der schwarze Kanal* (The Black Channel) encourages the viewer to hate the enemy in the West, which of course has now absorbed the East. In this short film, the infamous GDR propagandist Karl-Eduard von Schnitzler presents hatred of the West as a form of love for Germany. Too disturbing to be merely ironic, the uncomfortable cinematic confrontation with this crass exhortation to fear serves almost as a prelude to a subsequent exhibit in the same museum, where the viewer encounters a full-length mirror upon which is written "What did YOU do and who were YOU in this dictatorship?"[10] This mirror, like the segment of *Der schwarze Kanal*, dislodges viewers from the realm of reminiscence and presents them with silent questions about their own relation to dictatorship.

While Western visitors and younger-generation Easterners might view such visual dissonances with ironic distance or feelings of immunity, the true target audience in Perleberg falls primarily into the "history as personal trauma" category.[11] The political content in some of the Perleberg displays, especially the mirror's literal call to self-reflection and the notion of history as personal trauma, thus appear in tension with Vukov's aforementioned distinction between the (un)memorable as an apolitical category of worth that we find in *Alltag* museums and memory as the repression of politically generated trauma. The Perleberg museum purposely seeks to draw the connections between the two while remaining resolutely anti-political, concerned primarily with the question of personal moral conduct in the context of civil society, in both the past and present. In this way the Perleberg museum's otherwise banal presentation of everyday objects becomes a space for directly confronting the varied repressed traumas that accompanies the lived experience of the GDR. It is in this sense that the director, a former pastor, explained his understanding of his role as museum director "as a Christian, not as a historian" (Freimark). By this he means seeing his role as creating a therapeutic safe space where visitors can safely confront their own implication in the past.

Visitors are greeted with the immigration question "Do you want to be admitted [to the country]?" (*möchten Sie einreisen?*), and receive a "visa" in the form of a ticket, thereby entering a liminal space. The older visitors, the director told me, "at first express joy and recognition, and then remember what life was like." As they get deeper into the museum they feel allowed to feel, as in the case of a woman who stayed behind alone crying in one of the many rooms, not wanting her husband to see her tears. For "mixed couples," as he called them, an Easterner will bring his or her Western spouse, with the preface that "my partner doesn't believe what I lived through" and is eager to see what it was "really" like (Freimark).

As the visitors move through the museum, in Perleberg as almost everywhere else, they are accompanied by a soundtrack of GDR songs. The visitor browses the rows of radios or stacks of cleaning supplies to the strains of the *Das Lied der Partei* (*Party Song*, also known as *Die Partei hat immer Recht* [*The Party Is Always Right*]), the former GDR national anthem (now available in techno remix), or the peppy Free German Youth (FDJ) October Club song *Sag mir wo Du stehst* (*Which Side Are You On*). The uniformity of these songs across museums is striking. The songs work simultaneously as branding and atmospherics, the marches and rhythms providing a lively accompaniment to the primary colours of GDR plastics and FDJ banners, while the national anthem echoes suitably like a dirge. But sound is deployed not only as a soundtrack but as an exhibit itself, via headphones, that, as in Berlin, allow the visitor to listen to pre-selected clips of GDR rock music or listen privately to television shows on small screens set in a "Plattenbau"-style wall. In Radebeul a room full of stereo systems plays music with a slightly different purpose, not to highlight the music but, as the director emphasized to me, to showcase the high quality of GDR sound technology.

It is at the Berlin museum, however, that sound is fully employed in a synaesthetic sense with the expressed purpose of allowing the viewer to "experience" the Other in a double sense – the Other in the form of the now-disappeared East German average citizen and, within that imaginary space, the Stasi or party official. The role-playing between an "average citizen" and "party or state security official" almost feels like theme-park adaptations of the films *Goodbye Lenin!* (2003), and *Das Leben der Anderen* (*The Lives of Others*, 2006), a sense confirmed by the museum's research director that the museum serves as an "intellectual playground" that transmits history as "information, fun, and colour" (Wolle). Accordingly, the visitor is encouraged to lift the receiver of a telephone in the "authentic prefabricated apartment" (*originalgetreuen Plattenbauwohnung*) for an average person's experience, and later lift the phone on a high party official's desk, where the voice of a subordinate makes lame excuses.

Playing on this relationship between subject and object, the recreated *Plattenbau* apartment is bugged, and the viewer can squeeze into the narrow "Stasi corner," don headphones at a desk replete with listening equipment, binders, and a portrait of Honecker, and "spy" on fellow visitors down the hall in the "apartment" display. Interactivity connects touch, sound, and sight to give visitors a kind of authenticity in the form of authority born of experience. The mirror in Perleberg asking visitors what they did during the dictatorship can only be activated by the visitor's own history. In contrast, in the Berlin GDR museum, interactive elements are set in the context of numerous games that serve to educate the visitor and test their knowledge or just let them "experience" the past. Visitors can sit inside authentic Trabi (average citizen) or Volvo (high official) cars, turn the ignition, and "drive" them virtually through the city laid out on a screen in front of the car. Video games invite the visitor to match definitions, to use touch screens to dress virtual figures with period clothes, and to simulate making decisions to keep a State Owned Enterprise afloat. A digital board game beckons children to slam down bureaucratic stamps that call forth information on the game board.

Most interactive of all, however, is a soundproof, glass-walled interrogation room, where the visitor literally adopts the physical position of a detainee sitting across from an interrogator, portrayed here as a life-sized black wooden cut-out. The interrogator's questions are heard clearly in the room, but when the visitor puts her elbows on the table and hands over her ears the detainee's answers are transmitted through a special "bone sound technology" (*Knochenschalltechnologie*) and, as the museum's own exhibition description puts it, "The interrogation comes to life!" This mimetic act turns the visitor into the prosthesis of the unnamed, but voiced, victim. Intimacy is established at a new level here, one where authenticity is no longer about a safe zone for trust but a leaving of the self to enter a zone of indeterminate authority. As Sara Jones points to in her analysis of a similar interrogation exhibit at a Stasi prison, the effect of intimacy is produced when the visitor is put in the position of both expert and witness ("'At Home'" 215–22). These interactive exhibits about the Stasi complicate the claim made earlier by one director that the Stasi had no place in the everyday, and the Stasi appears as an inconsistent presence in the museums.

Conclusion

From one of the walls in the Berlin museum computerized LED portraits of the socialist triumvirate – Marx, Engels, and Lenin – stare down in familiar form, only to occasionally wink and smirk at the viewer, and suddenly change places with one another. These electronic portraits, combined with the various appropriations and juxtapositions of GDR symbolism both in the Berlin museum and beyond, "retrofit" GDR era iconography in the way that Serguei Oushakine uses the term. For Oushakine, retrofitting iconography provides a visual template that "offer[s] a recognizable outline without suggesting an obvious ideological strategy of its interpretation" (468). This echoes the museums' seeking of an authentic aura through political neutrality, though in this specific case in the Berlin museum authenticity lies in the aura of its retrofitted representation.

The aesthetics of authenticity in the museums also echo the spate of popular films about the GDR from the mid-2000s. The Berlin GDR museum was conceived in 2004, the year following the 2003 release of *Goodbye Lenin!* This film helped generate an "Ostalgia" wave built largely around authentic objects (or their simulacra), such as the infamous *Spreewald* brand of pickles, and both the film's promotional mock-ups of a GDR apartment and its interactive web game "the GDR in 79 square metres" prefigured the Berlin museum's later exhibits. In turn, the Berlin museum's *Stasi Corner* exhibit, which simulated spying, received new emphasis when the role of the Stasi gained visibility through *Das Leben der Anderen* and its interrogation scenes, which in turn may have inspired the subsequent interrogation display in the museum's expanded permanent exhibit.[12]

The strategies of authenticity described in the pages above address different audiences both spatially (East and West) and temporally (across generations). Yet they share the goal of allowing the GDR *Alltag* museums to represent the unmemorable objects of the era by creating a "semiotic loop" of images, texts, and objects, that, in Beverly James's phrase, "draws the viewer into an imagined past." This, she points out, makes museums spaces for forms of "semantic collaboration" between the objects and the viewers (138). In the GDR *Alltag* museums this semiotic loop elevates sound, touch, and even smell and taste in a kind of "pre-modern" form of museum where sight is less privileged. In this context it is perhaps not coincidental that the Berlin museum spokesperson used the comparison of eating hamburgers to touching the exhibits, for both are about in-corporation. Fittingly, the museum exit takes you directly to a GDR-themed restaurant that serves "authentic" food adjusted to contemporary high quality. The museum leaves a taste.

I have suggested that the form of semantic collaboration at work in the museums of everyday life under socialism in the GDR relies on modes of representation that use strategies of intimacy, tactility, and visuality to produce authenticity in the form of a post-socialist synaesthesia. These strategies attach "value" to a category of memory that is considered unworthy of memory (unmemorable), for reasons of both the seemingly banal form of the objects and the political risks of attaching value to them. Through the phenomenon of the GDR *Alltag* museums the "unmemorable" of the socialist past enters the realm of representation as objects of memory, and from there, in a small but significant way, enters the fray of the ongoing discursive construction of a united Germany.

NOTES

Research for this paper was generously supported by a grant from the German Academic Exchange Service (DAAD). I wish to thank the editors for their helpful comments.

1 For critiques of the state-supported museums see Berdahl (112–15). See also Scribner for an analysis of GDR *Alltag* museums as a "tender rejection" of the past rather than a "melancholy fixation" (186–7).
2 "Ex-DDR Bürger konnten ihre Alltagsdinge nicht schnell genug loswerden … [Mehr als einmal fischte ich mit Fotoapparat und Beutel bewaffnet] 'Schätze' aus Müllcontainern – achtlos wie Ballast über Bord geworfene Alltagskultur, vom Brigadebuch über Parteiabzeichen bis hin zum Jugendweihe-Geschenk und vieles andere mehr." The statistics on garbage bear this out: in 1990 West Germany produced 428 kg of garbage per capita. For the same period the East produced 1.2 tons per capita. See Ahbe (7).
3 On "the fringes" of everyday life see Sheringham (20).
4 "Jahrmarkt der Alltäglichkeiten." See also Sabrow, "Die DDR erinnern." The Berlin Museum's expanded permanent exhibition, opened in October 2010, seems to take some of this style of criticism into account by adding a focus on the State.
5 "möglicherweise eine falsche Strategie, weil sie die Aufforderung zur tendenziellen Entwertung nicht nur der Alltagskultur, sondern auch der Museumsarbeit darstellt … Nicht nur die Hinwendung der Kleinwelten scheint erforderlich, sondern – vermehrt – die Erinnerung an die großen Strukturen, Fragen und Linien."
6 "MfS und Verfolgung sind nicht wichtig im Alltagsbereich."
7 "Wir wollen erinnern – nicht provozieren."
8 "Als Besucher sollte man aktiv und neugierig einfach alles anfassen, was einem an Exponaten zwischen die Finger kommt. Ich würde es als Berlinerin zusammenfassen mit 'nur keine falsche Schüchternheit, immer ran an die Buletten' … oder in diesem Falle halt 'ran an die Exponate'!"
9 On tactility and McLuhan see especially Kadobayashi (26–31).
10 Was warst und tatest DU in dieser Diktatur?
11 On the role of irony in Ostalgia see Rethmann (22–3).
12 On *Goodbye Lenin!* see Bach, also Berdahl, and the *Goodbye Lenin!* official website. It is interesting to note that *The Lives of Others* is also echoed in the treatment of Stasi interrogations in Leipzig's Zeitgeschichtliches Forum (Contemporary History Forum), which in its focus on repression presents itself as a state-sanctioned counter-narrative to the Berlin GDR museum's focus on "normal" life. Thanks to Peter McIsaac for this observation.

7 Historical Museum Meets Docu-Drama: The Recipient's Experiential Involvement in the Second World War

STEPHAN JAEGER

Popularizing and Experiencing History

The last two decades have produced a remarkable number of popular representations of the Second World War geared towards the collective memory of the German people. History in general, but particularly that of the Second World War, has become increasingly popularized in genres which cater to a wide audience. These include feature films, documentaries, small-screen historical epics, television events and docudramas, permanent and temporary exhibits in museums and memorial places (*Gedenkstätten*), history magazines, and online history features. The intersection between TV documentary/docudrama and museum exhibit is particularly meaningful, since both genres and media have adapted representational practices of the other. Whereas TV docudrama employs representational techniques common to the historical museum to create the impression of physical authenticity, as well as spaces the viewer can experience in a three-dimensional way, historical museums use film for authentic documentation of historical arguments and to convey the atmosphere of the past, using filmic techniques to draw the visitor into the simulated and immersive experience of a stage set.

The popularization of history has been accompanied by an urge for authenticity. The intersection of the past on display in TV docudrama and museum shows two shifts in how to represent or display the past authentically. First, there is a general desire for authenticity of the past that overshadows the importance of historical analysis. Second, this intersection is marked by a tendency towards performative forms of authenticity: the viewer and the museum visitor re-experience the past or the past's authenticity in simulated ways (Assmann, *Geschichte* 153–4).[1]

The popularization of the Second World War has raised considerable criticism from German academic historians. For example, Horst Walter Blanke notes when analysing several of Guido Knopp's TV documentaries that Knopp has insufficiently conceptualized his use of historical sources, particularly in re-enacting historical scenes. Rather than reflect on historical processes, his films seem primarily interested in evoking emotions in the viewer (Blanke 73–4).[2] Yet, the trend of popularizing history has also found interest in German didactics of history. Thinking about the instructive functions of a historical museum or exhibit, Lukas Aufgebauer argues that there is a mediating role between experiencing the past – as if the visitor were entering or observing a stage set – and an archive of historically authentic objects (Aufgebauer 191–2). He posits that affective and cognitive processes must supplement each other in order for visitors to develop historical consciousness (*Geschichtsbewusstsein*). Consequently, the challenge for the "past on display" is whether perceiving and experiencing history through one's senses and cognitive understanding of processes and ideologies involved can supplement each other, so that viewers and visitors feel and understand a given portion of history which they can then relate to the present and future.

The examples analysed in this chapter – TV documentaries/docudramas and historical exhibits – are situated at the intersection of popular history and academic historiography. They claim to be accurate and factual, but a critical analysis of sources is not part of the representation. After Hayden White and the linguistic turn in historiography,[3] it is important to see that the narrativization of history is achieved not only through "storification" (or emplotment; White, *Metahistory* 7–11), but through the recipients' historical experiences – filtered through memories, previous experiences, and knowledge[4] – which Daniel Fulda has demonstrated in a case study of the Wehrmacht exhibit in Germany in the late 1990s (Fulda 173–94). Jonas Grethlein has noticed a revival of the concept of experience in the theoretical discussions about historiographic narrative: "One can therefore say that the recipients have experiences of experiences" (Grethlein 320). Frank Ankersmit sees the connection between historical experience and the sublime as a solution for the representational challenges posed by the linguistic turn. It enables the representation of the "real" (Ankersmit 248–9). The haptic feeling creates a way of blurring subject (the – for Ankersmit subjective – historian) and object (the past). For Ankersmit, historical experience is beyond truth or falsehood; it is organized around the unique, unrepeatable interaction between subject and object and does not depend on any interaction with an objective, verifiable reality. Experiencing the past seems similar to experiencing a work of art (Ankersmit 312–13).[5] Nevertheless, one can argue that, if a museum or a TV documentary uses an experiential approach in representing the past, it still remains subject to being measured against truth-claims.

Authenticity and Aura

The more historical experience is emphasized in representations of the past, the more these representations become centred on creating feelings of authenticity for the recipient. Historical authenticity can be defined in two ways: witnessing and experiencing the past (Pirker and Rüdiger 19). Witnesses, whether through first-hand accounts, auratic places, or objects from the past, seem to guarantee authenticity. At the same time, a viewer of a film or visitor of a museum is increasingly led to "experience" the past. This can be achieved through the use of replicas, historical re-enactment, and the evocation of an authentic feeling that relates to the mood or atmosphere of the past (Pirker and Rüdiger 17–18), even if such an experience is always constructed and on a secondary level (Jaeger 89–109).

Walter Benjamin's discussion of the auratic work of art and its displacement through technology in the late nineteenth and early twentieth century can help one to grasp more precisely the difference between witnessing and experiencing authenticity. If the authenticity of the past is represented because, for instance, the exhibit displays a real jeep in which soldiers from the *Bundeswehr* were injured in the conflict in Afghanistan[6] or if a TV documentary represents a fragment of an interview with an eyewitness in Dresden, the recipient has a similarly auratic feeling of the type to which Benjamin alludes, due to the feeling of originality that connects the recipient to the past: "The here and now of the work of art – its unique presence at the place of its existence" (Benjamin, *Kunstwerk* 437).[7] Yet, if one discusses the authenticity of the past – instead of an original work of art in the history of its production – Benjamin's auratic equation changes. The original – such as the jeep or the eyewitness – still guarantees the aura and links the past with the present, but unlike an original work of art, defined by its totality that a viewer regards in awe, history is rendered as a space that the recipient wants to access. Here the mode of experiencing authenticity becomes critical and Benjamin's idea of medial change provides an explanation for the importance of the aura while experiencing the past. The medial transformation that Benjamin sees in photography and film in the age of reproduction captures a newly simulated aura of the past that supplements the aura through witnessing. Modern techniques allow for the aesthetic reduction of distance to the past and enable simulated immersion experiences. The most radical theoretical concept of such an immersive experience has been developed by Alison Landsberg as prosthetic memories: "living memories produced in those who did not live through the event" ("America" 66). People enter experiential relationships with events beyond cognitive means as sensually or bodily immersive knowledge.[8] The genre of TV docudrama has been described as creating a "second-order" experience, using a historic event as its dramatic base (Paget 87–8; Ebbrecht 39–40). The intersections of film and museum are particularly suited to mutually raise the other genre's capacity for displaying the past, so that temporalities, past and present, can collapse, and the recipient can gain a simulated experiential access to the past.

Musealization through Film

Unlike with a movie that draws the viewer into a fictional reality, immersing him or her fully in a fictional world, the viewer of historical documentary film is always supposed to be aware of the difference between the present and the represented past. The viewer recognizes, in other words, the propositional nature of the representation.[9] The more a historical documentary attempts to bridge this gap and immerse its viewer into the past, the more it leaves analytic distance behind. The traditional documentary technique of witnessing (through eyewitnesses remembering the past) is supplemented by other authenticity techniques that the historical documentary takes from the historical museum. The film simulates the museum's function as a place of immediate experiencing, since the visitor comes in direct contact with auratic objects, witnessing authenticity, while simultaneously acting as an integral part of the historical space, which promises qualities of "immediate" experiencing impossible in any other medium.[10] Consequently, the first part of this chapter will examine the musealization of TV documentary/docudrama by analysing representational techniques to re-appropriate past space and create authenticity in Michael Kloft's Spiegel-TV documentary *Feuersturm: Der Bombenkrieg gegen Deutschland* (*Firestorm: The Allied Bombing of Nazi Germany*, 2003) and *Das Drama von Dresden* (*The Drama of Dresden*, 2005), written and directed by Sebastian Dehnhardt, under the supervision of Guido Knopp.[11]

The first authentication technique is one that was genuinely developed for the genre of film: Eyewitnesses give interviews fifty to sixty years after the Second World War in which they remember the events of the past with a particular emphasis on their thoughts and feelings at the time.[12] The complexity of the remembrance process and how memory changes over time is at best alluded to; the general idea is to give an authentic testimony through a historical eyewitness – usually an ordinary German to connect to a mass viewership – in order to create a proximity to the past. As Wulf Kansteiner has shown in his analysis of the evolution of Guido Knopp's filmmaking, Knopp has become increasingly efficient in creating an aura of authenticity by allowing the Nazi propaganda images to speak for themselves and by relegating discourse to a secondary position ("The Radicalization of German Memory" 156). Kansteiner also observes that Knopp often cuts eyewitness interviews into pieces in order to integrate them into the larger arc of the film. This enables the film to achieve what Kansteiner describes as a *Gesamtkunstwerkeffekt* ("total-work-of-art effect"), in which image, sound, speed, and scale are coordinated at the level of the film as a whole. Consequently, the archival footage seems to correspond exactly to the eyewitnesses' remembrances in the small interview fragments ("The Radicalization of German Memory" 162).

Michael Kloft uses fragmented eyewitness accounts in *Feuersturm* in a manner similar to Knopp's style. The film presents twenty-second pieces of an interview, usually beginning with the voice of the eyewitness coupled with corresponding images. The eyewitness is then seen in the interview situation before the narrator picks up the story. This segment typically also includes corresponding images, for example, footage of a battle between German striker planes and American bomber planes, or of a plane going down and an allied aircrew member being arrested on the ground and threatened by German civilians. Used this way, the eyewitness accounts do not become prominent enough to develop their own story. They have an exclusively exemplary function illustrating historical details or emotions that fit into the narrative plotline of the film.[13] Here, the film uses the traditional means of documentary films for witnessing authenticity: eyewitness blurbs are spliced into a film as arguments or examples to support a narrative controlled by a bird's-eye narrator (Nichols 44–56).[14] Speed and progress dominate, which differs vastly from the contemplation and slowness that a museum could provide (Benjamin, *Kunstwerk* 464; Flügel 111).

In line with Kansteiner's observation of the *Gesamtkunstwerk*, eyewitness testimonies can also be used to create or represent a historical space that exhibits the past to the viewer in a way that re-appropriates past space. For achieving authenticity so that the viewer experiences the past, the mere exemplary use of historical eyewitnesses is not sufficient. Instead, the viewer accesses the past as a multidimensional space, as in a museum. The DVD cover of *Das Drama von Dresden* calls the film a "historical 'real time reportage'"[15] that stages the last thirty-six hours in which Dresden "perished."[16] Dehnhardt relies heavily on two dozen eyewitness accounts (all first-hand with the exception of one expert in fire protection) that are spliced in up-to-twenty-second fragments into the film. In the opening sequence, three witnesses, captioned as "damals [at that time] in Dresden," remember the flair of Dresden's cultural and architectural grandness and beauty at the time, partly illustrated by footage of today's reconstructed Dresden. Then the narrator, accompanied by corresponding pictures of Dresden's old city from before the Second World War, objectifies these accounts by mentioning the metaphor of Dresden as the Florence on the Elbe. The film develops about ten of the eyewitness stories in detail, as different historical persons move through the city and talk about their experiences, feelings, and thoughts on 13 and 14 February 1945. By weaving these strands of personal remembrance into a larger spatial array, the film works to create a virtual map for the viewer.

Viewed from the perspective of musealization, this technique is effective. The viewer is emotionally introduced to individual biographies of people who personally experienced the bombing. For example, Elenore Stojek (twenty-two years old) had just arrived with her ten-year-old brother Achim in Dresden, after fleeing from Breslau. They stayed with their aunt in the Große Meißner Straße, a place to which the film returns several times during the night as it follows other witnesses through their fate. The focus of the eyewitness account is the witnesses' experience. Elenore Stojek describes the horror of sitting in the basements during the first wave and how she put her finger in her brother's ears to protect him from a burst eardrum. Later, at the beginning of the second attack, she describes how Achim started to bark like a dog in his terror. The film moves along with different witnesses through their experiences in that night, and consequently the viewer feels almost part of a three-dimensional space, moving in time and space through a virtual map of Dresden, sharing experiences that are exemplary but, unlike in *Feuersturm*, also individual.

Musealizing the past as a space for the viewer to experience is further reinforced in *Das Drama von Dresden* through more direct simulation, namely, the integration of re-enacted scenes. The eyewitness biographies are supported by three visual layers: today's eyewitness in the interview setting, corresponding historical footage and photographs, and re-enactment of scenes as described by the eyewitnesses. The film juxtaposes the images and memories of eyewitnesses of the bombing of Dresden from today's perspectives with staged or re-enacted scenes in which the viewer is led to a specific street address in Dresden, where they then see, in dimmed light underscored with dramatic music, shadowy scenes of people rushing into the basements and experiencing the bombing. One example starts with a photograph of Gerda Birnbaum, in front of the camera, underscored by dramatic music, and the voice of present-day Gerda Neumann over a re-enacted scene of a younger woman, representing Gerda, guiding her blind parents down the stairs to the basement in the Holbeinstraße. The next camera shot is of Gerda Neumann today, juxtaposed with another shot of the parents on the stairs, before her voice becomes silent and the viewer sees a re-enacted scene in a basement with sounds of bombing at the Große Meißener Straße. With this movement between testimony and re-enactment, the documentary attempts to transmit to viewers how it feels to have the living memory of being woken up by the alarm, rushing to the basements, and then enduring the bombing.

The viewer is even more drawn into the film in yet another sequence: footage of British airplanes and of the sky full of bombs is interspersed with the testimony from British pilot Leslie Hay. The film then begins a computer simulation of a bomb being dropped on a residential dwelling, briefly interspersed with technical explanations by bomb-squad expert Thomas Lange. At the moment when the simulated bomb hits the house, the screen bursts, and the next shot shows the face of a woman barely recognizable in a brownish, yellowish shadow light. Shot by shot, these images become more recognizable as another re-enacted scene.

Das Drama von Dresden, which presents itself as "historical real time reportage," puts the past on a musealized display by simulating the past space for the viewer. The documentary catches a historical temporal moment that musealizes the past in an experienced space. This technique allows for the re-enactment of the past while simultaneously demonstrating authentic remembrance. Testimonial authenticity is achieved auratically (through the eyewitness remembering or the aerial footage), as well as through the indexicality of real historic places in the re-enacted scenes. Yet an experiencing or performative authenticity is also accomplished by allowing the viewer to participate in the shadowy scenes of searching for shelter, particularly in the simulation of hearing and feeling the moment of impact when the bomb hits the house.

Whereas the *Drama von Dresden* produces an imaginary map in the viewer's mind to generate a sense of authentic space and experience, in *Feuersturm* Michael Kloft uses another musealization technique to create auratic experience: the accessing of physical ruins of history in combination with archival footage and accounts by eyewitnesses and prominent historians such as Richard Overy and Jörg Friedrich. Friedrich, known for his popular-historical publication *Der Brand* (The Fire) in 2002, carries as the historian-voice an authority the filmmaker himself cannot convey, and becomes a second narrator who uses the aura of select spaces to suggest the collective psyche of the German civilians.[17]

An exemplary sequence that illustrates Kloft's collaboration with Friedrich starts with an extant bunker in Brunswick. Through the narrator's and Friedrich's explication of the space, the bunker serves as threshold to the past and a key way of dramatizing Friedrich's assertion that one of the most important aspects of German suffering during the Second World War related to the fear ordinary Germans endured in the bunkers. Moving around the bunker, from which the public is now barred, the camera shows signposts ("Only for baby carriages")[18] as the narrator explains major facts about the Nazi air-raid defences and the functioning of the bunker. He also emphasizes that the bunker is still almost in its original condition. As the narrator goes on to say, "From 1942 these bunkers became fortresses essential for survival at the National Socialist home front,"[19] the audience sees the historian Jörg Friedrich walking through the bunker. Then Friedrich disappears for a few seconds, but the viewer hears his voice, before they see him again leaning at the banisters, showing his ability to move further into the past. By moving into a space off-limits to those without expert credentials, the historian gains authority as an archaeological historian who is able to dig out the past, except that, instead of material background, Friedrich's realm is historical experience. Correspondingly, Friedrich's voice provides the insights into the psyche of the German civilians in a register as seemingly objective as the narrator's earlier recounting of basic facts: "One's nerves became prepared, the anxiety that in the coming war civil life would be a target. This idea is still valid today. Nowadays, every student from elementary school on knows that they will be a target in war."[20] While exploiting the tendency of many viewers to empathize with narratives of personal suffering, Friedrich's collective claim allows for the viewer to become part of the abstract collective, an effect that can be described with Landsberg's concept of prosthetic memory ("America"). As with Dehnhardt's re-enacted scenes, this allusion to collective experience in real space musealizes the past in the sense that it allows the viewer to empathize with being in a position of helplessness in the bunkers during an air raid. Unlike a fictional representation, which allows for more identification, the viewer keeps some distance – as he or she would in the space of the museum – in order not to fully immerse her- or himself in the past. Dehnhardt and Kloft clearly reflect upon the simulation of the past that cannot replace past experience, but immerse the viewer in a secondary form of experiencing the past's aura and authenticity.

Despite this immersion of the viewer in secondary experiences of the past, Kloft and Dehnhardt's films keep their historiographic-documentary distance. German television clearly shies away from the most extreme form of re-enacting and musealizing the past in film, when actual people re-enact the past to gain direct experience, as can be seen in the BBC series *The Ship*, in which a crew of fifty so-called experts and volunteers sailed a replica of Captain Cook's *Endeavour* from Australia to Indonesia, following the path of Cook's first voyage around the world.[21] For German history, affective history – particularly in relation to the Second World War and the Holocaust – has long been a taboo. In Vanessa Agnew's argument, German re-enactments "tend to elegize certain aspects of the past and elide what remains uncomfortable and troubling" ("History's Affective Turn" 302). Such re-enactments seem to rely on the notion that the past has been mastered; they are neither explaining historical processes nor interrogating historical injustices. There is therefore a challenge for such theatrical re-enactment of history, which collapses temporalities and privileges experience over event and structure, to maintain historical depth: "Rather than eclipsing the past with its own theatricality, reenactment ought to make visible the ways in which events were imbued with meanings and investigate whose interests were served by those meanings" (Agnew, "Introduction" 335). Following Agnew's goal of self-reflection in historical re-enactment, it is apparent that the musealization in TV docudrama – such as in Dehnhardt's and Kloft's films – makes the viewer aware of the constructed nature of historical experience, yet neither of the examples analysed in this chapter contributes to an investigation of ideologies of meaning. At the same time, Kansteiner has shown that the representation of the Holocaust on TV is more successful with viewers when a film provides clear explanations – ultimately a master perspective from a bird's eye view or an apparently omniscient narrator. Knopp's TV series *Holokaust* (2000) was relatively unsuccessful with viewers since it was cautious with historical interpretation and merely represented the events, following the notion that the Holocaust is incomprehensible (Kansteiner, "Entertaining Catastrophe" 137).

In summary, the techniques of musealizing the past in films shown in this section – creating a space following eyewitnesses, the re-enactment of temporal sequences in space, and the entering of ruins from the past – rely on visual representation and on the movement of the camera to draw the viewer into the past, but they also let the past become an object as a three-dimensional space accessible to the viewer as if it was displayed in a museum so that the viewer can "touch" the authentic, "real" past.

Film in the Historical Museum

The second part of this chapter analyses how historical exhibits use film material and footage as well as how they mirror film techniques to achieve an experience of the past for the visitor in a historical exhibit / historical museum. As with musealization in the historical TV docu-drama, film in the museum tends to be used to achieve an effect of greater authenticity in the museum's visitor. It can be reduced to support a historical argument, but often intensifies the representation of the historical atmosphere.

First, film – footage, documentary, and feature film – is used as a resource to document or to supplement narratives of the past. The permanent exhibit, which opened in 2006, of the Deutsche Historische Museum in Berlin (DHM) and its Second World War section (actually 1933–45) serves as a good example.[22] As has been often noted, the DHM's collection is very object- and image-based (i.e., less film- and sound-based). Katja Köhr and Karl Heinrich Pohl observe that the curators exclusively rely on "the aesthetic-auratic effect of the objects" (585). Objects convey far more historical aura than the visitor experiences through simulated history. The exhibit has a documentary or encyclopaedic approach, presenting the path of Germans in the European context through 2000 years of German history from a "neutral" perspective.[23] The exhibit only uses film material if it can be perceived as historical material of the time. Past and present are clearly separated. As a result, all nine films/screens relating to the Second World War display wartime footage.[24]

At the beginning of the 1939–41 section, there is a mini atrium that shows about half an hour of newsreel pieces from Germany, Poland, France, the Soviet Union, and the United States. They are centred chronologically around major events of the war such as the invasion of Poland, the blitzkrieg against France, the siege of Leningrad, and so on, illustrated with *Deutsche Wochenschau* (German newsreel) clips and at least one clip from the Allied side. The chosen multi-perspectival approach creates a distance between historical event and viewer; the visitor can learn to a certain extent about the differences and similarities in propaganda and newsreels. The film theatre sets the historical tone for the subsequent parts of the exhibit. Most other films, often on little monitors such as the ones about the blitz in London or the firestorm in Hamburg or a clip from Goebbels's Total War Speech in the *Sportpalast* (sport palace), are set up locally within informational panels. Consequently, they mostly supplement the text, objects, and images of those sections. The last three screens – US footage from the liberation of a concentration camp, a clip from Juli Raisman's Soviet film *The Fall of Berlin*, and the US air-force special film project *Flight over Destroyed German Cities* at the beginning of the 1945–9 section – set a tone for the atmosphere of the time. Unlike the films on the small monitors, they are either hanging from the ceiling or projected so prominently on a wall that the footage conveys a message about the atmosphere of the time. Besides the newsreel pieces in the mini-atrium, only Goebbels's Total War Speech can be heard; all other film clips are reduced to being silent films. The contextualization of the film is minimal:[25] the visitor without a guide knows neither which concentration camp liberation is shown nor any production details of Juli Raisman's film *The Fall of Berlin*, except that forty cameramen accompanied the advance of the Red Army. Historians have consequently criticized the DHM for not showing the constructedness of history (Köhr and Pohl 578–90). The reliance on moving images from propaganda material intensifies this problem, insofar as the propaganda status of most of these films is not critically discussed. Thus, the possibility for the visitor to develop a critical view of history is reduced. The film clips – even in the newsreel atrium, where contextualization besides naming the sources is completely absent – leave the visitor on her or his own, so that the documentary material gets the same auratic status as other historical objects and images in the exhibit.

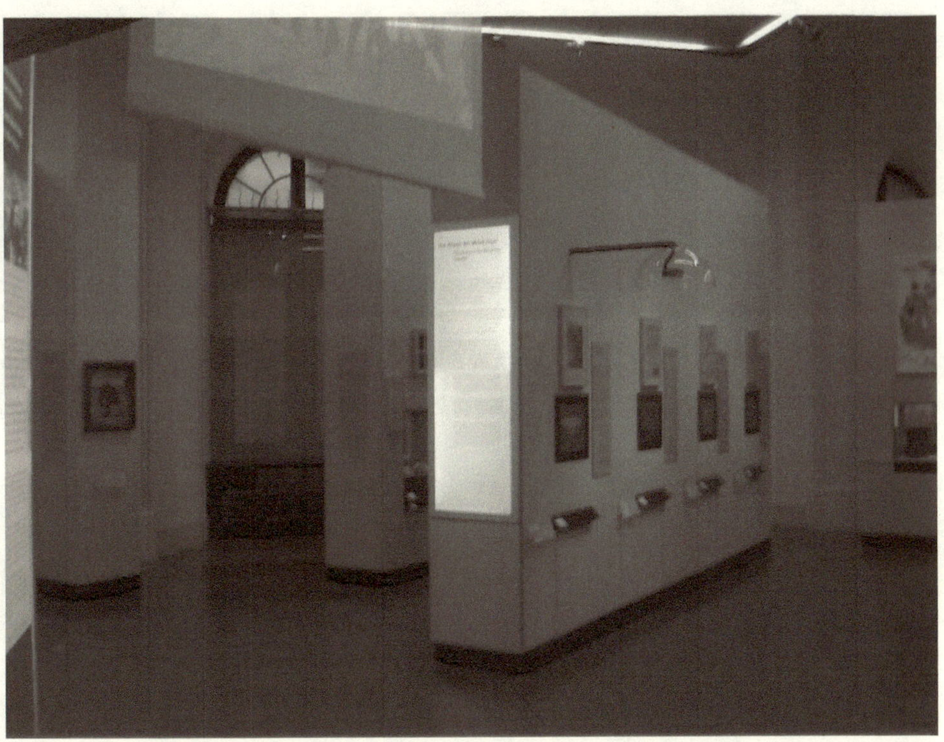

7.1 Four stations with monitor. Lead-up to the Second World War gallery. Permanent exhibit. Deutsches Historisches Museum, Berlin, 2011. Photo by author.

Does this approach to film documents in a historical museum also allow for experiencing authenticity? To an extent it does; one of the most interesting sequences is the actual lead-up to the Second World War. From right to left there are four stations at a wall (see figure 7.1): first on the annexation of Austria, with a clip from NS propaganda footage when the Wehrmacht entered Vienna; then the Sudeten crisis and the Munich Agreement, with a screen showing photographs; then the occupation of the rest of Czechoslovakia, with a clip from Johannes Häußler's and Walter Scheunemann's *Schicksalswende* (Twist of Fate, 1939); and finally the Hitler-Stalin pact to divide up Poland, with an audio news report from the weekly *Berliner Illustrirte.* All four stations are supplemented by cases with other documents and brief historical

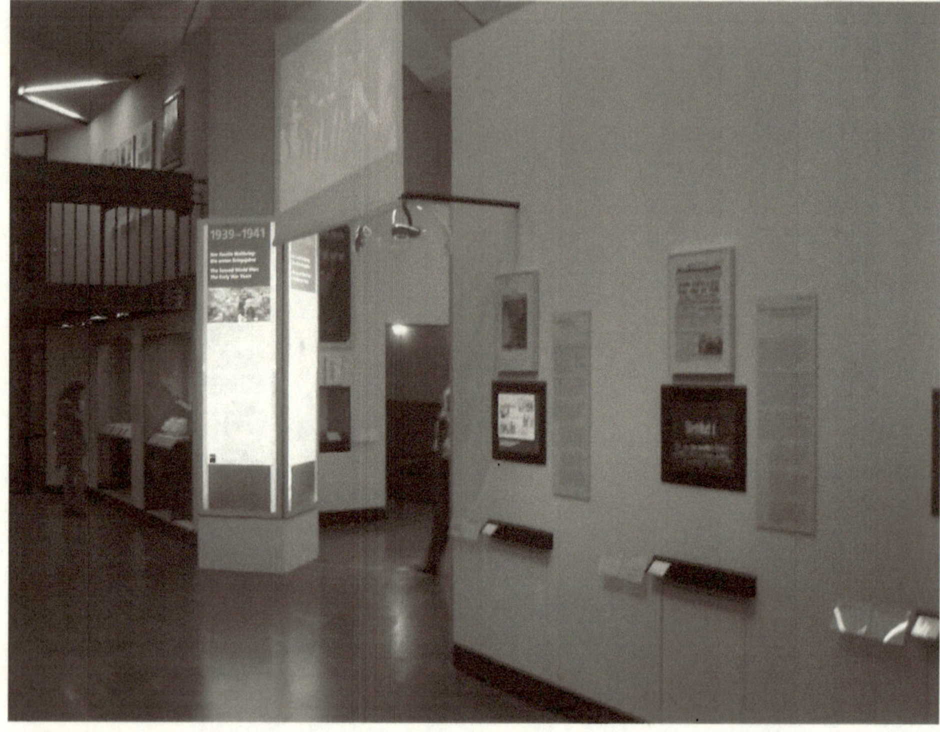

7.2 Entrance to section 1939–1941, beginning of the Second World War gallery. Permanent exhibit. Deutsches Historisches Museum, Berlin, 2011. Photo by author.

surveys. Again, the contextualization is fairly brief, but unlike most parts of the exhibit that are based on structural rather than on narrative order,[26] the visitor here experiences a visual (and partly aural) expression of how the Nazis started to expand their territory. Once the visitor walks along the four screens, he or she reaches the "entrance gate" to the Second World War, framed by the info post on the one side, the wall divider with the four screens on the other, and a translucent enlarged photograph of an iconic image of Wehrmacht soldiers tearing down the Polish border barrier at Gleiwitz (see figure 7.2).

Thus, the visitor moves along with Nazi expansion into the war, and then he or she can turn into the small atrium with wartime newsreels, giving the experience of a shower of propaganda, first by Nazi Germany, then supplemented by Allied voices. Consequently, the sources in this sequence promote less a testimonial form of expressing the authenticity of the past than an experiential one. The visitor can move with the propaganda of the main political events into the war and subsequently, in the mini-atrium, through the war. Film – in images and sounds – can reduce the auratic distance between visitor and historical subject matter. Particularly when set up in a narrative sequence, film allows for experiencing; however, it does not necessarily contribute to the understanding of historical reality. The visitor can lose his or her ability for contemplation, at least to an extent. Most film clips in the DHM, even the large projection of the *Flight over Destroyed German Cities*, though they influence the atmosphere of the room for the visitor, hardly immerse the visitor, since they lack narrativity and merely function as set pieces presenting history chronologically from a bird's eye view. There is a slight reduction of the visitor's distance from the past, and so the footage fulfils a supplementary function to recreate a kind of auratic authenticity.

Whereas the permanent exhibit in the DHM exclusively resorts to film as source material, which in the case of the Second World War and the Holocaust risks letting the visitors fall into similar propaganda traps as the people then experiencing the Nazi regime, film played a much more prominent role in the exhibit *Mythen der Nationen: 1945, Arena der Erinnerungen* (*Myths of the Nations: 1945 – Arena of Memories*),[27] curated by Monika Flacke, which could be seen in the Deutsche Historische Museum in Berlin from 2 October 2004 until 27 February 2005. The exhibit focused on the European perception of the Second World War in the sixty years after the war. In other words, it did not focus on the historical events, but on the perception and interpretation of history. The exhibit did not really represent new knowledge about the twenty-nine different national master narratives or myths about the war it presented; yet, besides its new comparative approach, it can also be regarded as a daring enterprise for the way it challenged prevailing differentiations of history and art, and between the representation of past reality and the performative creation of collective experiential worlds. In the sense of Benjamin's collapse of past and present, as seen above, it included a category of the present by integrating the perception of the visitor in the process of constructing the narratives of the past. Film played a particularly important role for achieving this presentism. The exhibit contained about fifty audiovisual stations with one two-to-three-minute film clip each.

In the exhibit, aesthetic effect overlapped with cognitive effect. The visitor could repeat the remembrance process by going through the exhibit – which melded with the visitor's pre-exhibit knowledge and attitude. It could be an active process of myth- or story-making and the questioning of those stories. In the panel on West Germany's remembering of the resistance, the film poster and a film clip of *Des Teufels General* (The Devil's General) was displayed.[28] On the one hand, the film scene represents the human element in the Wehrmacht and proves the existence of independent thinkers who opposed Nazism. On the other hand, the suicide of General Harras leaves room for interpretation and judgment. Is the suicide morally correct? Does it represent the most effective or wisest way to resist Nazism? Since the viewer only watches the fictional scene as Harras interviews his friend, one can easily form another impression of resistance in the Wehrmacht. The visitor reacts to the film clip on an aesthetic and emotional level. He or she experiences – from the present perspective – the interpretative choices and possible remembrance of many people in Europe in the last sixty years, who went to movies that shaped their ideas about the Second World War. This – in particular because of the fragmentary patchwork-and-collage character of the exhibit – creates a new historical world for each visitor, not based on historical fact, but on (especially visual) representations of perception. The use of film in this historical exhibit foregrounds the way that the reality and perception of the museum visitor contributes to the construction of a master narrative. To achieve this goal, the documentary and informational function of representation is supplemented by a performative one. The exhibit did not completely immerse the visitor in the past, since he or she could decide to see and understand the film clips as mere evidence of historical arguments that the exhibit made about myths and master narratives of the Second World War. But as used in *Mythen der Nationen*, film nonetheless offers an experiential function that puts processes of collective memory on display, allowing for a more open narrative. The visitor experiences the historical perception of the past, instead of events and actions from the past.

But even the most innovative approaches that let the visitor experience the past via film usually immerse him or her from a distance. In the new exhibit of the Militärhistorisches Museum der Bundeswehr (Military History Museum of the German Federal Armed Forces) in Dresden, which opened on 15 October 2011, one of the most provocative pieces is a clip from a Wehrmacht film showing a cat dying painfully after being exposed to chemical weapons. It expresses the horror of war and human atrocities in war and has a strong emotional impact on the viewer. Nevertheless, the viewer will be either shocked or sympathize with the cat, not empathize with it; the film cannot immerse the visitor in the perspective of the cat.

Film in museum representation can become more immersive, when, instead of merely employing the medium of film per se, exhibition layouts are created using film techniques. A historical museum can simulate the movement of a film for the visitor through its architectural and theatrical set-up so that visitors experience the museum's narrative in a linear fashion as if they are moving through the scenes of a film. The permanent exhibit *Kraków under Nazi Occupation 1939–1945* in Oskar Schindler's Enamel Factory (Fabryka Emalia Oskara Schindlera),[29] which opened in 2010, uses such a filmic technique. The visitor walks through narrow, corridor-like exhibit rooms, each organized according to a theme and generally following the timeline of the war. For instance, the visitor encounters Nazi announcements and swastika flags. The impression of Nazi propaganda taking over the city of Krakow is re-created through this performance. The visitor experiences the evolution of Nazi orders that regulated life in the city. When he or she enters the city square room of November 1939, the visitor sees a reconstructed tramcar as well as signs of the Adolf-Hitler-Platz and the shopping windows of Heinrich Hoffmann's store with Adolf Hitler portraits and books, the first German store on the square. When the visitor enters the market square for the second time in 1944, he or she walks between transparent Plexiglas panels which are spread throughout the room. The panels tell different stories of historical persons at that time in Krakow. In other words, the visitor feels as if he or she is meeting these people and encountering the everyday life on Krakow's main market square while trying to make their way through the panels. Moving through stage sets is not merely filmic because the film progresses in linear fashion, but because the visitor can experience each scene, so that the history of Krakow during the occupation becomes alive again. Consequently, the exhibit creates a cinematic perspective for the visitor. The exhibit uses sound, sight, and architecture to further simulate historical experience. It is as if a stage setting is unfolding before the visitor, who is drawn through the different scenes of the exhibit.

Conclusion: German Immersion and Its Limitations

The most interesting question that remains in this chapter is which intersectional representational techniques of film and museum are employed for which subject-matter in which historical context. In the context of the German museum – far more than in the context of an international one (such as in the US Holocaust Memorial Museum in Washington, DC), there is a hesitance to re-enact or stage the Holocaust or the Second World War. Conversely, in TV documentary, taboos arguably appear to be more readily given up. Nevertheless, because Germans are on the perpetrator side of Nazism, the Second World War, and the Holocaust, it is no coincidence that the documentaries mostly retreat to the German victim status, particularly raising the status of suffering civilians. Only then does immersive experience seem possible. In regard to film in the museum, it is mainly used for exemplary purposes and as documentation; the historical distance is maintained. In the permanent exhibit of the Deutsche Historische Museum, the few immersive experiences through film rely on the visitor taking on the role of mostly passive civilians or simply observers of events. The perception in the exhibit *Mythen der Nationen: 1945* is already more distant from the actual historical events in the Second World War, which allows for an immersive experience. Yet further immersion of the visitor into stage sets is either highly abstracted and universalized, such as in the Militärhistorische Museum der Bundeswehr in Dresden, or it is explicitly avoided.[30] The permanent exhibit *Topographie des Terrors* (*Topography of Terror*) in Berlin, for example, which opened in May 2010, evades any possibilities of immersion into the experience of the perpetrators and their crimes. It scarcely uses video and audio material, and clearly more to document than to immerse. It is certainly no coincidence that one of the most immersive Second World War exhibits can be found in Krakow, where the visitor can empathize with victims and heroes. Whereas the German cultural context still presents limitations to the possibility of using immersion to re-experience the Second World War, it seems much more straightforward to empathize with victims of the Stasi terror in the GDR, as can be seen in the Gedenkstätte Hohenschönhausen in Berlin (Jones, "Staging Battlefields" 105–7).

Despite these limitations and despite the necessary ongoing debate about a balance between affect and analysis, and between experience and critical reflection, film intensifies the aspect of perception in the setting of a historical museum, as musealization allows film documentaries to represent the past as physical space. Whether as ruins of the past, as re-enacted scenes, or as repetition of cinematic perception processes and simulation of historical experience through film for the museum visitor, documentary film and the historical museum clearly benefit from and rely on each other to evoke historical experience and authenticity. Thus, in creating historical space, docudrama meets the historical museum.

NOTES

1 Aleida Assmann discusses three basic forms to represent history: to narrate ("erzählen"), to exhibit ("ausstellen"), and to perform ("inszenieren"), either medially or locally (153–4). Although she recognizes that there can be infinite overlaps of these representational forms, she isolates the basic forms without discussing much hybridity between them. Consequently, the museum uses texts, images, objects, and digital media to exhibit, and the documentary is a media performance in film, on TV, video, or DVD.
2 Additionally, Keilbach (361) notes that dramatizing and emotionalizing history and the display of images predominate any analytic approach to history.
3 For a recent and mainly positive assessment of White's influence, see the essay collection *Re-Figuring Hayden White*.
4 See, for example, Tengelyi 185–99.
5 For a more detailed description and critique of Ankersmit's mutual exclusion of historiography and experience, see Jaeger 91–2.
6 This authentic object is one of the most prominent objects in the new exhibit of the Militärhistorisches Museum der Bundeswehr (Military History Museum of the German Federal Armed Forces) in Dresden.
7 "Das Hier und Jetzt des Kunstwerks – sein einmaliges Dasein, an dem Ort an dem es sich befindet."
8 For a discussion of recent European museum and memory places constructing an experience of authenticity, see Jones, *Staging Battlefields* 97–111.
9 "We enter the world in documentary through the agency of representation or exposition, that process whereby a documentary addresses some aspect of the world, allowing us to reconstruct the argument it proposes" (Nichols 112–13). For a structuralist analysis, focusing on cinematic documentary films, not on TV docudrama, discussing the representational technique to authenticate the past, see Hattendorf.
10 For the concept of the museum as a social space that allows for immediate experience, see for example Flügel 108.
11 It is difficult to point out the exact authorship in Knopp's productions, since they are produced by a team. Kansteiner argues that "the cutters, not the scriptwriters, are the real authors of these films" ("The Radicalization of German Memory" 154, note 2).

12 For a comprehensive summary of themes in recent representations of history in European television, see Bell and Gray 248–55. They list, among others, traumatic historiography, oral histories and testimony, reality and re-enactment, biography, topography, and absences.
13 See Lipkin for the persuasive powers that docudramas can develop through their emotional logic.
14 Though not the focus of the museum representation analysed in this article, video and audio testimonies of eyewitnesses who were victims in war and genocide have become an increasingly important method for authenticating the past. The travelling exhibit *Zwangsarbeit: Die Deutschen, die Zwangsarbeiter und der Krieg* (*Forced Labour: The Germans, Forced Laborers, and War,* since 2010) is a good example of this way of witnessing authenticity.
15 "Als historische 'Echtzeitreportage.'"
16 "die letzten 36 Stunden, in denen Dresden unterging."
17 Jörg Friedrich, in his voice-over narration, is always supported by matching footage. This correspondence of historical argument and images implies a synthesis of past and present and creates another layer of authenticity, whereas the voice of Richard Overy, who is always shown in his office, serves as objective relativization that cannot be obtained from eyewitnesses.
18 "Nur für Kinderwagen."
19 "Ab 1942 werden diese Bunker zu überlebenswichtigen Trutzburgen an der nationalsozialistischen Heimatfront."
20 "Es gab eine Vorbereitung der Nerven, der Ängste, dass im kommenden Krieg das Zivile Ziel sein würde. Das ist eine Vorstellung, die bis heute anhält. Jedes Schulkind weiß heute, dass es im Kriege Ziel sein wird."
21 See Cook 487–96. One of the "expert historians" on board, Alexander Cook, describes the challenges of re-enacting the past. He sees "a persistent tendency to privilege a visceral, emotional engagement with the past at the expense of a more analytical treatment," yet also marks the potential of investigative re-enactment to reduce the distance between viewers and the past (490).
22 For a survey on this section in the DHM, see Thiemeyer 42–5. For the genesis of the exhibit resulting in a lack of self-reflection and contextualization of objects, see Danker and Schwabe 591–606.
23 Robin Ostow calls it "a centralized, comprehensive, top-down narrative" (125).
24 The clips in the little film theatre contain twenty different newsreels from Germany, Poland, France, the United States, and the Soviet Union.

Additionally, one computer terminal, which allows the visitor to research the family story of the Jewish Chotzen family, contains five brief film clips.

25 This minimal contextualization of film can be observed throughout the permanent exhibit in the Deutsche Historische Museum, cf. Köhr and Pohl 586.

26 Ostow notes that the Second World War section "fails to represent this central trauma of the 20th century as a story" (131).

27 See http://www.dhm.de/ausstellungen/mythen-der-nationen/eng/gemeinsam_widerstanden_bundesrepublik_deutschland.htm.

28 Carl Zuckmayer's drama, which premiered in Zurich in 1946, was loosely based on the fighter pilot Ernst Udet. The play was made into a film by Helmut Käutner in 1955.

29 The museum belongs to the historical museums of Krakow (Muzeum Historyczne Miasta Krakowa).

30 For an overview of different ways that European First and Second World War museums emotionalize and immerse the visitor and stage war events, see Thiemeyer 236–53.

8 Framing the Past: Visual Musealizations of the Nazi Past in *Harlan – Im Schatten von Jud Süß* and *Jud Süß – Film ohne Gewissen*

ANNIKA ORICH AND FLORENTINE STRZELCZYK

"What is it with 'Jew Suess,'"[1] baffled critics asked at the unexpected success of the 2008 exhibition *Jud Süß – Propagandafilm im NS-Staat* (*Jew Suess – Propaganda Film during the Nazi Regime*) at the Haus der Geschichte Baden-Württemberg (Baden-Wuerttemberg House of History), which had devoted an entire show to the infamous 1940 film by Veit Harlan. The horrific, yet intriguing fate of Joseph Süßkind Oppenheimer, court Jew of Duke Karl Alexander von Württemberg and falsely executed for high treason, fraud, desecration of the Protestant religion, and lecherous relations with Christian women in 1738, has occupied Germans throughout the centuries. Oppenheimer's fate resulted in a plethora of artistic adaptations, Harlan's anti-Semitic propaganda piece being the most notorious. His film not only prompted the Stuttgart exhibition but also recently inspired two German filmmakers who used excerpts from the 1940 film in their respective works. In his 2008 documentary *Harlan – Im Schatten von Jud Süß* (*Harlan – In the Shadow of Jew Suess*), Felix Moeller traces how Harlan's work "resonates through the generations" by examining *Jud Süß*'s (*Jew Suess*) impact on the director's family (Buruma). Oskar Roehler investigates the making of Harlan's film by telling the story of Ferdinand Marian, the actor who played Jew Suess in the 1940 film, in his 2010 motion picture *Jud Süß – Film ohne Gewissen* (*Jew Suess – Rise and Fall*). The Stuttgart exhibition, Moeller's documentary, and Roehler's movie attest to Germans' continuing fascination with the National Socialist (Nazi) past and a desire to make sense of this history by putting its artefacts on display. These three latest engagements with the Jew Suess figure demonstrate the extent to which Oppenheimer and his many artistic explorations present a *lieu de mémoire* in German culture, one of those textual emblems that, together with places, concepts, and objects, constitute the sites where, according to Pierre Nora, "[cultural] memory crystallizes and secretes itself" (7; cf. Sheffi 422–37).

Organizers of the Stuttgart exhibition as well as the two filmmakers encountered the problem of how to investigate this *lieu de mémoire,* and how to display Harlan's *Jud Süß* in their own projects. The following discussion will primarily trace these questions in Moeller's and Roehler's films. Both films, we argue, function as distinct multilayered exploratory sites that articulate and negotiate a pedagogical mission regarding the significance of the Nazi past and its visual documents for the German present by engaging with Harlan's film and the Jew Suess figure through a variety of cinematic and museal techniques. Moeller's and Roehler's idiosyncratic approaches to one of the visual key artefacts of the Third Reich reveal a diametrically opposed understanding of the functioning of Harlan's film, thus resulting in conflicting assessments of how to remember and display National Socialist images. Both films, thus, throw into sharp relief the tensions that exist today between a broadly conceived obligation to collect, archive, and exhibit the Nazi past in order to educate the German public about the importance of the past in the present and about the seduction of Nazism that supposedly resides primarily in its visual legacy. By focusing on Veit Harlan's *Jud Süß* – arguably one of the most controversial *lieux de mémoire* in German history, Moeller's and Roehler's different approaches to this particular artefact from the country's fascist past raise larger questions regarding the memory of the Third Reich and the lessons to be drawn from it as well as the role that film as a medium plays in shaping, displaying, and remembering this chapter of German history.

History, Museum, Cinema

The present interest in Veit Harlan's *Jud Süß* echoes the film's success in the 1940s. *Jud Süß* showcases Joseph Süßkind Oppenheimer as an overambitious, scheming parvenu who insinuates himself into Duke Karl Alexander von Württemberg's confidence. As puppet master of the duke, Oppenheimer takes control of raising taxes and raises the prohibition on Jews living in the city. His persona and actions are met with civil unrest among the populace and the political representatives of the estates of the realm. Besides depicting the political and social conflict, Harlan's period drama centres on Oppenheimer's obsession with Dorothea Sturm, fiancée of his adversary Faber. After Oppenheimer tortures Faber and rapes Dorothea, the film ends with her suicide and Oppenheimer's public trial and eventual hanging. Harlan's melodrama was an international blockbuster[2] in the 1940s: the film, which drew more than 20 million people in Germany alone, and received critically acclaimed reviews at the Venice Film Festival, brought in over 6 million Reichsmark. While the film's actual role in inciting anti-Semitism continues to be debated,[3] Nazi officials clearly viewed *Jud Süß* as highly effective propaganda. The film appealed precisely because its anti-Semitic message was shrouded in cinematic modes of melodrama and entertainment, rather than in lecture-style documentaries such as Fritz Hippler's *Der Ewige Jude* (The Eternal Jew, 1940). The Propaganda Ministry described the movie as "'especially valuable regarding its national policies and artistic attributes' as well as 'worthwhile for a young audience'"[4] (Sheffi 434). Heinrich Himmler's enthusiasm for the film led him to order his fellow SS men to see the film, which also became compulsory viewing for the police force. In brief, *Jud Süß* played an integral role in Nazi authorities' efforts to provoke anti-Semitic sentiments and in propagandistic events across Germany and Europe.[5]

Consequently, the Allied Military Government labelled *Jud Süß*, along with other prominent Nazi propaganda films, a "Verbotsfilm" (banned film), prohibited public screenings, and decreed the destruction of the film.[6] During the post-war years, *Jud Süß* and its director gave Germans ample opportunities to confront the Nazi past, as several criminal and civil law suits scrutinized Veit Harlan's complicity in Nazi crimes in controversial, often highly publicized trials.[7] While Harlan was ultimately acquitted and even continued making movies, he never again experienced the same level of success and prominence he enjoyed during the Third Reich, and, to some extent, became a persona non grata. German courts, however, found it easier to pass sentence on the film:[8] in the 1960s, the Bundesgerichtshof (Federal Court of Justice) pronounced Harlan's *Jud Süß* to be "anti-constitutional," "inciting of racism," and "criminally libelous."[9] At the same time, the Friedrich-Wilhelm-Murnau-Stiftung (Friedrich Wilhelm Murnau Foundation) acquired the rights to the "Verbotsfilme."[10] These films are now called "Vorbehaltsfilme," films that, as the foundation explains, are only available under certain conditions: "The today so-called Vorbehaltsfilme are not available for general distribution. However, these films can be viewed anytime – at the Foundation's building – as long as the purpose of such viewing is for school, research, or production-related purposes. The many, constant public and nationwide screenings at movie theatres, schools, universities, etc. take place within the framework of an introduction and subsequent discussion."[11] Harlan's *Jud Süß*, then, is one of the most notorious Nazi artefacts in post-war Germany, not only a "Vorbehaltsfilm" but also a "Verdiktsfilm" (film that has been legally banned), and, as a result, has been mostly invisible – that is, not easily accessible and viewable – to Germans after 1945. In other words, Germans know of and about the film, yet few have actually seen it.[12]

Since the belief that Harlan had produced "an alarming film"[13] "with the most modern technology"[14] (Sheffi 434) dominated the debate about *Jud Süß* after 1945, the question of what to do about the film arose repeatedly.[15] These discussions centred on the problem of how to guide, if not control, the post-war audience's exposure to the film. The need to supervise access to the film seems to derive from the notion that Harlan's *Jud Süß* appears to set off a potentially perilous "cultural energy." For the purpose of our discussion, we appropriate the term "cultural energy," coined by Stephen Greenblatt in his 1990 essay "Resonance and Wonder." Greenblatt understands "cultural energy" as a felt intensity emanating from cultural artefacts on display – a concept that is reminiscent of Walter Benjamin's notion of "aura." Artefacts, Greenblatt explains, evoke resonance and wonder: "By 'resonance' I mean the power of the object displayed to reach out beyond its formal boundaries to a larger world, to evoke in the viewer the complex, dynamic cultural forces from which it has emerged and for which – as metaphor or, more simply, as metonymy – it may be taken by a viewer to stand. By 'wonder' I mean the power of the object displayed to stop the viewer in his tracks, to convey an arresting sense of uniqueness, to evoke an exalted attention" (19–20). In the case of Harlan's *Jud Süß*, resonance and wonder prove to be problematic, as its potentially dangerous resonance must be controlled carefully and framed didactically – its wonder, instead of being experienced by its audience, even contained and annihilated. The fact that one of the first post-war responses to *Jud Süß* and the role it allegedly played in proliferating anti-Semitism was the intent to destroy all copies of the film[16] demonstrates the virulence the film purportedly possesses. In other words, *Jud Süß*'s essentially destructive cultural forces have to be made visible to teach audiences about Nazi propaganda and the Holocaust, yet, at the same time, have to be confined to avoid unfolding their full anti-Semitic potency.

Museums have traditionally offered the space to negotiate and circumvent some of these issues associated with displaying Nazi artefacts. Indeed, few historical eras have been put on display as much as Germany's Nazi past, and even fewer have provoked the intense debates that the musealization of Nazism does. The term "musealization," often also described as "museum fever," refers to the broad, yet intense engagement with the museum in the wake of German unification (McIsaac 11; Koepnick 51), which saw the emergence of record numbers of cultural institutions and visitors (Korff "Aporien," 59; Korff "Reflections," 267).[17] For instance, the popular "Lange Nacht der Museen" (Long Night of Museums), now a yearly event where Berlin's museums open their doors all night long to the public, took place for the first time in 1997, and has been so successful that many other cities, even outside of Germany, have adopted the practice. In 2004, people stood in line for up to twelve hours to visit the temporary exhibit of the New York Museum of Modern Art (MoMA) at the Neue Nationalgalerie in Germany's capital. The show's success – over 1 million people from across Europe flocked to the exhibition – is mostly credited to a sophisticated marketing campaign, which cost over 1 million euros before its opening and sold the brand "MoMA" to mainstream Germany. The collaboration between the arts and other branches of the Berlin tourism industry was an integral part of this new marketing and branding approach to German museums, a strategy that has changed German museum culture permanently. Currently, exhibitions ranging from a glorious past of the cradle of European civilizations to recent German history, "from A like Allied Museum to Z like the Zucker Museum (Sugar Museum)" ("Museumspass Berlin"),[18] await buyers of the "Berlin Museumspass," which provides access to more than fifty museums for a period of three days.

The interest in museums and, especially, the Nazi past is, however, a manifestation of a larger cultural phenomenon that followed in the wake of German reunification: the widespread fascination with history and memory (Hockerts 15, 24–6). The unification process involved the merging of the divided cultural memories of the two Germanys after forty years. Not surprisingly, this cultural endeavour entailed thoroughly examining the period that last saw Germany as one nation, namely, the Third Reich. This coming to terms with the past often took place in museums, and increased interest in historical topics in general. Accordingly, exhibitions featuring historical themes tend to draw particularly high numbers of visitors (Hockerts 24). Cases in point are two of the most debated exhibits in recent years, the controversial *Wehrmachtsausstellungen* (*German Army Exhibitions,* 1995–9, 2001–4), which, for the first time, put on display the involvement of the

Wehrmacht in war crimes at the Eastern front and challenged the myth of the "saubere Wehrmacht" ("unblemished Wehrmacht"). The success of the Stuttgart exhibition on Harlan's *Jud Süß* is a more recent example of this greater interest in history, museums, and museum culture.

The appeal of history and memory – or, to be more precise, history and memory on display – translates into other audiovisual media: cinema and television, which have been invested in the representation of historical events from their very beginnings, reach an even larger audience and shape historical consciousness of today's mass-media societies to an even greater extent than the museum. As the example of Harlan's *Jud Süß* has already shown, displaying Nazi images is problematic if these images are themselves inherently seductive and degrading, if their undesirable "cultural energy" operates even beyond their own historical moment. From posters featuring mass graves of Holocaust victims and emaciated survivors aimed at the re-education of Germans during the early post-war years to the "Wehrmachtsausstellungen," from the intense fascination with Adolf Hitler in the 1970s to Guido Knopp's documentaries in the 1990s and films such as *Der Untergang* (*The Downfall*, 2004), the problem of how to reproduce Nazi images responsibly within contemporary film and other audiovisual media to access, explain, and demystify the Third Reich has always been a point of contention.

Yet, it is not only the showing of original footage that entails problems: although visual media can augment audience experience by offering immersive opportunities to access the past, they often, as both critics and artists have repeatedly pointed out, reproduce and recirculate the fascination and seduction emanating from fascist images. In his 1984 book *Reflections of Nazism: An Essay on Kitsch and Death*, Saul Friedlander explores what he labels "the new discourse" on Nazism that he sees playing out in literature and particularly in the cinema of the 1970s and 1980s (14–15). This discourse is marked by an earnest desire to approach and explain the Nazi period in a critical fashion, yet these films inevitably become mesmerized by the mystic, fantastic, and aesthetic aspects of fascism they set out to explore. Friedlander diagnoses an "overload of symbols; a baroque setting" (*Reflections* 45) and sees the dominant mode of emotional engagement of these films consisting in fascination, kitsch, nostalgia, and melodrama, exactly those modes, in other words, that were also the trademark of Nazi cinema. "The film experience is, par excellence, a site of mimetic emotions," Thomas Elsaesser argues. "Its ambiguous, libidinally charged play of identifications is therefore responding to a 'melodramatic' interpretation more obviously than a 'modernist' hermeneutics. Cinema, in this respect, is on the side of the excessive, perverse, or compulsive, rather than ruled by aesthetics of detachment and distance" ("Subject Positions" 150). What Lutz Koepnick labels German "heritage cinema," and Eric Rentschler has called the "cinema of consensus," is haunted by a similar dilemma: this nostalgic cinema presents the past as a cornucopia of suspenseful sights and sounds and turns "history into an object of consumption" (Koepnick 50–1; Rentschler, "From New German Cinema" 265). If anything, these debates are just a few examples of many that demonstrate the difficult relationship between visual material and media from the Nazi era and the ways in which our society of spectacle both mediatizes and didacticizes them.

Showing, appropriating, and seeing Nazi images and objects – original as well as fictional ones – are thus still fraught with anxieties and myths around their alleged seductive power and National Socialism's appeal. The institutions of both museum and cinema are faced with finding solutions to these issues, and both have developed strategies in response to this dilemma. In this chapter, we are, however, specifically interested in cinema's "museum function." In *Museums of the Mind: German Modernity and the Dynamics of Collecting*, Peter McIsaac has linked the renaissance of the museum to its alleged ability to organize material presence and to provide access to the experience of historical authenticity in an age of simulation. However, the task of collecting, archiving, and representing objects is not limited to the institutions of museums and other such cultural sites. To "describe inventoried consciousness in the museums and literary texts of a particular period," McIsaac coins the term "museum function," which indicates "the way objects are valorized, acquired and discarded, organized, displayed and hidden in a particular society and historical period" (12). Though McIsaac's usage of "museum function" focuses on museums and literature, we expand the scope of this term for the purpose of our discussion to also include cinema's role in engaging and shaping museal forms of representation and taking on a museum function when addressing the Nazi past. While visual material has always been appropriated to represent and access the past, "visual traces" themselves, as Stephen Greenblatt explains, "are put on display in galleries and museums specifically designed for the purpose" (19). How, then, does cinema engage with its "visual traces"? How does film collect, exhibit, contextualize, and didacticize – processes we will denote as museal and musealizing for the purpose of this chapter – its own visual history, especially if this history is traumatic and its original "energy" still potent?

Museal practices circumscribe different approaches and processes that are used to represent and make accessible cultural artefacts deemed to be worthy of preservation and, specifically, exhibition and display. One strategy of museal representation is, for instance, the attempt to "recreate the work imaginatively in its moment of openness" (Greenblatt 22). This goal is, for example, achieved by contextualizing and explaining the displayed artefact, by shedding light on its history and meaning across time and in different places. These processes of imagination – of embedding the artefact "in the contingencies of history" (Greenblatt 14) – are facilitated through diverse media, namely, catalogues, guides, signs, captions, and also visual material (cf. Greenblatt 22). Musealizing is thus always an act of interpretation and production of meaning, as artefacts become representatives of particular periods and events. As McIsaac argues, the "museum function" exerts a tremendous cultural force because it shapes the questions we ask about the past and formulates educational goals about the musealized objects and their past and present meaning (14). The relationship between the object on display and its viewer is thus a pedagogical one. Using film to display and explain Nazi film raises the question of how film can, in a pedagogically responsible way, frame a Nazi past accessible to us mainly through the cinematic images left behind. If fascism did not just employ visual media for its purposes, but could unfold its power and success only within these technologies, especially the medium of film (Strzelczyk 96), then the deployment of film in its "museum function," the relationship between the visual sources of photography and film from the Nazi period and the meaning generated from displaying them for a post-war audience, to contextualize the cinema of the Third Reich must become problematic. In other words, the seductive, dangerous power of Nazi images must henceforth be communicated through a framework without actually retaining these characteristics itself.[19]

In the case of Harlan's *Jud Süß*, these issues and possible answers continue to be explored and argued about. When the Jüdische Museum Fürth (Jewish Museum Fürth) announced in 2001 that it would screen *Jud Süß* as part of its special exhibition on Joseph Süßkind Oppenheimer, someone accused the museum's director of inciting the people. The public uproar that followed eventually forced the organizers to move the showing's location: the film was ultimately screened at a *Volkshochschule* (community college), instead of the museum.[20] While opponents of the showing, for example Ralph Giordano, particularly objected to the site and also feared the spread of anti-Semitism, supporters pointed to the educational benefits of confronting Harlan's film in a Jewish museum: "It would amount to a historical and pedagogical error, not to concern oneself with these [Joseph Süß Oppenheimer and Harlan's treatment] or not to address aspects of the NS era," Joel Cahen, curator of the Nachum-Goldmann-Diaspora-Museums in Tel Aviv, argued (Übelhack).[21] Similar opinions were expressed in 2006 when the travelling exhibition *Jud Süß – Geschichte(n) zu einer Figur* (*Jew Suess – (Hi)stor(ies) about a Figure*) opened in Göttingen, opting to only show excerpts of Harlan's piece. "As a teacher, I'm quite happy about the thoughtful didactics," one visitor commented. "The topic is presented in an exemplary manner. The exhibition allows older students to confront the issue of anti-Semitism" (Caspar).[22] In 2008, these issues then arose when the Stuttgart Haus der Geschichte opened its special exhibition on Harlan's *Jud Süß*, prompting some to ask whether "a museum is allowed to exhibit nasty Nazi propaganda," and whether "one [can] actually design an exhibition around one film"[23] (Böhm). The exhibition showed the film in its entirety, offering numerous screenings. The show proved to be so successful that, including the film's screenings, it had to be extended to satisfy the curiosity of Germans. While screenings of *Jud Süß* set out to enlighten Germans about the ways the Nazis abused and appropriated cinema, it is also crucial to see the film in its entirety in order to evaluate current attempts to come to terms with the Nazi past and its artefacts: "The viewer who has seen the original film [*Jud Süß*] can judge better if today's German cinema has been able to come to terms with the ghosts of the past," said some critics in response to Roehler's film (Zander).[24] Roehler as well as Moeller, thus, grappled with the questions of which parts of the original film and its alleged negative cultural energy to display, and in which way to frame its images.

To conclude, the question of how to best display and watch Harlan's *Jud Süß* continues to be an ongoing dispute, precisely because the belief the film allegedly possesses unparalleled seductive qualities and a dangerous "cultural energy" as well as the potential for gaining insight into the Nazi past remains equally unchallenged. In their respective efforts to display and musealize Nazi cinema within contemporary film, Moeller's and Roehler's diametrically opposed filmic treatments of Harlan's film both partake in this ongoing battle of the Jew Suess figure's museal imaginations, and further complicate the history and memory of its artistic and museal afterlife and its significance in German culture as a *lieu de mémoire*.

Musealizing Veit Harlan's *Jud Süß* in *Harlan – Im Schatten von Jud Süß* and *Jud Süß – Film ohne Gewissen*

The question of how to frame, display, and exhibit Veit Harlan's *Jud Süß* is thus fraught with indecision and the constant potential to cause controversy. Felix Moeller and Oskar Roehler, the two filmmakers who shared a desire to explore the 1940 film and its legacy cinematically, and embarked on their respective projects at the same time, also faced the problem of how to exhibit *Jud Süß* in their films. The first and most obvious differences in their choice of exhibition are the film genres they chose respectively and the focus they set on *Jud Süß*'s creators. Moeller's *Harlan – Im Schatten von Jud Süß* can be classified as an "expository documentary" (Nichols 167ff.), while Roehler's *Jud Süß – Film ohne Gewissen*, like the original 1940 film, meets all the pertinent characteristics of a melodrama. In the 2008 *Harlan – Im Schatten von Jud Süß*, Moeller traces how Veit Harlan's family has been impacted by their forefather's collaboration on *Jud Süß*, and how family members have reacted quite differently to Harlan's involvement and the Nazi past. He examines in interviews with family members how they view Harlan's responsibility, what they think about his work, and what lessons they draw from the family's participation in Nazi politics. Moeller fleshes out his excursion into the family memory by embedding the family members' exploration into the past into interviews with historians and film experts. Film footage from *Jud Süß* and other Harlan movies supplement Moeller's investigation, which culminates in the family's and Moeller's visit to the Stuttgart exhibition. Roehler's *Jud Süß – Film ohne Gewissen*, by contrast, does not centre on the director Veit Harlan but on the 1940s film's lead, Austrian actor Ferdinand Marian. The melodrama tells the story of *Jud Süß*'s inception, filming, and resonance in Nazi Germany by intertwining the history of making the Nazi propaganda film with the personal life and career of Marian. Marian played the charismatic Süß in 1940, and is portrayed by Austrian actor Tobias Moretti in Roehler's 2010 film. To narrate the production of Harlan's film and Marian's part in its making, Roehler re-enacts crucial parts of *Jud Süß* and sutures original footage from the 1940s film into these remade sequences.

By putting excerpts of the original film on display, both Moeller's and Roehler's films essentially become "guided tours" into the visual archival abyss of Nazi propaganda and *Jud Süß* in particular. Like curators, Moeller and Roehler selected, exhibited, and reframed footage from the 1940s film – thus, steering and channelling German audiences in their looking at the historical object "*Jud Süß*." To discuss the distinct approaches both filmmakers chose to musealize Harlan's *Jud Süß* in their respective films, our analysis will concentrate on the way Moeller and Roehler displayed and re-contextualized two of the most contested scenes of the 1940s film: namely, the scene in which Oppenheimer rapes Dorothea Sturm while torturing her fiancée Faber, and the scene that shows Oppenheimer's execution.

In fact, Joseph Süßkind Oppenheimer's death in 1738 ushers in the instrumentalization of his fate and persona as a visual and even museal phenomenon. His execution by public hanging in a red iron cage was staged as an outrageous, memorable spectacle for over 12,000 onlookers. The iron cage, where Oppenheimer's corpse remained rotting for another six years, became the second "museal showcase" – the trial ending with the death sentence being the first – that functioned as a pedagogical warning about the dangers of assimilated Jews for Germany society. His displayed body emerged as a central and highly mediated sight/site where the pleasures and thrills of looking and the disciplining of that gaze converged from the moment his persona entered the public eye. An early example are so-called *Schraubmedaillen*, double-sided lockets containing hand-painted images depicting Oppenheimer's fictionalized fate to inform, often mockingly, illiterate audiences of his alleged crimes, such as the corruption of Christian women, and ultimate doom. In line with this long tradition, the execution of Oppenheimer also served as the visual centrepiece of the anti-Semitic lesson Harlan's film sought to deliver. Not surprisingly, the trial and execution scenes from *Jud Süß*'s assume vital importance in Moeller's and Roehler's engagement with Harlan's film.

Of similar significance are the accusations against Oppenheimer regarding violating Christian women, which are mirrored in Dorothea's rape in Harlan's *Jud Süß*. "If this is propaganda, then we welcome propaganda," film director Michelangelo Antonio responded to *Jud Süß*'s highly praised screening in 1940 at the Venice film festival. "This is a convincing, incisive, extraordinary effective film ... The episode, in which Suess rapes the young girl, is stunningly skillfully done" (qtd. in Friedländer, *Jahre der Vernichtung* 480). The rape of Dorothea, played by Veit Harlan's wife Kristina Söderbaum, was an expression of artistic licence in regard to Oppenheimer's biography. However, the storyline has its origin in the charges regarding lecherous relations with Christian women that were brought against Oppenheimer. These accusations signify the anti-Semitic culmination of Oppenheimer's vileness and detrimental, even deadly, influence on the gentile community. Relating to Nazi propaganda, Dorothea's – the "Aryan" heroine – rape amounts to *Rassenschande*, the defilement of a female body through sexual intercourse with a Jew. In the context of the film, rape becomes the overarching trope to impress the notion of a violent penetration upon audiences, to which the German community depicted in the film is exposed through Jewish settlement, activities, and other ambitions. Often discussed as the most erotic episode, the rape scene in Harlan's film embodies all these elements: while Dorothea endures the rape by Jew Suess, Faber (Malte Jäger) is being violently tortured and thus emasculated by Suess's henchmen. Dorothea's loose hair, décolletage, and heavy breathing are captured by a voyeuristic camera that sadistically exposes her to the audience's gaze, making the rape and Faber's torture scene a both titillating and dreadful experience. In brief, the rape scene epitomizes not only the film's overall Nazi propagandistic morality tale but also post-war concerns about *Jud Süß*'s lingering potential to ignite anti-Semitic sentiments and promote Nazi ideals in contemporary German audiences.

Harlan's talent in drawing suggestively on the collective visual archive of National Socialism earned him the post-war label of "baroque fascist" (qtd. in Rentschler, *Ministry* 167) as well as a prosecution for crimes against humanity. He appropriated the enigmatic image of the caged Oppenheimer along with the victimized "Aryan" heroine to deliver cinematographic evidence of the danger that Jews, according to Nazi ideology, posed to the German people. In comparison to the "Aryan" heroes, Harlan's visualization and Ferdinand Marian's personification of Jew Suess render the Jewish protagonist an ambivalent character whose suave looks, compelling yet shifty features, and erotically charged personality make him the most fascinating figure in the film. Yet, the potential for the viewer to identify with Marian's ambiguous representation of Oppenheimer appears to only intensify the ultimate message of Harlan's propaganda, which climaxes in Dorothea's rape and death and in Suess's trial and execution. Designed as an exercise that guides the audience's gaze to recognize the imagined "true face of the Jew" underneath his numerous masks, the film shows Jews masquerading as Germans to infiltrate and destroy "Aryan" communities. The execution scene is the exact moment when Suess's panoptic gaze, which dominates most of the film and displays his initial mastery over actions, appearances, and characters, is completely transformed:

the power of his gaze is replaced by a presumably objective camera that turns Marian's character into the only object being exposed and exhibited, thus revealing the alleged "true essence of the Jew." Harlan's film channels the audience's erotically charged and violent impulses of aggressive scopophilia into supporting legalized genocide. The film's power lies, to use Eric Rentschler's words, in "learning how to look clearly" (*Ministry* 160) – how to recognize a Jew within German society by his alleged physical traits, behaviours, and discourse.

Ironically, the film functions in a similar manner today: it has become the training tool to re-educate contemporary audiences to see (behind) the propagandistic, potentially deadly anti-Semitism that the film propagates and, thus, to recognize the danger of National Socialism. At the centre of *Harlan – Im Schatten von Jud Süß* and *Jud Süß – Film ohne Gewissen* lies, we argue, the *Bildungsauftrag*, the educational and legally binding mandate that is defined in the laws governing the Öffentlich-Rechtliche Rundfunkanstalten (public broadcasting corporations) in Germany, and is meant to educate the German public – a directive generally accepted by both public and private media corporations as well as individuals when it comes to issues concerning the Nazi past and Germans' attempts to come to terms with it (Orich and Strzelczyk 294). Both Moeller and Roehler are examples of professionals internalizing this *Bildungsauftrag* and the Nazi past's inherent didactic message for their own work, and both films can be understood as a contribution to Germans' perennial attempt to come to terms with their Nazi past. In brief, both filmmakers approach and make use of Harlan's *Jud Süß* with this educational mandate in mind. Moeller's documentary film thus embeds sequences from Harlan's film in a didactical frame by situating the confrontation with *Jud Süß* in a museum. Roehler, by contrast, creates a melodrama that narrates the making of Harlan's film; the narrative functions as an interpretation of the Harlan film and its time. Yet, while both Moeller and Roehler, as we will discuss further, produce an interpretative, museal frame around the racist cultural energy of *Jud Süß*, both draw different lessons from and contradictory insights into the mechanism of the film, and its museal meaning in contemporary German society.

Limited Exposure: *Harlan – Im Schatten von Jud Süß*

In *Harlan – Im Schatten von Jud Süß*, Moeller examines *Jud Süß* and its Nazi history by asking questions about accountability and responsibility. Who is accountable for making *Jud Süß* into the "murder weapon"[25] it is perceived to be today? What accounts for its perceived negative "cultural energy"? How can the film be made accessible in a responsible manner today? "Those dark, unsettling times never leave you alone," Moeller confesses, adding, "My hope is that you learn from our lesson in history" (Rohter). Responsibility is thus not limited to the issue of how *Jud Süß* became the most successful propaganda film of the Nazi regime, but also extends to the question of how subsequent generations approach this "murder weapon" and the Third Reich in a responsible and productive manner to assign meaning to this historic document and its significance in the present. Both the rape scene and the execution scene demonstrate Moeller's approach and the conclusions he draws from his own engagement with Harlan's film: in short, Moeller promotes "limited exposure."

In his documentary, Moeller employs a multilayered and contextual approach to *Jud Süß* and its director to educate contemporary viewers about the film and the ongoing responsibility for the Nazi past. The documentary examines Harlan's film and its legacies in a number of ways that can best be described as pedagogically motivated distancing and reflection techniques that prompt audiences to critically reflect on Germany's darkest chapter. The documentary is designed around a visit of the third-generation family members of the Harlan clan to the 2008 Stuttgart exhibition, where Harlan's grandchildren, and by extension the documentary's viewers, primarily encounter their grandfather's work and his role in proliferating anti-Semitism. In other words, Moeller, whose film also ends with several shots and close-ups of Harlan's grandchildren viewing the exhibition, brings the museum into the cinema. He recognizes the museum as a cultural site that gives access to the past and transfers knowledge and insight to visitors, echoing Friedrich Knilli's sentiment that this exhibit and its accompanying catalogue might inspire the future generation's engagement with the story of Oppenheimer and his many media incarnations (111). Mirroring the tour through the museum and appropriating its instructional framework, Moeller's film teaches its audience about *Jud Süß* and its director through historical documents on display, explanations by the museum guide, the voice-over of the narrator August Zirner, a film scholar (Stefan Drößler), and selected screenings of several of Harlan's films (e.g., *Der Herrscher* [*The Ruler*, 1937], *Jud Süß*, *Immensee* [1942], *Kolberg* [1945]), designed to lay bare the anti-Semitic pedagogy of the film and the agency of individuals involved in its making. This pedagogically constructed, educationally streamlined viewing experience is enhanced by Moeller's interviews with different members of the Harlan clan. It is an unusual approach that shows how the director's family was affected by his notorious career and the way history resonates through the generations. The individual responses by family members, placed within the framework of educational instruction by professionals, create, at least at first sight, a complex, often downright contradictory space of possible reactions to and readings of Harlan's films and his personal responsibility. Moeller, however, ultimately guides viewers to adopt certain interpretations, since he strategically controls his audience's exposure to Harlan's film and the cultural context it emerged from. The documentary's viewers encounter most clips from *Jud Süß* as part of watching Harlan's family watching these excerpts within the Stuttgart exhibition, where clips are shown in showcases. At all times, the narrator's, film historian's, museum guide's, and family member's commentaries as well as additional documents frame the original clips cut from Harlan's notorious work. These excerpts, often tinted in different colours, only appear briefly on the full screen, without any extra didactic devices. Any clips from Harlan's film are, thus, only displayed within frameworks that establish distance and ensure supervision in order to lead viewers to recognize their responsibility in approaching the Nazi past and its documents as well as their own role in shaping history, memory, and cultural texts.

Moeller's museal approach to *Jud Süß* and his understanding of responsibility becomes most evident in the way he engages with the two aforementioned notorious sequences of Harlan's film. Both sections serve as a means to examine different notions of responsibility and agency regarding the production of the film as well as the making of history and memory. Moeller utilizes these iconic scenes to trace the extent of Veit Harlan's and his wife Kristina Söderbaum's involvement in the production of *Jud Süß*. In other words, Moeller examines their guilt in shaping Nazi culture and in creating a work of art that has played a part in the extermination of the Jews. He questions their self-perception – to some extent shared by most of their children – as innocent victims of the Nazi regime that relentlessly forced them into making a propagandistic film that was essentially under Goebbels's creative control. Moeller leads up to the sequence depicting the abuse of the "Aryan" couple by pursuing the question of how much knowledge Harlan and Söderbaum might have had about anti-Semitic propaganda and the persecution of the Jews to evaluate their guilt and accountability. After Thomas Harlan, Veit's most critical son, expresses his own puzzlement at his father's nonchalance about relying on Jews from the Prague and Lublin ghettos as extras in his films, Moeller shows a Nazi newsreel from September/October 1939: the clip discusses the subject of "this eastern Jewish sub-humanity" and the need to detain these "criminals," "dealers of girls," and "manipulators of international finances" while the camera pans across rows of emaciated Jewish prisoners, who lack any of the attributes that the voiceover ascribes to them. Likewise, Moeller contradicts Kristina Söderbaum's children's assessment that their mother was too naive and ignorant to have been aware of Nazi politics by showing an interview with the popular actress from 1973, in which she acknowledges her awareness of Nazi persecution of the Jews by 1938. By situating the torture and rape sequence in the context of official anti-Semitic propaganda and family and survivor memories, Moeller highlights the way in which *Jud Süß* visualizes centuries-old "anti-Jewish imagery and depictions" in the melodramatic mode of a feature film and in the portrayal of its Jewish protagonist, whose characterization is always contrasted with the depictions of the film's "Aryan" heroes personifying Nazi ideals. Moeller thus demonstrates how the film and its makers were deeply embedded in but also shaped Nazi discourse.

The inclusion of other sources and dissenting opinions by family members challenges and counterbalances the predominant familial, communicative memory, which remembers Harlan and his wife as being neither anti-Semites nor National Socialists. In this way, Moeller also questions common notions of what it means exactly to be an anti-Semite or a Nazi. The arrangement of different documents and voices suggests that Harlan not only must have been aware of the film's anti-Semitism but that he must have also made conscious decisions in regards to rendering these sentiments narratively and aesthetically on screen. While Moeller thus sheds doubt on Harlan's and Söderbaum's non-involvement in Nazi politics, he also does not provide a definite answer on the extent of their belief and support of National Socialism. Rather, he foregrounds the complexity of factors that lead to the creation of *Jud Süß* by emphasizing their creators' desire to pursue a career in Nazi cinema as a motivating factor. In other words, both Harlan and Söderbaum were committed to execute their jobs to the best of their abilities within the political context of the time, refusing to deliver mediocre performances. Their responsibility and agency lie in the fact that they contributed to making a "great film": in fact, that Kristina Söderbaum played the female lead ultimately points, as Thomas Harlan argues, more to Harlan's investment in and willingness to take on the film than to coercion by the Nazi regime. "The truth is the non-anti-Semite was the best person to sharpen the knives," Thomas Harlan explains, rejecting explanations based solely on his father's anti-Semitism as "too superficial." Moreover, he, and by implication Moeller, argues that his father's accountability did not expire with the completion of *Jud Süß*: "What makes this particularly dreadful is that the person who did this didn't comprehend what he had been complicit in. And by the time he might have been expected to understand it, he still hadn't realized that he no longer should practise this profession."[26] Moeller thus resurrects several cultural, social, and personal factors that contributed to the making of this Nazi text, disclosing the complicated mechanisms that make up history. Hatred of Jews, the documentary indicates, is not enough to explain the phenomena of Nazism, its racial policies, and, certainly not, *Jud Süß*. Moeller emphasizes the way people are entrenched in the historic fabric of their time by evoking "resonance": while cultural frameworks shape agency, Moeller makes an argument for the responsibility that individuals have in making and remembering history as individuals as well as members of families and larger social communities.

The notion of personal responsibility that Moeller promotes through his examination of Veit Harlan's and Kristina Söderbaum's complicity in making *Jud Süß* is mirrored in and extended to a more general appeal for approaching and handling media in a responsible way. Moeller's engagement with *Jud Süß* highlights cinema's ideological nature. Rather than simply vilifying Harlan's film, Moeller makes an argument that any text has the potential to be problematic: the cinematic image is inherently flawed as it easily carries ideological, propagandistic, or stereotypical messages. All cinematic images hold a seductive power that tends to manipulate the viewer through the powerful fictional worlds they create. While the characterization of Jew Suess points to the reproduction of "anti-Jewish imagery and depictions," Moeller particularly focuses on Kristina Söderbaum and her character Dorothea Sturm to discuss the way cinematic conventions contributed to making *Jud Süß* such a propagandistic success, a fact that thus problematizes any cinematic creation. As part of his attempt to contextualize the film historically, Moeller demonstrates how *Jud Süß* belongs to the melodramatic genre, echoing Linda Schulte-Sasse's efforts to disclose the similarities between *Jud Süß* and bourgeoisie tragedy. For instance, he situates the rape and death of Dorothea Sturm within the genealogy of other characters that Kristina Söderbaum played throughout her career.

Söderbaum, who only acted under her husband and aspired to become the next Elisabeth Bergner and Marlene Dietrich, embodied the "archetypical naïve childlike woman" who "became a screen idol with her natural blond Aryan looks." Since her characters often drowned on screen, Söderbaum soon acquired the nickname "[the Third Reich's] water corpse."[27] By showing several of Söderbaum's on-screen deaths (*Youth* [1938], *Jud Süß* [1940], *The Great City* [1942], *The Great Sacrifice* [1944]) – including in the post-war film *Hannah Amon* (1951), Moeller guides the viewer to understand how *Jud Süß* relied on common cinematic genres such as the melodrama and tropes originating in literature to have its storyline come to life and, thus, sheds light on the text's deliberate constructedness. By revisiting the circumstances around Harlan's decision to produce films supercharged with emotion and drama, Moeller emphasizes the agency and responsibility individuals hold in creating images: "If my films found favour, it was due to innocence and its loss, Eros and nature, cruelty, murder and suicide," Veit Harlan said of his work. Moeller, by quoting and focusing on this comment in his film, mines these themes by showing how they unintentionally also summarize the main themes of *Jud Süß* and thus provide an explanation for its success. "[My father] had a weakness for things heavenly," Thomas Harlan states in Moeller's film. "It was the postulations of feelings that didn't really exist. The synthetic creation of sentiment … I fear that 'The Great Sacrifice' and 'Immensee' are prime examples of this: Creating artificial sentiment and lending it … credibility." Moeller then shows a short clip from *Immensee* (1943) to illustrate Harlan's kitschy, affective style. Pointedly, the scene shown features the farewell between the film's two protagonists, Elisabeth (also played by Kristina Söderbaum) and Reinhardt: Elisabeth hands Reinhardt, already travelling on the train, a photo of herself, which Reinhardt immediately kisses, and which becomes a substitute for the real Elisabeth. Moeller thus highlights the affective, yet also life-like, power of images. "This is the cinema of illusion and of playing with emotions," film scholar Stephan Drößler explains in front of piles of film reels and other cinematic equipment. "And I'd say that was what was essential to him. And that this neatly coincided with the effects that Goebbels asked for and with the fundaments of the Third Reich." Moeller thus demonstrates how *Jud Süß* became what it is thought to be because of its intrinsic entrenchment in cinematic techniques and conventions and Harlan's brilliant understanding of cinematic technology. By doing so, Moeller, however, situates the film not only within familial and national history, but also in film history. In other words, Moeller does not simply put on display and musealize other films besides *Jud Süß*; more importantly, he also problematizes the medium itself in his documentary, and thus educates viewers about the power of cinema.

Moeller's engagement with film history indicates how he situates his own film within this framework and cinematic genealogy. *Harlan – Im Schatten von Jud Süß* functions as an intervention as he aims to interrupt the tradition of anti-Semitic imagery. His carefully constructed approach to Harlan's film and his educational endeavour is most explicit in the way he addresses the execution scene. He makes a conscious decision to omit the iconic cage and hanging scene, refusing to show the one image in which the anti-Semitic propaganda of the film most visibly culminated. Instead, he only selects clips from the final moments of Suess's life that serve as a critical comparative exercise about the notion of responsibility: he frames the trial/execution scene in *Jud Süß* through the lens of Harlan's trial and acquittal. The actual clips from Harlan's film are preceded by emotional interview segments with Maria Koerber, Harlan's daughter, and Jessica Jacoby, Harlan's half-Jewish granddaughter, who comment on Harlan's guilt and responsibility for the making of *Jud Süß* and assess his claim to have acted on Goebbels's orders alone. While he opts out of showing the actual execution scene, the visual centrepiece of almost all Jew Suess's representations, he focuses on another clip from the final sequences of the film, the trial scene, during which Suess rejects agency and responsibility, claiming to have only followed orders. This particular segment closes by cutting to Thomas Harlan, who explains, in no uncertain terms, that *Jud Süß*'s lesson in state-sanctioned genocide should have resulted in his father's conviction. Thomas Harlan's critique and outrage is thus directed not only at his father but also at post-war German society, which saw no contradiction in the fact that Harlan had been acquitted twice by a judge who was himself guilty of Nazi crimes. While Moeller consequently encourages the contemporary audience to draw parallels with the use and abuse of privilege, power, and responsibility, he remains so suspicious of the alleged seduction of the anti-Semitic images that he opts out of showing them altogether. In other words, Moeller believes that some images carry a certain destructive "cultural energy" that cannot be exhibited: these images of the past cannot be put on display because it is impossible to escape the position of the anti-Semitic gaze. Moeller thus opts for discussion instead of display, limiting the viewers' exposure to Harlan's images that had allegedly such devastating effects during the 1940s. *Harlan – Im Schatten von Jud Süß* employs both an actual museum as well as the "museum function" to frame his investigation into the German Nazi past, the filmic oeuvre of Harlan, his most infamous work *Jud Süß*, and the ripples that Harlan's work have caused into the present among his family as well as German society.

Melodrama and Museum: *Jud Süß – Film ohne Gewissen*

Jud Süß – Film ohne Gewissen investigates Veit Harlan's making of *Jud Süß* by exploring, through the genre of melodrama, the figure of Ferdinand Marian, the Austrian actor who played the role of Suess. The film's melodramatic narrative serves as the frame that interprets and explains the making of *Jud Süß* and provides the explanatory context for the infamous scenes and sequences from the original film. The narrative shows Marian to be a victim of the German propaganda machine and reinforces this message by inventing a number of unhistorical details, such as a Jewish wife who perishes in a camp, an act of rebellion against Goebbels that results in smashing a glass ashtray in the minister's office, refusing to take on the role of Suess, or an ardent Nazi maid blackmailing the actor. The narrative context, as with many history films, shapes historical representation less according to known facts than in response to the dramatic demands of the genre, such as sexual tension, redemption, closure, or political-ideological viewpoints. By extending the notion of museum function to the cinema, we argue, *Jud Süß – Film ohne Gewissen* utilizes its narrative frame to exhibit and reinterpret crucial aspects of *Jud Süß*.

Similarly to Felix Moeller's documentary, the centrepiece of Oskar Roehler's *Jud Süß – Film ohne Gewissen* forms the staging of the infamous rape sequence and the insidious execution scene from Harlan's *Jud Süß*. The 2010 film tells the story of the inception of Harlan's *Jud Süß*, filming, and resonance in Nazi Germany and intertwines the history of making this film with the personal life and career of Ferdinand Marian, the Austrian actor who played the charismatic Suess in 1940, who in Roehler's movie is played again by an Austrian actor, Tobias Moretti. Roehler re-enacts crucial parts of *Jud Süß* to narrate the production of Harlan's film and Marian's part in its making by suturing original footage from the 1940s film into these remade sequences. To achieve the greatest possible verisimilitude to Harlan's film, Roehler not only enlists actors in almost all major roles who possess a striking resemblance with the cast of the 1940s film, but his remade episodes also mimic the setting, camera angle, lighting, costumes, background, and sepia tone of the original film. "Some scenes we re-enacted one to one," explains Roehler, "others we even copied digitally into the original" (Kniebe).[28] These reproduced sections thus become almost indistinguishable from the original in terms of the actors' diction, intonation, gestures, and movements, with Moretti often "interacting" with the original actors in Harlan's film. Roehler then screens this hybrid simulation throughout his film. For instance, Roehler re-performs the rape scene with Tobias Moretti and Paula Kalenberg acting as Marian/Suess and Söderbaum/Dorothea and then splices footage from Harlan's original into the episode. The resulting mash-up thus intersperses the rape re-enacted by Moretti and Kalenberg with the simultaneous torturing of the original Faber (Jaeger). During the execution scene, Roehler again has Moretti acting as Marian in the role of Suess, with the effect that Moretti/Marian/Suess pleads with a court (scene) from the original Harlan film. The rape and torture sequences then are screened at the occasion of the film festivals in Venice and Berlin.

Both these scenes are staged in parallel fashion and invite comparison. Roehler asks spectators to "see for themselves" how 1940s audiences may have received Harlan's film. Roehler pans across the festively decorated auditoriums, taking in audience excitement in anticipation of *Jud Süß*'s premiere. In fact, the two scenes consist of tightly edited cross-cutting between audiences, close-ups of Marian/Moretti watching his onscreen performance as Suess, and the modified *Jud Süß*'s episodes themselves. The two scenes also mark different stages of insight that the protagonist gains by watching himself on screen and perceiving the effects of his performance on the audience. The Venice film screening of the rape scene represents the climax of Roehler's film. In Venice, the titillating rape and torture scene, which Roehler imbues with historical accuracy by providing Italian subtitles, is shown to have an arousing effect on Söderbaum (Kalenberg), who watches together with Marian (Moretti) their performance during the premiere in a packed cinema. Roehler stages the success of Marian as the Jewish seducer, who allegedly received large amounts of female fan mail, as the success of the romantic lead: after the screening, Marian is inundated with requests for autographs by young female fans. In an ensuing discussion during the film's after-party, a prominent Italian film producer, who is smitten by Marian's charisma on and off screen, discusses Marian's potential as an international film star: "I see you as a lover – how should I say – with a certain edge."[29] The response by Marian's fictional Jewish wife, "How come you know my husband so well?,"[30] alludes not only to his many affairs she is aware of but also to Marian/Moretti's self-perception as an actor in control of his performance that has managed to seduce fans, the Nazi elite, and Goebbels alike. The following sequence that takes place at *Jud Süß*'s premiere in Berlin and features the execution scene also marks the turning point for Marian's career.

In Germany's capital, the movie theatre and stage are flanked and framed by Nazi banners and swastikas, and the Berlin audience stares mesmerized at the modified *Jud Süß* film while Marian/Moretti watches his own execution on film. The triangulated cross-cutting between Marian/Moretti, the modified Harlan film, and the stunned audience functions to inform about Marian/Moretti's growing awareness that he is not just the seducer but also the seduced. *Jud Süß*'s performance and the reaction it receives demonstrate how his performance in the film emotionally manipulates Germans to accept anti-Semitism and National Socialism. The sequence also positions Marian, whose fate and career are sealed with the making of the film, as the affective touchstone that solicits for the audience of Roehler's film access to both the historical pressures and ideologies of the time, but also the individual ambitions and the conditions for filmmaking.

The excerpt ends with the original film's warning to ban Jews from German cities, directed at next generations. Roehler then cuts to a speech by Joseph Goebbels (Moritz Bleibtreu), who uses the ending of Harlan's film to call for the annihilation of the Jews before the Nazi elite. Afterwards, the film's cast mingles at the reception party where the sinister Goebbels introduces Marian to the oversexed wife of a concentration camp commandant, Frau Frowein (Gudrun Landgrebe), who longs to live out her fantasy about having sex with a Jew. Marian (Moretti) has fervent, rather aggressive sexual intercourse with Frowein, which restages the rape of Dorothea Sturm by Suess. Marian and Frowein simulate the rape sequence they– and Roehler's audience in the previous sequence – just watched, with Marian reciting the dialogue from *Jud Süß* while Frowein impersonates Dorothea, including the famous white handkerchief that the original Suess used as a sign to prompt and interrupt the torture of Faber. The alleged seductive and destructive "cultural energy" of Harlan's film materializes in Roehler's film as increasingly transgressive sexuality and death.

As in Felix Moeller's documentary, Roehler equally displays excerpts from Harlan's *Jud Süß* and thus musealizes Harlan's film within his own film. Roehler also relies on similar distancing devices: his viewers watch the imagined 1940s audiences watch a mashed-up, altered, *Jud Süß*.[31] Roehler, like Moeller, is also interested in the production and producers and cast of Harlan's original. Like Harlan's career in Moeller's film, Marian's story also unfolds as an ambivalent one: the desire to advance one's career and other personal motivating factors played as much into the creation of the film as the ideologies of the time. However, Roehler's strategy of appropriating the original and positioning these simulations in his film point to a different understanding of the way Harlan's work functioned as an anti-Semitic propaganda piece in the past and present, of the possibilities and limits of the genre of narrative cinema, and of the nature of the cinematic image and apparatus in general. For Roehler, the dangerous "cultural energy" of Harlan's film lies, in fact, outside and detached from the audiovisual images per se, but is anchored in the cinematic narrative that was shaped by the ideological forces at work at the time. In other words, if certain sequences from Harlan's film and any remakes are situated within a different narrative and context, the images themselves lose their suspected toxic quality. According to Roehler, the tradition of "anti-Semitic imagery and depiction" can be remembered and put on display if one approaches and contextualizes these artefacts in a morally conscious and educational framework. Roehler credits narrative cinema with the ability to realize this task.

If one were to follow Roehler's assessment, Harlan's film was simply missing a moral conscience when telling its story of Oppenheimer: the film, as Roehler's title indicates, is a film "ohne Gewissen" (without conscience). Thus, Roehler supports the ongoing censorship of Harlan's film. "Of course, *Jud Süß* must remain censored. Today's audiences lack the necessary political consciousness even more so than ever before," Roehler says just before the premiere of his film at the 2010 Berlinale, Germany's annual international film festival in Berlin. "Unbelievable casting, cutting dramaturgy, brilliant manipulation. If one shows *Jud Süß* to any Neo-Nazis from Brandenburg today, they would put on their battle gear and march towards the Jewish synagogue," he explains (Kniebe).[32] Seventy years after its making, Harlan's anti-Semitic propaganda piece has, Roehler admits almost admiringly, not lost any of its seductive allure and ideological assault power, against which contemporary audiences are as defenceless as audiences in the 1940s if they were to watch the film in its entirety. Although Roehler follows the general consensus that Harlan's film is a "murder weapon," he seems to believe that excerpts from the film can be displayed through simulation and contextualization – while Moeller's documentary argues that any of the individual images of Harlan's film cannot be separated from the film's overall anti-Semitic message and, indeed, cinema's ambiguous relationship to the dissemination of ideology. That Roehler does not locate the fascism of Nazi images in their mesmerizing surfaces but in an ideological, cultural content separable from cinematic form and apparatus determines his approach to the original scenes from Harlan's film.

Jud Süß – Film ohne Gewissen then displays many fewer scruples with exposing contemporary Germans to the power of Nazi images and paraphernalia. The film happily delves into all worn clichés about Nazi kitsch and its cinematic renderings, from Nazi flags and swastikas to overpowering architecture and spaces, from transgressive sex to smashing uniforms, from allusions to István Szabo's *Mephisto* to Quentin Tarantino's *Inglorious Basterds*. The Nazi past in Roehler's film unfolds as a grand melodramatic spectacle of trauma, destruction, and redemption, in which both the seduction of Nazism and the pressure of the regime conform to make and break the individuals caught in its web. Following the conventions of "heritage cinema" (Koepnick), exposing fascist ideology for Roehler is thus a question of narrative: "A completely legitimate plot device" as a way to convey "historical inner truth," Roehler says about the way he crafted the plot and used cinema's melodramatic properties to offer his audience insight into the workings of the Nazi film and propaganda machinery (Scholl).[33]

The depiction of the 1940s captivated audience and actors mesmerized by their own performance, the mash-up of re-enactments and original footage, and the 2010 film's own narrative of Marian's life as a victim of Nazism, furnished with fictional, emotionally charged bits to increase the story's dramatic effect, amount to a gradual build-up of emotion and affect. "It was Oskar's desire to intensify the melodramatic aspects," Klaus Richter, who wrote the original script for *Jud Süß – Film ohne Gewissen*, notes (Rodek).[34] This strategy of "carving out feelings,"[35] which Richter believes to be Roehler's greatest strength, also includes the use of "kitsch" (Rodek). Roehler's decision to tell the story of Harlan's *Jud Süß* by maximizing its portrayal's melodramatic and emotional effects explains his approach to the original and the Nazi past: for Roehler, insight into the way this notorious "murder weapon" was created and functioned can be gained through emotions. In other words, historical artefacts and history can be accessed by being "felt." In his essay "Sympathy for the Devil: Cinema, History, and the Politics of Emotion," Johannes von Moltke diagnoses a widespread infusion of history with emotion in post-unification culture. Audiovisual media, that is, television and film, "arguably take pride of place in the production of a diffuse but distinctly new feeling for history" (18). Such "media," he explains, "have supplied a stream of historical representations characterized by strong affect and emotion" (18). To create historical consciousness and conscience, Roehler generates "excess," which is supposed to tap into and elicit an emotional understanding of Germany's most contentious and conflicted chapter of history. "Melodrama, however, refers to a much broader category of films and a much larger system of excess," Linda Williams states in her 1991 article "Film Bodies: Gender, Genre, and Excess." "It would not be unreasonable, in fact, to consider all three of these genres [pornography, horror, and melodrama] under the extended rubric of melodrama, considered as a filmic mode of stylistic and/or emotional excess that stands in contrast to more 'dominant' modes of realistic, goal-oriented narrative" (3).

The screening of the rape and execution mash-ups serves Roehler as a means to generate precisely such melodramatic, affective excess. This section of Roehler's film features excessive sex: the hybrid version of "Dorothea's" rape by a sexually charged Suess; the scene's arousing effect on the 1940s audience; rather quiet intimate moments between Marian (Moretti) and his wife; and, ultimately, "Anti-Semitism as SM-roleplay"[36] (Buß), when Marian fervidly takes Frowein from behind at the window while they both watch as Berlin is destroyed by Allied bombing. The episode thus offers its viewers the experience of horror: it not only creates representations of war, persecution, and anti-Semitism, but also mythologizes a sinister Goebbels as an obscure Mephisto figure who lures Marian on to a path of self-destruction through his contribution to one of the most infamous propaganda films of all time. Caught up in this thick web of inevitable destruction and lurking death is the fate of the abstruse hero Marian, with whom Roehler's contemporary audience ultimately "aligns" itself (von Moltke 29–31, 33). Over the span of this sequence, Marian's personal downfall takes place: he experiences the height of his career and a moment of marital bliss in Venice, while, by the end of the Berlin scene, his personal as well as professional life has all but fallen apart. For Roehler, then, education about the Nazi past and its visual artefacts can be achieved through emotions, affect, and empathy with the fictional portrayal of historic characters and events. His approach suggests a trust in the melodramatic genre's ability to provide, through the generation of excessive feelings, a deeper insight into history than any analytical approach aimed purely at creating distance could. The most troubling and problematic aspect of Roehler's film does not lie in his choice of genre per se, but in his refusal to problematize the corruptibility of melodramatic cinematic forms that can be filled not just with any ideological content, but also convey this content convincingly via affect, emotion, and empathy. Roehler's approach to *Jud Süß* thus illustrates the limits and impossibilities of cinema putting its own history on display: "We only observed the laws of cinema – not a good philosophy for a film that traces catastrophes that result from observing the laws of cinema"[37] (Rosenfelder).

Conclusion

In conclusion, both Moeller's and Roehler's films address similar issues associated with coming to terms with the Nazi past and its visual artefacts. Both filmmakers explore questions surrounding the production of film, the nature of the cinematic image, and the role of individuals in shaping cinematic texts. When engaging with *Jud Süß*, both Moeller and Roehler borrow strategies traditionally associated with the museum, that is, the collecting, exhibiting, contextualizing, and didacticizing of historical objects. Both Moeller and Roehler make use of the museum function of cinema, its ability and interest to frame and explain the past visually, yet arrive at different conclusions about how to display Harlan's *Jud Süß* and, by implication, the "visual traces" of the Nazi past. While Moeller's musealization of the film points to a certain amount of wariness in regards to the cinematic apparatus, Roehler makes use of one of cinema's most common but also traditionally controversial genres to recreate the past and expose the toxic "cultural energy" of *Jud Süß*. Both films thus raise a number of interesting questions: first, the ongoing status of *Vorbehaltsfilme* in Germany at a time when the rest of the world has moved on to freely fantasize about space and surf Nazis; second, the enormous anxieties for Germans connected with how to display the past preserved in these films that have been shrouded in mystery, especially at a moment of generational change; finally, the problem of how to remember, musealize, and display films that have, not least by our own expectations, been corrupted by political abuse in the past.

NOTES

1 "Was ist bloß dran am 'Jud Süß'?"
2 Cf. Schulte-Sasse, Rentschler.
3 Cf. Przyrembel and Schönert.

4 "'staatspolitisch und künstlerisch besonders wertvoll' und als 'Jugendwert'"
5 Cf. Przyrembel and Schönert.
6 The Friedrich-Wilhelm-Murnau-Stiftung lists Harlan's film as an example of these Verbotsfilme (http://www.murnau-stiftung.de/geschichte1933).
7 Cf. Henne.
8 Cf. Henne for detailed discussion regarding the film's legal status.
9 "verfassungsfeindlich, volksverhetzend, strafrechtlich beleidigend"
10 Previously, Terra Film, the Allied Government and the Bundarchiv held the rights.
11 "Die heute sogenannten Vorbehaltsfilme sind nicht für den allgemeinen Vertrieb freigegeben, jedoch sind diese Filme jederzeit – in den Räumen der Stiftung – für schulische, wissenschaftliche und produktionstechnische Zwecke zur Sichtung verfügbar. Die vielfältigen und fortwährenden bundesweiten öffentlichen Aufführungen in Kinos, Universitäten, Schulen etc. sind eingebunden in einen einführenden Vortrag und eine anschließende Diskussion. " http://www.fwm-stiftung.de/geschichte1933; cf. Henne 285.
12 Cf. Przyrembel and Schönert; Henne reports that the question of which film genre is best suited to engage with *Jud Süß* has been previously discussed (8).
13 "einen beängstigenden Film"
14 "[m]it modernster Technik"
15 This assessment is by no means limited to Germany. Linda Schulte-Sasse sums up the post-war reception of the film in North America: "Veit Harlan's *Jud Süß* (1940) ranks among the most infamous of Nazi films, having been branded one of the 'most vicious … dangerous and notorious motion pictures of all times,' and as a film appealing to 'the lowest instincts of man.' It is likewise often cited as an exemplary specimen of propaganda whose effect is 'undeniable'" (22).
16 While being tried for crimes against humanity, Veit Harlan stated that he had indeed done so (cf. Sheffi 435–6). Yet, the film reappeared in the Middle East, as a propagandistic tool against Israel after 1945, making its way back into global circulation (cf. Sheffi 436).
17 Cf. also Hockerts who links the fascination with museums to other audiovisual media, such as television and film (24). In a recent article, Bernhard Schulz reports that the Deutscher Museumsbund (German Museums Association) in collaboration with the Institut für Museumsforschung (Institute for Museum Research) in Berlin are in the process of rethinking the function of the museum, in particular its ability to exhibit. The sheer number of museums raises the question what the priorities of these cultural

institutions are anew, even more so "in the age of the virtual availability of all objects" ("im Zeitalter der virtuellen Verfügbarkeit aller Objekte").

18 "[v]on A wie Allierten-Museum bis Z wie Zucker-Museum"

19 A similar debate has been taking place in regards to Adolf Hitler's *Mein Kampf*.

20 At this one-time screening, with approximately 40 people, tickets were sold out relatively soon. A lecture was part of the event.

21 Sich damit [Joseph Süß Oppenheimer and Harlan's treatment] nicht zu beschäftigen oder auch Aspekte aus der NS-Zeit nicht darzustellen, wäre ein historischer und auch pädagogischer Fehler."

22 "Als Lehrerin freue ich mich über die durchdachte Didaktik," one visitor commented, "Das Thema is vorbildlich aufbereitet. Für ältere Schüler ist die Ausstellung gut geeignet, um sich mit dem Thema Antisemitismus auseinanderzusetzen." The website to the exhibition: http://www.jsoppenheimer-ausstellung.de/

23 "Darf ein Museum üble Nazi-Propaganda ausbreiten? Lässt sich ein Film ausstellen?"

24 "Denn ob das deutsche Kino heute in der Lage ist, mit den Gespenstern der Vergangenheit fertig zu werden, kann besser beurteilen, wer den Originalfilm gesehen hat."

25 Shortly following the introduction about Veit Harlan's success during the Third Reich, his oldest son Thomas Harlan labels his father's notorious film a "murder weapon" ("Mordinstrument") in an interview conducted by Alfred Biolek. See below for further discussion of this subject.

26 The significance that Moeller attributes to Thomas Harlan's insight is evident in the fact that this conclusion about the responsibility of his father is indeed quoted twice in the documentary. When first introduced through an interview with Alfred Biolek at the very beginning of the documentary, Thomas Harlan says: "It became a murder weapon. And once you've seen that the fruit of your work turns into a murder weapon, it is difficult to say, I am a filmmaker and will carry on making films. That was the end for me. That's where my, let's say, extreme prejudice towards him comes from."

27 "Reichswasserleiche." The English subtitles do not translate the "Reich."

28 "Es gibt einige Szenen, die haben wir eins zu eins nachgestellt ... Andere haben wir sogar digital in das Original hineinkopiert."

29 "Ich sehe Sie als einen Liebhaber – wie soll ich sagen – mit gewissen Abgründen."

30 "Woher kennen Sie meinen Mann so gut?"

31 Besides the screening in Venice and Berlin, *Jud Süß* is also shown at a private screening of Goebbels and in Auschwitz.

32 "Klar muss *Jud Süß* zensiert bleiben. Das nötige politische Bewusstsein fehlt dem heutigen Publikum doch mehr als je zuvor. Unglaubliches Casting, messerscharfe Dramaturgie, geniale Manipulation. Wenn man *Jud Süß* heute irgendwelchen Brandenburger Neonazis zeigt, dann ziehen die ihre Kampfanzüge an und marschieren Richtung Jüdische Synagoge." Thomas Henne points out that Neo-Nazis seem to prefer Harlan's film *Kolberg* (1945) instead of *Jud Süß* (290).

33 "man kann das einen dramaturgischen Kniff nennen, aber uns schien das dann am Ende vollkommen legitim. Weil was wir einfach machen wollten, ist einen historisch wahren Film zu machen, der von einer starken, inneren Spannung lebt."

34 "Es war Oskars Wunsch, melodramatisch zuzuspitzen"

35 "Gefühle herausarbeiten"

36 "Antisemitismus als SM-Rollenspielchen"

37 "Wir haben doch nur die Gesetze des Kinos befolgt – keine gute Philosophie für einen Film, der den Katastrophen nachspürt, die dabei herauskommen können, wenn man nur die Gesetze des Kinos befolgt."

9 Moving Statues: Arthur Grimm, the *Entartete Kunst* Exhibition, and Installation Photography as *Standfotografie*

KATHRYN M. FLOYD

An installation photograph, a flat and static condensation of the temporal and spatial experience of the body moving through the narrative of an art exhibition, reveals a dialogue among three fundamental roles. At the centre of the photo are the artworks that embody the agency of the artist or artists and operate like figures in a painting or actors in a scene. Their photographic traces are substitutions for their actual presence in the museum. Conditioned by memories of encounters with auratic artworks, the gaze seeks them out first in the photograph. But the surrounding architectural space and gallery staging soon exert themselves; the markers of history found in many installation shots add another layer to this spatial context. Doorways, hallways, walls, and floors, and images of visitors moving and observing in the past shift attention away from the objects and suggest that there is more to see beyond the frame of the photo. The ability to draw the eye further in and redirect its focus, even if only temporarily, away from the singular artworks to the broader narrative of the museum, is the power of the museum director or curator who, like a film director, coordinates and embodies the collaborative work and networks of influence that merge to produce the display. The curator personifies the museal process of defining and categorizing the objects on view.

Installation photographers negotiate the shifting boundaries between singular objects on display and the complex environments in which they are positioned, as well as the unstable terrain between the stillness of the photograph and the kinetic experience of the museum narrative. In both respects, gallery pictures are therefore fixed fragments of larger wholes. They also document the push and pull between the creative agencies represented by the artwork and the museum, or, put another way, they capture the interaction between the artist's and the curator's authorship. In this sometimes friendly, sometimes fraught relationship between the two, there exists an unresolved tension: neither artist nor curator maintains complete authority nor is fully independent. Each role needs the other. In the midst of the never-resolved negotiations between these authors, and between stasis and movement, image and experience, fragment and whole, the photographer finds a platform on which to exert his or her authority, which has everything to do with the capacity to "fix" this difficult landscape. The photographer is equally reliant upon the artist and curator, but may also be the more powerful "author" when the photograph survives as a record of these ephemeral encounters. Installation photographers not only represent the conditions of the museal, they also help to author its history and therefore re-enact the process of musealization itself.

While the capacity of installation photographers to formulate new, "permanent" images from transitory exhibition situations attests to their agency, they are almost never given credit. Although the constructed nature of all photographs is a commonplace, the recognition of the gallery photographer as an "artist" is drowned out by his or her proximity to the "louder" voices of the artist and curator. It is difficult to "see" the photograph as a composition because the eye focuses on the authority of the artwork and museum context inside its frame.[1] That installation photographers often remain unknown proves a challenge to scholars who want to understand their work, but the anonymous photographer's status can also be an opportunity for transgression.

Arthur Grimm, the Nazi photojournalist who made one of the most recognized images of the 1937 Munich exhibition *Entartete Kunst* (*Degenerate Art*) (figure 9.1), also remains obscure. His photograph of Wilhelm Lehmbruck's 1911 sculpture *Die Kniende* (*The Kneeling Woman*), in room 6 of the show, survives as an important historical record of this exhaustively researched "anti-exhibition." Despite the image's significant role in analysing this visual argument against vanguard art, scholars have rarely acknowledged Grimm or adequately investigated his work.[2] As a historical document, his photo, along with seventeen others he shot that day, allows visual entry "into" the exhibition at its opening on 19 July. But the photograph also disrupts this illusion of access and instead substitutes a narrative about a moving statue. Little by little a surreal fantasy begins to take shape and we begin to see Grimm's constructed photograph. His ambiguous image documents the event, but also authors a new narrative belonging only to the photographer.

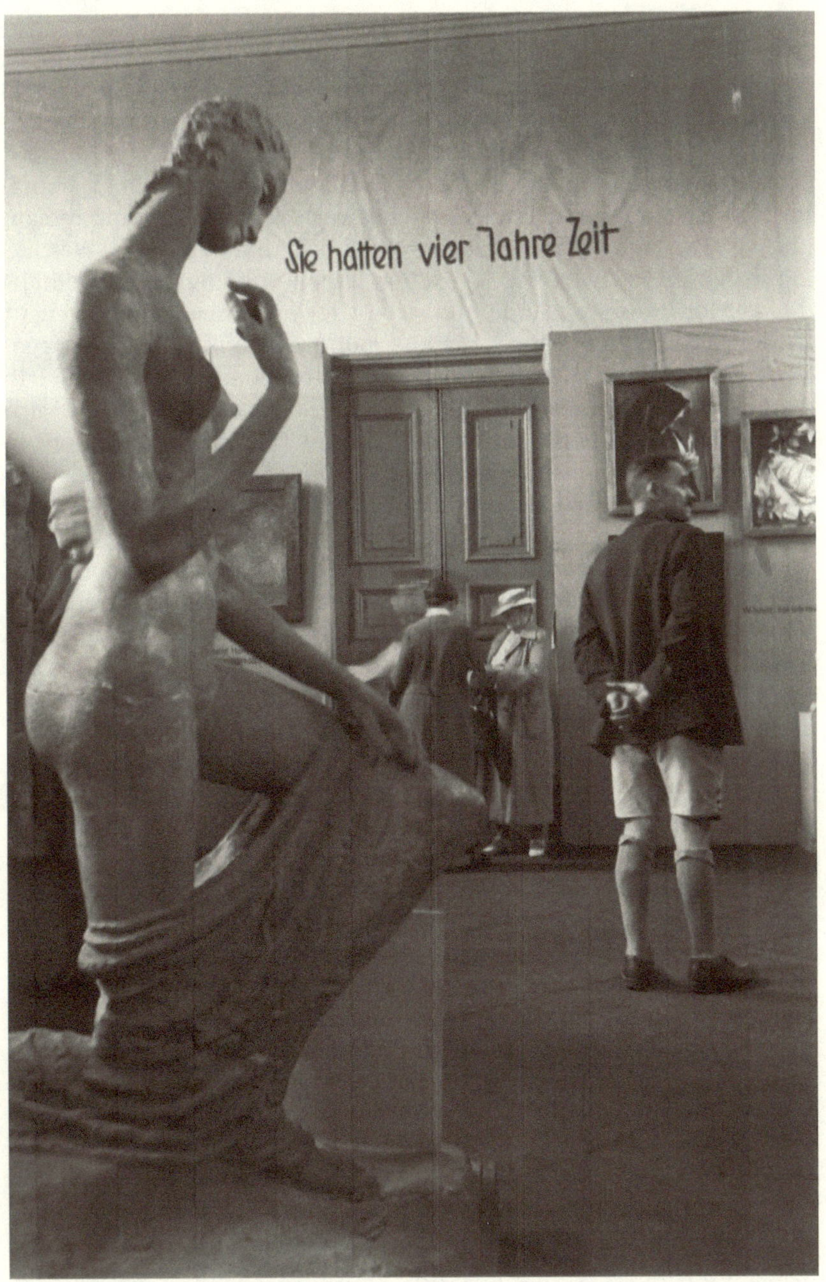

9.1 Photograph by Arthur Grimm of Room 6 of the 1937 *Entartete Kunst* exhibition. Wilhelm Lehmbruck's sculpture *Die Kniende* (1911) is in the foreground. *Source*: bpk, Berlin/Arthur Grimm/Art Resource, New York.

The complex image is made more mysterious by the fact that little is known about Grimm's political attitudes, his beliefs about modern art, or his intentions for these photos.[3] Born in 1908, he joined the National Socialist German Workers' Party (NSDAP) on 1 May 1933 in his hometown of Rehau (Upper Franconia). His early life and training remain unclear. The archival record, however, shows that by 1934 he was living in Berlin and working actively as a press photographer, perhaps directly for the propaganda ministry or for a German photo agency.[4] Evidence of his early career may be found in the thousands of negatives, contact sheets, and photographic prints that he sold in 1971 to the Bildarchiv Preussischer Kulturbesitz. They document a wide variety of subjects, from the activities of various NSDAP organizations to German industry, science, and sport to portraits of individuals and records of military actions in France, Poland, Serbia, and Russia. Sometimes Grimm's camera also recorded the work of other image-makers. In addition to the *Entartete Kunst* exhibition, he also photographed the spaces of the art academy in Berlin-Charlottenburg, the Ateliergemeinschaft Klosterstrasse, and the studios of Albert Speer and Arno Breker.

The photographic archive also shows that the year before he attended the *Entartete Kunst* exhibition, Grimm worked on Leni Riefenstahl's *Olympia* (1938), her unique cinematic remediation of the 1936 Berlin Olympic Games. For this project he served as a stills photographer, or *Standfotograf.* Stills photographers, like installation photographers, translate the staged display of artistic work, in this case the performances of actors on a film director's set. Stills photographers not only documented "behind the scenes" activity. They recreated in static images the moving scenes shot by the cinematographer either alongside the rolling camera, just after a scene wrapped, or at a later time when the shot was restaged.[5] The pictures functioned as archival documents for the studio, study images for the director, or publicity photographs for advertisements (Müller 19). The challenge for the stills photographer was to encapsulate the temporal and physical performance of the actors and embody the broader narrative of the film in a single still shot (Campany 7). He had to translate the dynamism of the moving picture, the passage of time, and the narrative flow of the plot, all within the confines of a singular, consumable object that could be mobilized for other purposes (Stezaker 113). Both stills and installation photographers therefore share the task of summarizing the creative work of others and walk a fine line between the movement and temporality inherent in the media of exhibitions and films and the static character of their own form of image making. They also share a lack of recognition, despite their work's potential importance as historical documentation.[6]

This essay argues that Grimm's record of room 6 at the 1937 *Entartete Kunst* exhibition serves as an interesting place from which to consider whether the translation of film through *Standfotografie,* an idea predicated on the arguments of Mieke Bal and others that an exhibition can be like a filmic narrative experience, might be a useful analogy for understanding the relationship of installation photographs to the museums and exhibitions they embody ("Exhibition as Film"). Grimm's photograph becomes a valuable point of departure not only because of his experience with both modes of picture making, but because the subject matter of the image evokes themes fundamental to these images. In particular, the motif of the moving statue, a metaphor for creative power and a symbol of the tensions between movement and stasis, stands at the centre of the work. The context of *Entartete Kunst* furthermore raises questions about the power relationships attached to the remediation of artworks, museums, and exhibitions. Most of all, the photograph demonstrates what histories can be gleaned when images of remediation are looked *at,* rather than simply *into.*

Wilhelm Lehmbruck's Moving Sculpture

Before Grimm encountered Lehmbruck's *Die Kniende* in 1937, the work was already associated with the theme of the moving statue. From 1911 on, the critical literature often described it in terms of sound and physical movement, often with recourse to religious imagery. Critics sometimes conceived of the work as a flat composition and debated which of its "two-dimensional" profiles best awakened its expressivity. Julius Meier-Graefe, one of Lehmbruck's supporters, discussed these two points but also commented on the effective mediation of the work in museums, exhibitions, and photography.

Die Kniende represented an important milestone for Wilhelm Lehmbruck (1881–1919), who left Düsseldorf for Paris in 1910.[7] There, under the influence of Rodin and Archipenko, he shifted his style from a naturalistic mode to "proto-Expressionism." *Die Kniende,* originally produced in plaster, was a turning point in this regard. Only slightly larger than life size, it portrays a woman kneeling or possibly bowing, but operates also as a study in expressive line and form.[8] Its elements evoke a languid movement, neither completely still nor fully in motion, but always in transition. She is frozen between getting up and bowing down (Stecker 8).

Lehmbruck made additional versions of the work in cast stone, a coloured concrete-like material more durable than plaster, but breakable nonetheless, and *Die Kniende* made the rounds at the important contemporary art exhibitions of the day. Lehmbruck also had it photographed to further extend its reach (Bornscheuer 21, 33). His first reproduction, taken in his studio, captured the work's left profile, accentuating the lines of the bent leg, long left arm, and drapery. This same photograph, with its studio background blacked out, became a souvenir postcard for the 1913 New York Armory Show, where it was prominently displayed (Bornscheuer 29). Lehmbruck no doubt understood that the translation of a large three-dimensional sculpture into a flat portable photograph not only garnered the work wider attention, but also significantly affected its meaning. When asked by the organizers of the 1912 Sonderbund exhibition if they could photograph it, Lehmbruck agreed, but asked that he be present at the shoot (Bornscheuer 32).

Critics also analysed the work in terms of its flat, planar compositions, discussing its various profiles and the primary viewing perspective that Lehmbruck intended. No doubt Lehmbruck's many sketches of kneeling figures influenced this debate, but the photographs of the work in monographs and journals must have also coloured the dialogue (Bornscheuer 34). Paul Westheim's 1919 monograph reproduced several plates in which *Die Kniende* materializes from a flat black background like the earlier postcard. Lehmbruck seemed to prefer this expressive, almost painterly style that isolated the work (Bornscheuer 36). Westheim's photo displayed *Die Kniende*'s right profile with the upraised arm, which he argued was the most powerful perspective (Bornscheuer 30, 37, 38). This view also paralleled critics' comparison of the figure to Gothic and Renaissance Annunciation imagery, specifically, to the figure of the angel.[9] Critic Max Raphael specifically identified the Annunciation fresco in Orvieto as an appropriate comparison.[10] However, Jan Van Eyck's Annunciation panel (Washington, DC) also displays remarkable correspondences to *Die Kniende*, especially in the gesture of the upraised hand.[11]

In the climate of growing hostility towards modernist art, critics sympathetic to Lehmbruck's work took up the themes of life and animation suggested by these religious comparisons. Julius Meier-Graefe, for example, praised Lehmbruck's expressive abilities by describing the sculpture as a living being and using metaphors of speech and music to discuss its form.[12] Remembering the work at the 1911 Salon d'Automne, he noted in 1932 that the figure called out to him in such a way that the other works in the gallery were muted in her presence (Meier-Graefe, "Pariser Reaktionen" 444). He later felt that he needed to hear again the "language of the limbs, of the raised hand"[13] (Meier-Graefe, "Paris" 9). To understand the figure's form, he continued, "one must investigate the parts, just as one does the gestures and gaze of an individual with whom one speaks"[14] (ibid.). Meier-Graefe's descriptions themselves animate the static object. His metaphors of life and vitality, common in art criticism at the time (Nead 53–5), communicated the creative depth of the artist and the expressive power of the artwork, which Meier-Graefe argued was so great that upon seeing it, one felt compelled to "sink down before it"[15] ("Paris" 9). This gesture of devotion, coupled with his animating descriptions, evokes the Greek myth, told by Ovid, of the sculptor Pygmalion. Through his imagination and technical skill, Pygmalion creates an original female form so beautiful that, out of love, he kneels down before it. When Venus sees his desire, she brings the statue to life. But as Viktor Stoichita points out, it is not only Pygmalion and Venus who animate the statue. Ultimately, it is Ovid's text that preserves her life over time (Stoichita 20).

The paradox of the narrative of the animated statue, which involves the quickening of the inanimate, but also the preservation of an "ideal" female body in stone, complicates the long-standing argument of writers like Theodor Adorno that the museum functions as a mausoleum of relics disconnected from life. Nineteenth- and early-twentieth-century paintings, Gothic novels, and early films told stories of gallery spaces populated by fantastic, moving statues that originated in the Pygmalion myth and recreated the museum as a place that suspended art in a timeless state beyond life and death (Nead 45, 48). In the real world of art and museum politics, the theme of the "museum of the living" likewise provided a foil to the concept of the museum-as-tomb. In the nineteenth century, these galleries of recent art by living artists were Europe's first contemporary art museums. The Musée du Luxembourg, for example, opened in 1818 as a museum dedicated to modern French masters. The museum's concept involved a cyclical historical process. As contemporary artists (ideally) became "Old Masters," their works were transported to the art historical galleries of the Louvre. But as John Elderfield writes, the museum of the living was really a kind of "purgatory" where artworks waited to meet their fate (101). "The principle was to display works of art ... in the Luxembourg Museum until five or ten years after the artist's death and then one would decide whether they went to the Louvre," depending on their perceived quality (100). This movement from the temporary, "unstable" space of the contemporary art gallery to the permanent narrative of the art history museum was therefore not a removal to a lifeless tomb, but rather a kind of apotheosis. Transferred to the art history museum, works perceived as canonical were entered into the safety of the timeless museal realm, forever protected from the vagaries of "criticism" and "life."

In modern Germany, the "Galerie der Lebenden" ("Museum of the Living") came out of late-nineteenth-century calls to reform national museums by making them more relevant and appealing to the lives of everyday citizens. Proposals included expanding the types of objects on display (e.g., to include applied art) as well as opening up their historical scope to embrace new art. Because the French dominated the modern canon, the debate about what to acquire for these institutions was bound to questions of nationhood. The scandal surrounding Hugo von Tschudi's acquisition of modern French art for the Nationalgalerie in Berlin is perhaps the most famous event in this early debate about how to define German art and art history through the concept of the museum.[16]

In the wake of the November Revolution, calls also came from champions of Expressionism to include works from this movement in German museums as a way to further education about progressive goals and to advocate for state support for contemporary art (Weinstein 39–40). That same year, Ludwig Justi, von Tschudi's successor and also a supporter of modernism, purchased a handful of Expressionist artworks. A year later, as part of the expansion of the Nationalgalerie, he opened his "Galerie der Lebenden" in the recently acquired Kronprinzenpalais, where he displayed these and other contemporary artworks, including Lehmbruck's *Die Kniende*. Justi organized his new displays around living artistic personalities; his belief in the deeply emotional character of German art was emphasized in his focus on individuals (Steinkamp 49–50). Older works originally from the former princely residence were moved to the historical galleries on the Museumsinsel to make room for these "living" objects. Justi's "Galerie der Lebenden" became the central location through which Expressionism entered German museums and, in turn, the canon of German art history (Joachimides 199).

Lehmbruck's liberal supporters Julius Meier-Graefe and Paul Westheim were critical of Justi's new museum. Despite their shared support of Expressionism, they felt his reforms came too late and did not go far enough (Weinstein 40). These disagreements may in part have led Meier-Graefe to write in 1932: "*Die Kniende* today is in the Kronprinzenpalais and doesn't have the right space to be heard completely ... An ideal space that can absorb her whole language, can hardly be found anywhere" (Meier-Graefe, "Paris" 9). He notes, however, the valuable antidote to this poor viewing space are the photographs in Westheim's monograph on Lehmbruck. Meier-Graefe states that in these images we see "more of the incalculable beauty than the view of the work in the museum" (ibid.).[17]

Politics aside, the idea that a photograph of an artwork might provide a better viewing experience than its original context did not originate with Meier-Graefe. Since the nineteenth century, photographs had become important art historical tools because they made objects accessible, made side-by-side comparisons possible, and provided a high degree of visual detail. Even very different thinkers like Bernard Berenson and Walter Benjamin noted that photographs provide superior viewing strategies for works of art. Most important, photographs preserved ruined, fragile, or damaged objects indefinitely, so that they might remain a part of art history, suspended beyond life and death in a timeless photographic museum.[18]

The need to protect *Die Kniende* had already become a necessity when Meier-Graefe wrote about her photographic "life" in 1932. After Lehmbruck committed suicide in 1919, his widow continued to cast and circulate his works. But by the 1930s the sculpture was experiencing an unwelcome kind of movement, its removal from public collections. In 1927 the city of Duisburg, Lehmbruck's birthplace, installed a bronze version of *Die Kniende* in a public garden. In the growing right-wing atmosphere, the press attacked the expressive work, calling it a "deformity" and a "mutilation" of the park (Salzman 6). After calls for its destruction, city officials removed it. Ten years later Nazi officials seized versions of *Die Kniende* from the Kronprinzenpalais and the Kunsthalle Mannheim as part of the action called the "Säuberung des Kunsttempels" ("Cleansing of the Art Temple"). That summer they also confiscated the Munich Städtische Galerie's cast-stone version, damaging it in the process. On 19 July it appeared at *Entartete Kunst*, where Grimm documented it. One week later it was mysteriously removed.

(Re)moving Sculptures: The Exhibition *Entartete Kunst*

The 1937 exhibition *Entartete Kunst* was the culmination of a broader campaign, begun years earlier by groups like the Kampfbund für deutsche

Kultur ("The Fighting League for German Culture") to define modernist art as a "degenerate" influence infiltrating German culture. At issue were the avant-garde styles considered to be Jewish, Bolshevik, decadent, or cosmopolitan.[19] What tenuously held together these varying definitions of degeneracy were vague ideas that focused on what degenerate art was *not* (Zuschlag 56). In short, it was "not-German," and therefore "not-art." This weak definition created a number of artists as "borderline" cases. First-generation German Expressionists, many of who had fought in the First World War, posed a particular problem. Were the expressive styles of Ernst Barlach, Ludwig Gies, Emil Nolde, or Wilhelm Lehmbruck in fact foreign and unhealthy or was their work a contemporary "gothic" form of Nordic expression? The rivalry between Joseph Goebbels and Alfred Rosenberg represented two sides of this debate; Goebbels initially supported a more liberal attitude towards modern art, while Rosenberg, head of the Kampfbund, supported only *völkisch* styles.[20]

The so-called *Expressionismusstreit* ("Expressionism Debate") was not truly settled until *Entartete Kunst* in 1937. Until the radical "purification" of German museums that year, Nazi officials applied the category "degenerate" unevenly and contradictorily. Furthermore, the campaign against avant-garde art entailed more than just the classification of individuals. Although the identification of Jewish or Communist artists, the censorship of their work, and the destruction of their careers and lives was certainly widespread, the struggle against modern art also targeted "Aryan" avant-gardists who might be redeemed. These figures were exhorted to give up their elitist ways and support art that reflected the *Volk*. In these cases, it was not necessarily the individual whom the Nazis labelled "degenerate," but instead particular works of art. Many formerly celebrated paintings and sculptures were redefined in this way. Abstraction, expressive figurative distortions, critical subject matter, non-traditional media, or avant-garde techniques might cause a work to be categorized as "not-art." Party officials inspected temporary exhibitions and galleries to remove offending works. Just as often, however, they closed down entire shows (Zuschlag 50). Most important, the party targeted individuals with the power to define art, attacking art historians as well as German art critics who had popularized modern art (Petropoulos, *Art as Politics* 53–4). Public museum directors especially came under fire for their acquisitions of new art from the previous decades. Nazi critics berated them for spending the everyday German's hard-earned money on degenerate or foreign artworks that appealed only to "art snobs" and damaged the larger cause of German culture.[21]

The attack on museums and museum directors eventually culminated in the 1937 action "Die Säuberung des Kunsttempels," when Reich officials confiscated thousands of works from public collections, thereby stripping them of their status as "art." But even earlier, officials were seizing artworks from museums and galleries, just as they had begun to steal the personal property of Jewish collectors and dealers or oust art professors and critics from their jobs. The first instance of the removal of works from a public museum happened in 1930 at the Weimarer Landesmuseum, when officials removed a set of Expressionist works (including images by Lehmbruck) from view (Zuschlag 35). Nevertheless, immediately after the Nazis' seizure of power in 1933, museums received no explicit directives about how to deal with potentially "degenerate" artworks. The inconsistent application of definitions and policies left many directors confused about how to carry on. Ludwig Justi wrote in 1933 to a colleague asking about the Kronprinzenpalais's response to the political situation that "the position of the government on new German art is in no way clear,"[22] and that he had removed nothing (Zuschlag 52). In 1936, however, in the lull after the international attention of the Olympic Games, Goebbels shut down the exhibits of new art in Justi's museum (Barron 15).

The 1937 "Säuberung des Kunsttempels," the cleansing of the timeless and permanent "temple of German art," a metaphor for German culture, was perhaps fittingly instigated by plans for a temporary exhibition. Organized for the anniversary of the Nazi takeover, *Gebt mir vier Jahre Zeit* (*Give me four years' time*) displayed evidence of the general progress made under National Socialism. Goebbels, who had already brought his attitudes in line with those of Rosenberg and Hitler, organized an art exhibit for the show to illustrate the contrasts between Weimar era "art" and the art of the Third Reich. Goebbels and the secret police gave Walter Hansen, a former art teacher, and Wolfgang Willrich, a painter and critic, authorization to seize works from various collections for use in the display. They visited museums like the Kronprinzenpalais and removed original works of their choosing (Zuschlag 176). In the end, however, the concept for the display changed and the two left the project for others to finish. It is unclear whether the works they seized appeared in the display or if in the end only photographic reproductions of artworks were put on view.

Goebbels selected Willrich to assist with the project because of the critic's inflammatory publication *Säuberung des Kunsttempels* (*Cleansing of the Art Temple*, 1937). He had produced the book, he wrote, to clarify the debate about degenerate art and educate individuals duped by art professionals about the avant-garde. The book was to be a weapon in the fight for German culture against the tyranny of modernism advocated by those same dark forces (Willrich 7–8). In his introduction, Willrich noted two basic beliefs that kept people from taking action against these powers in the field of *Kunstpolitik*. The first was an incorrect notion that art was a harmless entertainment. Willrich argued that art fundamentally affected a culture either positively or negatively. The second false belief was the notion that history and art history were forces beyond the control of human agency. "The facts of history, and also of art history, are not the result of chance or of a higher power, with which one simply must come to terms: 'That is the line of development and one must accept it as a given'"[23] (Willrich 8). Willrich's book went on to "prove," through images from German museums and periodicals and texts taken from progressive art journals and books, that both sinister and foolish individuals had steered German culture and art history from its proper path. The German people, he argued, should not take this false historical narrative as a fact, but must take action to purify the "temple" and re-author German (art) history.

Willrich's book influenced the plans for *Entartete Kunst* and he became a member of the commission, headed by Adolf Ziegler, head of the Reich Chamber of Fine Art, charged on 30 June with clearing public museums of all offending work produced after 1910. The action, however, was not simply a necessity undertaken to fill an exhibition. The seizure of "unacceptable" works was instead an extreme reactionary gesture of the symbolic purge of German art and culture through the metaphor of the museum. While many objects went to Munich for *Entartete Kunst*, even more were sold off or destroyed. Between the end of June and the middle of July the team, armed with an unlimited power to select and confiscate works they deemed degenerate, travelled to twenty-eight different cities, where they removed approximately 700 objects, which they sent to Munich. By the end of the summer 16,000 works had been "purged" from public collections. Those not exhibited in Munich went to Berlin to be warehoused, sold, or destroyed (Barron 19).

The team installed over 600 works by over 100 artists which were seen from July to November in Munich by approximately two million visitors who squeezed through seven narrow rooms, normally occupied by the archaeology department's permanent collection of antique plaster casts. The works, organized by vague themes like Jewish art or religious subjects, created a visual definition for the notion of "degeneracy." Like the earlier exhibition, the show also defined "degeneracy" through contrast, in particular its contrast to the *Grosse Deutsche Kunstausstellung* at the nearby Haus der Deutschen Kunst. The exhibition also used strategies of ridicule and shame by juxtaposing large wall texts composed of decontextualized avant-garde statements with the artworks. Seemingly "rational" statements by Hitler and Goebbels provided foils. The collage of texts and images hung haphazardly formed an atmosphere of impermanence. But the visual "terrorism" evoked by the exhibition also emanated from the exhibition's focus on the themes of seizure and removal that differed fundamentally from the works' former lives as museum objects.

The exhibit employed a consciously makeshift character. The organizers transformed the gallery walls with sheeting that barely shrouded the permanent architectural details; the stucco decorations and wall murals of the archaeology department were covered but could still be seen through the thin cloth. Temporary panels projected out from, but also left visible, the taller permanent walls to which they were attached. The impermanence of the spatial structure proved a meaningful contrast not only to the neoclassical Haus der Deutschen Kunst (House of German Art), but also to the idea of permanence, stability, and protection generally associated with the art history museum, ideally the destination for valuable contemporary works. The unstable space communicated the de-accessioned works' devalued status and diminished historical worth and represented a direct reversal of the cycles of "museums of the living." *Entartete Kunst* transported works not from an unstable purgatory towards a static canon of history, but reversed their flow away from the sacred space of the *Kunsttempel* and back out into the wilderness. This narrative of "de-musealization" was accomplished not only through the show's makeshift aesthetic, but also through reminders of the works' past "lives." The team labelled objects with red text stating that each painting or sculpture had been paid for with the taxes of hardworking Germans and they gave information about the museums from which each work had been seized. The text told the viewer how much the museum director had paid for the object and when it had been acquired (von Lüttichau 45). In short, the information about each work revolved around its museal history. Viewing each artwork thereby called up awareness, or perhaps even a personal memory, about its former status and location.[24]

In two instances, organizers created what might be understood as "flashbacks" by pairing an artwork with a photograph showing it in its former location. At the very beginning of the exhibition, as visitors came up the stairs to the galleries, they encountered Ludwig Gies's crucifix confiscated from Lübeck Cathedral. At the bottom of the sculpture, organizers attached a photograph of the work in situ in the cathedral. At the opposite end of the exhibition, Lehmbruck's *Die Kniende* was also paired with a photograph. Propped up on its plinth was a photograph of the artist's sculpture *Sitzender Jüngling* (*Seated Youth*, 1917), which replaced *Die Kniende* after it was removed on 29 July, as it had been installed in a cemetery in Duisburg. These images "preserved" the history of these objects, but only as a way to make a case about their vulnerability in the face of more powerful forces.

While the positive literature on *Die Kniende* proposed an animated and lively being emanating from inanimate material, the degenerate art exhibition subtly defined the "bodies" of modern artworks not only as distorted and diseased, but also as weak, uprooted, and capable of being mobilized from the outside. The show responded to Willrich's argument that art and art history were not forces beyond all control, but rather could be forcibly redefined and reauthored. German culture, through the metaphor of the German museum, could indeed be cleansed and this process of purification, of de-musealization, was the true subject of the exhibition. That the bodies of the moving viewers enacted this narrative again and again no doubt suggested a further correspondence between the fate of unacceptable art and that of undesirable bodies. The narrative of de-musealization was also a narrative of terror.

Constructing the Moving Statue: Leni Riefenstahl and Arthur Grimm

Arthur Grimm seems to have approached the narratives of *Entartete Kunst* with a filmic eye. As a member of the press, he attended the exhibition opening with a smaller, more exclusive crowd. With fewer visitors present, he could compose his images carefully; his style balances a snapshot's transitory character with the staged photograph's formal structure. Instead of wide perspectives of the environment or tight shots of individual works, Grimm favoured unusual angles signifying a controlled movement through the exhibition. The first photograph in the series, for example, offers a long view down a wall in room 5 replicating the sensation of a tracking shot (figure 9.2). The image is less focused on the "degenerate" works and more interested in creating motion. Although the wall text reads "Verrückt um jeden Preis"

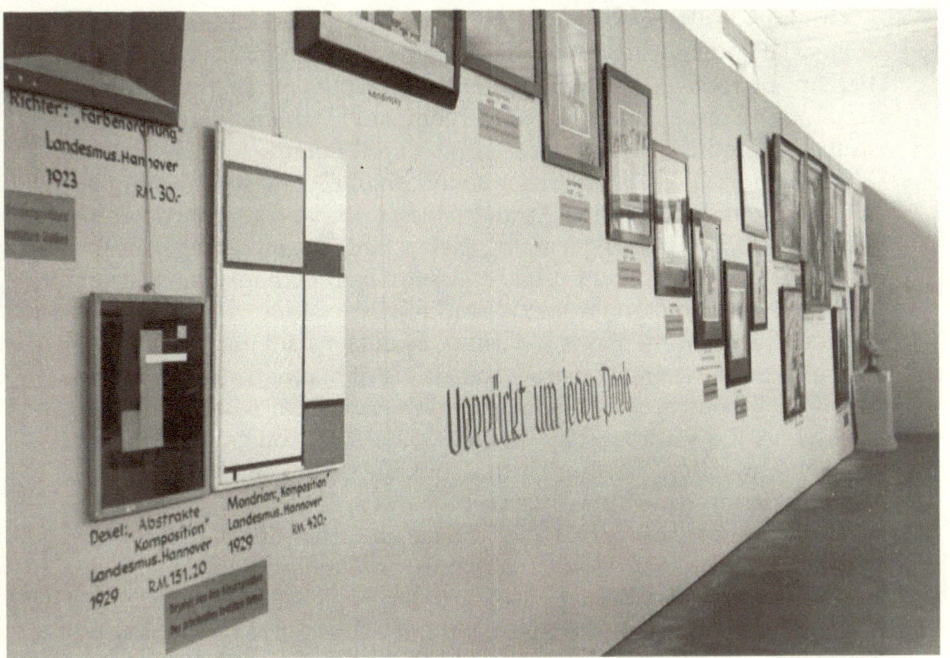

9.2 Photograph by Arthur Grimm of room 5 of the *Entartete Kunst* exhibition (1937) showing paintings by Walter Dexel, Piet Mondrian, and Wassily Kandinsky. *Source*: bpk, Berlin/Arthur Grimm/Art Resource, New York.

("Crazy at any price"), the structured pattern of "movement" over the cascade of paintings nearly forms an abstract composition.

When shooting individual paintings, Grimm rejected the head-on viewpoint typically used to document artworks; he positioned himself at an angle so as to include the wall. The technique turns flat images into three-dimensional objects and mimics the viewpoint of approaching visitors. Grimm consistently used this technique to photograph paintings by Kurt Schwitters, Max Beckmann, Otto Dix, and Oskar Kokoschka. For the religious work *Christ and John* (1926) by Barlach, he portrays the sculpture illuminated by a spotlight. Grimm furthermore made only four conventional photos of visitors looking at artworks. It seems that he preferred to invent his own narrative of motion from static objects, rather than illustrating the haphazard movements of actual visitors.

Grimm's aesthetic was surely influenced by his work in 1936 on Leni Riefenstahl's film *Olympia*. How he came to the project is unknown. Perhaps he received the assignment through the propaganda ministry, or through a press outlet or newsreel company.[25] His family connections in the film industry might have also secured him the job. His brother Hans Grimm (1905–2001) was a sound engineer for Tobis-Klangfilm, where his credits included Arnold Fanck's *Stürme über den Montblanc* (*Avalanche*, 1930), starring a young Riefenstahl. The project was the first sound film for Fanck and it had to be dubbed; perhaps Hans Grimm and Riefenstahl met in the sound studio.

From the scant mentions of Grimm by Riefenstahl and other *Olympia* colleagues, we can construct something of his contribution. Riefenstahl's 1937 book *Schönheit im Olympischen Kampf* (*The Beauty of Olympic Competition*), a photographic essay on the film, constitutes his only official recognition. "Arthur Grimm took the stills. The photographs of work in progress are by Arthur Grimm and Rolf Lantin," reads part of her brief acknowledgment, which did not credit specific photographers for particular images; as she maintained throughout her life, *Olympia* and all of its imagery belonged solely to her (Riefenstahl, *Schönheit* 283). Grimm probably worked under Lantin, the director of the photo division for the film (Graham 293). As Steven Bach recounts, Lantin and an unnamed assistant constantly trailed Riefenstahl to document her work (154–5). Perhaps this assistant was Grimm. It is certain he served as a *Standfotograf* during Riefenstahl's trip to Greece to film the Olympic torch ceremony; the Bildarchiv retains these images. His photographs also show that he was present at the Haus Ruhwald, *Olympia*'s headquarters during the Games. Ernst Jäger, the publicity director, also mentions Grimm's attendance at track and field events (Graham 84).

The film was a challenge and opportunity for Riefenstahl. With money from the Reich, special favours from Hitler, and little daily oversight by Goebbels and the Ministry, she had unprecedented creative control over her artistic vision. An *auteur* in every way, she rejected the idea of conventional newsreel-style documentary and instead chose to "stylize" the event, sometimes going so far as to create "fantasy" from reality (S. Bach 162–3). Planned by the Reich as a display of German strength, the Games were already a spectacle of athletic prowess, beautiful bodies, a healthy people, and a civilized nation. As with her earlier party films, Riefenstahl documented the Nazi staging, but also recreated it using narrative film techniques such as atmospheric lighting, montage, music, visual symbolism, and animation, to express broader ideals (Rother 96–7). Working without a script, Riefenstahl first shot miles of film and later created a narrative by editing the raw material. In this way, *Olympia,* says Rother, is more akin to painting than to documentary photography (36). The film was clearly marked with her authorial imprint.

One might also argue that her approach to the Games was "sculptural." In addition to the year she spent quite literally "constructing" the film from miles of footage, *Olympia*'s formal treatment of bodies moving in space and time, for example, sometimes multiplied across the screen or silhouetted against an expressive sky, makes aesthetic "objects" of the ideal figures and creates an artificial, even surreal, atmosphere. This sensibility was most evident in the film's ten-minute prologue that begins with a series of tracking shots over and around the ruins of the Athenian Acropolis. As the camera travels through the misty landscape, ancient sculptures appear in a shadowy gallery and "move" through the camera's actions. This suggestion of "living sculptures" is fulfilled by a slow dissolve from Myron's marble *Discobolus* to the real body of German athlete Erwin Huber, who completes the action. The climactic transition from sculpture to living body represents "a bridge from Antiquity to the present," as Riefenstahl put it (*Memoir* 171). The prologue continues with modern-day athletes, mostly nude and silhouetted against a dramatic sky, the running of the Olympic torch, a sequence of temple dancers, and an animated "flight" over Europe and down into the Olympic Stadium. The ancient "museum" of living sculptures in the prologue gives birth to ideal German bodies in the present. The moving statue links modern German culture to the classical past.

Riefenstahl's prologue is also interesting because in a sense "her" film begins with a prologue that "belongs" to someone else. While Riefenstahl later claimed it was her concept from the beginning, surrealist director Willy Zielke, responsible for the prologue, identified her original inspiration as a painting by Arnold Böcklin (Graham 42–3). It was actually Zielke who went to Greece, unsupervised, at the beginning of June. There, he filmed the Acropolis, where he used smoke powder and veiled lenses to evoke a mysterious Greek past, and visited the National Museum to shoot the sculptures (Graham 45). In July, Riefenstahl, Lantin, Grimm, and a small group of journalists flew to Greece for the torch lighting and to check in on Zielke's progress. When they arrived, the group screened his footage and then proceeded to the torch ceremony. Grimm photographed Riefenstahl's shots of the proceedings as well as her recreation of event; she had been unsatisfied with the ceremony so she recreated her own (Graham 60–2).

Riefenstahl eventually re-edited Zielke's materials, but left the beginning scenes of temples and "moving statues" intact. The dissolve of the discus thrower was a kind of collaboration. Zielke had a cast of the sculpture created and shot it as it rotated on a turntable. Riefenstahl captured the footage of Huber and edited the scenes together (Graham 141–2). The dissolve from the *Discobolus* to Huber represents the point in the prologue where Zielke's work ends and Riefenstahl's begins. In the case of Riefenstahl and Zielke, the ability to make sculptures move also became a kind of competition and mark of their respective creative abilities. Seen often in early cinema, scenes of sculptures coming to life also symbolized an idea of creative superiority: moving statues represented the new media's ability to make still images (both sculptures and individual still frames) appear lifelike. Versions of the Pygmalion story in film were therefore also stories of the filmmaker's and, in turn, the medium's superiority over other types of (still) image-making (Nead 48–52). The living Greek sculptures in *Olympia* embody the competitive, powerful bodies of the modern athletes, but also suggest the power of cinema, and in particular that of Riefenstahl, who claimed creative authorship and personal responsibility for the collaborative effort of the film and for the remediation of the entire spectacle. "It was my prologue," said Zielke (Graham 45). "It was my vision," wrote Riefenstahl (*Memoir* 171).

The Return of the Moving Statue

Grimm must have learned a lot working on the *Olympia* project, from innovative camera angles and surreal effects to lessons about strong personalities, creative control, and most important, about restaging staged events and distilling moving narratives. The assignment must have constituted a lesson about the balance between the real and the constructed and between personality and anonymity, narrative and object, film and photography, movement and stasis, and sculptures and bodies. At the very least, he must have brought some aspects of his recent experiences in film to bear on his encounter with *Die Kniende*.

Grimm's photograph of room 6 merges these concepts into an uncanny vision that is also "betwixt and between." Taken from a low angle close to the sculpture, Grimm's perspective of the statue's right profile makes it seem much larger than its actual size; it towers over the space, curving to the right as if about to move. The camera's large depth of field flattens out the gallery. Through this uniform focus, Grimm makes the sculpture speak the words "Sie hatten vier Jahre Zeit" ("They had four years' time") painted on the back wall. Like a medieval speech scroll, common in the type of Annunciation imagery mentioned by Lehmbruck's critics, the words become visible and issue from the sculpture's mouth. They represent sound, but they remain silent. The composition of the image also suggests elements of Annunciation scenes, specifically, *Die Kniende*'s position to the left of a second figure. In this case, the individual is a man who looks away, not hearing or seeing her announcement, rather than a female figure interacting with an angel. The man also mirrors the position of Pygmalion before his statue in traditional illustrations of Ovid's story. Again, there is a reversal. Rather than sinking down before *Die Kniende*, the man turns his back. The life of the sculpture, its status as a moving and speaking, possibly even dangerous, creature seems to exist only for Grimm's camera and the viewer of his photograph.

In addition to its status as an installation photograph that documents the exhibition, could this moving yet static, sound-filled, yet silent image of a moving statue be considered *Standfotografie*? Mieke Bal makes the case for thinking about exhibitions as "films." Not only do exhibitions create kinetic, temporal narratives that unfold through movement and time, they also sometimes cause the viewer to experience filmic strategies like the demarcation of "scenes," or the creation of "close ups" ("Exhibition as Film" 71–93). In the case of *Entartete Kunst*, the series of "flashbacks" to the objects' former locations and values, or the narrative of de-musealization, might also be considered "cinematic," especially where organizers used photographs. Typical installation shots, like typical film stills, remediate the (filmic) narrative of the exhibitionary space, but normally do so by creating a (fragmented) version of the whole. They author a new still image that suggests or replicates the original work. To do otherwise undermines the still's work as publicity or the installation photo's use-value as illustration or documentation. Just as early photographs of Lehmbruck's sculpture isolated and preserved one definition of its form, these images condensed and "fixed" a particular view of the exhibition or film. They may have shifted its meaning by reframing it, but they remained documentary to the point that they never obliterated the larger narrative.

If we choose to consider Grimm's complex photograph as *Standfotografie*, then we are obliged to ask exactly what narrative the photograph distils. In short, to what "film" is this image attached? It is not clear, for example, that Grimm condenses the *Entartete Kunst* organizers' story of forced removal and de-musealization. While the photo references Hitler's "Four Year Plan" (or the exhibition *Gebt mir vier Jahre Zeit*) through the "speech scroll," it does not create a contrast between the work's former and current state. Although it may "flash back" to the object's past as a musealized artwork (by bringing images related to the notion of the creative force into the photo), it does not depict the work as weakened, mobilized, or "cast out" by the exhibition. Rather, *Die Kniende*'s animated state, its ability to speak and to move, is brought out of the past and into the present through the photograph. The powerful, living sculpture (whether angelic or demonic) haunts the gallery.

Rather than simply replicating the positive narrative of Lehmbruck's *Die Kniende* or the negative strategies of *Entartete Kunst*, Grimm does something more akin to Leni Riefenstahl's supreme directorial approach to documentary. He dismantles and reconstructs what he sees to the point that the result belongs more to him than to its original "authors." He exerts his own artistic agency in the presence of outside creative forces. The photograph of room 6, with its living statue and balance of movement and stasis, suggests *Standfotografie* or a conventional installation shot, but in many ways the film or exhibition it "documents" takes place only in Grimm's imagination. That the picture includes not only references to photography and film, but also to painting and sculpture, puts Grimm's work as a press photographer on a level with these formats, but also beyond them as he commands their strategies through his camera. Grimm's surreal image at its core represents a narrative about his power to remediate.

In the 1970s and 1980s, the second-hand markets became flooded with old film stills as Hollywood studios dumped their archives of outdated photographs. Unsigned by any photographer and circulating unattached to their original contexts and meanings, some were found and used by scholars and some by artists or collectors (Campany 9). Many have simply been lost or forgotten, and with them, important data not just about films, actors, and directors, but about an anonymous, yet influential type of still photography. The same is true for installation photographs of exhibitions and museums. Their continuing anonymity keeps these photographs, along with their makers, strategies, and histories, unrecognized, invisible, and, therefore, outside of the archive of (art) history. Scholars must look not only into these images for what they can offer, but also *at* them. In the end, Grimm's moving statue insists upon it.

NOTES

1 It should also be noted that often the artists whose works are documented in the images are the names given in the photo caption. Depending on the situation, the artist or curator rather than the photographer retains the copyright to such images.

2 Grimm's photos of *Entartete Kunst* were important documents in the reconstruction of the event by Mario-Andreas von Lüttichau (see von Lüttichau).

3 The function of Grimm's photographs is not known. They may have been made for personal use or for the propaganda ministry or a photographic agency. The Bildarchiv Preussische Kulturbesitz retains no information about their publication before 1945 and a survey of articles about the exhibition in major German newspapers and journals in 1937 reveals nothing.

4 For a discussion of press photography in the Third Reich, see Sachsse.

5 Film stills are sometimes confused with frame stills, the individual "photograms" or individual frames that make up a motion picture, which were theorized by Roland Barthes. Film stills (*Standfotografs*) are always independent photographs made by a still camera that often represent the idea of the single fragmentary frame still (see Campany 11).

6 Stills photographers were at the bottom of the hierarchy of the film set. Their works were unsigned and the copyright for the images belonged to the studio. They have therefore remained largely unknown (see Müller 19).

7 For an overview of Lehmbruck's oeuvre, see Schubert.

8 A recent exhibition in Duisburg for the 100th anniversary of the sculpture proposes that the work portrays a bowing dancer and is closely related to the culture of dance in Paris around 1911 (see Stecker).

9 Julius Meier-Graefe was the first to make this comparison with Annunciation imagery in 1914 (Bornscheuer 27).

10 "Reden wir, um konkret zu bleiben, von den Gesetzen der Plastik, von dem Unterschied zwischen Plastik und Pseudoplastik, wie er sich aus einem Vergleich dieses gotischen Verkündigungsengels aus Orvieto mit Lehmbrucks in Haltung und Proportion sehr ähnlichen Knienden ergibt" (Raphael 137).

11 Schubert outlines the various comparisons of the work to Annunciation imagery and suggests Donatello's Annunciation in Santa Croce in Florence (42–3).

12 Kurt Badt also used similar metaphors, describing the work's melody: "Die Melodie, die Kopf und Hand beginnen, klingt durch die ganze Figur fort" (176).

13 "Man muss die Kniende Gestalt des öfteren sehen, um die Sprache der Glieder, der erhobenen Hand … zu vernehmen."
14 "Wohl muss man jetzt auf Teile eingehen wie auf Gebärde und Blick eines Menschen, mit dem man redet, um erst nachher die Bindung der Teile zu gewinnen."
15 "Es … zwang den Betrachter … niederzusinken."
16 For a nuanced discussion of the so-called Tschudi Affair, see Paret.
17 "Die Kniende steht heute im Kronprinzenpalais und hat nicht den richtigen Raum, um ganz vernommen zu werden, aber es gehört zu ihrer Eigenart, dass der ideale Raum, der die ganze Sprache aufzunehmen vermöchte, kaum irgendwo zu finden wäre. Manche photographischen Ausschnitte, die Westheim in seinem Buch reproduziert hat, geben fast mehr von der unabsehbaren Schönheit als der Anblick des Werkes im Museum."
18 This idea was most fully developed by André Malraux, who argued that photographic reproductions of artworks construct an art historical "museum without walls."
19 Christoph Zuschlag outlines the history of the concept of degeneracy in art (20–30).
20 For a description of this debate, see Petropoulos, *Art as Politics* 19–50.
21 For a discussion of the position of museum directors during the Third Reich, see Petropoulos, *The Faustian Bargain* 13–61.
22 "Die Stellung der Regierung zur neuen deutschen Kunst ist noch keineswegs geklärt." For a detailed account of the Kronprinzenpalais's history in the years of the Third Reich, see Janda.
23 "Die Tatsachen der Geschichte, auch der Kunstgeschichte sind nicht Auswirkungen des Zufalls oder einer höheren Fuegung, mit der man sich einfach abzufinden hätte: 'Das ist so die Linie der Entwicklung, man muss sie hinnehmen als etwas Gegebenes.'"
24 One such example may be found in Peter Guenther's recollection of the exhibition in which he states, "I was confronted on all sides by images with which I had grown up, which I admired and loved, and which were now labelled "degenerate" (Guenther 43).
25 Two photos in the Bildarchiv show him standing near newsreel cameras at NSDAP events.

10 "In a Hundred Years of Cinema ...": History and Musealization in Harun Farocki's *Arbeiter verlassen die Fabrik in elf Jahrzehnten*

CHRISTINE SPRENGLER

In 2008 the Hirshhorn Museum in Washington, DC, staged an ambitious two-part exhibition called *The Cinema Effect*. With the intention of reflecting and, to a certain extent, complicating the "dual poles of cinema," part one was subtitled "Dreams" and part two, "Realisms." Co-curated by Kerry Brougher and Kelly Gordon, "Dreams" sought to foreground how artists like Rodney Graham, Kelly Richardson, and Anthony McCall take on the history of cinematic illusion and fantasy through explorations of its apparatus and imagery. Whereas Méliès's presence is felt, sometimes acutely, throughout this first part of the exhibition, the Lumière brothers haunt the corridors of the second. Anne Ellegood's and Kristen Hileman's curatorial vision for "Realisms" is one that focuses on issues of representation and mediation, confronting the distinctions between fiction and reality through the work of Candice Breitz, Isaac Julian, and Runa Islam, among others. In all, *The Cinema Effect*, like other exhibitions of its kind, showcased a wide range of artistic practices invested in the history of cinema and the concept of the cinematic, broadly and variously defined.[1]

But the Lumière brothers do more than inaugurate a history of imaging practices invested in questions of the real. Their landmark 1895 film *Workers Leaving the Factory* (figure 10.1) forms an integral part of a multi-monitor installation enlisted to serve as the transition piece between "Dreams" and "Realisms," namely, Harun Farocki's *Arbeiter verlassen die Fabrik in elf Jahrzehnten* (*Workers Leaving the Factory in Eleven Decades*, 2006). First, however, I want to deal briefly with Farocki's earlier, single-screen version of this work, *Arbeiter verlassen die Fabrik* (*Workers Leaving the Factory*, 1996). By doing so, I hope to set the groundwork for analysing how the reinvention of a single-screen television and film

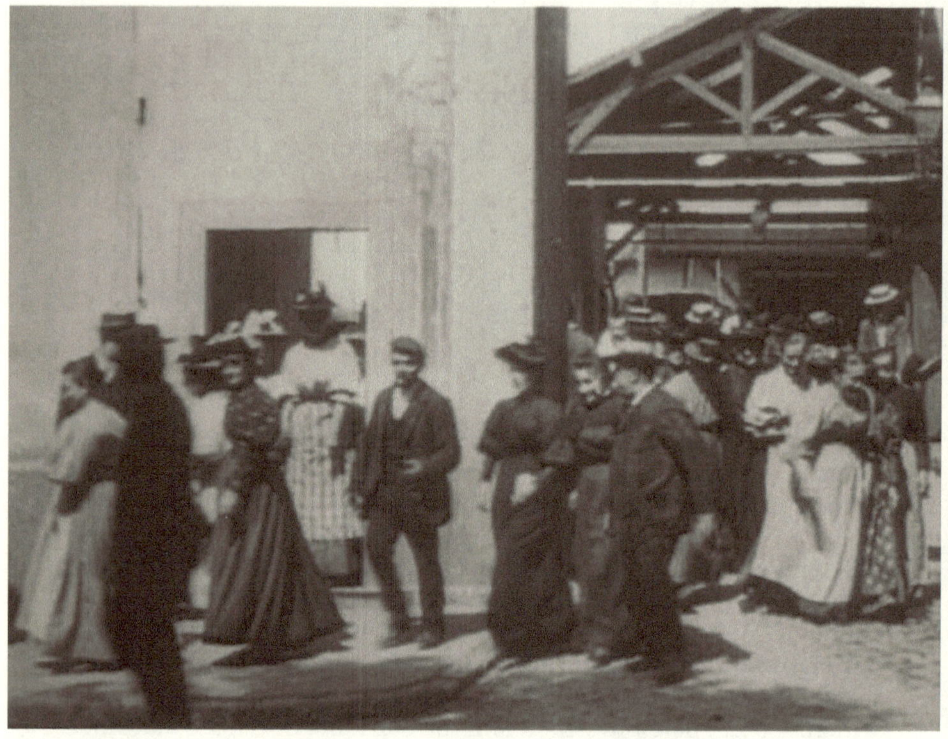

10.1 Still of Lumière's *Workers Leaving the Factory* from *Arbeiter verlassen die Fabrik in elf Jahrzehnten* (*Workers Leaving the Factory in Eleven Decades*). Dir. Harun Farocki. Harun Farocki Filmproduktion, Berlin, 2006. Video installation.

project as a multi-monitor installation presents us with an opportunity to think about essay films in what I call their "expanded" form. In particular, I want to attend to how the historiographical project initiated in its first incarnation is transformed in critically productive ways when installed in an art gallery and how its original focus on argument and analysis develops into a nuanced engagement with the processes of musealization. To conclude, I argue that *Arbeiter verlassen die Fabrik in elf Jahrzehnten* does more than simply reflect on the complexities inherent in the relationships among history, media, and institutions, but has the capacity to yield vital knowledge about the nature of these relationships and to prompt important, even if unanswerable, questions about these issues.

Mediations, Meditations, and Filmic Expressions

Labelled "Germany's best-known *unknown* filmmaker" in 1993, Harun Farocki has since become quite well known as a political filmmaker, film essayist, and, more recently, installation artist (Elsaesser, "Introduction"). An artist active since the mid-1960s, Farocki's works engage broad questions about war, labour, power, institutions of social control, mediation, and technologies of representation, surveillance, and vision. For Thomas Elsaesser his cinema is, above all, a metacinema, one in "constant dialogue with images, with image making, and with the institutions that produce and circulate these images" (Elsaesser, "Introduction"). For Hal Foster, Farocki's works also operate as "myth critiques" in the Barthesian sense, as "analytical rearticulations of ideological images" (158). Indeed, like Barthes, Farocki aims to demystify the machinations of capitalism – its forms, tools, and expressions – for as wide an audience as possible. Broadcast-television viewers, filmgoers, and now museum visitors are all among the constituencies that Farocki seeks to persuade with his incisive social and political critiques such as *Nicht löschbares Feuer* (*Inextinguishable Fire*, 1969), *Bilder der Welt und Inschrift des Krieges* (*Images of the World and the Inscription of War*, 1988), *Leben – BRD* (*How to Live in the German Federal Republic*, 1990), *Videogramme einer Revolution* (*Videograms of a Revolution*, 1992), and *Ich glaubte Gefangene zu sehen* (*I Thought I Was Seeing Convicts*, 2000).

Initially shown in 1995, the single-screen version of *Arbeiter verlassen die Fabrik* was not conceived to fete cinema's centenary, but to reflect on its evolution, histories, and the types of commemorative gestures defined by the extraction and circulation of iconic clips.[2] But while Farocki's film begins with a familiar first in the history of cinema, the various re-presentations of this trope do not belong to any kind of established canon. They are drawn from a hundred years of Hollywood and European narrative film, from silent and sound film, documentaries, newsreels, surveillance, and promotional industrial video. They chart the movement of individuals and masses, workers and workforces, strikes and strikebreaking, and the spaces and technologies that contain, confine, and regulate people. It is a film about labour and about how, as Farocki explains, "the visible movement of people [can stand] in for the absent and invisible movement of goods, money and ideas" ("Workers Leaving the Factory" 243). But it is also a meditation on how images become recognizable and the role of the cinema in determining how and what we see, and how and what we remember.

The first few moments of Farocki's *Arbeiter verlassen die Fabrik* reveal it to be a deeply analytical work. Sequences are described, contextualized, and their meaning and significance interpreted for us. Some are identified, others historically situated in broader social upheavals and political events. Some are repeated, others paused in order to subject the stilled image to closer scrutiny. The text, like the images, is repetitive, and, for both, each iteration introduces some sort of variation. Early on in the film the narrator introduces us to three distinct factory sites and times that are linked by the trope "the workers are running."[3] In 1975 in Emden at the Volkswagen Factory, the "workers are running as if something were drawing them away." In 1926 in Detroit, they are running "as if they had already lost too much time," while in 1957 in Lyon it is "as if they knew somewhere better to be." These analytical statements, though grounded in little more than sheer speculation, unite these sequences under the banner of "workers running" and introduce a strategy of repetition that links spaces and gestures that belong to different histories, establishing comparisons between times, sites, and genres and encouraging us to acknowledge the nuanced articulations of the sub-tropes under the rubric of "workers leaving a factory." It is a strategy pursued throughout with dramatic effect. Later, "in one hundred years of film" is followed first by "there have probably been more prison gates than factory gates" and then by "we can see more prisons and houses of correction than factories and factory gates." The phrase: "Workers leaving the factory" is appended with "as soldiers," or "to join a Nazi rally," among others. However, these repetitive statements are not exclusively descriptive of Farocki's visual dictionary of tropes. They also introduce the ideas that constitute the arguments about media and history advanced by this film. For instance, "an image like an expression" is followed by "which can be suited to many statements" and then "so often used that it can be understood blindly."

Indeed, these last two phrases speak not only to the complex relationships between what we see and hear in Farocki's work; they also reveal something of the structuring logic and aesthetic sensibilities underpinning this film. As Trond Lundemo suggests, *Arbeiter verlassen die Fabrik* is very much an "archival project, where the constant re-organization and repetition of isolated items and files are made in accordance with the criteria of the search" (qtd. in Wahlberg 19). This archival impulse, at play throughout Farocki's oeuvre, has also been described as encyclopaedic, iconological, and focused on the status and possibilities of the trace (Blümlinger 319). For Farocki, these "filmic expressions" constitute a kind of "film thesaurus" and stock what he calls his "archive for research into the development of concepts" (Hüser 308).[4] Motifs are tracked across media, genres, periods, and cultural contexts, shedding and accruing meaning in the process. They are deconstructed – dissected into their constituent parts and variations. Workers leave different types of factories, wear different types of clothing, move in different types of ways, and ultimately do different types of things once they've left. In the process, Farocki reveals the fluidity and malleability of this trope. He shows us what changes with each iteration or re-imaging, but also what persists. He exposes the extent to which cultures, histories, and contexts both preserve and shape what it means to leave a factory and the ways in which visual media, whether fictional or documentary, define the significance of this ostensibly simple act and the significance of its actors. Workers here are as much the product of a documentary strike reel as they are of an Eisenstein film and our knowledge of them is moulded and circumscribed by the discursive strategies at work in different forms of cinema.

This approach has earned *Arbeiter verlassen die Fabrik* its description as archival and, despite Farocki's hesitation about this term, its designation as an "essay film."[5] As such, Farocki's project shares certain affinities with others similarly defined, including kindred works like Chris Marker's *Sans soleil* (1983), Daniel Eisenberg's *Persistence* (1997), or Jean-Luc Godard's *Histoire(s) du cinéma* (1988–98). At its core a self-reflexive genre (and I use that word rather loosely), the essay film has been described as a "meeting ground for documentary, avant-garde and art film impulses" (Arthur, "Essay Questions" 62). It is seen as a point of encounter between "fact and fiction," "the real and the artificial," and an interrogative practice "consciously engaged in the activity of representation itself" (Biemann 10). For Laura Rascaroli, "essay films pose searching questions about the cinema as a repository of memory, as museum and as archive" (64). Its near "axiomatic" reliance on found footage, as Paul Arthur characterizes it, necessitates what I would argue is a near axiomatic engagement with history, memory, and representation (*A Line of Sight* 66). *Arbeiter verlassen die Fabrik* is and/or does all these things and it does them rather well. But what I want to focus on in what follows is what Rascaroli's and Arthur's statements intimate:

the capacity for essay films to do historiography, to question how and through what means history is produced, how cultural memories are shaped and disseminated. And to see how this is affected by its transition from a single screen work into an installation, and one that, in the process, presents us with an opportunity to consider an added dimension of the work: its incisive engagement with musealization and the museal nature of much contemporary media.

By selecting clips from one hundred years of cinema, *Arbeiter verlassen die Fabrik* presents us with an array of sequences with very different aesthetic sensibilities, ones that become readily apparent through frequent cross-cutting. A montage organized by the sub-trope "the factory as a scene of crime" begins with a promotional video from 1987 demonstrating the effectiveness of a subterranean barrier, cuts to robbers posing as workers in Siodmak's *The Killers* (1946), which itself is first stilled to enable the narrator to explain what is happening and then interrupted by an undated sequence of surveillance footage showing "real" robbers hopping a factory fence. The space outside the factory – absent but imagined in the first, staged in the second, and actual in the third example – is captured on 35 mm and video, and contextualized by a range of genres. Each incarnation of "the factory as a scene of crime" certainly looks different, a result of varying approaches to framing and editing and the fundamental technological distinctions between film and video. With these juxtapositions, Farocki alerts us to the ways in which diverse technologies and formal strategies represent – and thereby construct and preserve – space. Noir, promotional, and surveillance all contribute to a visual discourse of sorts that constitutes our understanding of this space as a site of contest and one whose status as public or private has itself been contested.[6] As such, it also functions as a site of memory, one where history happened, where political struggles were initiated and fought out. Farocki's inclusion of multiple and divergent visions of this space promote an awareness of the role played by representational practices in framing and memorializing sites, times, and events. He reminds us that we cannot have any kind of direct, unmediated access to our past, but that history is available to us only in mediated fragments or, in other words, what Linda Hutcheon calls its "textualized remains" (*Poetics* 30).

And yet, Farocki's argument here is not that we cannot access history in any unproblematic way, so we might as well not try. Instead, he proposes that though we need to be cognizant of how visual media inflect representations of history, we still have something historical to learn from these images, from the practices that created them, and indeed as much from fiction as that which is ostensibly factual. In part, this argument is advanced through the relationship established between found footage and Farocki's script. Whereas the appropriated materials are highly diverse, the narration is not. It describes and analyses fictional and documentary sequences in remarkably similar ways. Both are treated as significant historical objects – as implicated in the construction of our knowledge of the past, as vestiges of it, and as conduits to both histories of representational practices and histories of events. For example, around the sub-trope of "policing the exit of workers from their factories," we again see a clip from the promotional film for gates, this time demonstrating their resistance to the elements – rain, snow, and hot desert winds. This sequence is absolutely silent. Next, we see workers escorted off factory property while hearing: "Workers are leaving the factory here because the police are clearing the grounds and locking them out. Among the workers is one particularly concerned about his personal honour." The voice-over describes what is happening, in the same way it does in a Pathé newsreel of a Birmingham strike in 1965 or workers outside Detroit's Ford factory in 1926. But in this instance, it describes Charlie Chaplin without ever identifying the sequence's source as *Modern Times* (1936). Here Farocki suggests that Chaplin might give as much insight into work at the Ford plant as the documentary footage witnessed earlier. And, indeed, in other instances, it is fiction – Griffiths, Lang, Pudovkin – that initiates Farocki's more searching political commentary about broader social and historical forces.

So, what happens to these historiographical engagements and the film's "essay" status when the single-screen version broadcast on television and in film theatres becomes *Arbeiter verlassen die Fabrik in elf Jahrzehnten*, an installation destined solely for art galleries and museums? For the curators of *The Cinema Effect*, this piece was supposed to play a very specific role. As noted, it was tasked with bridging and also challenging the Dreams/Realisms binary that structured the show. And indeed it does through its choice and arrangement of clips from the history of film. However, I think it is useful to spend some time with this incarnation of the work for two further reasons. First, it is noteworthy how this expanded version continues to function historiographically and essayistically, albeit in different ways. Second, the ways in which it tackles questions of history and media lead directly into a critical engagement with the museum site and with processes of musealization. In doing so, *Arbeiter verlassen die Fabrik in elf Jahrzehnten* does much

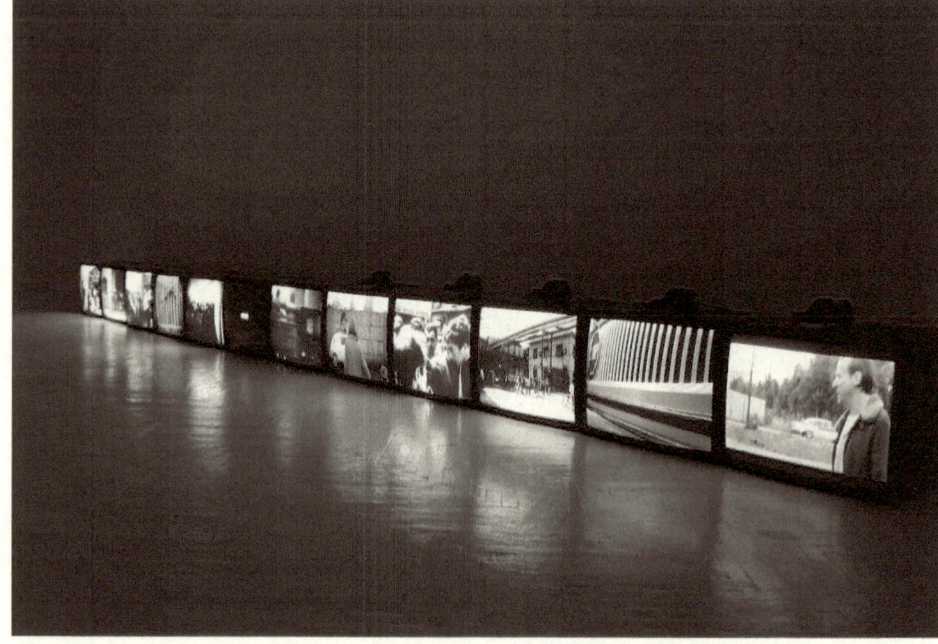

10.2 Exhibition view of *Arbeiter verlassen die Fabrik in elf Jahrzehnten*. Photo credit: Harun Farocki, "Arbeiter verlassen die Fabrik in elf Jahrzehnten," in *tranzitdisplay*, Prague. © Jiří Thýn 2009.

more than connect two halves of the Hirshhorn exhibition; it confronts a set of issues related to history and media, exemplifying along the way how art not only reflects, but also offers tremendous insight into, broader contemporary cultural concerns.

Expanding the Essay Film: History and Historiography

Arbeiter verlassen die Fabrik in elf Jahrzehnten is comprised of twelve monitors placed in a row on the gallery floor, each looping a different, single sequence (figure 10.2).[7] Monitor one plays the Lumière film, while the rest play clips both familiar and new in chronological order: another Lumière film from 1899, documentary footage of Moscow in 1912, D.W. Griffith's *Intolerance* (1916), Fritz Lang's *Metropolis* (1926), Charlie Chaplin's *Modern Times*, Slatan Dudow's *Frauenschicksale* (1952),

Michelangelo Antonioni's *Il deserto rosso* (1964), Jacques Willemont's *La reprise du travail aux usines Wonder* (1968), Danièle Huillet and Jean-Marie Straub's *Trop tôt, trop tard* (1982), a promotional film, *Durchfahrtssperren DSP* (1987), demonstrating gates, and Lars von Trier's *Dancer in the Dark* (2000).[8] The narration is gone. Instead, visitors can listen to the original soundtracks of some of the films on offer. None are translated. I am calling this an "expanded essay film" in order to evoke the tradition of expanded cinema that Farocki cites as influential on his recent installation work – though less in Gene Youngblood's sense of expanding consciousness than Birgit Hein's more general assessment of a practice that, in some way, goes "beyond the individual film projection" to include multiple projections, mixed media, as well as spatial and temporal expansions (qtd. in Export). Though some, including Philip Lopate, might suggest that translating the single-screen *Arbeiter verlassen die Fabrik* into its multi-monitor format disqualifies it as an essay film (245), I would argue with Nora Alter that "the nature of the essay encourages and promotes its translation … into other media and forms" (55). Her important work on the audiovisual essay as installation makes a compelling case for how essayistic explorations and arguments are not at all compromised by this shift from two to three dimensions. Instead, she argues for the need to appreciate how these explorations and arguments function differently. In the case of *Arbeiter verlassen die Fabrik in elf Jahrzehnten*, it is now up to the images, their juxtaposition, and an active, critical spectator to do the analytical work accomplished (in part) by Farocki's script in the original.

There are a number of ways in which *Arbeiter verlassen die Fabrik in elf Jahrzehnten* continues the historiographical project initiated by the single-screen version. The integration of fiction and documentary, sound and silent film, various aesthetic strategies and media formats continues Farocki's project of addressing the cinematic image as historical and of construing history itself as a representational practice necessarily mediated and implicated in relations of power. It reflects on the search for origins and acts of iteration. It also explores the role of images in the production and circulation of cultural memory and cinema's role in the creation of what Alison Landsberg has called "prosthetic memory," memories "that circulate publicly, that are not organically based, but that are nevertheless experienced with one's own body – by means of a wide range of cultural technologies – and as such, become part of one's personal archive of experience, informing not only one's subjectivity, but one's relationship to the present and future" (*Prosthetic*

Memory 66). Farocki's expanded essay film is invested in complicating the notion of prosthetic memory, showing how media shape and circulate historical memory but also how the vicissitudes of historical memories, their multiple and complex typologies, are based on subsequent re-presentations in different forms.

Crucially, *Arbeiter verlassen die Fabrik in elf Jahrzehnten* also pursues its historiographical project by extending what Farocki calls his "soft montage" from its typical double-screen articulation to the use of multiple monitors, leading to a near infinite number of juxtapositions between the images on offer. For Farocki, soft montage trades in a "general relatedness" rather than a "strict opposition or equation" (*Speaking about Godard* 142). Associations are suggested by the images, but it remains the work of the spectator to pursue the significance and parse the meanings of these associations. As such, this project is part of a series of explorations – including *Schnittstelle* (*Interface*, 1995), *Ich glaubte Gefangene zu sehen* (*I Thought I Was Seeing Convicts*), and *Gegen-Musik* (*Counter-Music*, 2004) – that activate various forms of spatial montage, returning us to the earliest histories of cinema, including histories of experimental film and video practices. With soft montage, Farocki aims to usher in a series of moments that lend themselves to comparative analysis and to dialogical encounters, rather than provide an exclusively temporal succession of images where one image replaces another, where one image speaks directly to another and establishes a dichotomy that restricts instead of expands the possible parameters of analysis. In *Arbeiter verlassen die Fabrik in elf Jahrzehnten*, as in other multi-projection works like *Deep Play* (2007), the simultaneous presentation of several images at once spatializes time and history, whether across an entire century or a few short moments that defined a single event. While a degree of linearity remains in the chronology of the clips, the filmic sequences themselves and, quite literally, in the placement of the monitors in a row, the twelve distinct streams of images come into multiple, fleeting points of contact with each other. And they do so for a variety of reasons both formal and content-driven, as when shots of similar distance, tropes, objects, or gestures momentarily unite disparate decades, sites, and genres. Thus, the work unsettles the historical linearity that it initially and superficially appears to promise, and complicates the criteria by which historical narratives are extracted from the sounds and images that constitute the past. History, in all this, starts to look like the increasingly random endeavour that it is, one that is less positivist and rational than accidental, intuitive, and variable.

Expanding the Essay Film: Museal Practices and Museum Spaces

Part of what Farocki's soft montage strategy also contributes, in its physically expanded form, is a reflection on the processes of musealization and the museal nature of the cinema. It does so in especially productive ways in the context of *The Cinema Effect* exhibition, and in a manner that draws on and thus preserves the historiographical thrust of the work. In its broadest terms, musealization speaks to what Andreas Huyssen, referring to the work of Hermann Lübbe, calls the "expansive historicism of our contemporary culture" and to the ways in which museological operations have become the purview of other cultural practices – including the cinema (*Twilight Memories* 25). Invoking Godard, Rascaroli suggests that "the whole history of cinema ... may be viewed in terms of musealization" and that essay films especially "which select, store, recontextualizing and disseminate images of the past," function according to a museal sensibility (67). Certainly this is what *Arbeiter verlassen die Fabrik in elf Jahrzehnten* accomplishes. It does so as a single-screen work, but in more direct if not self-reflexive ways as a multi-monitor installation. As an installation, each clip ostensibly becomes an object. These fragments, from celebrated and forgotten films, are endowed with a physical materiality and, in the process, are transformed into the kind of art objects that recall the collecting, preserving, and contextualizing functions of the museum. But encasing these mostly cinematic clips in television monitors goes beyond these functions. It speaks, on the one hand, to *Arbeiter verlassen die Fabrik*'s own history as a television work, encouraging us to think about the institutional and cultural pressures that have forced its migration into this new space. Farocki explains that he had no choice but to leave the cinema for the art world. Dwindling cinema audiences for his kind of films, lack of exhibition venues and what he perceives to be the "less narrow idea of how images and sound should conform" on the part of art viewers, are some of the reasons behind this shift ("Cross Influence/ Soft Montage" 73). On the other hand, Farocki's move to the art world draws our attention to the ways in which distinct presentational formats mediate the expressions they contain, and are themselves mediated in turn through further iterations in an unending process – an important historiographical point to be sure and one that builds on the critical project of the single-screen version.

In this way, Farocki's installation presents itself as a set of Russian dolls, each stratum associated with its own sets of museal practices:

history is encased in the cinema which is encased in the television monitor which is encased in the museum. As practices, forms of media, and distinct institutions, history, cinema, television, and the museum are each understood through their relations with the past, with the means and extent to which they conserve the past, and foster expressions of cultural or national memory. Each frames the past in particular ways and, quite crucially, each frames the other. Their dependencies, differences, and points of contact emerge in this work and each is understood through the other: history becomes understood through cinema, and cinema through history; the cinema is understood through television, and television through cinema, and so on. Farocki's framing strategies also suggest the extent to which history, cinema, and television are all implicated – if not united – in a similar historical project to preserve and contextualize objects and images, those mobilized as conduits to the past. While each medium or practice might approach this project somewhat differently and to different effect, the forms of history, cinema, television, and the museum are all governed by a similar museal impulse.

By drawing our attention to the operations of the museum, *Arbeiter verlassen die Fabrik in elf Jahrzehnten* also echoes Volker Pantenburg's warning to think critically about the implications of film's relocation into this context. While some celebrate the new aesthetic and spectatorial modes enabled by this shift, Pantenburg rightly reminds us that museums are not neutral spaces, that the "black box" is as much an ideological framework as the film theatre or the "white cube" (4–5). And this is what Farocki's installation ultimately does by occupying a transitional space in ways beyond those imagined by Hirshhorn's curators. Positioned near the escalators in the second floor lobby, it is neither inside the exhibition proper, nor outside the museum space, neither in the type of black box that housed the majority of the projection pieces, nor in the brightly lit, white-walled space one floor up.[9] In many respects it activates a kind of grey area, both literally and figuratively. It turns a thoroughfare into a space in which one feels obliged to stop, to look and contemplate – that is, to perform the labour that sites marked as exhibitionary prompt us to do. As such, it ushers in an awareness of how certain sites are defined by and encourage certain types of labour and thus how space and labour are interconnected if not interdependent in determining ways. However, it also turns us, the visitor, into another manifestation of Farocki's key trope, and implicates us in his archive of concepts. "Workers leaving the factory" is extended through our involvement to visitors leaving the gallery. Aligning visitors with workers certainly makes us think about what might have been produced through our encounter with the installation. And, of course, the museum in this equation becomes aligned with the factory, a site that operates according to industrial logic and one that manufactures standardized parts.[10]

Moreover, through its specific choice of clips, Farocki's work also evokes the way in which both factories and museums operate as institutions of social control, spaces under constant surveillance that promote an internalized managerial gaze and, in the process, regulate our behaviour. Spaces that transform individuals into masses – workforces and audiences – and discourage expressions of agency or "concern for personal honour." Spaces that carefully structure our movements in and through them, despite the freedom of mobile spectatorship promised by museum rhetoric. Spaces with very specific and somewhat parallel histories of their own become sites of memory and memorialization, sites implicated in changing dynamics of power through changes to exhibitionary complexes. Therefore, *Arbeiter verlassen die Fabrik in elf Jahrzehnten* not only alerts us to the collecting, preserving, and contextualizing aspects of musealization, but also its controlling, standardizing, and regulating impulses as well. Indeed, it allows us to think through how these impulses manifest themselves across the spectrum of museal practices at issue here, including history as a discipline and cinema both fictional and documentary.

In other words, with the collaboration of spectators who actively "co-perform" analysis along with the art object, *Arbeiter verlassen die Fabrik in elf Jahrzehnten* has the capacity to illuminate and accomplish plenty of things.[11] Like a traditional essay film, it makes a series of arguments about labour, factories, the cinema, and history. But it does so in a way that furnishes us with the tools to reflect critically on the issues associated with these subjects, to participate in the formulation of such arguments, and to acknowledge what is at stake in making claims about the past. It sparks realizations about the complexities and dynamics that govern relations between institutions and representational practices. As such, Farocki's expanded essay film does more than simply argue a position as it did in its first incarnation. Now, it also teaches. And what it teaches is not a set of historical or cinematic facts, nor a series of claims that can be easily refuted, but rather which intractable problems borne out of increasingly intertwined museal practices require further inquiry in our contemporary age. For instance, whereas the single-screen version of *Arbeiter verlassen die Fabrik* sought to advance the claim that since cinema and the factory's first encounter in 1895, the two have repelled each other, the multi-monitor version encourages us to confront the dynamics of musealization, media, and history and the web of connections between them. It prompts us to consider the significance of relations between media genres and histories, the impact of certain strategies of representation, and the function of institutions – factories, museums, and prisons.

Thinking in Film

To suggest that art teaches us something is not a radical notion. Art's faculty for generating knowledge has been recognized in very general terms, and its edifying potential has been the subject of philosophical debate for centuries. Questions about art's capacity to improve us in some way, drive us to political action, or help us better understand our world have emerged in a variety of iterations throughout the history of art. More recently, these questions have been broached by those reflecting on the idea of art as research, art as theory, and art as knowledge.[12] These paradigms are especially useful for engaging with Farocki's filmic installations and shed light on how and why *Arbeiter verlassen die Fabrik in elf Jahrzehnten* succeeds in a pedagogical vein.

Part of the success of *Arbeiter verlassen die Fabrik in elf Jahrzehnten* can be attributed to the features it shares with what Hubert Damisch calls a "theoretical object." Damisch explains:

> A theoretical object is something that obliges one to do theory. Second, it's an object that obliges you to do theory but also furnishes you with the means of doing it. Thus, if you agree to accept it on theoretical terms, it will produce effects around itself ... Third, it's a theoretical object because it forces us to ask ourselves what theory is. It is posed in theoretical terms; it produces theory; and it necessitates a reflection on theory. But I never pronounce the word theory without also saying the word history. Which is to say that for me such an object is always a theoretico-historical object. (qtd. in Bois, Hollier, and Krauss 8)

A theoretical object can be an artwork in its entirety or one of its constituent elements. For instance, Damisch regards clouds in Renaissance and Baroque painting as emblematic of pictoriality itself, as objects that complicate the paradigm of perspective by opening up a set of theoretical questions about the achievements and failures of perspective as a representational device (Bois, Hollier, and Krauss 8). Clouds have this capacity because they elude the structuring force of perspective and are thus, under this system, unrepresentable and consequently unknowable to a degree, and thereby bring into sharp focus concerns of an epistemological character. They also operate like a hinge, an all-too-often neglected tool that performs an important function by linking the visual components and ideas that constitute a painting, for example, heaven and earth (Damisch 146). They derive their meaning from the spaces or realms they connect, but also enable consideration of the nature of these spaces and the concepts in which they are grounded, not to mention the nature of representation itself.

For Damisch, and for Farocki too, art is an agent with the capacity to confront theoretical issues, an agent historical in nature and inevitably historically determined, but one that nevertheless allows for the pursuit of certain transhistorical concerns, like labour. *Arbeiter verlassen die Fabrik* and *Arbeiter verlassen die Fabrik in elf Jahrzehnten* are certainly theoretical objects in their own right, objects that work on and through a series of theoretical projects associated with cinema, the history and future of film, and historical questions about access, representation, mediation, and, in the case of the latter, museal practices of preservation, organization, display, and regulation. The status of these works as essay – or expanded essay – films only heightens their theoretical bent. In fact, what makes video essays like these so interesting to scholars, including Ursula Biemann, is their "commitment to theory" and how they manage to "test the possibility of theory-building through visual means" (89). One might say, following Mieke Bal's lead, that art of this nature "thinks" (*Travelling Concepts* 61).[13] Indeed, this comment is a fitting assessment given Farocki's assertion that he tries "to think in film so that the ideas come out of filmic articulation" (Foster, "Vision Quest" 157). Elsewhere, Bal proposes that if "visual art makes any sense at all beyond the narrow domain of beauty and the affective domain of pleasure, it is because art, too, thinks; it is thought" (*Quoting Caravaggio* 117). This thought is not something generated in response to an artistic gesture, nor does it refer to an idea or narrative made manifest through visual form. Instead, it is "visual thought, the thought embodied in form" (117).

The importance of history to theory and, more generally, of history in conceptions of art's capacity to do theory or produce knowledge, surfaces in other permutations of these ideas. While Ernst van Alphen does not appeal to "theory" in the way Damisch or Bal do, he convincingly shows us how an artwork might "practice cultural philosophy" by functioning as a "historical agent" rather than a "historical product"(xiii). Art, for van Alphen, has successfully intervened in our "thinking, imagining, and representing such key aspects of human existence as individuality, identity, and space" (xvi). In the case of Farocki's expanded essay film, we see an intervention into aspects of labour, history, cinema, and the museum. And, more than simply intervene, art, from this perspective, has the capacity to undertake philosophical projects, to explore the cultural issues that occupy our thoughts, and to make very real contributions to how ideas take hold and develop. In fact, van Alphen argues that art does more than simply contribute to existing discourses. It can "transform the ways in which cultural issues are being conceived" (xiii).

That is what *Arbeiter verlassen die Fabrik in elf Jahrzehnten* accomplishes best. It transforms the ways in which cultural issues surrounding media practices and institutions are being conceived and thought about. It allows us to see with a critical gaze how history operates, not alone as an independent, empiricist discipline, but as one intricately connected to a set of institutions and media practices. It reveals the web of connections and cross-influences among history, cinema, museums, and, of course, factories. And it allows us to recognize how history and the cinema each operate according to a museal sensibility, how the process of musealization in terms of its collecting and preservational practices as well as its ideological functions structures and mediates our views of the past.

NOTES

1 Other exhibitions include *Spellbound: Art and Film* at the Hayward Gallery (1996), *Into the Light: The Projected Image in American Art 1964–1977* at the Whitney (2001), *Future Cinema* at ZKM (2002–3), and *Projections* at the Justina M. Barnicke Gallery (2007), to name just a few.

2 It is important to note that *Workers Leaving the Factory* was created at a time during which such practices were "ripe with clips and cuts" (Rebhandl 123).

3 The narrator in the German version of *Workers Leaving the Factory* is Harun Farocki and in the English version, Kaja Silverman.

4 Consider Farocki's statement: "More than anything it's a great pleasure to have … versions of the same process before your eyes. I would love to have a book with a thousand versions of the motif 'A woman takes something away from a sleeping man'" (qtd. in Hüser 308).

5 Of the essay film, Farocki voices concern about its dilution and vagueness in contemporary practice. He states: "This category is just as unsuitable as 'documentary film,' sure. When there is a lot of music on TV and you see landscapes – they've started calling that an essay film as well. A lot of stuff that's just relaxing and not unequivocally journalistic is already called an essay. That's terrible of course" (qtd. in Hüser 313).

6 However, though differences seem most noteworthy here, we are also struck by similarities and realize the slippages between fiction and documentary and the ways in which these genres borrow heavily from one another.

7 Please note that this installation view was from an exhibition at Tranzitdisplay. An installation view from the Hirshhorn was not available.

8 Clearly not all "eleven" decades are represented here. In fact, the 1940s, 1970s, and 1990s are missing, with two examples each from the 1960s and 1980s. Perhaps this rather blatant diversion from the descriptive title of the work is a remark on the artificiality of decades as periods and the pitfalls of periodization as a practice.

9 Douglas Gordon's work *Off Screen* (1998) established a distinct inside to the exhibition by requiring visitors to walk through a heavy cinema curtain onto which red light was projected.

10 Hito Steyerl has pursued the connection between factories and museums in her analysis of the affinities between these two spaces and the practice of turning former industrial sites into art museums – Tate Modern being a prime example (see Steyerl).

11 The idea that art objects and spectators "co-perform" analyses is an idea pursued by Jill Bennett and grounded in her reading of Mieke Bal's work on art's capacity to think or produce knowledge, points that will be pursued momentarily in the conclusion. Bennett also, quite rightly, argues that such practices "operat(e) at the intersection of different discourses, practices and aesthetics [and] constitute an intermedial space through which new ways of seeing and new terms for analysis can emerge" (436).

12 Consider, for instance, the explosion in recent years of PhD programs in art *practice*, wherein research and writing constitute a significant component of the degree. It is also a very practical concern given present-day funding structures in the arts and humanities. This is particularly true in Canada, where the Social Sciences and Humanities Research Council introduced a funding competition for major "research-creation" grants.

13 Mieke Bal, too, shares Damisch's belief in the power of art to function theoretically. Bal writes that theory "is not an instrument of analysis, to

be 'applied' to the art object supposedly serving it but in fact subjecting it. Instead, it is a discourse that can be brought to bear on the object at the same time as the object can be brought to bear on *it*" (*Travelling Concepts* 61). For her, the capacity for artworks to exist as theoretical objects speaks in more general terms to an artwork's ability to behave in a conceptually self-reflexive way, to offer and articulate thought about art (see Bal, "Narrative Inside Out").

11 Sex on Display: Sexual Science and the Exhibition *PopSex!*

MICHAEL THOMAS TAYLOR AND
ANNETTE F. TIMM

N.O.Body, a fifteen-minute film from 2008 by Pauline Boudry and Renate Lorenz, opens with a bearded woman, or perhaps a man in drag, who walks slowly down the steps of an empty nineteenth-century lecture hall. Standing on a display table at the front of the room – a space the viewer has been invited to inhabit – she takes a remote control and turns on a projector to superimpose an image over her body. The image is in fact a photograph recognizable as one possible iteration of herself: Annie Jones, the circus attraction and most famous bearded lady of the nineteenth century, as we know from the artists' description of the work (Boudry and Lorenz 20; see also Lorenz 15, 25). What follows is a disruptive play of identities that unfolds as the performer projects images onto her body and the screen, exploring herself in the light and the shadows she casts. The diverse identities and images coincide in the sense that all articulate dimensions of *Geschlecht*, a German word that can mean both sex and gender, as well as race, generation, and genus.

The images come from popular culture, from magazines and other print media, from private archives, and from the pages of medical and sexual science journals. They are identities defined and created as images that have been objectified, pathologized, stigmatized, and commercialized. At the same time, they invoke but do not explain their subjects' hidden, perhaps unknown histories. The possible agency of these lives is evoked when the object of medicalized investigation presents herself as a performer; her position as a subject within this scene complicates the discourses of knowledge production, which define supposedly natural sexual identities. Her performance thus disrupts the structure of the "gaze," be it understood in Foucauldian or feminist terms.[1] This disruption intensifies when she turns on the radio to listen in to the background noise of the universe. The radio blares out pop music as well as cosmic science-fiction sounds that seem to enter into her body to produce a snorting, explosive laugh. Bodily experience – bodily happening, really – reasserts itself over the subject–object relations of visual display. But at the same time, this fit of laughter is in danger of being medicalized once again as we follow our modern prejudices to diagnose it as hysteria. It performs a relationship that Renate Lorenz has theorized as "contagion" – an infectious affect that defers and suspends structures of recognition and normalization (Lorenz 17).

These transpositions and superimpositions articulate a series of shifts that characterize the history of the museum. They outline first a history of display in circuses, fairs, panopticons, and cabinets of curiosities that were, in the course of the nineteenth century, institutionalized in museum spaces and appropriated by new sciences such as anthropology. They also reflect the commercialization and spread of this knowledge in popular culture. *N.O.Body* encapsulates these themes by tracing a tension between the overwhelmingly visual nature of display in the late nineteenth and early twentieth centuries and the ostensibly corporeal, physical truths of which it was taken as evidence. It exposes the categories and identities this display was supposed to make visible, the abstract taxonomies used to categorize the bodies and desires of the "subjects" of sexual science, while reminding us with its title that there is "no body" here, no material, physical essence independent of the gaze of the scientist or voyeur. To take inspiration from the work of Mieke Bal, the film thus transforms a scene of gazing into a dialogic happening that unfolds and can be analysed the way a narrative can (Bal *Looking In*). The film makes explicit and explores the positions characterizing the situations of speech that are inherent within these various scenes of display. It acts out a shift from an understanding of spectatorship as a static relationship, in which an absent third-person narrator projects knowledge onto passive recipients, to a more complex, dialogic relationship in which the spectator is an active participant in this happening. The film constructs a narrative, in other words, about itself and about structures of the Gaze that challenge the conditions by which it is viewed.

In short, then, *N.O.Body* can be read as a film about the musealization of sex. For this reason among others, we chose to show this film in Calgary, Canada (on DVD), as part of an exhibition called *PopSex!* Staged at the Alberta College of Art + Design in January 2011, the exhibition combined images from the history of sexual science – and in particular the history of Magnus Hirschfeld – with artistic responses to this history.[2] Hirschfeld, whose period of work and influence stretched from just before 1900 to his death in 1935, was among the leaders of the world's first movement for minority sexual rights and a key founder of sexual science. By introducing him to a Calgary audience unlikely to be very familiar with his work, we sought to promote a discussion about the origins of modern sexual identities and the place of this history and its images in our own sexual present. This essay reflects upon our practice as scholars and curators; more broadly, our aim is to think about the role of sexual display for the history of museums in this history.

The World's First Sex Museum

Magnus Hirschfeld's Institut für Sexualwissenschaft (Institute for Sexual Science), founded in Berlin in 1919, was arguably the world's first widely known sex museum.[3] In a former aristocratic villa in the Tiergarten district of Berlin, members of the institute spatially and conceptually combined the goals of research, clinical practice, and public advocacy. In terms of research, Hirschfeld followed the universally accepted scientific practice of the day in believing that scientific research needed to be buttressed with extensive material collections.[4] He built a collection of sexual artefacts and photographs that he saw as analogous to the carefully ordered archives of Ernst Haeckel's phylogenetic institute in Jena, Louis Pasteur's biological institute in Paris, and Rudolf Virchow's Pathology Institute at the Charité hospital nearby (Herrn 4). But Hirschfeld took this impulse to display objects as evidence of scientific research into a new dimension by blurring the boundary between the objective researcher, the object of research, and the museum visitor. As patients seeking advice about physical or psychological sexual concerns made their way through the hallways and staircases of the institute, and even in the consultation rooms themselves, they passed display cases containing a wide assortment of fetish items, dildos, masturbatory aids, birth control devices, and photos of hermaphrodites, castrati, and nudes of every description. The institute thus borrowed from techniques of display found in existing museums while also highlighting the continuity of this display with traditions from which the museum had differentiated itself as it developed during the nineteenth century. In this regard, it reflected the anxieties shared by curators of ethnological and anthropological museums of the time – above all, worries about the commercialization of this display and about crowds motivated by little but "Schaulust" – a lust to look. Despite the institute's pedagogical and scientific goals, the nature and placement of its objects could not help but evoke earlier *Wunderkammer* – those early-modern collections of exotic objects used to provide entertainment and prove the worldliness of aristocratic families.[5] And the private tours that Hirschfeld provided to prominent visitors (particularly other scientists, politicians, and interested foreigners like André Gide and Christopher Isherwood) were not far removed from the practice of rich treasure hunters proudly displaying their trophies to honoured guests.

Like the museums it resembled, the institute adopted strategies to minimize these dangers. Both the placement of objects within the institute and the specific content of each tour were structured with a variety of sensibilities in mind. Explanations were customized to the knowledge of the particular audience: the less enlightened were shielded from objects that had the potential to unduly shock, and captions were minimal, so that the amount of information conveyed could be customized (Herrn 12; Giese 142). Importantly, Hirschfeld made a point that visitors should view the collections only as part of a tour in which a guide could explain what they were seeing. Karl Giese, the institute's archivist (and Hirschfeld's companion), usually led these tours, which were offered weekly to the public at large beginning in 1924. Visitors often had the opportunity to meet members of sexual minorities, particularly transvestites (a word that Hirschfeld coined), who were symbols of the institute's threefold purposes of research, treatment, and advocacy. Hirschfeld and his colleagues made a conscious attempt to distinguish their practice from the unsubstantiated claims and sensationalistic tactics of the popularizers. The institute's museal function was thus compatible with other ethnographic and anthropological projects of the day that sought to distinguish scientific displays from mere entertainment (Bennett, *Birth* 41, 59; Penny 168).

In short, the institute's goal was to educate rather than to titillate. Institute members saw their work as scientific, but they also viewed themselves as public educators rather than simply as researchers. As Giese explained in the popular sex-reform magazine *Die Aufklärung* ("The Enlightenment" – in this case referring to sexual enlightenment), public tours were a conscious attempt to appeal directly to the general population, bypassing the often very unenlightened teaching about sex common in medical circles. These "predetermined orthodoxies," Giese argued, presented "a particularly difficult obstacle for [the] unprejudiced approach" to sexual subjects advocated in the institute (Giese

142). While other anthropological museums also made direct appeals to the public, Hirschfeld's institute was unique in both its direct challenge to established scientific (in this case medical) teaching and the sexual nature of its collection. As public interest grew in the early 1920s, and daily tours became the rule, Hirschfeld and his co-workers became increasingly sensitive to the danger that a public desire for entertainment and sensation would overwhelm their pedagogical and reformist mission. Giese implied as much when he insisted that despite the obvious focus on "abnormal" manifestations of the sexual, the displays were intended to "strip the objects of the sensational" in order to thwart the "danger of confusion rather than explanation" (Giese 141–2). And yet, as Rainer Herrn argues, there was also clearly some manipulation of prurient curiosity to serve educative goals – "'the sensational' dimensions of the displays certainly spoke directly to the expectations of the visitors" (Herrn 12).

Science, clinical treatment, and entertainment thus sat in particularly fraught tension with each other in the Institute for Sexual Science. On the one hand, there was an enormous emphasis placed on objectively observable biological "facts." Hirschfeld's scientific taxonomies proliferated in the sexual scientific literature of the day because of the explanatory power of his basic assumption that both sexuality and gender were characteristics expressed as a continuum of varying natural traits. Although he believed in the diversity of human sexual identity, and despite the fact that he objected to the schemas of traditional medicine, which he claimed masked prejudice behind the claim of sexual enlightenment (Giese 139), he developed a theory of sexual transitions (*sexuelle Zwischenstufen*) and placed all those who came to him for help into a naturalized category of sexual attributes and character. One can interpret this categorization as part of a project to discipline the bodies and reactions of the institute's subjects and visitors. Through specific strategies of public education and scientific classification, the display of sex in the institute produced and disciplined both knowledge and experience. And yet, the fact that both the physical displays and the presence of individuals from sexual minorities revealed previously taboo sexual practices and biological anomalies meant that the institute could not escape continuity with the history of public exhibitions, fairs, circuses, and other spectacles that had drawn attention to "freaks" since the Middle Ages.

This is precisely the connection that Boudry and Lorenz underline and which Lorenz has more recently taken as an occasion to elaborate a theory of queer art as "freak theory" (Lorenz 23–30). By having their bearded lady perform in a medical lecture hall, the artists highlight the similarities between nineteenth-century methods of medical education and the still-popular freak shows, panoptica, and vaudeville performances of the day. This artistic re-appropriation of the era and its dilemmas helps us to understand what was troubling about some of the practices at the institute. The "performances" of Hirschfeld's patients/exhibits shared many features with the *Völkerschauen* made famous by the wild animal merchant and impresario Carl Hagenbeck. These travelling "people shows" – displays of *Naturvölker*, or ethnic groups that German anthropologists considered closer to nature – attracted not only a huge popular audience but also significant attention from anthropologists and scientists, like Rudolf Virchow, who believed that housing family units in zoos and carefully observing their habits in captivity could serve the interests of anthropological science (Bruckner 137). The fact that these spectacles were given a scholarly stamp of approval from the leading anthropologists of the day did not, however, hide the fact that they involved a complicated and exploitative relationship between the human exhibits and their scientific observers, who in fact became part of the show when they arrived to take notes, measure limbs and skulls, and symbolize Western advancement in their role as all-knowing experts (Bruckner 139). The exchanges between visitors to Hirschfeld's institute and the objects of their interest – often very human objects with very real political and social vulnerabilities – could not escape similar power dynamics. Despite intense efforts to educate and scientifically ground the display, the prying eyes of the medical gaze laid bare intensely private identities, and the display of fetish objects always contained the danger of both commodification and the arousal of *Schaulust*.

Hirschfeld's practices gave the physical presence, voice, and agency of the subjects displayed an entirely new framework in comparison to earlier medical demonstrations or freak shows. This display was embedded within a project of enlightenment, education, and emancipation. Unlike the *Völkerschauen*, this was emphatically not a colonialist project. The goal was neither to transform the appearance or behaviours of these members of sexual minorities to fit accepted norms, nor was it to reveal them as somehow inferior or in need of civilization. The physical presence of subjects as objects of display and as patients meant that the dynamic of the recognition of identity unfolded as a matter of performance that prioritized individual choices of presentation and comportment. Even in the more mediated photographs and scientific displays, where subjects were sometimes literally the objects of medical experts who almost violently revealed their physical abnormalities to the camera, institute patients clearly display not only their consent but their active desire to reveal themselves.

Several images of Friedericke Schmidt, one of the patients Hirschfeld diagnosed as hermaphroditic, vividly document these possibilities. In the earliest images of Schmidt, taken in 1905, her face is obscured with a blindfold. In photographs published in 1930, she gazes at the camera confidently without a blindfold. Hirschfeld had provided an important expert opinion in a legal petition to have her recognized as a man, but despite the petition being successful, Schmidt chose instead to continue living as a woman (Herrn 7–8). The triptych of images of Schmidt dressed as a man, as a woman, and naked (except for shoes and stockings) underscores the variability of gender identity and the lack of obvious correspondence between the body and its social presentation. It is without doubt a document of the scientific gaze. But it also suggests a single subject confidently exploring, claiming, and inhabiting these several selves.

Furthermore, the nature of the subject made it difficult, if not impossible, for this display to "happen" without an explicit consideration of the audience's reaction. The topic of sex was fraught with shame, stigma, and embarrassment – not to mention with desire – and these emotions could not simply be ignored. Another archival image unexpectedly illustrates the complications that could result. It depicts an institute tour: a group of people looking at a man who is clearly Karl Giese. But closer inspection reveals that none of the visitors' faces are visible; the image depicts only the backs of their heads. And when this image was recently shown to a surviving employee of the institute, she revealed that the picture had in fact been staged, with workers from the institute posing as visitors because no actual visitors wanted to be photographed in the space (Herrn 14). Hirschfeld's insistence on guided tours and the open aims of education and enlightenment thus reveal a contrast with the strategies followed by the museums it otherwise resembled. Although he shared the same conviction in the authority of science, Hirschfeld refused to entirely emulate the mode of presentation in classical natural history museums, where – as Mieke Bal argues about the American Museum of Natural History in New York – the position of scientific authority both dominates and disappears because it presents the art of the exhibition as nature (*Looking In* 120).

The practices of the institute also highlighted the ways in which visitors could not be excluded from the construction of meaning it attributed to its objects of display.

Hirschfeld's sex museum thus contained all of the contradictions that structured natural historical and anthropological museums in Germany, and which differentiated them from their counterparts elsewhere in Europe and North America. It also reflected the debates these museums had prompted about the most appropriate way to display collections for both scholars and the public in order to facilitate the production of knowledge. As Andrew Zimmerman has shown, two paradigms had been competing for dominance since the late nineteenth century. In one, championed by Adolf Bastian, museums should be organized according to an ideal of "totality"; Bastion therefore organized each section of Berlin's Royal Museum of Ethnology as an overview of all objects available from various "natural peoples" (*Naturvölker*), hoping that this simultaneous display of humanity would allow the viewer to abstract out timeless, universal truths (Zimmerman 177–8). This strategy, informed by the history of German humanism (as well as debates about the difference between "natural" and "civilized" forms of culture, and an extreme aversion to blurring the boundaries between humans and animals), was opposed to the more Darwinian practice of ordering objects – and cultures – according to an evolutionary narrative, be it biological or cultural.

Hirschfeld fell somewhere in between these two poles. Although he believed that many sexual traits such as sexual orientation or transvestitism were hereditary, his perspective was not originally an evolutionary one. On the contrary, his practices of display aimed to demonstrate ever-proliferating taxonomies of identities as part of a system of simultaneously existing natural variation. At the same time, his careful attention to the life stories and personal choices of his subjects demonstrated attention to the importance of social constructs and their influence on behaviour. The displays at the Institute for Sexual Science thus fused an underlying code of biological classification with an appreciation of the interplay between in-born sexual characteristics, social norms, and individual subjectivities. Images of bodies that were clearly meant to provide visual evidence of natural types stood next to photographs of individuals who defied the "natural" signs of their bodies through their clothing choices and general comportment. Thus, while Hirschfeld's sexual types seemed to simply increase the number of still essentialized categories, his attention to individual life stories and his focus on fighting for the rights of sexual minorities put an emphasis on the need for political change and the transformation of social norms.

N.O.Body in Berlin and Calgary

Nothing encapsulates this dynamic more vividly than the *Wall of Sexual Transitions*, an arrangement of photographs that Hirschfeld designed first as a travelling exhibition for a conference in 1910, and which hung in the institute. Divided into four quadrants, the wall displayed images of so-called hermaphrodites, homosexuals, androgynous individuals, and transvestites; the idea was that this arrangement would make visible the natural transitions between various combinations of sexual traits. In photographs of this wall, as blurred as they may be, one can make out, in the upper right quadrant devoted to androgyny, an image of Annie Jones, the bearded lady we meet in the film *N.O.Body*. In the context of this film, however, the appearance of this figure from Hirschfeld's wall also points beyond Hirschfeld's practices of display. *N.O.Body* refers to the title of an autobiography of a hermaphrodite, also one of Hirschfeld's patients, that was published anonymously in 1907. The title thus also refers to the longer history of sexual science, which grew out of confessional narratives solicited and collected by scientists (and by criminologists) as evidence. As the publication of this autobiography makes clear, however, the collection and publication of these case studies also made these newly diagnosed identities available to the wider public, making them a part of popular culture and encouraging "literary" confessions that re-claimed medical and criminal categories.[6]

N.O.Body plays on all of these layers of sexual science, staging an archaeology, as it were, of Hirschfeld's institute. But it also reimagines a future that the institute made possible. For, as a work that highlights the dynamics of display, performance, and self-fashioning that characterizes both the presence and representation of Hirschfeld's subjects, it also reminds us of the proximity of the institute to another kind of exhibition space, namely, the art gallery. It provides a retrospective view of the institute, one that emphasizes aspects of the history of the museum that have become more apparent, and more important, to contemporary observers. It lets us see, in short, how Hirschfeld's display of sex in the institute moved beyond existing paradigms of museums to anticipate many of the issues that have since come to define what we call musealization. This display registered the historical shift to scientific, institutionalized museums while also pointing forward to several key innovations that became more prominent in the following decades: the implication of the museum in identity politics, the shift from the museum as a place that imparts knowledge to a place in which an "experience" happens, and the incorporation of that experience into the very structure of the display.

N.O.Body was originally created in 2008 for an exhibition curated by Rainer Herrn in Berlin, *Sex brennt* (*Sex burns*). This exhibition aimed to counteract the historical silence that had developed around the seminal importance of Magnus Hirschfeld as a target of the Nazi book burnings in May 1933. Histories of the book burnings almost entirely left out the fact that the plundering of Hirschfeld's institute on 10 May 1933 was the first act in the carefully staged series of book burnings that were repeated throughout Germany and made into a media spectacle. Herrn's exhibition aimed to engage with Berlin's culture of memory in order to exploit the gaps in individual visitors' knowledge of these events. He combined *N.O.Body* with several other works of art that reacted to a selection of archival materials presented as postcards, which visitors could take home if they wished. He thus encouraged individuals to reconstruct their own narratives of this past while also challenging the official, public narrative of this history. Herrn countered the ritual erasure of Hirschfeld's work by the Nazis and its effects on post-war memory with a form of individual memorialization. His hope was to disseminate Hirschfeld's history in the same form in which it had survived: as individually constructed stories – private archives – removed from the organizing authority of political and scientific institutions. *Sex brennt* thus emulated Hirschfeld's own strategies of fusing education and museal display in order to engage the general public. On the one hand, a few precious objects from the institute (painstakingly reassembled by Herrn and his colleagues at the Magnus Hirschfeld Gesellschaft) physically authenticated the past, while images testified to its destruction. And on the other hand, the works of art performed a unique act of musealization by imagining new forms of memory. The invitation to visitors to create private archives from the postcards gave this experience a material basis for future remembrance.

Even if many of the visitors to Herrn's 2008 exhibition were likely surprised that the famous book burning at Opernplatz was fed with books from Hirschfeld's library, they had almost certainly heard of Hirschfeld himself, and they had likely come to the exhibition to learn more about Germany's most famous sexual scientist. *Sex brennt* was an enormous success because it could draw on the existing historical knowledge of visitors, while asking them to view this somewhat known history through an artistic lens that destabilized the comfortable boundaries between the supposedly enlightened sexual present and this earlier period of experimentation, exploration, and tragedy. The distributed postcards placed history in the visitors' hands and directly involved them in a conversation about the creation of sexual identities, a conversation that crossed temporal boundaries and was then visualized in the newly created art.

Taking inspiration from this powerful technique, we quickly realized that we would have to reconceptualize this process of curation for a Calgary audience that lacked a specific connection to this history. While images from Christopher Isherwood's novels and the various films depicting the cabaret scene of the 1920s have certainly created the common impression of interwar Berlin as the site of sexual experimentation and gender bending, in North America, the story of Alfred Kinsey dominates the narrative of the history of sexual science, and Hirschfeld's pioneering research and advocacy is rarely mentioned. Our challenge, then, was to provide enough historical context – just enough didactic content – for visitors to make sense of the juxtaposition we were making between this history and the present while still respecting the power of the art to speak for itself.

Our decision to curate *N.O.Body* as part of an exhibition in Calgary therefore had several important consequences tied to the particular space of our exhibition and our local audience. In Calgary, where visitors would have at best only the most vague ideas about this context, *N.O. Body* acquired new functions. To be sure, it teased and titillated as a curiosity. But this exhibition was placed in a context meant to underscore surprising moments of relevance to the present. In Alberta, gender reassignment surgery had been a hot topic over the past several years, as the government made a controversial decision to de-fund treatment through the provincial health-care plan (which, as elsewhere in Canada, covers all individuals; happily, this decision was reversed in June 2012). And conservative, rural clichés aside, Calgary is also an open, tolerant, multicultural city of immigrants in which sexual minorities arouse relatively little public interest, let alone ire. Perhaps ironically, in a city like this it becomes difficult for queer minorities to gain any real visibility at all. Curating *N.O.Body* in this context inevitably made the work a comment on these local forms of identity politics. And finally, the particular placement of the film in our exhibition made it into a commentary on our own endeavours. The film was shown in a space set apart by walls in which we reimagined the institute, which was also the only space in which we placed a traditional historical narrative about the archival images we displayed. This space was also used on one weekend as a meeting room for an international conference of scholars that we organized, making us part of the exhibition display. In this context, the space was also the site of work that reflected the positions of spectatorship implied in our own production of knowledge and, more concretely, the forms of musealization in which scholarship is often presented to the public at large.

In short, our exhibition was conceived to allow visitors to deconstruct Hirschfeld's practices of visual display, viewing them through the lens of history, while also seeing the contemporary display of sex with a similarly critical perspective. As one attempt to analyse these imagined positions of spectatorship, we will now describe in more detail our process of curating *PopSex!* We will then conclude this essay by briefly examining two other videos in the exhibition in order to ask about the contemporary importance of museums as spaces for examining the history and significance of sexuality and for asking about the place of sex in the museum. These videos offer particularly clear examples of how the display of sex, even in a setting that consciously avoids titillation, inevitably engages the viewer in ways that undermine the goals of the traditional museum to narrate knowledge from a distanced, objective position. Seen in the context of Hirschfeld's history, our exhibition also raised questions about the particular challenges of the musealization of sex and the historical contextualization of our present-day sexualities. If Hirschfeld's history might be seen as contributing to a kind of "cosmopolitan memory" that now influences perceptions of the history of sexuality around the world,[7] then how might exhibitions like ours participate in the "collective memory-making" exercise that Sharon MacDonald describes in her book *Memorylands*? Just as Hirschfeld's institute served not only scientific but also politically reformist impulses, sex museums and exhibitions generally serve not only to display memory but also to influence future perceptions: to create – as MacDonald puts it – imaginings of the future (MacDonald 17).

PopSex!

Perhaps even more than other forms of knowledge, knowledge about sex circulates through images that resonate across cultures and geographic boundaries.[8] Our first curatorial act was thus to choose images from Hirschfeld's archives that might immediately resonate with our local audience. We asked ten artists (eight from Calgary and three who are currently based in Berlin) to work with us. Meeting individually with most of the artists over the course of several months, we showed them the postcards from *Sex brennt* and answered their questions about the historical context. The artists were thus in a sense the first visitors to the exhibition – they began our process of communication by viewing images that they had never seen before and by deciding which of these stories from history held the most meaning for them. Our first act of curation was to act as interlocutors between history and the artists. Our goal was not to provide them with historical knowledge as something distant and static but rather to facilitate the production of new knowledge through a juxtaposition of these archival images and the concerns of their current work. After our individual conversations over the shuffled postcards and two joint meetings as a group, the artists created new works that drew upon both the historical inspiration and their present-day concerns.

This curation was conducted in a somewhat unique mode, because what we had in mind was a hybrid beast, somewhere between the museum and the art exhibition. Although the final staging took place in the classic white cube of the Illingworth Kerr art gallery, the artists themselves recognized that we were playing with classical modes of artistic curation. Our aims straddled boundaries between the art world and the history museum, assembling artistic reactions to historical information with the goal of engaging viewers in a conversation about the relationship between this past and our present. At the same time, the strategies we chose for presenting the archival material itself made these postcards (taken from another exhibition in another context) themselves seem more akin to the other works of art. Presented as a single row of framed images without any explanatory text, in a space filled with other images and objects created by artists, the postcards appeared as another installation; they thus implied that the museal presentation of history is itself a form of staging. But apart from an invitation to experience the juxtaposition of history and art, and a decision to present these images largely independent of any context or narrative, our staging of this history was not part of a larger strategy to guide or prompt a particular experience. In this regard, it differed from the growing emphasis on creating visitor "experiences" in contemporary history museums. (Perhaps the most famous example of this practice is the way that the US Holocaust museum asks visitors to perceive its displays through the eyes of a single victim of the Holocaust.) Rather, we wanted to emphasize the difficulty of distinguishing an objective historical perspective from a presentation of history that seeks to integrate the participation of the viewer. We sought a way of showing these images together with the art that would not deny the immediate, subjective impact they might have on a viewer unfamiliar with their history, while also making it possible for the viewer to re-evaluate that experience in light of new historical knowledge and the artists' own perspectives, or rather that of their work, on the display of sex.

That is to say, our efforts to engage visitors depended on a refusal to simply present the historical material as a lesson to be swallowed whole. Apart from three brief sentences, the exhibit was not therefore prefaced with historical explanation. This text was intended only to make clear our aims and the issues at stake:

> Magnus Hirschfeld's Institute for Sexual Science put sex on display. Hirschfeld was unique in his trust that this display could serve aims of enlightenment, education, reform, emancipation, and community. His theory of gender as a continuum rather than a binary is still revolutionary. *PopSex!* explores the legacy of this history and the futures it made possible.

Our approach to the historical images followed a similar strategy. Eschewing didactic historical wall plates, we instead grouped the historical images into five categories ("Coming out to the Camera," "Pop Science," "Sex in Public," "Taxonomies," and "Private Selves") and in front of each grouping we placed a gallery-case table with two quotations – one from Hirschfeld's era and the other from the Canadian present. We hoped that visitors would be struck first by the visual power of the images – images of transvestites, transsexuals, and hermaphrodites, of marital advice manuals, and of schematic models of sexual types and human sexual response from the research of the Institute for Sexual Science – and that they would then make their own connections to quotations from the present and to the art that filled the room.

The art in this section of the gallery included a range of works: a triptych of photographic juxtapositions by Jean-René Leblanc; an installation of filing cabinets and magnetically attached drawings by RICHard SMOLinkski; an installation of a rug knitted by Wednesday Lupypciw, which was used in a video about two Vancouver prostitutes that played on a television put on top of the rug; David Folk's installation of erotic and violent drawings, evoking mythological scenes, set into a filing cabinet; and finally, a mixed-media installation by Mireille Perron and Heather Stump that took the form of a living room of sorts, a collection of objects that explored the boundaries of public and private by reflecting on the place of subjectivity in the history of "enlightened" science. We expected and welcomed some shock and confusion as visitors tried to make sense of these juxtapositions, particularly on the part of those unfamiliar with the forms and methodologies of scientific research in the early twentieth century.

As an example of some of the resonances that developed in this space, we could point to a triptych of photographs created by Jean-René Leblanc. Leblanc juxtaposed several of the historical images with photographs of scenes in which subjects were invited to explore self-presentation with post-it notes. One of the images he chose was also displayed across the room under the category of "Taxonomies": itself a photographic triptych, a form that Hirschfeld often used to document the "true" characters of cross-dressers and forms of androgyny. We have already described this triptych of Friederike Schmidt, who appears first dressed as a woman, then as a man, and then nude. Hirschfeld expected us to take this visual evidence as proof of an inborn sexual type that might be masked by clothing but was objectively readable in the unadorned body. On the table below this image, we quoted Hirschfeld: "The most valuable result of research into homosexuality is the discovery that there are only gradual quantitative differences between men and women in all mental and corporeal points ... Nature did not depart here from the law she confirms everywhere: that she works in transitions rather than leaps" (17). We then quoted a recent article in the *Edmonton Journal* that reported on the discovery that outdated diagnostic codes were still being used to bill the province for medical treatment: "In Alberta, homosexuality still falls under the heading of Mental Disorders: Sexual Deviations and Disorders. It is at the top of the list and is followed by bestiality, pedophilia, transvestism, exhibitionism, transsexualism, disorders of psychosexual identity, frigidity and impotence" ("Homosexuality"). (This policy, too, was happily changed in June 2012.) In any case, a number of connections between the historical information and current attitudes were possible. The archival images certainly served a museal function in that there was a recovery of a history that has been lost – not least because Hirschfeld's archive was actually dispersed and burned. But in this essay (as in the exhibition itself) we leave the production of knowledge – the tracing of precise connections between this past and our present – up to our audience.

We did want to convey meaning, but not in the didactic mode of an historical museum.

Our only overt step in the direction of traditional musealization was to provide a set of footnotes to the archival images. Gallery visitors could pick up a small booklet of historical annotations to the archival images displayed. There was, admittedly, some self-deprecating irony in our use of the title "Footnotes" for this booklet. As scholars, we found ourselves irresistibly tempted to supplement our curation with evidence for our assertions about the authenticity of the past we were displaying. But we were careful to put this supposed assertion of objectivity in its place – not on the wall, but in the hands of the viewer. Footnoting our exhibition was our way of revealing our own curatorial stance without representing ourselves as omnisciently objective purveyors of knowledge. Footnotes, after all, support an argument; they are attached to essays as evidence for a thesis and thus represent an implicit admission that that thesis is debatable. As Anthony Grafton has argued, they are more than merely the visible infrastructure of scholarly production; they "form an indispensable if messy part of that indispensable, messy mixture of art and science: modern history" (235). Calling our historical descriptions "footnotes" thus allowed us to highlight the messy connections within the exhibition itself. Rather than tracing a seamless line from Hirschfeld's history to our sexual present, our curation of the archival images was meant to prompt reflection about both continuities and discontinuities and about the dangers of assuming objectivity.

To some degree, providing footnotes in a separate booklet also prevented words from detracting from the powerful sexual images on display. As Noël Coward once remarked: "having to read a footnote resembles having to go downstairs to answer the door while in the midst of making love" (Grafton 70). Although, following the tradition of the Institute for Sexual Science (our aim was not to titillate), we did not want to shy away from the power of desire, sexual identification, or even feelings of shame, alienation, or embarrassment. This meant a conscious break with historiographical and museal practice. In both written history and historical presentations in museums, sex is often presented in almost consciously unsexy terms. To avoid the charge of sensationalism, historians and curators often de-sensualize their material, presenting it in clinical language and settings. In part, this is a function of disciplinary training and the urge to prove professional credentials. And while many historians have come to terms with the inevitably narrative and thus subjective nature of our discipline, we are still accustomed to creating a comfortable distance between ourselves and historical subjects.[9] Thus, even as Foucault's arguments about the historicity of sex and sexuality have influenced more and more subfields of historical research, there is still a certain discomfort in historically examining histories of desire and pleasure – bodily experiences that seem to preclude a definitive distancing between our analyses and our identification with historical subjects. One of the reasons we chose art as a means of promoting a discussion about this particular past was that art refuses to accept this kind of distancing. It plays directly to emotions and to sensuality – to affects that range from identification to alienation, and which may thus challenge both.

That said, the space as a whole prompted experiences on various levels – experiences that were more emotional and immediate, as well as more distanced and analytical in a traditionalist historical mode. As described above, the main entrance hall relied upon modes of juxtaposition, while we also used walls to set apart a space in which we reimagined the institute itself. This institute space contained *N.O.Body* and a second video installation by Kurtis Lesick, *mis(read)*, that reflected on parallels between the Nazi book burnings and contemporary forms of censorship and commercial pressures to control the media. In this space, we also used archival material to present Hirschfeld's personal history and the history of the institute in a more conventional, linear fashion. But the room itself was dominated by a very large reproduction of Hirschfeld's *Wall of Sexual Transitions* – blown up and printed so that as viewers came closer, the images of these sexual freaks dissolved into printed dots on a page. The wall clearly belonged to the space of the reimagined Institute, set apart and yet visible – if partly occluded – from anywhere in the first gallery; it functioned as a title, as it were, for the menagerie of images and experiences to be encountered. With this institute-space, then, we intended to speak most directly to our visitors about the institute, its modes of display and Hirschfeld's popularization of sexual science, and about the significance of this history for our practice as scholars. The space also served, however, as a pivot between the juxtapositions of the main hall and an additional gallery that was part of the exhibition – a second hall entered through heavy curtains and darkened entirely except for two video installations, in which we intended to create a very different kind of experience for the viewers. To conclude this essay, we will now briefly describe that experience and use it as a point of reference to draw some overall conclusions and ask some questions about the musealization of sex.

Future Histories of Sexualities

The second hall of the *PopSex!* exhibition contained two video installations: *Glitter Bike Ride,* by Anthea Black and Mr and Mrs Keith Murray, and *Legacy,* by Benny Nemerofsky Ramsay. Visitors arrived in this darkened gallery last, after having passed through the institute space with its *Wall of Sexual Transitions,* and the two videos *N.O.Body* and *mis(read).* Moving into the dark hall thus brought visitors from a reflective, almost analytical space into a more immersive – even absorptive – experience of spectatorship. Each of these videos drew viewers into witnessing intensely intimate experiences of loss, wounding, and mourning that also conjured new forms of belonging. And each video used this experience to develop visions of sexual futures that were also calls to action. But perhaps most importantly in the context of *PopSex!*, each of the videos was also part of an installation that included what could be considered aspects of musealization. As Sharon MacDonald emphasizes in *Memorylands,* musealization is as much about the future as the past; it consists of "anticipations of the future" (MacDonald 17).

Each of the videos achieved its absorptive effect in different ways. In *Glitter Bike Ride,* Anthea Black and Mr and Mrs Keith Murray embodied transgendered beings of the future, riding their bikes through Central Park in New York City. This outing into the city was conceived as a memorial to a friend lost recently in a bike accident; it followed a tradition of leaving white "ghost bikes" to memorialize bicyclists killed this way. In a silent landscape of colour, the Glitter Twins publicly shared their common solitude. They exude a dream-like joy that absorbed viewers, a reaction that could be seen in the faces of the spectators in Central Park, but which also kept viewers of the video at a distance, reminding them that this was a private act of mourning. The video presented a dream world that engulfed viewers and yet remained inaccessible except through this witness of its having happened.

Legacy, by Benny Nemerofsky Ramsay, is a work equally luscious in its visual composition, its sound, and its presentation on a baroque-like screen that hung in the middle of the room, which thus appeared as an illuminated portal into another world. But the protagonist of the story, a seeker in an enchanted cruising forest, also demonstrated to viewers the limits of spectatorship and gazing. Wearing a mask of mirrors that reflects what he sees but prevents him from seeing out, the seeker encounters four oracles who speak to him words taken from gay elders of the recent past. The oracles speak of the pain and wounds that come from the authenticity of "coming in" and "coming out," of disrupting subject/object relations to make intimacy the basis of a new subject/subject people; and of the triumph of growing through this pain and standing one's ground until society has come to change. Part of the story's power depends upon the viewers' knowledge of the background (if not the specific origins) of the quotations uttered by the oracles, which originate in part from the gay rights struggles and the AIDS crisis of the 1980s and 1990s. At the same time, the poetry of the piece speaks to all those who have felt objectified by social norms and expectations. The video's encounters conclude with a fierce tribal cry, as each oracle and finally also the seeker joins, one by one, in a unified howl that resonated throughout the exhibition space. This howl enveloped viewers, making them witness to an embodied, visceral community that represents the fulfilment of the seeker's journey. The triumph of the seeker was also the triumph of the desiring self – an embodied and emphatically sexual self – that promises to be an agent of the future.

Equally importantly, however, both videos were also accompanied by objects on display that made explicit the museal nature of this witness. At the exhibition opening, the Glitter Twins performed a recreation of their bike ride, ritually installing the bicycles they had ridden in the park on a reflecting pedestal covered with glitter. And *Legacy* was accompanied by a display of the mask worn by the seeker, presented on a plinth in a Plexiglas case, together with a hand-printed bookwork containing the words spoken by the oracles, a work of art that itself could be purchased by visitors. Moreover, of course, these words themselves have a history – a very specific queer history – that some viewers were undoubtedly prompted to seek out.

By placing these works in constellation with the history of Hirschfeld's institute and its contemporary resonance, *PopSex!* made them legible as examples of what a future queer history might look like – a history poised between the particular, marginalized groups it recovers from the past and its vision of a future in which sexual difference might bring about new possibilities of emancipation and new kinds of belonging. Our exhibition took up this queer history as a history of resistance to dominant norms, sexualities, and desires. But more fundamentally, it attempted to make possible individual experiences that are nevertheless also perceived as part of a common project of sexual history, a history and a future of histories in which embodiment and desire are at the core of experience and of historical memory. It thus also challenges more common, ostensibly less sexual modes of writing history and musealizing the past.

Conclusion

The resonance of our exhibition – which had over 2000 visitors in ten days, a record for an exhibition of this length at ACAD – suggests that we were not wrong in assuming that a conversation about sex between history and the present could touch a chord. Both the artists' enthusiastic reception of our rather unorthodox curatorial strategy and the viewers' identification with the art suggest that there is a kind of "collective memory" about the history of sexuality that can be activated to imagine and shape our sexual futures. Musealizing sex was part of this experience. Revealing Hirschfeld's subjects – individuals often called "freaks" in their time – and displaying images from an era of unprecedented interest in sexual identity highlighted both the continuities and discontinuities with our sexual present. Revealing sex in its various forms, we would assert, is thus a critical aspect of taking it seriously as a social and psychological force. As Karl Giese noted in 1929, displaying sex always risks the charge of sensationalism and voyeurism. And our visitors probably did feel discomfort when they viewed the archival image of Hirschfeld holding open the genitals of a hermaphrodite or when they watched the Glitter Twins writhe under Wednesday Lupypciw's rug in a piece of performance art. These are the kinds of frank portrayals of embodied and desiring sexual selves that we are used to seeing only in medical textbooks, consciously erotic forms of entertainment, or pornography. But putting sex on display in this way also allows us to understand and honestly examine the power of sexual identities past, present, and future. This sometimes uncomfortable confrontation with the bizarre and yet still familiar sexual identities and practices of both the past and an often hidden present places us – embodied sexual subjects ourselves – within an evolving story of human sexual self-definition.

NOTES

1 Both the panoptic and medical versions of Foucault's definition of "the gaze" would be relevant. See Foucault, *Discipline* and *Birth*. But particularly in the world of imagery and display, we must add a feminist perspective, like that of Laura Mulvey, that emphasizes the gendered power

dynamics of the gaze and describes how sexual imagery in modern culture generally assumes the perspective of the erotically desiring heterosexual male. See Mulvey, "Visual Pleasure and Narrative Cinema" and *Visual and Other Pleasures*.

2 *PopSex!* was also shown in Edmonton, Alberta, in the summer of 2012 as part of the Works and Design Festival. Among the large team involved in preparing and staging this exhibition, we would especially like to thank and acknowledge our designer, Andreas Puskeiler, the curator of the Illingworth Kerr Gallery at the Alberta College of Art + Design, Wayne Baerwaldt, and the staff at the gallery, who mounted the show.

3 Those who ran the institute believed that this was true. See Giese 141.

4 For an extensive discussion of the nineteenth-century practice of scientific collecting and display see A. Zimmerman.

5 For a general definition and background to the *Wunderkammer*, see Hooper-Greenhill 78–104.

6 On the use of case studies in early sexual science, see Oosterhuis.

7 The term "cosmopolitan memory," coined by Daniel Levy and Natan Sznaider with reference to the Holocaust, does not suggest that memories will be the same everywhere, but rather that certain key world events will resonate in memories across the globe, forming unique interactions between global and local creations of meaning. See: Levy and Sznaider 8 and 23-38.

8 This phenomenon has received considerable attention from historians of colonialism: See Burton, McClintock, and Stoler 51–101.

9 The classic exploration of narrative structures in historical writing is White, *Metahistory*. See also White, *The Content and the Form* and T.R. Ankersmit 182–93.

12 Spaces in Motion and Cinematic Experiences: The Permanent Exhibition *Film* of the Deutsche Kinemathek – Museum für Film und Fernsehen

PETER MÄNZ

The importance of the moving image has increased since the beginning of the twenty-first century. With the use of digital media and the Internet as a key medium, we are surrounded by moving images in our daily life. Cinema still plays an important role, but television, home video, and the permanent presence of the computer draw our attention to screens with moving images everywhere – even in public spaces and in public transport. Today, with tablet PCs and smart phones, moving images are available at any place and at any time. Under these circumstances museums on film history have become more and more important. As we are permanently surrounded by floods of moving images which we mostly perceive in fragments, film museums should lead us to more competence in using moving images by showing us the development of film aesthetics and presenting a canon of important films and filmmakers. Furthermore, film museums can increase the awareness of the relations between film and politics. The existing film museums in the German-speaking countries have different approaches to the exhibition of film history. Some people say that the cinema is the only place to communicate film history. For institutions like the Österreichisches Filmmuseum (Austrian Museum of Film) in Vienna or the Filmmuseum München (Munich Film Museum), the black boxes of their cinemas are considered their exhibition halls, and their curated film programs the exhibitions.[1] Other film museums such as the Deutsches Filminstitut (German Film Institute) in Frankfurt am Main, the Filmmuseum Düsseldorf, the Filmmuseum Potsdam, and the Deutsche Kinemathek – Museum für Film und Fernsehen (Museum for Film and Television) in Berlin screen films, but present permanent object-based exhibitions as well. One of the advantages of a permanent exhibition is that unlike screened films, it is always accessible to visitors. It has to function for people who do not know anything about film history, but it also has to be attractive for visitors with much prior knowledge. Thus, an object-based permanent exhibition is the most suitable way to provide an overview of film history for an institution like the Deutsche Kinemathek, which, in addition to its archives and exhibitions, offers screenings, panels, literature on film history, and archives.

The permanent exhibition *Film* of the Deutsche Kinemathek, designed by the architect Hans Dieter Schaal, was opened in September 2000 and provides a walk through German film history with references to Hollywood.[2] On the basis of this installation, I would like to investigate the potential of an object-based exhibition on film history, focusing on strategies of displaying moving images and objects in relation to spatial constellations.

When visitors to the Deutsche Kinemathek – Museum für Film und Fernsehen enter the *Film* exhibition, they leave the outside world behind and immerse themselves into another. The first room of the exhibition, the "mirror cabinet," which guides visitors from contemporary film back to silent film, has an overwhelming effect on most people. This immersion into a new experience is documented by many comments in the guest book of the museum, such as "Thank you for the immersion into film history."[3] The strategy for the design of this film museum goes back to the "Musée du Cinéma" in Paris, which opened in 1972 and was curated by Henri Langlois, the founder of the Cinémathèque française. In 1961, Langlois developed his concept of a "Louvre du Cinéma," in which he describes the spatial strategies of his upcoming museum:

> The Musée du Cinéma is essentially a museum of evocation and suggestion in which everything must combine to immerse the visitor in a succession of atmospheres and states of soul corresponding to the significance intended for each gallery, each one having its own accent. [It is necessary] to create a climate, room by room, which puts the spectator in a state to understand and better sense the works which are shown. (Robinson 244)

If we relate this concept of "evocation and suggestion" to the permanent exhibition of the Deutsche Kinemathek – Museum für Film und Fernsehen, then the mirror cabinet has the function of a prologue. If we regard the permanent exhibition as a film (to walk through), the mirror cabinet functions as the opening credits. In this gallery, shots of actors and actresses taken from different feature films can be seen on three screens. The quotations belong to films that appear again later in the exhibition. There are mirrors everywhere – including on the ceiling and on the floor – which evokes a feeling of boundlessness. For media scholar Andrea von Kameke, who interprets the concept of the permanent film exhibition in relation to Walter Benjamin's theory of "Reception-in-Distraction," the mirror cabinet evokes a cinematic experience:

> By making the gaze the theme of the prologue to the whole exhibition, the film museum places a concept at the center that is crucial to the immersive character of film ... Here almost everything is missing that belongs to a traditional cinema situation. There is not even a bench to sit on to watch the film excerpts. Not only the room is not dark, but the mirrors reflect the light and make it brighter. The large monitors are multiplied in the mirrors. We cannot leave our own body behind, but perceive it in relation to the images of the monitors. Far from seeing one unified work, we are presented with the shortest snippets of film, and taken from one short fragment to the next. We can walk through the corridor quickly with the mode of distraction. However, the gazes that confront us on the screens demand our own gaze to meet them – if only for the short moment that they last. At this moment, when the characters are either looking at us directly or gazing at someone within the diegetic universe, we cannot help but be drawn in. If we know the film, we remember it, if we do not, our desire to go and see is kindled. Cinematic illusionism thus continues to work on us even outside the cinema. (228)

After the visitor is brought back to the beginnings of cinema, the presentation of objects starts in the next room. The theme of this section, "Pioneers and Divas," is the German film between 1895 and 1918, focusing on three film pioneers (Max Skladanowsky, Oskar Messter, and Guido Seeber) and three early female stars (Fern Andra, Asta Nielsen, and Henny Porten). The room is dominated by a large projection screen at the back showing film sequences that demonstrate the different ways of acting and the different star images of the three women. The screening is accompanied by music, typical for silent-movie cinema, and there is a bench in front of the screen for sitting. The large screen and the music evoke the atmosphere of an early cinema and the floor plan is comparable to a "Ladenkino,"[4] but this atmosphere is disturbed by various architectural elements: from the right side white cubes break into the room – diagonally from the top or from the bottom. In these white cases objects and moving images are displayed. While the large projection with the images of early female stars stands for the cinema as a place of longing and dreams, the attention of the visitor is also drawn to the white cases and the exhibits at the front of the room. Two important objects are displayed in showcases on the left: a historic camera and projector. Two films are displayed in white cases on the right: in the front of the room, a short documentary of German soldiers leaving for the war in China in 1900 (*Ausfahrt der Chinakrieger* [Departure of the China Warriors], 1900), and in the back of the room, an advertising film showing the actress Henny Porten campaigning for *Kriegsanleihen* ("war bonds") during the First World War. The moving images and the objects speak to the beginnings of stardom, to technical and aesthetic developments of the medium, and to political resonances. But what are the real exhibits in an object-based film exhibition, the objects or the moving images?

Sabine Lenk, former director of the Filmmuseum Düsseldorf, describes the problem as follows:

> So how can we exhibit film when film requires the viewer to sit still and silent for more than an hour? In an ordinary museum the visitors stroll through the building looking at the objects arranged in a specific order. They are able to exchange ideas about what they see, communicating their interest, enthusiasm, or even their dislike to those accompanying them. This could also be possible – if a group was on its own and would not disturb others – in the in-house cinema of a film museum. But film on display in the exhibition space has to be short, as the desire of the visitors to move on and "see the rest of the museum" is too strong to keep them in front of a screen for more than 10 to 15 minutes at most … So a film from the very early period of cinematography can be shown in its entirety, but for longer ones, extracts must be selected. (320)

Like von Kameke, Lenk draws on the thought of Walter Benjamin in looking for ways of addressing this issue, noting the importance of the auratic original in particular:

> In art museums, as in film museums, to enable visitors to "get in touch with the original" is still the main objective. In a film museum to pretend that "contact with the original" means watching the moving images is, as already explained, an unrealistic claim. Furthermore film as an object is just a celluloid strip in a can. Put in a display cabinet, it looks like decoration. The "aura of the original" is much better provided by associated

> objects, especially those which a movie star or director has once used. Mentally projecting recollections of scenes from the film into the object, the spectator's imagination recreates the flair of Hollywood or Babelsberg, thus creating the object's aura. (320)

If we refer Lenk's considerations to the room "Pioneers and Divas," her questions about the original and the aura have to be discussed again. Typical for the program of early cinema was a variety of short films of different genres (dramas, slapsticks, news) that were screened as numbered episodes and then repeated again. The cinematic experience of this era was more one of an "original program" than of an original film. The longer feature film, endowing the actors and actresses and the creation of stars with a certain image, started after 1910, but the program with short numbers still dominated the cinema during the 1910s. Under these circumstances, cinematic experience in the first two decades of the twentieth century was a disparate one and differed from the rest of the century. It was not dominated by the feature-length movie in ways that seem obvious today.

Sabine Lenk's statements that "contact with the original means watching the moving images is an unrealistic claim" or that "film as an object is just a celluloid strip in a can" can also be rethought, as the exhibited moving images from *Ausfahrt der Chinakrieger* and the exhibited camera help to show. One of the key advantages of an object-based film museum is that it can demonstrate the operation of technical equipment. By displaying a camera prototype of the early twentieth century that can be cranked by the visitor by pressing a button – showing all the technical functions from closing the lens to the transport of the perforated film in slow motion – the celluloid strip is put into an illuminating context. This object creates an aura as a historic original, demonstrating its functions rather than being seen through those who once held it in their hands.

The short film about the battleship presented opposite the camera tells the viewer something about the foci of early cinema, mainly as news used for political propaganda. As the film is shown in its original length, this exhibit communicates something about the beginnings of film aesthetics and the challenges of early film technology. In 1900, cinematographer Guido Seeber tried one of the first pan shots in film history, but created a very jerky picture because of the historic static tripods. The second technical exhibit, displayed at the back of the room, is a historic projector that can be put in motion by the visitor through the push of a button. The advertising film for war bonds shown opposite is also screened in its original length. It demonstrates important developments in the aesthetics of the moving image in the early twentieth century, such as dissolves, while also showing how the star Henny Porten was used for propaganda purposes in Imperial Germany.

If we regard the permanent exhibition as a film to walk through, the room "Pioneers and Divas" has several components. The screen with the three early stars evokes a cinematic experience, but this experience is interrupted by objects and screenings. Visitors enter into a space with "its own accent" (Robinson 244) and can explore this "early cinema" environment on their own terms, like a camera that moves on a set. But they can also sit down and watch the excerpts of feature films with Fern Andra, Henny Porten, and Asta Nielsen. As the excerpts on the large screen are composed in a way that conveys the atmosphere of the new star worship and the differences between the three actresses, this screened compilation should also be seen as an exhibit.

Following a gallery dedicated to the film *Das Cabinet des Doctor Caligari* (The Cabinet of Dr Caligari, 1920), the visitor enters the next large section about film during the Weimar Republic. The gallery is structured by round columns, the first of which depicts the set "forest" of Fritz Lang's movie *Die Nibelungen* (The Nibelungs, 1924). But then the room widens into the modern city of Berlin at the end of the "Roaring Twenties" and the trees of the forest change into *Litfaßsäulen* ("advertising columns"). The *Nibelungen* forest stands for the heroic, conservative, and nationalistic Ufa style of the 1920s. The advertisement columns represent the modernity and open-mindedness of the Weimar Republic. This gallery is designed as a metaphorical environment with changing spatial components and can again be seen as a space in motion. Along with the change of the spatial situation, the displayed objects and films change as well. The exhibits (objects, film sequences, or short films) introduce four important German-speaking directors (Ernst Lubitsch, Friedrich Wilhelm Murnau, Fritz Lang, and G.W. Pabst) and other genres of German cinema in this period, including the *Bergfilm* (mountain film), proletarian film, and the sound film operetta. Technical and aesthetic developments of moving images are also on display in this section: the importance of German film architecture and the large studios, the moving camera, and the invention of sound film.

At the back of the room there is a huge projection screen again, showing compiled sequences of two German feature films around 1930:

Asphalt (Joe May, 1929) and *Schleppzug M 17* (Tugboat M 17, 1933). The "particular atmosphere" (Robinson 244) of this room is evoked by transforming the buzz of Berlin in the 1920s into moving images. Many visitors see the compiled sequences of *Asphalt* and *Schleppzug M 17* as the main attractions, as interpreted by von Kameke: "The two short films are characterised by fast movements, volatility and proximity. They depict a big city traffic location in the 1920s … A multitude of impressions do not only stream in on the spectator, but almost overwhelm him/her. While the room also contains other exhibits, such as pictures, posters and documents, the fast moving images of the two short films and the music accompanying them dominate the whole room" (227). If we compare the atmospheres of the two rooms, "Pioneers and Divas" and "Weimar Republic," it is evident that "Pioneers and Divas" is inspired by an early cinema, whereas the design of "Weimar Republic" evokes the experience of the urban Berlin in the Roaring Twenties. One can perceive the large screen at the back of the room as a cinematic apotheosis of metropolitan Berlin similar to Walter Ruttmann's movie *Berlin. Die Sinfonie der Großstadt* (*Berlin. Symphony of a Great City*, 1927). If we relate this screening to the objects presented in this room, it is evident that the sound film *Schleppzug M 17* was shot on location in Berlin (the screened sequence takes place on Potsdamer Platz, where the Museum für Film und Fernsehen is located today), whereas the Berlin street in *Asphalt* was constructed in the studio. Set design drawings for *Asphalt* are displayed on a wall opposite the screen, and visitors who compare the two film sequences realize the difference between studio and location shooting.

Fritz Lang's *Metropolis* (1927) is the second film to which a section in the permanent exhibition is dedicated. Inspired by the vertical production design and settings of this film (The Upper City, The Machine Rooms and the Worker's City, The Catacombs), architect Hans Dieter Schaal used the double height of the ceiling to connect two levels of the building. A bridge guiding the visitor from the section "Weimar Republic" to "Metropolis" provides a view of a large video installation entitled "Wall of Catastrophes." On eighteen monitors, scenes of catastrophes taken from movies by Fritz Lang are shown. Looking down at this installation, which is accompanied by a corresponding sound track, the viewers experience a threatening atmosphere. They see, for instance, a sequence taken from *Das Testament des Dr. Mabuse* (The Testament of Dr Mabuse, 1933) in which a barrel with gasoline rolls in the direction of the spectator and then explodes, or the assassination of a politician in a car (reminiscent of Walther Rathenau's assassination). They see the workers destroying the machine, the explosions, and the floods of water in the Worker's City of Metropolis. The moving images sometimes jump from one monitor to the next and are composed to a new artistic form. Thus, the atmosphere of catastrophes is intensified.

In the section dedicated to *Metropolis* the visitors go down a spiral staircase, comparable to the spiral staircase in Rotwang the mad scientist's house in the film. Again, the design functions as a film to walk through. Even visitors who do not know the film experience the vertical structure of the film design, which represents the differences between the social classes. Here, beside other objects, a camera is on display, the so-called Stachow Filmer, a lightweight camera developed in Germany during the 1920s. Chief cinematographer Karl Freund used it in *Metropolis* for the shooting of special effects. Freund was one of the pioneers of new film aesthetics with a subjective, moving camera. One of the advantages of the Stachow Filmer was that it did not need to be cranked – it worked with an electric motor. The Stachow Filmer is on display on a swing, "flying" – just as it was used for shooting in *Metropolis*. The captions are combined with photographs taken during the shooting of *Metropolis*; they show Karl Freund beside Fritz Lang, who starts moving the swing. This presentation shows different aspects: first, it highlights technical innovations that in the 1920s helped German cinematographers and directors develop new film aesthetics, and it also situates them within a specific historical context.

The shaky, quick camera movements in *Metropolis* convey the experience of explosions and shock waves. One of the first experiences of Freder, the movie's young hero, after he goes down to the "Hall of the Machines" is that of a blast from the so-called M-Machine. This sequence – like the entire film – can be related to the impact of the First World War, the first industrial war in history. In his book *Shell Shock Cinema: Weimar Cinema and the Wounds of War*, Anton Kaes describes Freder's confrontation with the M-Machine and the explosion: "From afar, in a long shot, Freder watches helplessly as the gauge exceeds its limit and, as feared, the machine explodes, emitting large clouds of white smoke. It is as though a shell had detonated: the force of the blast lifts one worker up in the air, the other workers are thrown down from the top of the gigantic machine. Freder runs toward them but is hurled back, blinded by the flash of light" (178). Filmed with a subjective camera moving quickly back and forth, the explosions can be experienced again by the museum visitors in front of the "Wall of Catastrophes," since they pass this wall once more when they continue their way through the exhibition. In reviewing the dangerous scene in this different context, visitors can now also reflect on the camera techniques that evoked this atmosphere.

While the exhibit focuses on technical innovation, it also illustrates the way in which these innovations were documented and published by the advertisement department of Ufa in magazines, which are included in the display. With this installation, the era of cinema of the Weimar Republic in the permanent exhibition ends. Thus, the moving images can be seen in relation to the First World War, or as an anticipation of the catastrophes that followed after 1933.

The next section of the permanent exhibition is dedicated to German-speaking filmmakers and actors who made their career in Hollywood before 1933. The title of this section, "Transatlantic," and the design remind the visitor of the deck of a ship. Three rooms about Marlene Dietrich's Hollywood career follow.[5] In the main hall some of Dietrich's film costumes are shown and film clips and portraits are displayed. The designer Hans Dieter Schaal again combined the objects with mirrors: "The person – the star – is absent and has, in reality, never been present: merely her images are visible. Only through the visitor's mind do the exhibits, mere dead objects, recover their fictitious lives. The power of imagination nourished by images blossoms" (Jacobsen et al. 332).[6]

After the last room, dedicated to Dietrich's return to Germany and Billy Wilder's film *A Foreign Affair* (1948) and a section on Leni Riefenstahl's *Olympia* (1938), the visitor enters the section about German film under National Socialism. The design of the room is a metaphor reflecting on the burden of Nazi dictatorship and the difficulties of the German people in dealing with it. The walls and the display cases are made of stainless steel. The walls contain drawers, and thus the atmosphere is evocative of a mortuary or an archive. The drawers can be opened and closed; they contain objects and moving images on flat screens reflecting on problems that German post-war society did not want to be confronted with. There is no projection or large screen in this room: all images and objects can disappear in the drawers. The central object in this room is the installation "Wall of Victims," with portraits of filmmakers, actors, and actresses who were killed by the Nazis or ended their persecution by committing suicide. The selected exhibits in this section focus on three aspects of film during the Nazi dictatorship: politics, propaganda, and entertainment. Again, the moving images in the drawers are exhibits; some of them are compilations of documentaries and feature films, others short films in full length, like the trailer for Veit Harlan's film *Jud Süss* (*Jew Suess*, 1940). This trailer intensifies the atmosphere and the message of the film and gives an overview of all the German stars cast in this film. Another drawer shows a report of the SD, or Sicherheitsdienst der SS (security service of the SS), about the reception of *Jud Süss* in Germany. Although the atmosphere in this area is a quiet one and visitors concentrate on the exhibits in the drawers, sound from different exhibits can be heard because normally more than one drawer with moving images is opened.

This room is followed by a section about German-speaking exiles in Hollywood. We find a cabinet with documents, letters and objects. For example, on display is the little Chinese "God of Luck" that Bertolt Brecht gave to Fritz Lang after arriving in Los Angeles with Lang's help. The room is dedicated to the film agent Paul Kohner, who came to Hollywood in the 1920s, worked for Carl Laemmle's Universal Studios, and helped many German exiles as a film agent. In 1938, Kohner founded the "European Film Fund" to support German-speaking filmmakers in Hollywood.

The last section of the permanent exhibition *Film* consists of two rooms on German film history from 1946 until today. One of the challenges of this section is that it deals with almost seventy years of film history in East and West Germany. The atmosphere of both rooms is dominated by large display cases on the right side that look like shop windows, a design that refers to the so-called economic miracle in postwar Germany. The first room is dedicated to German film between 1946 and the beginning of the 1980s, and on its back wall the visitor sees a photograph of Hanna Schygulla and Rainer Werner Fassbinder taken during the shooting of *Die Ehe der Maria Braun* (*The Marriage of Maria Braun*, 1978). The objects in the display cases on the right are presented in chronological order, and the room's last cases concern two of the most important East and West German film directors of the 1960s and 1970s: Konrad Wolf and Rainer Werner Fassbinder. On the left side – again in chronological order – forty-eight filmmakers and films are on display, starting with Gerhard Lamprecht's *Irgendwo in Berlin* (*Somewhere in Berlin*, 1946) and ending with Michael Haneke's *Das weiße Band* (*The White Ribbon*, 2010) in the second room.[7] Every director is introduced with his or her portrait. When the visitor presses a button, a significant sequence of the selected film starts. On the "Wall of Directors," the visitors find filmmakers from East and West Germany, men and women, directors of documentaries and feature films. Every screen (with two directors) is combined with a display case where various objects related to the films are shown, such as personal notebooks, location photos, costume drawings, props and awards, or personal screenplays with annotations and sketches by the directors. One can see the "Wall of Directors" as a large installation and a documentary about East and West German filmmakers who reflected on German society and German history.

The Wall of Directors is continued in the second room on German film history between the beginning of the 1980s and today. Large objects, for example a more than three-metres-long model of the steamship used in Werner Herzog's *Fitzcarraldo*, are on display.[8] At the end of the room, there is a projection screen showing scenes taken from the films of this section that present images of actors and actresses looking directly at the spectator. This presentation of actors can be related to the first room of the show, the mirror cabinet, and short moments of exposure that may kindle the visitors' interest in watching the movies they are taken from after having walked through their own movie about German film history.

Conclusion

If we regard the permanent exhibition *Film* of the Deutsche Kinemathek – Museum für Film und Fernsehen as a film to walk through, it can be seen as a documentary with elements of a feature film, an interactive film about more than one hundred years of German film history which guides the visitor through different environments related to the magic of cinema. Deeply impressive cinematic experiences alternate with object-based exhibits and are conceived to lead to new perspectives on cinematic art. In the twenty-first century, at a time when the moving image is a permanent part of our daily life, an attractive design and various offers to explore the different aspects of film history are necessary. Historical originals with an aura are suited to this concept, as well as moving images that are composed in an artistic way. With the digitalization of film there are many opportunities: historical films in full length are available on DVD or BluRay and can be watched at any time at home. This does not replace the screening of a film in a real cinema; more than one cinema should be an essential part of every film museum. One advantage of an object-based film exhibition is that the equipment and techniques that are necessary to create a movie can be made comprehensible through objects. Visitors can move through the rooms like cinematographers; they can make cuts like directors and repeat takes several times. The moving images are exhibits like the objects. Often the objects create new views; sometimes film extracts are compiled into new artworks.

A permanent object-based exhibition is the most suitable offering to the public for film museums. In Berlin, the focus lies on the relations between film and politics. The environments reminiscent of film sets, combined with moving images, might motivate our guests to immerse themselves in German film history and might provide them with new views on German film. Like one of our visitors wrote in our guest book on 24 March 2012: "An excellent and stylishly presented museum. It has inspired me to watch more German films in the future."

NOTES

1 For a more detailed discussion, see *Filmmuseum*.
2 The permanent exhibition *Film* was curated by the former director of the Deutsche Kinemathek, Hans Helmut Prinzler, and Wolfgang Jacobsen and Werner Sudendorf. In 2006, the permanent exhibition on television opened and the Deutsche Kinemathek changed its name into "Deutsche Kinemathek – Museum für Film und Fernsehen." In 2009, two new rooms with the name "From Post-war to Present" were added to the *Film* exhibition. Since 2006, Dr Rainer Rother has been the artistic director of Deutsche Kinemathek.
3 "Danke für das Eintauchen in die Filmgeschichte"
4 A cinema in a former shop of a tenement house in Berlin. The first permanent cinemas opened around 1905.
5 The "Marlene Dietrich Collection Berlin" is an important part of the collections of the Deutsche Kinemathek.
6 "Der Mensch selbst, der Star, ist abwesend, war in Wirklichkeit nie hier, nur seine Bilder sind zu sehen. Nur in der Phantasie der Besucher erhalten die Exponate, tote Gegenstände bloß, ein fiktives Leben zurück. Die Vorstellungskraft wird von den Bildern genährt und blüht auf." See also Käthow 74–8.
7 One can say that this "Wall of Directors" is a homage to the "Autorenfilm."
8 One important aspect of these display cases is their focus on German filmmakers who are internationally successful.

Bibliography

Abraham, Nicolas, and Maria Torok. *The Shell and the Kernel*. Trans. Nicholas Rand. Vol 1. Chicago: U of Chicago P, 1994. Print.

Adorno, Theodor W. *Aesthetic Theory*. Ed. Gretel Adorno and Rolf Tiedemann. 1970. Ed. and trans. Robert Hullot-Kentor. Minneapolis: U of Minnesota P, 1997. Print.

– *Minima Moralia: Reflections on a Damaged Life*. Vol. 1. Trans. Edmund F.N. Jephcott. London: Verso, 2005. Print.

– "Valéry Proust Museum." In *Prisms*. Cambridge, MA: MIT Press, 1983. 173–86. Print.

Agnew, Vanessa. "History's Affective Turn: Historical Reenactment and Its Work in the Present." *Rethinking History* 11.3 (2007): 299–312. Print.

– "Introduction: What Is Reenactment?" *Criticism* 46.3 (2004): 327–39. Print.

Ahbe, Thomas. *Ostalgie: Zum Umgang mit der DDR-Vergangenheit in den 1990er Jahren*. Erfurt: Landeszentrale für politische Bildung Thüringen, 2005. Print.

Alfrey, Judith, and Tim Putnam. *The Industrial Heritage: Managing Resources and Uses*. New York: Routledge, 2004. Print.

Alter, Nora. "Translating the Essay into Film and Installation." *Journal of Visual Culture* 6.1 (2007): 44–57. Print.

Angst essen Seele auf [*Fear Eats the Soul*]. Screenplay by Rainer Werner Fassbinder. Dir. Rainer Werner Fassbinder. Tango-Film. 1974. Film.

Ankersmit, Frank. *Sublime Historical Experience*. Stanford: Stanford UP, 2005. Print.

Ankersmit, T.R. "Hayden White's Appeal to the Historians." *History and Theory* 37.2 (1998): 182–93. Print.

Arbeiter verlassen die Fabrik [*Workers Leaving the Factory*]. Dir. Harun Farocki. Harun Farocki Filmproduktion, Berlin, WDR, Köln, 1995. Video.

Arbeiter verlassen die Fabrik in elf Jahrzehnten [*Workers Leaving the Factory in Eleven Decades*]. Dir. Harun Farocki. Harun Farocki Filmproduktion, Berlin, 2006. Video Installation.

Arthur, Paul. "Essay Questions: From Alain Resnais to Michael Moore." *Film Comment* 39.1 (January–February 2003): 58–62. Print.

– *A Line of Sight: American Avant-Garde Film since 1965*. Minneapolis: U of Minnesota P, 2005. Print.

Assmann, Aleida. *Geschichte im Gedächtnis: Von der individuellen Erfahrung zur öffentlichen Inszenierung*. Munich: Beck, 2007. Print.

– "Transformations between History and Memory." *Social Research* 75:1 (2008): 49–72. Print.

Aufgebauer, Lukas. "Förderung von Geschichtsbewusstsein bei Schülerinnen und Schülern im Museum – Chancen und Probleme der 'sinnlichen Erfahrung von Geschichte.'" In *Kulturwissenschaft(en): Konzepte verschiedener Disziplinen*, ed. Jürgen Joachimsthaler and Eugen Kotte. Munich: Meidenbauer, 2010. 187–202. Print.

Aust, Stefan. *Der Baader-Meinhof Komplex*. 3rd ed. Munich: Wilhelm Goldmann, 2010. Print.

Baader-Meinhof Komplex, Der. Dir. Uli Edel. Prod. Bernd Eichinger. Constantin. 2008. DVD.

Bach, Jonathan. "Vanishing Acts and Virtual Reconstructions: Technologies of Memory and the Afterlife of the GDR." In *Memory Traces: 1989 and the Question of German Cultural Identity*, ed. Silke Arnold-de Simine. Oxford: Peter Lang, 2005. 261–80. Print.

Bach, Steven. *Leni: The Life and Work of Leni Riefenstahl*. New York: Knopf, 2007. Print.

Badt, Kurt. "Die Plastik Wilhelm Lehmbruck's." *Zeitschrift für bildende Kunst* 31.8/9 (1920): 169–82. Print.

Baker, Steve. *The Postmodern Animal*. London: Reaktion Books, 2000.

Bal, Mieke. *Double Exposures: The Subject of Cultural Analysis*. New York: Routledge, 1996. Print.

– "Exhibition as Film." In *Exhibition Experiments*, ed. Sharon Macdonald and Paul Basu. London: Blackwell, 2007. 71–93. Print.

– "Exhibition Practices." *PMLA* 125.1 (2010): 9–23. Print.

– "Exposing the Public." In *A Companion to Museum Studies*, ed. Sharon Macdonald. Malden: Blackwell, 2006. 523–42. Print.

– *Looking In: The Art of Viewing*. Amsteldijk: Overseas Publishers Association, 2001. Print.

– "Narrative Inside Out: Louise Bourgeois' Spider as Theoretical Object." *Oxford Art Journal* 22.2 (1999): 102–26. Print.

– *Quoting Caravaggio: Contemporary Art, Preposterous History*. Chicago: U of Chicago P, 1999. Print.

– *Travelling Concepts in the Humanities: A Rough Guide*. Toronto: U of Toronto P, 2002. Print.

Barron, Stephanie. "1937: Modern Art and Politics in Prewar Germany." In *"Degenerate Art": The Fate of the Avant-Garde in Nazi Germany*, ed. Stephanie Barron. Los Angeles: Los Angeles County Museum of Art, 1991. 9–23. Print.

Barthes, Roland. *Camera Lucida: Reflections on Photography*. Trans. Richard Howard. New York: Hill and Wang. 1981. Print.

– *Image, Music, Text*. Trans. Stephen Heath. New York: Hill and Wang, 1977.

– *S/Z*. Trans. Richard Miller. London: Cape, 1974. Print.

Bartmanski, Dominik. "Successful Icons of Failed Times: Rethinking Post-Communist Nostalgia." *Acta Sociologica* 54.3 (2011): 213–31. Print.

Bauer, Richard, and Michael Brenner, eds. *Jüdisches München: Vom Mittelalter bis zur Gegenwart*. Munich: Beck, 2006. Print.

Bauman, Zygmunt. *Wasted Lives: Modernity and Its Outcasts*. Cambridge, UK: Polity, 2004.

Baxandall, Michael. "Exhibiting Intention: Some Preconditions of the Visual Display of Culturally Purposeful Objects." In *Exhibiting Cultures: The Poetics and Politics of Museum Display*, ed. Ivan Karp and Steven D. Lavine. Washington: Smithsonian Institution Press, 1991. 33–41. Print.

Bazin, André. "The Ontology of the Photographic Image." In *What Is Cinema?*, ed. and trans. Hugh Gray. Berkeley: U of California P, 1967. 9–16. Print.

Beier-de Haan, Rosmarie. "Re-Staging Histories and Identities." In *A Companion to Museum Studies*, ed. Sharon Macdonald. Oxford: Blackwell, 2006. 186–97. Print.

Bell, Erin. "Televising History. The Past(s) on the Small Screen." *European Journal of Cultural Studies* 10.1 (2007): 5–12. Print.

Bell, Erin, and Ann Gray, eds. "Conclusion: Broader Themes and Televisualization." In *Televising History: Mediating the Past in Postwar Europe*. Basingstoke: Palgrave Macmillan, 2010. 248–55. Print.

Benjamin, Walter. "Das Kunstwerk im Zeitalter seiner technischen Reproduzierbarkeit." In *Gesammelte Schriften*, ed. Rolf Tiedemann and Hermann Schweppenhäuser, vol. I.2, Frankfurt a.M.: Suhrkamp, 1991. 431–508. Print.

– "The Work of Art in the Age of Its Reproducibility: Second Version." In *Walter Benjamin: Selected Writings, Volume 3: 1935–1938*, ed. Howard Eiland and Michael W. Jennings. Cambridge: Harvard UP. 2002. 101–33. Print.

Bennett, Jill. "Aesthetics and Intermediality." *Art History* 30.3 (2007): 432–50. Print.

Bennett, Tony. *The Birth of the Museum: History, Theory, Politics*. New York: Routledge, 1995. Print.

– "Civic Seeing: Museums and the Organization of Vision." In *A Companion to Museum Studies*, ed. Sharon Macdonald. Oxford: Blackwell, 2006. 263–81. Print.

Berdahl, Daphne. "Expressions of Experience and Experiences of Expression: Museum Re-Presentation of GDR History." *Anthropology and Humanism* 30.2 (2005): 156–70. Print.

– "Expressions of Experience and Experience of Expression: Museum Re-Presentations of GDR History." In *On the Social Life of Postsocialism: Memory, Consumption, Germany*, ed. Matti Bunzl. Bloomington: Indiana UP, 2010. 112–22. Print.

– "Goodbye Lenin, Auf Wiedersehen GDR: On the Social Life of Socialism." In *On the Social Life of Postsocialism: Memory, Consumption, Germany*, ed. Matti Bunzl. Bloomington: Indiana UP, 2010. 123–34. Print.

– "'(N)ostalgie' for the Present: Memory, Longing, and East German Things." *Ethnos* 64.2 (1999): 192–211. Print.

Berger, John. "Why Look at Animals?" In *The Animals Reader: The Essential Classic and Contemporary Writings*, ed. Linda Kalof and Amy J. Fitzgerald. Oxford: Berg, 2007. 251–61. Print.

Betts, Paul. "The Twilight of the Idols: East German Memory and Material Culture." *Journal of Modern History* 72.3 (2000): 731–65. Print.

Biemann, Ursula. "The Video Essay in the Digital Age." In *Stuff It: The Video Essay in the Digital Age*, ed. Ursula Biemann. New York: Springer, 2003. 8–11. Print.

Bilder der Welt und Inschrift des Krieges (*Images of the World and the Inscription of War*). Dir. Harun Farocki. Harun Farocki Filmproduktion, Berlin-West, with financial support from the kulturellen Filmförderung NRW, 1988. 16mm. Film.

Bilski, Emily D. "How Can Germans and Jews Speak to Each Other about Germany? How Can We *Not* Speak about Germany?", ed. Jutta Fleckenstein and Bernhard Purin. *Jüdisches Museum München*. Munich: Prestel, 2007. 70–71. Print.

Blanke, Walter. "Stichwortgeber: Die Rolle der 'Zeitzeugen' in G. Knopps Fernsehdokumentation." In *Geschichtskultur: Die Anwesenheit von Vergangenheit in der Gegenwart*, ed. Vadim Oswalt and Hans-Jürgen Pandel. Schwalbach am Taunis: Wochenschau-Verlag, 2009. Print.

Blumenstein, Ellen. "Zur Vorstellung des Terrors und Möglichkeiten der Kunst." In *Zur Vorstellung des Terrors: Die RAF*, ed. Klaus Biesenbach. Göttingen: Steidl, 2005. 16–24. Print.

Blümlinger, Christa. "Harun Farocki: Critical Strategies." In *Harun Farocki: Working on the Sight-Lines*, ed. Thomas Elsaesser. Amsterdam: Amsterdam UP, 2004. 315–22. Print.

BMW Museum. "BMW Konzeptfahrzeuge." June 2008–April 2010. Web.

– "Die zweite Wechselausstellung: Museen im 21. Jahrhundert." Web.

Böhm, Roland. "Jud Süß wird enttarnt." *Der Tagesspiegel*, 13 December 2007. Web.

Bois, Yves Alain, Denis Hollier, and Rosalind Krauss. "A Conversation with Hubert Damisch." *October* 85 (1998): 3–17. Print.

Boltanski, Christian. *Das fehlende Haus*. 1990. Berlin.

Bolter, Jay David. "Formal Analysis and Cultural Critique in Digital Media Theory." *Convergence* 8.4 (2002): 77–88. Print.

Bolter, Jay David, and Richard Grusin. *Remediation: Understanding New Media*. Cambridge, MA: MIT Press, 2000. Print.

Bornscheuer, Marion. "Lehmbruck's Kneeling Woman, Paris 1911." In *Kneeling Woman 100 Years*, English ed., ed. Raimund Stecker and Marion Bornscheuer. Duisburg: Lehmbruck Museum and Cologne: Dumont, 2011. 16–50. Print.

Boudry, Pauline, and Renate Lorenz. "*N.O.Body*." In *PopSex! Footnotes*, ed. Michael Thomas Taylor and Annette Timm. Calgary, n.p., 2011. Pamphlet for an exhibition held at the Illingworth Kerr Gallery, Alberta College of Art + Design, Calgary, Alberta, 6–22 January 2011. Print.

Boym, Svetlana. *The Future of Nostalgia*. New York: Basic Books, 2001.

Bruckner, Sierra A. "Spectacles of (Human) Nature: Commercial Ethnography between Leisure, Learning, and Schaulust." In *Worldly Provincialism: German Anthropology in the Age of Empire*, ed. H. Glenn Penny and Matti Bunzl. Ann Arbor: U of Michigan P, 2003. 127–55. Print.

Buchner, Katharina. "*Der Baader-Meinhof Komplex*: Das sagen Jugendliche zum RAF Film." *Stern*, 30 September 2008. Web.

Burt, Jonathan. *Animals in Film*. London: Reaktion Books, 2002. Print.

– "The Illumination of the Animal Kingdom: The Role of Light and Electricity in Animal Representation." In *The Animals Reader: The Essential Classic and Contemporary Writings*, ed. Linda Kalof and Amy J. Fitzgerald. Oxford: Berg, 2007. 289–301. Print.

Burton, Antoinette, ed. *Gender, Sexuality and Colonial Modernities*. London: Routledge, 1999. Print.

Buruma, Ian. "Himmler's Favorite Jew." *New York Review of Books*, 1 March 2010. Web.

Buß, Christian. "Der Nazi in meinem Bett: Film über das Dritte Reich." *Spiegel Online*, 21 September 2010. Web.

Calle, Sophie. *Die Entfernung – The Detachment*. 1996. Marie-Elisabeth Lüders Building, Berlin.

Campany, David. "Once More for Stills." In *Paper Dreams: The Lost Art of Hollywood Still Photography*, ed. Christoph Schifferli. Paris: Edition 7L, 2007. 7–13. Print.

Carey, Jessica. "Humane Disposability: Rethinking 'Food Animals,' Animal Welfare, and Vegetarianism in Response to the Factory Farm." Diss. McMaster U, 2011. Print.

Caspar, Michael. "Jud Süß in Göttingen: Stimmen zu einer schwierigen Ausstellung über Joseph Oppenheimer." *Jüdische Allgemeine*, 13 July 2006. Web.

Clifford, James. *Routes: Travel and Translation in the Late Twentieth Century*. Cambridge, MA: Harvard UP, 1997. Print.

Coe, Sue. *Dead Meat*. New York and London: Four Walls Eight Windows, 1995. Print.

Conrad, Vera. *Der Baader-Meinhof Komplex: Materialien für den Unterricht*. 2008. Education GmbH. Web.

Cook, Alexander. "The Use and Abuse of Historical Reenactment: Thoughts on Recent Trends in Public History." *Criticism* 46.3 (2004): 487–96. Print.

Cooke, Paul. *Contemporary German Cinema*. Manchester: Manchester UP, 2012. Print.

– "*Ostalgie*'s Not What It Used to Be." *German Politics and Society* 22.4 (2004): 134–50. Print.

– "Surfing for Eastern Difference: *Ostalgie*, Identity, and Cyberspace," *Seminar – A Journal of Germanic Studies* 40.3 (2004): 207–20. Print.

Corner, John. "Epilogue. Sense and Perspective." *European Journal of Cultural Studies* 10.1 (2007): 135–40. Print.

Crane, Susan. "Memory, History and Distortion in the Museum." *History and Theory* 36.4 (1997): 44–63. Print.

Crary. Jonathan. *Suspensions of Perception: Attention, Spectacle and Modern Culture*. Cambridge, MA: MIT Press, 1999. Print.

Damisch, Hubert. *A Theory of /Cloud/: Toward a History of Painting*. Trans. Janet Lloyd. Stanford: Stanford UP, 2002. Print.

Danker, Uwe, and Astrid Schwabe. "Orientierung in der Geschichte der Deutschen? Die Dauerausstellung des Deutschen Historischen Museums." *Geschichte in Wissenschaft und Unterricht* 58.10 (2007): 591–606. Print.

"Die Darsteller im *Baader-Meinhof-Komplex*: Verstörend ähnlich." *RP online*, 4 February 2008. Web.

DDR Museum Berlin. N.d. Website introduction (English). http://www.ddr-museum.de/en/exhibition. Web.

– Statistiken. N.d. http://www.ddr-museum.de/de/presse/statistiken. Web.

Dean, Tacita. "Palast." In *Tacita Dean: Film Works*. New York: Charta, 2007. 74–5. Print.

De Certeau, Michel. "Ghosts in the City." In *The Practice of Everyday Life*, vol. 2. Trans. Steven F. Rendall. Berkeley: U of California P, 2002. 133–44. Print.

– "Walking in the City." In *The Practice of Everyday Life*, vol. 1. Trans. Steven F. Rendall. Berkeley: U of California P, 2002. 91–110. Print.

Deep Play. Dir. Harun Farocki. Harun Farocki Filmproduktion, 2006. Multichannel Video Installation.

Derrida, Jacques. *The Animal That Therefore I Am*. Ed. Marie-Louise Mallet. Trans. David Wills. New York: Fordham UP, 2008. Print.

Derrida, Jacques, and Elisabeth Roudinesco. *For What Tomorrow: A Dialogue*. Trans. Jeff Fort. Standford, CA: Standford UP, 2004. Print.

Deutscher Bundestag. *Fortschreibung der Gedenkstättenkonzeption des Bundes: Verantwortung wahrnehmen, Aufarbeitung verstärken, Gedenken vertiefen*. Drucksache 16/9875, 2008. Web.

Drama von Dresden, Das. Dir. Sebastian Dehnhardt. Broadview TV, Cologne, 2005. Television.

Drama von Dresden, Das. Dir. Sebastian Dehnhardt. Warner Home Video, Hamburg, 2006. DVD.

Ebbrecht, Tobias. "Docudramatizing History on TV: German and British Docudrama and Historical Event Television in the Memorial Year 2005." *European Journal of Cultural Studies* 10.1 (2007): 35–53. Print.

Eichinger, Katja. *Der Baader-Meinhof Komplex: Das Buch zum Film*. Hamburg: Hoffmann und Campe, 2008. Print.

Elderfield, John. *Imagining the Future of the Museum of Modern Art*. New York: Museum of Modern Art, 1998. Print.

Elsaesser, Thomas. *New German Cinema: A History*. New Brunswick, NJ: Rutgers UP, 1989. Print.

– "Subject Positions, Speaking Positions: From *Holocaust, Our Hitler*, and *Heimat* to *Shoah* and *Schindler's List*." In *The Persistence of History: Cinema, Television, and the Modern Event*, ed. Vivian Sobchack. New York: Routledge, 1995. 145–86. Print.

– "Introduction: Harun Farocki." *Senses of Cinema* 21 (July–August 2002): n.p. Web.

Engell, Lorenz. "'Virtual History': Geschichte als Fernsehen." *Zeithistorische Forschungen / Studies in Contemporary History*, Online-Ausgabe, 6.3 (2009). http://www.zeithistorische-forschungen.de/16126041-Engell-3-2009. Web.

Erll, Astrid, and Ann Rigney. "Introduction: Cultural Memory and Its Dynamics." In *Mediation, Remediation and the Dynamics of Cultural Memory*, ed. Astrid Erll and Ann Rigney. Berlin and New York: de Gruyter, 2009. 1–11. Print.

Erll, Astrid, and Stephanie Wodianka. "Einleitung: Phänomenologie und Methodologie des 'Erinnerungsfilms.'" In *Film und kulturelle Erinnerung*, ed. Astrid Erll and Stephanie Wodianka. Berlin and New York: de Gruyter, 2008. 1–20. Print.

Export, Valie. "Expanded Cinema as Expanded Reality." *Senses of Cinema* 28 (October 2003): n.p. Web.

Fall of Berlin. Dir. Yuli Raizman, Yelizaveta Svilova. Central Documentary Film Studio (USSR), 1945. Film.

Farocki, Harun. "Cross Influence/Soft Montage." In *Harun Farocki: Against What? Against Whom?*, ed. Antje Ehmann and Kodwo Eshun. London: Koenig Books, 2009. 69–74. Print.

– "Workers Leaving the Factory." In *Harun Farocki: Working on the Sight-Lines*, ed. Thomas Elsaesser. Amsterdam: Amsterdam UP, 2004. 237–44. Print.

Farocki, Harun, and Kaja Silverman. *Speaking about Godard*. New York: New York UP, 1998. Print.

Feuersturm – Der Bombenkrieg gegen Deutschland. Dir. Michael Kloft. Spiegel TV, Hamburg 2003. Television.

Filmmuseum. Spec. issue of *Film-Dienst* 64.16 (2011): 6–38. Print.

Firestorm: The Allied Bombing of Nazi Germany. Dir. Michael Kloft. First Run Features, New York, 2008. DVD.

Fish, Stanley Eugene. *Is There a Text in This Class? The Authority of Interpretive Communities*. Cambridge, MA: Harvard UP, 1980. Print.

Fleckenstein, Jutta. "Stimmen_Orte_Zeiten / Voices_Places_Times." In *Jüdisches Museum München*, ed. Jutta Fleckenstein and Bernhard Purin. Munich: Prestel, 2007. 25–78. Print.

Fleckenstein, Jutta, and Bernhard Purin, eds. *Jüdisches Museum München*. Munich: Prestel, 2007. Print.

Flügel, Katharina. *Einführung in die Museologie*. 2nd ed. Darmstadt: Wissenschaftliche Buchgesellschaft, 2009. Print.

Foster, Hal. "An Archival Impulse." *October* 110 (2004): 3–22. Print.

– "Vision Quest: The Cinema of Harun Farocki." *Artforum* 43.3 (2004): 156–61, 250. Print.

Foucault, Michel. *The Birth of the Clinic: An Archeology of Medical Perception*. New York: Vintage Books, 1973. Print.

– *Discipline and Punish: The Birth of the Prison*. Trans. Alan Sheridan. New York: Random House, 1977. Print.

Freimark, Hans-Peter. Personal interview. 4 November 2010.

Friedländer, Saul. *Die Jahre der Vernichtung: Das Dritte Reich und die Juden 1939–1945*. München: C.H. Beck, 2007. Print.

– *Reflections of Nazism: An Essay on Kitsch and Death*. 1984. Bloomington: Indiana UP, 1993. Print.

Friedrich, Jörg. *Der Brand: Deutschland im Bombenkrieg 1940–1945*. Munich: Propyläen, 2002. Print.

Fulda, Daniel. "'Selective' History: Why and How 'History' Depends on Readerly Narrativization, with the Wehrmachtsausstellung as an Example." In *Narratology beyond Literary Criticism*, ed. Jan Christoph Meister. Berlin: de Gruyter, 2005. 173–94. Print.

Gegen-Musik (*Counter-Music*). Dir. Harun Farocki. Olivier Rignault, Harun Farocki Filmproduktion, Berlin, Lille, capitale européenne de la culture, Délégation aux Arts Platiques, Fonds Image/Mouvement Centre National de la Cinématographie, Fonds DICREAM, 2004. Video.

Giese, Karl. "Eros im Museum." *Die Aufklärung* 1.5 (1929): 141–2. Print.

Goodbye Lenin! X-Verleih AG. 2005. Web.

Goodbye Lenin! Dir. Wolfgang Becker. X-Filme Creative Pool, 2003. Film.

Grafton, Anthony. *The Footnote: A Curious History*. Cambridge: Harvard UP, 1999. Print.

Graham, Cooper C. *Leni Riefenstahl and Olympia*. Metuchen, NJ: Scarecrow Press, 1986. Print.

Greenblatt, Stephen. "Resonance and Wonder." *Bulletin of the American Academy of Arts and Sciences* 43.4 (January 1990): 11–34. Print.

Grethlein, Jonas. "Experientiality and 'Narrative Reference,' with Thanks to Thucydides." *History and Theory* 49.3 (2010): 315–35. Print.

Greub, Suzanne, and Thierry Greub, eds. *Museen im 21. Jahrhundert: Ideen. Projekte. Bauten*. Munich: Prestel, 2008. Print.

Griffiths, Alison. "Media Technology and Museum Display: A Century of Accommodation and Conflict." In *Rethinking Media Change: The Aesthetics of Transition*, ed. D. Thorburn and H. Jenkins. Cambridge, MA: MIT Press, 2003. 375–89. Print.

Grimm, Arthur. *Room 5 of the Entartete Kunst Ausstellung*. Munich, 1937. Bildarchiv Preussischer Kulturbesitz. Berlin. Photograph.

– *Room 6 of the Entartete Kunst Ausstellung*. Munich, 1937. Bildarchiv Preussischer Kulturbesitz. Berlin. Photograph.

Groys, Boris, "The Artist as Consumer." In *Shopping: A Century of Art and Consumer Culture*, ed. Christoph Grunenberg and Max Hollein. Frankfurt: Hatje Cantz, 2002. 55–60. Print.

Grusin, Richard. "Premediation." *Criticism* 46.1 (2004): 17–39. Print.

Guenther, Peter. "Three Days in Munich, July 1937." In *"Degenerate Art": The Fate of the Avant-Garde in Nazi Germany*, ed. Stephanie Barron. Los Angeles: Los Angeles County Museum of Art, 1991. 33–43. Print.

Gurian, Elaine Heumann. *Civilizing the Museum: The Collected Writings of Elaine Heumann Gurian*. New York: Routledge, 2006. Print.

Halbwachs, Maurice. "Space and the Collective Memory." In *On Collective Memory*. New York: Harper & Row, 1980. 128–56. Print.

Hanquinet, Laurie, and Mike Savage. "'Educative Leisure' and the Art Museum." *Museum and Society* 10.1 (2012): 42–59. Web.

Harlan – Im Schatten von Jud Süß. Dir. Felix Moeller. 2008. Salzgeber, 2010. DVD.

Hattendorf, Manfred. *Dokumentarfilm: Ästhetik und Pragmatik einer Gattung*. Constance: Ölschläger, 1994. Print.

Hein, Hilde S. *The Museum in Transition. A Philosophical Perspective*. Washington, DC: Smithsonian, 2000. Print.

– *Public Art: Thinking Museums Differently*. Lanham, MD: Mira Press, 2006. Print.

Henne, Thomas. "Der Umgang der Justiz mit Veit Harlans *Jud Süß* seit den 1950er Jahren: Prozesse, Legenden, Verdikte." In *"Jud Süß": Hofjude, literarische Figur, antisemitisches Zerrbild*, ed. Alexandra Przyrembel and Jörg Schönert. Frankfurt am Main: Campus Verlag, 2006. 263–92. Print.

Henning, Michelle. "Legibility and Affect: Museums as New Media." In *Exhibition Experiments*, ed. Sharon Macdonald and Paul Basu. Oxford: Blackwell, 2007. 25–46. Print.

– *Museums, Media and Cultural Theory*. New York: Open UP, 2006. Print.

Henze, Sylvia. "Die RAF und die DDR: Zur künstlerischen Darstellung eines 'blinden Flecks.'" In *Ikonografie des Terrors: Formen ästhetischer Erinnerung an den Terrorismus in der Bundesrepublik 1978–2008*, ed. Norman Ächtler and Carsten Gansel. Heidelberg: Winter, 2010. 179–98. Print.

Herrn, Rainer. "Eros im Museum: Magnus Hirschfelds Sammlungen im Institut für Sexualwissenschaft." Unpublished paper, cited with permission. Print.

Hetherington, Kevin. "The Unsightly: Touching the Parthenon Frieze." *Theory, Culture and Society* 19 (2002): 196–9. Print.

Himmel über Berlin, Der [*Wings of Desire*]. Screenplay by Wim Wenders and Peter Handke. Dir. Wim Wenders. Road Movies. 1987. Film.

Hiroshima Mon Amour. Dir. Alain Resnais. Argos Films, 1959. Film.

Hirschfeld, Magnus. *Geschlechtsübergänge – Mischungen männlicher und weiblicher Geschlechtscharaktere*. Expanded edition. Leipzig: Verlag der Monatsschrift für Harnkrankheiten und sexuelle Hygiene, 1906. Print.

"History in the Making." *Der Baader-Meinhof Komplex*. Dir. Uli Edel. Prod. Bernd Eichinger. Constantin. 2008. DVD.

Hockerts, Hans Günter. "Zugänge zur Zeitgeschichte: Primärerfahrung, Erinnerungskultur, Geschichtswissenschaft." *Politik und Zeitgeschichte* 28 (2001): 15–30. Print.

Hoffmann, Hilmar. *Kultur für alle. Perspektiven und Modelle.* Frankfurt/M.: S. Fischer, 1984. Print.

Holokaust. Dir. Maurice Philip Remy, Friederike Dreykluft. Prod. Guido Knopp. MPR Film und Fernsehproduktion/Zweites deutsches Fernsehen, Munich, 2000. Television.

Homewood, Chris. "From Baader to Prada: Memory and Myth in Uli Edel's *The Baader Meinhof Complex* (2008)." In *New Directions in German Cinema*, ed. Paul Cooke and Chris Homewood. London: IB Taurus, 2011. 130–48. Print.

Hooper-Greenhill, Eilean. *Museums and Education. Purpose, Pedagogy, Performance.* New York: Routledge, 2007. Print.

– *Museums and the Interpretation of Visual Culture.* New York: Routledge, 2000. Print.

– *Museums and the Shaping of Knowledge.* London and New York: Routledge, 1992. Print.

"Homosexuality Continues to Be Listed as 'Mental Disorder.'" *Edmonton Journal*, 22 December 2010. Print.

Hüser, Rembert. "Nine Minutes in the Yard: A Conversation with Harun Farocki." In *Harun Farocki: Working on the Sight-Lines*, ed. Thomas Elsaesser. Amsterdam: Amsterdam UP, 2004. 297–314. Print.

Hutcheon, Linda. *A Poetics of Postmodernism: History, Theory, Fiction.* New York: Routledge, 1988. Print.

– *The Politics of Postmodernism.* London: Routledge, 1989. Print.

Huyssen, Andreas. *Present Pasts: Urban Palimpsests and the Politics of Memory.* Stanford: Stanford UP, 2003. Print.

– *Twilight Memories: Marking Time in a Culture of Amnesia.* New York: Routledge, 1995. 13–35. Print.

Ich glaubte Gefangene zu sehen [*I Thought I Was Seeing Convicts*]. Dir. Harun Farocki. Harun Farocki Filmproduktion, Berlin, Generali Foundation, Wien, 2000. Video.

Inglorious Basterds. Dir. Quentin Tarantino. Universal Pictures, Hollywood, 2009. Film.

International Council of Museums. *International Council of Museums.* Web. http://icom.museum/who-we-are/the-vision/museum-definition.html.

Jacobsen, Wolfgang, Hans Helmut Prinzler, and Werner Sudendorf, eds. *Filmmuseum Berlin – Der Katalog.* Berlin: Nicolai, 2000. Print.

Jaeger, Stephan. "Historiographical Simulations of War." In *Fighting Words and Images: Representing War across the Disciplines*, ed. Elena Baraban, Stephan Jaeger, and Adam Muller. Toronto: U of Toronto P, 2012. 89–109. Print.

James, Beverly. *Imagining Postcommunism: Visual Narratives of Hungary's 1956 Revolution.* College Station: Texas A&M UP, 2005. Print.

Janda, Annegret. "The Fight for Modern Art: The Berlin National Gallery after 1933." In *"Degenerate Art": The Fate of the Avant-Garde in Nazi Germany*, ed. Stephanie Barron. Los Angeles: Los Angeles County Museum of Art, 1991. 105–19. Print.

Joachimides, Alexis. *Die Museumsreformbewegung in Deutschland und die Entstehung des modernen Museums 1880–1940*. Dresden: Verlag der Kunst, 2001. Print.

Jones, Sara. "At Home with the *Stasi*: Gedenkstätte Hohenschönhausen as Historic House." In *Remembering the German Democratic Republic: Divided Memory in a United Germany*, ed. David Clarke and Ute Wölfel. Basingstoke: Palgrave Macmillan, 2011. 211–22. Print.

– "Staging Battlefields: Media, Authenticity and Politics in the Museum of Communism (Prague), the House of Terror (Budapest) and Gedenkstätte Hohenschönhausen (Berlin)." *Journal of War and Culture Studies* 4.1 (2011): 97–111. Print.

Jüdisches Museum München. Jüdisches Museum München. http://www.juedisches-museum-muenchen.de. Web.

Jud Süß. Dir. Veit Harlan. Terra, 1940. Film.

Jud Süß – Film ohne Gewissen. Dir. Oskar Roehler. 2010. Concorde, 2011. DVD.

Kadobayashi, Takeshi. "Tactility, This Superfluous Thing: Reading McLuhan through the Trope of Sense." *UTCP Bulletin* 4 (May 2005): 26–35. Print.

Kaes, Anton. *From Hitler to Heimat: The Return of History as Film*. Cambridge, MA: Harvard UP, 1989. Print.

– *Shell Shock Cinema: Weimar Cinema and the Wounds of War*. Princeton: Princeton UP, 2009. Print.

Kansteiner, Wulf. "Entertaining Catastrophe: The Reinvention of the Holocaust in the Television of the Federal Republic of Germany." *New German Critique* 90.3 (2003): 135–162. Print.

– "The Radicalization of German Memory in the Age of Its Commercial Reproduction." In *In Pursuit of German Memory: History, Television, and Politics after Auschwitz*. Athens: Ohio UP, 2006. 154–80. Print.

Käthow, Stephanie. "Mit allen Mitteln der Kunst: Der Film baut sich ein Museum. Staunende Blicke im Filmmuseum Berlin und anderen Tempeln der 'zehnten Muse.'" In *Museum und Film*, ed. H.C. Eberl, J.T. Frieghs, G. Kastner, C. Oesch, H. Posch, and K. Siefert. Vienna: Turia und Kant, 2003. 74–88. Print.

Keilbach, Judith. "Mit dokumentarischen Bildern effektvoll Geschichte erzählen: Die historischen Aufnahmen in Guido Knopps Geschichtsdokumentationen." *Medien + Erziehung* 42.6 (1998): 359. Print.

Kellerhof, Felix. "Zentralrat will Roehlers 'Jud Süß' verbieten." *Welt Online*, 11 March 2010. Web.

Kirshenblatt-Gimblett, Barbara. *Destination Culture: Tourism, Museums, and Heritage*. Berkeley: U of California P, 1998. Print.

Klonk, Charlotte. *Spaces of Experience: Art Gallery Interiors from 1800 to 2000*. New Haven: Yale UP, 2009. Print.

Kniebe, Tobias. "Der Teufel und sein Schmierenkomödiant." *Süddeutsche.de*, 11 February 2010. Web.

Knilli, Friedrich. "Dreißig Jahre Lehr-und Forschungsarbeit zur Mediengeschichte des 'Jud Süß': Ein Bericht." In *"Jud Süß": Hofjude, literarische Figur, antisemitisches Zerrbild*, ed. Alexandra Przyrembel and Jörg Schönert. Frankfurt am Main: Campus Verlag, 2006. 75–121. Print.

Koepnick, Lutz. "Reframing the Past: Heritage Cinema and Holocaust in the 1990s." *New German Critique* 87 (Autumn 2002): 47–82. Print.

Köhr, Katja, and Karl Heinrich Pohl. "Affirmation statt Kritik? Das Deutsche Historische Museum in Berlin und seine Ständige Ausstellung." *Geschichte in Wissenschaft und Unterricht* 58.10 (2007): 578–90. Print.

Kolker, Robert Phillip, and Peter Beicken. *The Films of Wim Wenders*. New York: Cambridge UP, 1993. Print.

Kopytoff, Igor. "The Cultural Biography of Things: Commoditization as Process." In *The Social Life of Things*, ed. Adjurn Appadurai. Cambridge: Cambridge UP, 1986. 64–94. Print.

– "Reflections on the Museum." *Journal of Folklore Research* 36.2 (1999): 267–70. Print.

Korff, Gottfried. "Aporien der Musealisierung: Notizen zu einem Trend, der die Institution, nach der er benannt ist, hinter sich gelassen hat." In *Zeitphänomen Musealisierung: Das Verschwinden der Gegenwart und die Konstruktion der Erinnerung*, ed. Wolfgang Zacharias. Essen: Klartext Verlag, 1990. 57–71. Print.

– *Museumsdinge: Deponieren – Exponieren*. Cologne: Böhlau Verlag, 2002. Print.

– "Die Popularisierung des Musealen und die Musealisierung des Popularen." In *Museum als soziales Gedächtnis? Kritische Beiträge zu Museumswissenschaft und Museumspädagogik*, ed. Gottfried Fliedl. Klagenfurt: Kärntner Dr.-u. Verl.-Ges., 1988. 9–23. Print.

– "Reflections on the Museum." Trans. John Bendix and Regina Bendix. *Journal of Folklore Research* 36.2/3 (1999): 267–70. Print.

Kraushaar, Wolfgang. *Die RAF und der linke Terrorismus*. 2 vols. Hamburg: Hamburger Edition, 2006. Print.

Kreuder, Friedemann. "Hotel Esplanade: The Cultural History of a Berlin Location." *PAJ: A Journal of Performance and Art* 22.2 (2000): 22–38. Print.

Kristeva, Julia. *Black Sun: Depression and Melancholia*. Trans. Leon Roudiez. New York: Columbia UP, 1989.

Kunstraum München. *"Dream City" – Ein Münchner Gemeinschaftsprojekt – 25. März bis 20. Juni 1999*. Munich: Museum Villa Stuck, 1999. Print.

Kuspit, Donald. *Redeeming Art: Critical Reveries*. Ed. Mark Van Proyen. New York: Allworth Press, 2000. Print.

Kuzniar, Alice. "Where Is the Animal after Posthumanism? Quivering Life in Sue Coe's Art." *New Centennial Review* 11.2 (2011): 17–40.

Landsberg, Alison. "America, the Holocaust, and Mass Culture of Memory: Towards a Radical Politics of Empathy." *New German Critique* 71.2 (1997): 63–86. Print.

– *Prosthetic Memory: The Transformation of American Remembrance in the Age of Mass Culture*. New York: Columbia UP, 2004. Print.

Leben – BRD (*How to Live in the German Federal Republic*). Dir. Harun Farocki. Harun Farocki Filmproduktion, Berlin-West, ZDF, Mainz, La Sept, Paris. 1990. 16 mm.

Leben der Anderen, Das [*The Lives of Others*]. Dir. Florian Henckel von Donnersmarck. Wiedemann & Berg Filmproduktion. 2006. DVD.

Lederle, Josef. "So ist die Welt: Der 'Extremdokumentarismus' des Nikolaus Geyrhalter." *Filmdienst* 60.2 (2007): 6–9. Print.

Lehmbruck, Wilhelm. *Die Kniende*. 1911. Plaster cast.

Lenk, Sabine. "Collections on Display: Exhibiting Artifacts in a Film Museum, with Pride." *Film History* 18.3 (2006): 319–25. Print.

Levinas, Emmanuel. "As If Consenting to Horror." *Critical Inquiry* 15.2 (Winter 1989): 485–8. Print.

Levy, Daniel, and Natan Sznaider. *Holocaust and Memory in the Global Age*. Philadelphia: Temple UP, 2005. Print.

Lidchi, Henrietta. "The Poetics and Politics of Exhibiting Other Cultures." In *Representation: Cultural Representations and Signifying Practices*, ed. Stuart Hall. London: Sage, 1997. 151–222. Print.

Lifschitz, Sharone. "Speaking Germany." 2006–7. Exhibition Poster.

Lipkin, Steven N. *Real Emotional Logic: Film and Television Docudrama as Persuasive Practice*. Carbondale: Southern Illinois UP, 2002. Print.

Lives of Others, The. Dir. Florian Henckel von Donnersmarck. Arte, 2006. Film.

Lopate, Phillip. "In Search of the Centaur: The Essay-Film." In *Beyond Document: Essays on Non-Fiction Film*, ed. Charles Warren. Middletown, CT: Wesleyan UP, 1996. 243–70. Print.

Lorenz, Renate. *Queer Art: A Freak Theory*. Bielefeld: Transcript Verlag, 2012. Print.

Lowenthal, David. *Possessed by the Past: The Heritage Crusade and the Spoils of History*. New York: The Free Press, 1996. Print.

Lübbe, Hermann. *Die Aufdringlichkeit der Geschichte: Herausforderungen der Moderne vom Historismus bis zum Nationalsozialismus*. Graz: Verlag Styria, 1989.

M. Dir. Fritz Lang. Perf. Peter Lorre, Gustaf Gründgens, Inge Landgut. Nero-Film AG, 1931. Film.

Macdonald, Sharon. *A Companion to Museum Studies*. Vol. 12. Oxford: Blackwell Publishers, 2006. Print.

– *Memorylands: Heritage and Identity in Europe Today*. New York: Routledge, 2013. Print.

Macdonald, Sharon and Gordon Fyfe, eds. *Theorizing Museums: Representing Identity and Diversity in a Changing World*. Oxford: Blackwell, 1996. Print.

MacLeod, Suzanne. "Towards an Ethics of Museum Architecture." In *The Routledge Companion to Museum Ethics: Redefining Ethics for the Twenty-First Century Museum*. London: Routledge, 2011. 379–92. Print.

Malamud, Randy. "Zoo Spectatorship." In *The Animals Reader: The Essential Classic and Contemporary Writings*, ed. Linda Kalof and Amy J. Fitzgerald. Oxford: Berg, 2007. 219–36. Print.

Malraux, André. *Museum without Walls*. Garden City, NY: Doubleday, 1967. Print.

Marks, Laura U. *The Skin of the Film: Intercultural Cinema, Embodiment, and the Senses*. Durham: Duke UP, 2000. Print.

Marstine, Janet C., ed. *The Routledge Companion to Museum Ethics: Redefining Ethics for the Twenty-First Century Museum*. London: Routledge, 2011. Print.

Marquard, Odo. "Verspätete Moralistik. Bemerkungen zur Unvermeidlichkeit der Geisteswissenschaften." *Kursbuch* 91 (March 1988): 13–18.

McClintock, Anne. *Imperial Leather: Race, Gender and Sexuality in Colonial Conquest*. New York: Routledge, 1995. Print.

McIntosh, Alison J., and Richard C. Prentice. "Affirming Authenticity: Consuming Cultural Heritage." *Tourism Management* 18.2 (1997): 75–87. Print.

McIsaac, Peter. *Museums of the Mind: German Modernity and the Dynamics of Collecting*. University Park: U of Pennsylvania P, 2007. Print.

McLuhan, Marshall. *Understanding Media: The Extensions of Man*. Cambridge: MIT Press. 1994. Print.

Meier-Graefe, Julius. "Pariser Reaktionen." *Kunst und Künstler* 10.9 (1912): 444–8. Print.

– "Paris 1910/11." *Frankfurter Zeitung*, international ed., 5 January 1932: 9–11. Print.

Mephisto. Dir. István Szabo. Hessischer Rundfunk, 1981. Film.

Mercedes Museum. http://www.mercedes-benz-classic.com/content/classic/mpc/mpc_classic_website/en/mpc_home/mbc/home/museum/home.flash.html#. Web.

Metropolis. Screenplay by Thea von Harbou and Fritz Lang. Dir. Fritz Lang. UFA. 1927. Film.

Morris, Errol. *Believing Is Seeing. Observations on the Mysteries of Photography*. New York: Penguin, 2011. Print.

Müller, Alois. "Prototypes and After-Images." In *Film Stills: Emotions Made in Hollywood*, ed. Annemarie Hürlimann and Alois Martin Müller. Zurich: Museum für Gestaltung Zürich and Edition Cantz, 1993. 19–21. Print.

Müller, Michael, and Andreas Kanonenberg. *Die RAF-Stasi-Connection*. Berlin: Rowohlt, 1992. Print.

Mulvey, Laura. "Visual Pleasure and Narrative Cinema." In *Media and Cultural Studies: Keyworks*, ed. Meenakshi Gigi Durham and Douglas M. Kellner. Oxford: John Wiley & Sons, 2006. 342–52. Print.

– *Visual and Other Pleasures*. 2nd ed. Houndmills, New York: Palgrave Macmillan, 2009. Print.

"Museumspass Berlin. Eine Karte öffnet 55 Tore." *Visit Berlin*. 2012. Web.

Museumsnews. DDR Museum Berlin. 12 October 2010. http://www.ddr-museum.de/de/blog/museumsnews. Web.

Nadkarni, Maya, and Olga Shevchenko. "The Politics of Nostalgia: A Case for Comparative Analysis of Postsocialist Practices." *Ab Imperio* 2 (2004): 487–519. Print.

Nead, Lynda. *The Haunted Gallery: Painting, Photography, Film c. 1900*. New Haven: Yale UP, 2007. Print.

Nichols, Bill. *Representing Reality: Issues and Concepts in Documentary*. Bloomington: Indiana UP, 1991. Print.

Nicht löschbares Feuer (*Inextinguishable Fire*). Dir. Harun Farocki. Harun Farocki, Berlin-West für WDR, Köln, 1969. 16 mm.

Night and Fog. Dir. Alain Resnais. Argos Films, 1955. Film.

Nora, Pierre. "Between History and Memory: *Les lieux de mémoire*." *Representations* 26 (1989): 7–24. Print.

Olle DDR Daueraustellung. Museumsbaracke "Olle DDR." N.d. Web.

Olympia, Fest der Völker, Fest der Schönheit. Dir. Leni Riefenstahl. Olympia-Film G.m.b.H. 1938. Film.

Oosterhuis, Harry. *Stepchildren of Nature: Krafft-Ebing, Psychiatry and the Making of Sexual Identity*. Chicago: U of Chicago P, 2000. Print.

Orich, Annika, and Florentine Strzelczyk. "'Steppende Nazis mit Bildungsauftrag': Marketing Hitler Humor in Post-Unification Germany." In *Strategies of Humor in Post-Unification German Literature, Film, and Other Media*, ed. Jill Twark. Newcastle upon Tyne: Cambridge Scholars Publishing, 2011. 292–329. Print.

Ostalgie-Kabinett. DDR Museum "Ostalgie-Kabinett." N.d. Web.

Ostow, Robin. "From Memory to History: Displaying World War II in the German Historical Museum." In *Recalling the Past – (Re)constructing the Past: Collective and Individual Memory of World War II in Russia and Germany*, ed. Withold Bonner and Arja Rosenholm. Jyväskylä: Aleksandri Institute, 2008. 123–36. Print.

Oushakine, Serguei Alex. "'We're Nostalgic but We're Not Crazy': Retrofitting the Past in Russia." *Russian Review* (2007): 451–82. Print.

Paget, Derek. *No Other Way to Tell It: Dramadoc/Docudrama on Television*. Manchester: Manchester UP, 1998. Print.

Pantenburg, Volker. "Post Cinema? Moving, Museums, Mutations." *SITE Magazine* 24 (2008): 4–5. Print.

Paret, Peter. "The Tschudi Affair." *Journal of Modern History* 53.4 (December 1981): 589–618. Print.

Parry, Ross. *The Museum in a Digital Age*. New York: Routledge, 2010. Print.

Patterson, Charles. *Eternal Treblinka: Our Treatment of Animals and the Holocaust*. New York: Lantern Books, 2002. Print.

Pearce, Susan M. "Objects as Meaning; Or Narrating the Past." In *Interpreting Objects and Collections*, ed. Susan M. Pearce. London: Routledge, 1994. 19–29. Print.

Penny, H. Glenn. *Objects of Culture: Ethnology and Ethnographic Museums in Imperial Germany*. Chapel Hill: U of North Carolina P, 2002. Print.

Peters, Butz. *Terrorismus in Deutschland*. Stuttgart: Deutsche Verlags-Anstalt, 1991. Print.

Petropoulos, Jonathan. *Art as Politics in the Third Reich*. Chapel Hill: U of North Carolina P, 1996. Print.

– *The Faustian Bargain: The Art World in Nazi Germany*. Oxford: Oxford UP, 2000. Print.

Pichler, Barbara. "The Construction of Reality: Aspects of Austrian Cinema between Fiction and Documentary." In *Cinema and Social Change in Germany and Austria*, ed. Gabriele Mueller and James Skidmore. Waterloo: Wilfrid Laurier UP, 2011. 269–83. Print.

Pirker, Eva Ulrike, and Mark Rüdiger. "Authentizitätsfiktionen in populären Geschichtskulturen: Annäherungen." In *Echte Geschichte: Authentizitätsfiktionen in populären Geschichtskulturen*, ed. Eva Ulrike Pirker, Mark Rüdiger, et al. Bielefeld: Transcript, 2010. 11–30. Print.

Porsche Museum. http://www.porsche.com/international/aboutporsche/porschemuseum/. Web.

Pressemitteilung. "DDR Museum für das 'Europäische Museum des Jahres' nominiert." Berlin: DDR Museum. 11 January 2008. Web.

Przyrembel, Alexandra, and Jörg Schönert. *"Jud Süß": Hofjude, literarische Figur, antisemitisches Zerrbild*. Frankfurt am Main: Campus Verlag, 2006. Print.

Radley, Alan. "Artefacts, Memory and a Sense of the Past." In *Collective Remembering*, ed. David Middleton and P. Edwards. London: Sage, 1990. 46–59. Print.

Raphael, Max. *Idee und Gestalt: Ein Führer zum Wesen der Kunst*. Munich: Delphin, 1921. Print.

Rascaroli, Laura. *The Personal Camera: Subjective Cinema and the Essay Film*. London: Wallflower, 2009. Print.

Rebhandl, Bert. "Enemy at the Gate: Harun Farocki's Work on the Industrial Disputes of Film History." In *Harun Farocki: Against What? Against Whom?*, ed. Antje Ehmann and Kodwo Eshun. London: Koenig Books, 2009. 122–7. Print.

Rectanus, Mark. *Culture Incorporated: Museums, Artists, and Corporate Sponsorships*. Minneapolis: U of Minnesota P, 2002. Print.

– "Globalization: Incorporating the Museum." In *A Companion to Museum Studies*, ed. Sharon Macdonald. Oxford: Blackwell, 2006. 381–97. Print.

– "Moving Out: Museums, Mobility, and Urban Spaces." In *Museum Media*, ed. Michelle Henning. International Handbook of Museum Studies, general eds. Helen Rees Leahy and Sharon Macdonald. Malden and Oxford: Wiley-Blackwell, forthcoming 2015. Print.

Reid, Susan Emily, and David Crowley, ed. *Style and Socialism: Modernity and Material Culture in Post-War Eastern Europe*. New York: Berg, 2000. Print.

Rentschler, Eric. "From New German Cinema to the Post-Wall Cinema of Consensus." In *Cinema and Nation*, ed. Mette Hjort and Scott MacKenzie. Routledge: London, 2000. 260–77. Print.

– *Ministry of Illusion: Nazi Cinema and Its Afterlife*. Cambridge, MA: Harvard UP, 1996. Print.

Rethmann, Petra. "Post-Communist Ironies in an East German Hotel." *Anthropology Today* 25 (2009): 21–3. Print.

Riefenstahl, Leni. *Leni Riefenstahl: A Memoir.* New York: St Martin's Press, 1992. Print.

– *Schönheit im Olympischen Kampf.* Berlin: Deutscher Verlag, 1937. Print.

Riegel, Henrietta. "Into the Heart of Irony: Ethnographic Exhibitions and the Politics of Difference." In *Theorizing Museums: Representing Identity and Diversity in a Changing World*, ed. Sharon MacDonald and Gordon Fyfe. Oxford: Blackwell Publishers, 1996. 83–104. Print.

Rieger, Susanne. "Eine neue Synagoge für München: Die Chronik des 'Projekts St.- Jakobs-Platz' 1999–2007." *Rijo Research*. 2008. Web.

Riegl Alois. "Der moderne Denkmalkultus: Sein Wesen und seine Entstehung." In *Gesammelte Aufsätze*. Vienna: WUV-Universitätsverlag, 1996 [first pub. 1903]. 139–84. Print.

Ritvo, Harriet. *The Animal Estate: The English and Other Creatures in the Victorian Age*. Cambridge, MA: Harvard UP, 1987. Print.

Robinson, David. "Film Museums I Have Known and (Sometimes) Loved." *Film History* 18.3 (2006): 237–60. Print.

Rodek, Hanns-Georg. "*Jud Süß* sollte Spiel-, kein Dokumentarfilm sein." *Welt Online*, 21 September 2010. Web.

Rohter, Larry. "Nazi Film Still Pains Relatives." *New York Times*, 1 March 2010. Web.

Rother, Rainer. *Leni Riefenstahl*. Trans. Martin Bott. New York: Continuum, 2002. Print.

Rosenfelder, Andreas. "'Jud Süß' hätte ein guter Film werden können." *Welt Online*, 22 September 2010. Web.

Rosenstone, Robert A. *History on Film – Film on History*. Harlow: Pearson, 2006. Print.

Rubin, Martin. *Thrillers*. Cambridge, MA: Cambridge UP, 1999. Print.

Rubin, Martin, ed. *Vom Ausstellen*. Spec. issue of *Recherche Film und Fernsehen* 7–8 (2010). Print.

Rundbrief. "Mitglieder stellen sich vor: Jürgen Friedhoff." Berlin: Verein zur Dokumentation der DDR-Alltagskultur e.V., 3 (1997): 9. Print.

Rundbrief. "Mitglieder stellen sich vor: Jan Faktor." Berlin: Verein zur Dokumentation der DDR-Alltagskultur e.V., 5 (1999): 7. Print.

Sabrow, Martin. "DDR-Alltag im Museum." In *2 Jahre DDR Museum: Eine Kritische Bilanz*. Berlin: DDR Museum, 2008. 7–13. Print.

– "Die DDR erinnern." In *Erinnerungsorte der DDR*, ed. Martin Sabrow. Munich: C.H. Beck, 2009. 11–30. Print.

Sachsse, Rolf. *Die Erziehung zum Wegsehen: Fotografie im NS-Staat*. Hamburg: Philo Fine Arts, 2003. 23–47. Print.

Salzman, Siegfried. *"Hinweg mit der 'Knienden'": Ein Beitrag zur Geschichte des Kunstskandals*. Duisburg: Museumsverein Duisburg, 1981. Print.

Sander, August. "Remarks on My Exhibition at the Cologne Art Union" [1927]. In *The Weimar Republic Sourcebook*, ed. Anton Kaes, Martin Jay, and Edward Dimendberg. Berkeley: U of California P, 1994. 645–6. Print.

Saunders, Anna. *Honecker's Children: Youth and Patriotism in East(ern) Germany, 1979–2002*. Manchester: Manchester UP, 1997. Print.

Schabbing, Bernd. "Mega-Trend Kulturtourismus." *Kulturmanagement* 54 (2011): 10. Web.

Schlanstein, Beate. "Echt wahr! Annäherungen an das Authentische." In *Alles authentisch? Popularisierung der Geschichte im Fernsehen*, ed. Thomas Fischer and Rainer Wirtz. Konstanz: UVK, 2008. 205–25. Print.

Schleider, Tim. "Der Jud Süß zieht noch immer." *Stuttgarter Zeitung*, 8 July 2008. Web.

Schicksalswende. Dir. Johannes Häußler and Walter Scheunemann. Deutsche Filmherstellungs- und -Verwertungs- GmbH, Berlin, 1939. Film.

Scholl, Joachim. "Oskar Roehler: Dramaturgischer Kniff ist voellig legitim." *Deutschlandradio*, 18 February 2010. Web. Radio.

Schubert, Dietrich. *Wilhelm Lehmbruck: Catalogue Raisoneé der Skulpturen 1898–1919*. Worms: Wernersche Verlagsgesellschaft, 2001. Print.

Schulte-Sasse, Linda. "The Jew as Other and National Socialism: Veit Harlan's *Jud Süß*." *German Quarterly* 61.1 (Winter 1988): 22–49. Print.

Schulz, Bernhard. "Im Fieber. Deutsche Museen stoßen an ihre Wachstumsgrenzen." *Tagesspiegel*, 21 May 2012. Web.

Schulze, Gerhard. *Die Erlebnisgesellschaft. Kultursoziologie der Gegenwart*. Frankfurt/Main: Campus, 1992. Print.

Schnittstelle (*Interface*). Dir. Harun Farocki. Musée Moderne d'art de Villeneuve d'Ascq, Harun Farocki Filmproduktion, Berlin, 1995. Video.

Schulze, Gerhard. *Die Erlebnisgesellschaft: Kultursoziologie der Gegenwart*. Frankfurt/Main: Campus, 1992. Print.

Scribner, Charity. "Tender Rejection: The German Democratic Republic Goes to the Museum." *European Journal of English Studies* 4.2 (2000): 171–87. Print.

Sheffi, Na'ama. "Jud Süß." In *Deutsche Erinnerungsorte 1*, ed. Étienne François and Hagen Schulze. Munich: C.H. Beck, 2001. 422–37. Print.

Sheringham, Michael. *Everyday Life: Theories and Practices from Surrealism to the Present*. New York: Oxford UP, 2006. Print.

Sherrill, Martha. "Painting Herself into a Corner: Sue Coe Is 'Hot.' Does That Make Her a Hypocrite?" *Washington Post*, 19 March 1994: D1. Print.

Shevchenko, Olga, and Maya Nakdarni. "The Politics of Nostalgia: A Case for Comparative Analysis of Postsocialist Practices." *Ab Imperio* 2 (2004): 487–519. Print.

Ship, The. Dir. Christopher Terrill. British Broadcasting Company, London, 2002. Television.

Shukin, Nicole. *Animal Capital: Rendering Life in Biopolitical Times*. Minneapolis: U of Minnesota Press, 2009. Print.

Simon, Nina. *The Participatory Museum*. Santa Cruz: Museum 2.0, 2010. Print.

Sobchack, Vivian. *The Address of the Eye: A Phenomenology of Film Experience*. Princeton, NJ: Princeton UP, 1992. Print.

– "The Insistent Fringe: Moving Images and Historical Conciousness." *History and Theory* 36.4 (1997): 4–20. Print.

Sontag, Susan. *On Photography*. New York: Farrar, Straus, and Giroux, 1977. Print.

– *Under the Sign of Saturn*. New York: Farrar, Straus, and Giroux, 1980. Print.

Stadtgeschichtliches Museum Leipzig and Bundestiftung zur Aufarbeitung der SED-Diktatur. *Die Musealisierung der DDR: Wege, Möglichkeiten und Grenzen der Darstellung von Zeitgeschichte in Stadt- und Regionalgeschichtlichen Museen*. Leipzig: [Stadtgeschichtliches Museum Leipzig], 2011. Print.

Stecker, Raimund. "The Kneeling Woman – She Kneels Down before Us." In *Kneeling Woman 100 Years*, English ed., ed. Raimund Stecker and Marion Bornscheuer. Duisburg: Lehmbruck Museum and Cologne: Dumont, 2011. 6–11. Print.

Steinkamp, Maike. *Das unerwünschte Erbe – Die Rezeption "entarteter" Kunst in Kunstkritik, Ausstellungen und Museen der SBZ und der frühen DDR*. Berlin: Akademie Verlag, 2008. Print.

Stendel, Sarah. "Die RAF im Kino: Verblüffende Ähnlichkeit." *Süddeutsche.de*, 2 April 2009. Web.

Stephan, Hans-Joachim. Personal interview. 8 July 2009.

Steyerl, Hito. "Is a Museum a Factory?" *e-flux Journal* 7.6 (2009): n.p. Web.

Stezaker, John. "The Film-Still and Its Double: Reflections on the Found Film Still." *Stillness and Time: Photography and the Moving Image.* Ed. David Green and Joanna Lowry. Brighton: Photoforum 2006. 113–127. Print.

Stock, Wolfgang Jean. "Ein Haus der Begegnung / A Meeting Place." In *Jüdisches Museum München*, ed. Jutta Fleckenstein and Bernhard Purin. Munich: Prestel, 2007. 79–89. Print.

Stoichita, Victor I. *The Pygmalion Effect: From Ovid to Hitchcock.* Trans. Alison Anderson. Chicago and London: U of Chicago P, 2008. Print.

Stoler, Ann Laura. "Carnal Knowledge and Imperial Power: Gender, Race and Morality in Colonial Asia." In *Gender at the Crossroads of Knowledge: Feminist Anthropology in the Postmodern Era*. Berkeley: U of California P, 1991. 51–101. Print.

Strzelczyk, Florentine. "Facism – Fantasy – Fascination – Film." *Arachne* 7.1/2 (2000): 94–111. Print.

Stürme über dem Montblanc [*Avalanche*]. Dir. Arnold Fanck. Perf. Leni Riefenstahl, Sepp Rist, Ernst Udet, and Friedrich Kayßler. Aafa-Film AG, 1930. Film.

Suchsland, Rüdiger. "*Jud Süß – Film ohne Gewissen*! von Oskar Roehler im Wettbewerb." *Tip Berlin*, 17 February 2010. Web.

Ten Dyke, Elizabeth A. "Memory and Existence: Implications of the Wende." In *The Work of Memory: New Directions in the Study of German Society and Culture*, ed. Alon Confino and Peter Fritzsche. Urbana: U of Illinois P, 2002. 154–68. Print.

Tengelyi, László. "In Verteidigung der Geschichtserfahrung: Zur Auseinandersetzung von Paul Ricœur mit Hayden White." *Erfahrung und Geschichte: Historische Sinnbildung im Pränarrativen*, ed. Thiemo Breyer and Daniel Creutz. Berlin: de Gruyter, 2010. 185–201. Print.

Teufels General, Des. Dir. Helmut Käutner. Real-Film GmbH, Hamburg,1954.

Thiemeyer, Thomas. *Fortsetzung des Krieges mit anderen Mitteln: Die beiden Weltkriege im Museum.* Paderborn: Schöningh, 2010. Print.

Tilley, Christopher. "Interpreting Material Culture." In *Interpreting Objects and Collections*, ed. Susan M. Pearce. London, New York: Routledge, 1994. 67–75. Print.

Todd, Richard. *The Thing Itself: On the Search for Authenticity.* New York: Penguin, 2008. Print.

Todesspiel. Dir. Heinrich Breloer. ARD. 1997. Television film.

Torres, Bob. *Making a Killing: The Political Economy of Animal Rights.* Oakland: AK Press, 2007. Print.

Tschumi, Bernard. *Architecture and Disjunction.* Cambridge, MA: MIT Press, 1994. Print.

Übelhack, Andrea. "Darf ein Museum den Nazifilm 'Jud Süß' zeigen?" *HagGalil*, 13 February 2001. Web.

Unser täglich Brot [*Our Daily Bread*]. Dir. Nikolaus Geyrhalter. Mongrel Media, 2005. Film.

Untergang, Der [*Downfall*]. Dir. Oliver Hirschbiegel. Prod. Bernd Eichinger. Constantin. 2004. Film.

Urry, John. *Consuming Places.* London: Routledge, 1995. Print.

– "How Societies Remember the Past." In *Theorizing Museums: Representing Identity and Diversity in a Changing World*, ed. Sharon MacDonald and Gordon Fyfe. Oxford: Blackwell Publishers, 1996. 45–65. Print.

van Alphen, Ernst. *Art in Mind: How Contemporary Images Shape Thought.* Chicago: U of Chicago P, 2005. Print.

Veenis, Milena. "Cola in the German Democratic Republic: East German Fantasies on Western Consumption." *Enterprise & Society* 12.3 (2011): 489–524. Web.

Vergo, Peter, "The Reticent Object." In *The New Museology*, ed. Peter Vergo. London: Reaktion, 1989. 41–59. Print.

Videogramme einer Revolution [*Videograms of a Revolution*]. Dir. Harun Farocki. Harun Farocki Filmproduktion, Berlin, Bremer Institut Film/Fernsehen Produktionsgesellschaft GmbH, Bremen, 1992. Video transferred to 16 mm.

von Kameke, Andrea. "Film Museums as 'Cinematic Spaces'?" In *The Cinematic Experience: Film, Contemporary Art, Museum*, ed. Alice Autelitano. Pasian di Prato, Udine: Campanatto Editore, 2010. 223–32. Print.

von Lüttichau, Mario-Andreas. "'Deutsche Kunst' und 'Entartete Kunst': Die Münchener Ausstellung 1937." In *Die "Kunststadt München 1937": Nationalsozialismus und "Entartete Kunst,"* ed. Peter-Klaus Schuster. Munich: Prestel, 1987. 83–118. Print.

– "Rekonstruktion der Ausstellung 'Entartete Kunst.'" In *Die "Kunststadt München 1937": Nationalsozialismus und "Entartete Kunst,"* ed. Peter-Klaus Schuster. Munich: Prestel, 1987. 120–81. Print.

von Moltke, Johannes. "Sympathy for the Devil: Cinema, History, and the Politics of Emotion." *New German Critique* 34:3.102 (Fall 2007): 17–43. Print.

Vukov, Nikolai. "The 'Unmentionable' and the 'Unforgettable': Museumizing the Socialist Past in Post-1989 Bulgaria." In *Past for the Eyes: East European Representations of Communism in Cinema and Museums after 1989*, ed. Oksana Sarkisova and Peter Apor. New York: Central European UP, 2008. 275–306. Print.

Wahlberg, Malin. "Inscription and Re-Framing: At the Editing Table of Harun Farocki." *Konsthistorisk Tidskrift / Journal of Art History* 73.1 (2004): 15–26. Print.

Ward, Janet. *Weimar Surfaces*. Berkeley: U of California P, 2001. Print.

Ward, Simon. "Globalization and the Remembrance of Violence: Visual Culture, Space, and Time in Berlin." In *Globalization, Violence and the Visual Culture of Cities*, ed. Christoph Lindner. London: Routledge, 2009. 87–106. Print.

– "Obsolescence and the Cityscape of the Former GDR." *German Life and Letters* 63.4 (2010): 385–7. Print.

Wasson, Haidee. *Museum Movies: The Museum of Modern Art and the Birth of Art Cinema*. Berkeley: U of California P, 2005. Print.

Weil, Stephen E. *Making Museums Matter*. Washington, DC: Smithsonian, 2002. Print.

Weinstein, Joan. *The End of Expressionism: Art and the November Revolution in Germany, 1918–1919*. Chicago: U of Chicago P, 1990. Print.

Wenders, Wim. *The Act of Seeing: Essays and Conversations*. London: Faber and Faber, 1997. Print.

– "An Attempted Description of an Indescribable Film: From the First Treatment of *Wings of Desire*." In *The Logic of Images: Essays and Conversations*. Trans. Michael Hoffmann. London: Faber and Faber, 1992. 73–83. Print.

– Audio commentary. *Der Himmel über Berlin* (*Wings of Desire*). Dir. Wim Wenders. Perf. Bruno Ganz, Solveig Dommartin, Otto Sander. Axiom, 2008. DVD.

– "On Making It Up as You Go Along (Conversation with Friedrich Frey)." In *The Act of Seeing: Essays and Conversations*. Trans. Michael Hoffmann. London: Faber and Faber, 1997. 183–89. Print.

– *On Film: Essays and Conversations*. Trans. Michael Hoffmann. London: Faber and Faber, 2001. Print.

Werner, Frank R. "Himmelblauer Wolkenbügel über München." In *Coop Himmelb(l)au BMW Welt, München*. Stuttgart: Edition Axel Menges, 2009. 7–15. Print.

Westheim, Paul. *Wilhelm Lehmbruck*. Potsdam and Berlin: Gustav Kiepenheuer, 1919. Print.

White, Hayden. *The Content and the Form: Narrative Discourse and Historical Representation*. Baltimore: Johns Hopkins UP, 1987. Print.

– *Metahistory: The Historical Imagination in Nineteenth-Century Europe*. Baltimore: Johns Hopkins UP, 1973. Print.

Williams, Linda. "Film Bodies: Gender, Genre, and Excess." *Film Quarterly* 44.4 (Summer 1991): 2–13. Print.

Williams, Paul. *Memorial Museums: The Global Rush to Commemorate Atrocities*. Oxford, New York: Berg, 2007. Print.

Willrich, Wolfgang. *Säuberung des Kunsttempels: Eine kunstpolitische Kampfschrift zur Gesundung deutscher Kunst im Geiste nordischer Art*. Munich: J.F. Lehmann, 1937. Print.

Wilson, Emma. *Alain Resnais*. Manchester: Manchester UP, 2006. Print.

– "Material Remains: *Night and Fog*." *October* 112 (2005): 89–110. Print.

Winkler, Anne. "'*Kept Things*': Heterotopic Provocations in the Museal Representation of East German Everyday Life." *Laboratorium: Russian Review of Social Research* 6.2 (2014): 101–122. Print.

– "'Not Everything Was Good, but Many Things Were Better': Nostalgia for East Germany and Its Politics." In *Ecologies of Affect: Placing Nostalgia, Desire and Hope*, ed. Tonya K. Davidson, Ondine Park, and Rob Shields. Waterloo, ON: Wilfrid Laurier UP, 2011. 19–42. Print.

Wirtz, Rainer. "Das Authentische und das Historische." In *Alles authentisch? Popularisierung der Geschichte im Fernsehen*, ed. Thomas Fischer and Rainer Wirtz. Konstanz: UVK, 2008. 187–203. Print.

Wolf, Christa. *Stadt der Engel oder The Overcoat of Dr. Freud*. Berlin: Suhrkamp, 2010. Print.

Wolfe, Cary. *What Is Posthumanism?* Minneapolis: U of Minnesota P, 2010. Print.

Wolle, Stefan. Personal interview. 3 November 2010.

Wollen, Peter. "Godard and Counter Cinema: Vent d'est." *Afterimage* 4 (1972): 6–17. Print.

Zander, Ulrike. "Jud Süß: Der Originalfilm, seine Hinter- und Abgründe." *Museums Magazin Online* 1 (2011). Web.

Zeitreise, Lebensart DDR 1949–1989. Concept paper (Entwicklungskonzept). Radebeul: n.d. Print.

Zeller, Christoph. *Ästhetik des Authentischen: Literatur und Kunst um 1970*. Berlin and New York: de Gruyter, 2010. Print.

Zimmerman, Andrew. *Anthropology and Antihumanism in Imperial Germany*. Chicago: U of Chicago P, 2001. Print.

Zimmermann, Martin. "Der Historiker am Set." In *Alles authentisch? Popularisierung der Geschichte im Fernsehen*, ed. Thomas Fischer and Rainer Wirtz. Konstanz: UVK, 2008. 137–60. Print.

Žizek, Slavoj. *Violence: Six Sideways Reflections*. New York: Picador, 2008. Print.

Zuckmayer, Carl. *Des Teufels General*. Frankfurt a.M.: Fischer, 2006. Print.

Zuschlag, Christoph. *"Entartete Kunst": Ausstellungsstrategien im Nazi-Deutschland*. Worms: Wernersche Verlagsgesellschaft, 1995. Print.

Contributors

Jonathan Bach is associate professor in the Graduate Program of International Affairs at the New School, New York.

Catriona Firth is project manager of the Warwick Commission on the Future of Cultural Value at the University of Warwick, UK.

Kathryn M. Floyd is assistant professor of art history at Auburn University, Alabama, USA.

Stephan Jaeger is professor of German at the University of Manitoba, Canada.

Alice Kuzniar is professor of German and English at the University of Waterloo, Canada.

Peter Mänz is head of exhibitions at the Deutsche Kinemathek in Berlin.

Peter M. McIsaac is associate professor of German and museum studies at the University of Michigan, Ann Arbor, USA.

Gabriele Mueller is associate professor of German studies at York University, Toronto, Canada.

Annika Orich is a PhD candidate in German at the University of California Berkeley, USA.

Mark W. Rectanus is Professor of German studies at Iowa State University, USA.

Florentine Strzelczyk is Professor of German at the University of Calgary, Alberta, Canada.

Christine Sprengler is associate professor of art history at Western University, Ontario, Canada.

Michael Thomas Taylor is associate professor of German and humanities at Reed College in Portland, Oregon, USA.

Annette Timm is associate professor of history at the University of Calgary, Alberta, Canada.

Simon Ward is senior lecturer in German at Durham University, UK.

Anne Winkler teaches in the Department of Sociology at the University of Alberta, Edmonton, Canada.

Index

www.ingramcontent.com/pod-product-compliance
Lightning Source LLC
LaVergne TN
LVHW090152080826
844660LV00013B/771/J

* 9 7 8 1 4 4 2 6 4 9 6 5 1 *